Communicating to Manage Health and Illness

Communicating to Manage Health and Illness is a valuable resource for those in the fields of health and interpersonal communication, public health, medicine, and related health disciplines. This scholarly edited volume advances the theoretical bases of health communication in two key areas: 1) communication, identity, and relationships; and 2) health care provider-patient interaction. Chapters aim to underscore the theory that communication processes are a link between personal, social, cultural, and institutional factors and various facets of health and illness. Contributors to the work are respected scholars from the fields of communication, public health, medicine, nursing, psychology, and other areas, and focus on ways in which patient identity is communicated in health-related interactions. This book serves as an excellent reference tool and is a substantial addition to health communication literature.

Dale E. Brashers is the David L. Swanson Professorial Scholar and Head of the Department of Communication, and Professor of Medicine at the University of Illinois at Urbana-Champaign. He has received the National Communication Association Golden Anniversary Monograph Award, the International Communication Association Young Scholar Award, and the National Communication Association Outstanding Health Communication Article Award. His work has been published in *Communication Monographs*, *Health Communication*, *Human Communication Research*, *Journal of Communication*, *Journal of Social and Personal Relationships*, *AIDS Care*, *Issues in Mental Health Nursing*, and in numerous edited books.

Daena J. Goldsmith is Professor of Communication at Lewis and Clark College. She has professional affiliations with the National Communication Association, International Communication Association, and International Association for Relationships Research. Her scholarly interests include interpersonal communication, health communication, social support, self-disclosure, gender, and culture. Her current research focuses on couples in which one person is coping with a chronic health condition such as heart disease, cancer, or HIV. Her book, *Communicating Social Support*, was published in 2004, and her research has appeared in *Communication Monographs*, *Human Communication Research*, *Social Science and Medicine*, *Journal of Social and Personal Relationships*, *Health Communication*, and *Communication Yearbook*.

Communicating to Manage Health and Illness

Edited by
Dale E. Brashers
Daena J. Goldsmith

Routledge
Taylor & Francis Group

NEW YORK AND LONDON

First published 2009
by Routledge
270 Madison Ave, New York, NY 10016

Simultaneously published in the UK
by Routledge
2 Park Square, Milton Park, Abingdon, Oxon OX14 4RN

Routledge is an imprint of the Taylor & Francis Group, an informa business

© 2009 Taylor & Francis
Typeset in Goudy and Gill Sans by EvS Communication Networx, Inc.
Printed and bound in the United States of America on acid-free paper by Walsworth Publishing
Company, Marceline, MO

Library of Congress Cataloging in Publication Data
Communicating to manage health and illness / [edited] by Dale E. Brashers and Daena J.
Goldsmith.
p. ; cm.
Includes bibliographical references and index.
1. Communication in medicine. I. Brashers, Dale E. II. Goldsmith, Daena J., 1964-
[DNLM: 1. Communication. 2. Health Education--trends. 3. Health Behavior. 4. Pathologic
Processes. WA 590 C7339 2009]
R118.C614 2009
610.1'4—dc22
2008055152

ISBN 10: 0-8058-4428-7 (hbk)
ISBN 10: 0-8058-4429-5 (pbk)
ISBN 10: 0-203-92918-7 (ebk)

ISBN 13: 978-0-8058-4428-3 (hbk)
ISBN 13: 978-0-8058-4429-0 (pbk)
ISBN 13: 978-0-203-92918-6 (ebk)

This book is dedicated to Professor David L. Swanson, who encouraged us in so many ways.

Contents

Introduction

Communicating to Manage Health and Illness

Daena J. Goldsmith and Dale E. Brashers

Our experience of health and illness is shaped by our personal background, social networks, cultural context, and community affiliations. We undertook this edited volume because we believe communication processes are a link between personal, social, cultural, and institutional factors and various facets of health and illness. For example, social networks and the social support they can provide are associated with mortality, morbidity, recovery, and coping with illness (for reviews, see Cohen, Underwood, & Gottlieb, 2000; Sarason, Sarason, & Gurung, 1997). Communication constructs and maintains networks and is one of the chief means through which information, aid, and emotional support are sought and provided (for review, see Albrecht & Goldsmith, 2003). Likewise, there is substantial evidence that the quality of interactions with health care providers affects health outcomes, provider-patient relationships, and patients' satisfaction (for reviews, see Brown, Stewart, & Ryan, 2003; Roter & Hall, 2006; Sans-Corrales et al., 2006; Suarez-Almazor, 2004) and that interventions to improve provider-patient interactions can improve communication skills and outcomes (for reviews, see Cegala & Broz, 2003; Griffin et al., 2004; Haywood, Marshall, & Fitzpatrick, 2006).

Beliefs about health and illness are another example of how communication links health experiences and outcomes with individual and cultural factors. We know patient labels, metaphors, beliefs, and explanatory models shape health behavior and that these cognitive schemas may vary from one individual to another and from one cultural group to another (e.g., Kirmayer & Sartorius, 2007; McElroy & Jezewski, 2003; Whaley, 1999). Interpersonal communication is one way cultural ideas are passed on, both through explicit instruction and socialization and also through everyday talk in which beliefs are applied to particular experiences (Cline, 2003; Walker & Dickson, 2004). Mass communication also shapes our beliefs, through the images and information that are presented (for review, see Kline, 2003, 2006) and through mass media campaigns designed to change health behaviors and attitudes (for reviews, see Murray-Johnson & Witte, 2003; Noar, 2006; Salmon & Atkin, 2003). Our understanding of health and illness is socially constructed and embedded in ideologies and power structures (for reviews, see Kline, 2003, 2006; Lupton, 2003). Cultural discourses related to managing health and illness circulate through mass and interpersonal communication, in interactions with health care agencies and providers, and in personal life as well.

The authors included in this volume share in common an interest in distinctively communicative forms, processes, and functions related to health and illness that occur in non-mass-media communication, not only in provider-patient interactions but also in everyday interactions with friends, family, peers, care-providers, and coworkers. Several recent assessments of the state of the art in health communication have recognized the need for further research on health-related interpersonal interactions in everyday life. For example, Parrott (2004) stated,

> Ultimately, strategic health communication seen from the vantage of communication emphasizes the reality that people's physical and mental well-being depends far more on the ability to manage health day-to-day than on the teachable moments that occur via health promotion and education or via medical interaction. (p. 751)

She went on to observe the opportunities that exist for interpersonal communication scholarship to address how stigma, privacy management, and self-disclosure processes bear on our ability to communicate about health with diverse populations. Duggan (2006) similarly summarized progress made in the study of relational dynamics in provider-patient communication and communication about health in close relationships. She observed, "Research in interpersonal communication in health contexts in the past decade has provided a solid foundation for developing theoretically based communication interventions for provider-patient interactions or for close relationships in which illness is a concern" (pp. 102–103). In their description of published health communication research in the last decade, Beck and her colleagues (2004) found one quarter of the studies were of interpersonal interactions among health care participants (e.g., provider-patient communication, social support interactions, and interactions among health care providers).

This volume originated in a seminar that took place at the University of Illinois at Urbana-Champaign, to which we invited prominent researchers to discuss how interpersonal and organizational communication shape health and illness. By bringing together scholars from diverse fields whose interests spanned communication in personal relationships and organizations as well as provider-patient communication, we hoped to synthesize common themes and set an agenda for issues in need of further research. As the book took shape, we invited others whose expertise could contribute to the themes that emerged from our initial discussions. The chapters that follow represent a blending of review, empirical report, and calls for future research in several different domains.

Communication Between Providers and Patients

The importance of interpersonal communication between health care providers and patients is well-established. In chapter 1, Kelly Haskard, Summer
Williams, and Robin DiMatteo synthesize evidence that provider-patient communication shapes outcomes of health care interactions, including not only
participant satisfaction but also adherence and treatment response. We know
provider-patient communication matters, and it is imperative that we theorize
the dimensions of interaction that differentiate better and worse outcomes as
well as the psychosocial, emotional, and mental health challenges providers
and patients encounter. This chapter shows communication is central to managing the physical and mental health outcomes of patient-provider interactions
and proposes a new synthesis of findings around the notion of the therapeutic
alliance. When providers exhibit relational qualities such as empathy, genuineness, respect, and concern, then patients are more affectively satisfied, more
likely to disclose emotional concerns that impinge on treatment, and more
likely to trust their physician. This alliance can improve patient adherence,
with corresponding improvements in treatment outcomes. It also increases the
likelihood that primary care physicians can detect depression—an important
consideration given the incidence of depression, its inter-relationship with
physical symptoms and comorbid conditions, the suffering it causes, and the
likelihood that a primary care physician is the first (and maybe only) connection to care for more than half of those in the United States who have mental
illness. The authors conclude with a summary of evidence that training can
improve physician and patient communication skills.

Provider-patient interactions occur in the context of societal health care
trends and institutional constraints. In chapter 2, Bernice Pescosolido, Thomas
Croghan, and Joel Howell focus on the trend toward large scale measurement
of outcome data, including "reports of patient satisfaction, an assessment of
costs, evaluations of whether procedural guidelines were followed, or tracking the impact of the provision of medical care" (p. 41). These assessments
frequently are justified as necessary to improve the quality of care; however,
the processes of collecting and distributing this information have potentially
complex effects on health care access, provider-patient communication, and
policies regarding health care organization and financing. Internally focused
assessment is nothing new—there is a long tradition of physicians communicating amongst themselves about treatment and practice—however, the last
50 years have seen a shift toward external assessments conducted by health
services researchers and disseminated to various publics, including health
care organizations, patient-consumers, insurance companies, and government
policy makers and regulators. In this modern Health Outcomes Movement,
assessment is a communicative act. Measurement entails communication
between researcher and researched, and the results often are communicated
strategically to influence health behavior, medical practice, and health policy.

The chapter provides historical perspective on how and why an emphasis on patient voice and public stakeholders has taken hold at this particular time. The authors then analyze what is communicated by the methods for measuring outcomes and by the patterns of publishing results. They conclude by examining what the Health Outcome Movement communicates to the lay public and how culturally diverse groups respond differently to attempts to solicit their feedback. The authors' analysis reveals contested meanings of outcomes: instead of scientific measurement to promote empowerment and improve care, those who are subjected to measurement often interpret it as irrelevant or as an excuse to deny care.

Communication in Health Care Organizations

Provider-patient interactions occur in the context of health care organizations. The managed care context is the focus of Kevin Real and Rick Street's chapter 3. Real and Street ask, "In what way do health care organizations affect processes and outcomes of communication in medical consultations?" (p. 65). Although the question seems straightforward enough, the answer is complicated by the wide variety of ways health care is organized and by the emphasis in previous research on patient-provider-level outcomes and processes without attention to the broader contexts in which individual and dyadic factors occur. Yet, the import of the organizational context is readily seen when we consider how the structure of organizations and their financing arrangements influence what patients can see which providers when and for how long. Recent changes in health care organizations have reduced physician autonomy and increased the influence of organizational factors, resulting in trends toward conflicting physician loyalties to patients versus employers, reduced patient trust in providers, and disruption of continuity in the provider-patient relationship. The authors' ecological model not only demonstrates the significance of organizational context for provider-patient communication but also reveals how providers and patients can use communication to overcome organizational constraints. For example, providers may attempt to manage conflicting loyalties by using ambiguity or building an "us against the organization" alliance with patients. New communication technologies also can provide avenues for disclosing information, coordinating care, and improving patient education and participation in decision-making. Communication practices take shape within organizational constraints and new ways of communicating may enable participants to adapt to new organizational structures.

Managed care has had far-reaching effects not only on patients' experiences and care but also on physicians' professional roles and working conditions. In chapter 4, John Lammers and Josh Barbour point out how individual and institutional factors create variability in how physicians respond to managed care. Structuration theory provides a framework for considering how a physician's role and practice setting shape her or his expectations for and experiences of managed care. The authors report results of a survey of primary practice and specialist physicians in a community with three quite different institutional settings: a specialty clinic, a public clinic, and an independent practitioner association. Taking individual differences and institutional arrangements into account enabled Lammers and Barbour to predict variation in how physicians felt about managed care. Different individual roles and practice settings resulted in different experience with managed care—both in terms of number of patients with managed care arrangements and in the length of time one had dealt with managed care—and this, in turn, predicted physicians' attitudes about how managed care affected professional autonomy, integrity, authority, and earnings. Physicians in this study were not uniformly dissatisfied with managed care; instead, their reported satisfaction varied with role and setting.

Communication in a Culturally Diverse Society

Two chapters show how cultural differences enter into health care interactions. Howard Waitzkin's chapter 5 draws from his influential book, *At the Front Lines of Medicine: How the Healthcare System Alienates Doctors and Mistreats Patients and What We Can Do About It*. He details the cultural barriers that complicate primary care providers' ability to identify and diagnose somatic conditions arising from traumatic experiences among refugees and immigrants. Somatoform symptoms are those for which no organic pathology can be identified. Although these symptoms are not unique to refugees and immigrants, cross-cultural differences make their diagnosis and treatment more challenging. These include language barriers, cultural differences in communication patterns and expected medical roles, different explanatory models of the body, and cultural taboos and stigmas associated with illness. In addition, the patient's life world and use of traditional healing practices are part of a social context that affects symptoms yet may be unknown or unfamiliar to health care professionals. The contributions of stress (socioeconomic, environmental, and political) to somatoform symptoms may go unrecognized. Traumatic events may be processed in "terrible narratives" that patients find too horrific and/or incoherent to tell; in-depth, culturally sensitive interviewing is important if health care practitioners are to identify the link between somatization, culture, and trauma. The chapter concludes with a discussion of the challenges for health care professionals in identifying and changing social contextual factors that affect their patients.

In chapter 6, Elaine Hsieh examines what role medical interpreters play in interactions between health care providers and patients with limited English proficiency. Theory, training, and policy related to medical interpreters have promoted a *conduit* metaphor to describe the work interpreters do: they are seen as neutral transmitters of information between providers and patients. In this view, an interpreter's job is to passively relay information, reinforce the patient-provider relationship, and remain as invisible as possible. In contrast, Hsieh's observations of what interpreters actually do revealed interpreters as active participants in a complex process of meaning negotiation. Interpreters must purposefully and strategically translate not only the words used but also the cultural assumptions and values that provide context for their words. In addition, if they are to promote an effective patient-provider relationship, interpreters must sometimes act strategically to edit, explain, or enhance what is said. In interviews about their work, interpreters sometimes recognize and articulate this active role, including the tensions and contradictions they experience as they seek to comply with the institutionally preferred conduit role while honoring the larger goal of securing quality health care for all patients. Hsieh suggests a more productive metaphor for interpreter's work is that of a mediator who intervenes in the communicative process in a way that ensures the patients' and providers' equal access to and control over information.

Communicating Patient Identities, Meanings, and Narratives

Several chapters share an emphasis on recognizing that patients who live with illness are more than their medical diagnosis; they are persons with identities and their desire to perform valued identities shapes medical interactions. In chapter 7, John Heritage examines how concerns for appearing to be a reasonable person, ever present in ordinary conversations, also shape interactions between patients and physicians. Visits to a physician are governed not only by a dispassionate desire to determine the facts of a patient's condition, but also by value-laden concerns for legitimacy. Patients who seek medical care are normatively expected to have a "doctorable" problem, one that is worthy of medical attention, advice, and sometimes treatment. Consequently, justification for the visit is part of what occurs during provider-patient interactions. Heritage's analysis shows how this issue emerges not only during the initial part of a visit, in which the patient presents his or her problem, but also may persist through history taking, physical examination, diagnosis, and counseling phases. This concern with establishing doctorability clearly illustrates how identity concerns shape the ways patients interact with physicians.

In chapter 8, Bruce Lambert, Naomi Levy, and Jerome Winer seek to improve psychiatric treatment for persons with mental illness by understanding what medication means to patients and how illness and treatment impinge on valued identities. They document how psychiatric treatment trends show a dramatic increase in drug therapy and brief medication management for the treatment of outpatients. Despite the successes and popularity of psychopharmacology, high rates of nonadherence, poor appointment keeping, and patient and provider dissatisfaction with treatment suggest room for improvement. The authors consider how drug therapy prescribed in brief, medically-oriented consultations can lead providers to overlook the impact of illness and medication on patients' sense of self. Mental illness and medication often disrupt a patient's biography and threaten the activities that sustain a patient's valued identities. The side effects of medications extend beyond physical symptoms to take on symbolic import, including the interpretation of "being on" any medication at all. When medication regimens fail to take into account patients' meanings and experiences, patients suffer and they may choose nonadherence rather than further loss of self. The authors propose an expanded model of mental health care that includes communicating with patients about what drug therapy means to them and how to take into account not only bodily side effects but also meanings for biography and identity. The chapter shows how the ability to communicate a desirable self and a coherent life story shape how patients self-manage their illness. Improved provider-patient communication can create better medication management by alerting providers to patients' meanings and collaborating to find a regimen patients can follow.

Some illness identities are highly stigmatized. In chapter 9, Lance Rintamaki develops a model of social identify for people living with HIV that reflects the reciprocal relationships between identity and communication. People living with HIV vary in the value they associate with HIV, and this orientation develops through processes of managing negative meaning, managing positive meaning, and orienting to stigma. Individuals also vary in how salient HIV is to their identity and the actions they take to heighten or diminish their awareness. Giving and receiving social support, developing peer relationships, and engaging in self-advocacy are among the communication behaviors that shape one's social identity as a person living with HIV. In turn, the value and salience of one's identity as HIV positive influences the willingness to seek or give support, resist stigma, self-advocate for health care, or participate in peer relationships or HIV organizations. This chapter holds implications not only for understanding the experience of living with HIV but also for broader models of how social identities develop and change. Understanding the diverse orientations individuals may take to an HIV-positive identity also helps account for important outcomes such as seeking care, adhering to regimens, practicing safe sex, and enhancing mental health.

Illness narratives have been an important discursive site for studying illness identity and a potentially powerful tool patients use to reconstruct and enact identity. Kathy Charmaz's chapter 10 considers how our emphasis on patient illness narratives can obscure the meanings of silence. She asks, "Do stories encompass all experience? How do we account for silences?" (p. 240) and she observes that, "what participants do not say may be as telling as what they do say" (p. 241). Charmaz points out the importance of studying not only stories, but also silences, and all that falls in between, including "unspoken signals, impassive responses, implied messages, emotive signals, fragmented sentences, and false starts" (p. 241). The meanings of silence may be especially subjective, differing for a patient, friends, family, and researchers. Consequently, attention to silence may help correct a tendency to focus on our interpretation of a story *product* so that we may see the *process* through which layers of meaning are constructed by multiple interactants. Attention to silence also can balance the order of stories with the chaos, uncertainty, and emotion that accompany illness. Silence also draws attention to overwhelming and indescribable bodily experiences and to those who cannot speak, choose to remain silent, or have been silenced. Finally, attention to silence calls researchers to reflect upon the stories we tell about patient experience. We can provide participants with opportunities to tell silenced stories and distill unspoken meanings but we must reflect upon our own interpretive practices and accept suffering, silence, fragmentation and ambiguity alongside orderly, coherent narrative. Throughout her chapter, Charmaz emphasizes how stories and silences are occasioned by social contexts and take on meaning in interactions with others.

Communication in Relational Contexts

Finally, personal relationships provide a context in which patients experience illness and communicate about that experience. In chapter 11, Ashley Duggan, Beth Le Poire, Margaret Prescott, and Carolyn S. Baham detail how patterns of dyadic communication may inadvertently promote unhealthful conditions, such as substance abuse, domestic violence, disordered eating, and depression. Inconsistent nurturing as control theory (INCT) provides a framework for understanding how one partner's behaviors may sustain unhealthful behaviors in the other person. Conflicting desires to nurture and control produce a pattern of inconsistent responses that end up rewarding unhealthful behavior. Even when partners recognize problematic behavior, they are often caught up in varying motives, including not only desires to change problem behaviors but also wanting to feel needed, desiring control in an uncontrollable situation, fearing an end of a valued relationship, and feeling concern and love for one another. Communication patterns mirror conflicting motives, alternating between punishing problem behaviors and rewarding them—a pattern that further conditions and entrenches those behaviors. INCT synthesizes findings from studies of diverse conditions and points the way to changes in communication that can break out of dysfunctional patterns. This theory makes clear how individual health problems are intertwined with social relationships through the processes of communication.

Personal relationships can also serve as an important form of social support for persons coping with illness. Similarities between the functions of social support and the benefits of spirituality are the focus of Jennifer Peterson's chapter 12. In her interviews with women living with HIV, she found many women spoke of spirituality in social and relational terms; thus, for some spirituality served as a source of social support. Just as a friend or loved one might provide appraisal support, emotional validation, directive guidance, or tangible help, Peterson's interviewees spoke of how their spirituality helped them re-appraise stressful situations, gave them a sense of affirmation and care, and provided a powerful connection that gave guidance and even instrumental aid. For many women, spirituality also facilitated connection with a church that functioned as a social network. This was particularly important when women felt rejected by their families or friends and excluded from other HIV communities. Whereas some conceptualizations of spirituality might focus on a belief system or a way of viewing the world, the women in Peterson's study revealed ways that spirituality may also be experienced as a social and relational phenomenon sustained by communication with a spiritual being and with other members of a community who share that spiritual connection.

Overarching Themes

Roxanne Parrott concludes this volume by examining how three broad classes of communication (societal, scientific, and lay) shape a wide range of significant outcomes. "Communicating as a society about health" (p. 323) entails as public discussion, such as debate and decision making related to health resource allocation. "Communicating the science of health" (p. 326) involves disseminating research findings. "Communicating our experience with health" (p. 329) refers to lay discourses that often go unnoticed because they are woven into daily life. In the chapters in this volume, Parrott finds numerous significant outcomes of communication that arise within each of these three arenas, including: "resource allocation; gate-keeping; identity formation and/or maintenance; comprehending and comparing; uncertainty; fear; accountability; effort; excuse and/or justification accounts; stereotypes; compliance; hope and/or optimism; guilt, embarrassment, and/or shame; sanctions; and policy and/or behavior change" (p. 324). These outcomes are interwoven within fields of discourse that give them salience and meaning. Parrott traces several important health issues (e.g., prenatal care, health behavior change, and risk reduction to mention just a few) through societal, scientific, and lay domains of discourse to show how communication shapes interrelated outcomes. Examining the discourses surrounding managing health and illness reveals tensions between competing interests. How we communicate shapes whose interests are served, which policies prevail, and which values are honored; in turn, communication is contextualized by interests, institutions, values, policies, and social and cultural factors. Parrott concludes with a call for communication advocacy.

The authors in this volume collectively address several major themes that link health and illness to the communicative forms, processes, and functions we enact in relationships with health care providers as well as others in our everyday lives. One theme concerns how personal meanings, beliefs, identities, and narratives are presented in interactions. Health beliefs, illness identities, and illness narratives have garnered much attention over the past two decades. Several authors in this volume make the distinctive contribution of *examining how identities and narratives are communicated to particular audiences in particular contexts.* Stories and silences are performances designed for particular moments (Charmaz) and the ability to integrate illness into one's unfolding life story shapes treatment adherence (Lambert et al.). A therapeutic relationship in patient-provider interactions (Haskard et al.) may improve the chances that those coping with mental and physical illness find ways to integrate their medications and their illness into the identity performances they value outside the doctor's office.

A second theme running through this volume is to study *how health beliefs and behaviors are situated in particular cultural communication contexts*, including national and ethnic subgroups. Health care inequities and folk beliefs about illness are manifested in conversations and patterns of interaction and several chapters reveal how information, beliefs, and resources are transmitted in interaction as well as how abstract differences in health beliefs create concrete moments of interactional discomfort, misunderstanding, and/or asymmetry. Communication processes are often the mediating link between social statuses or cultural beliefs and health care outcomes such as access, quality of care, and satisfaction. Providing high quality care is not only a matter of translating the words spoken in patient-provider interaction but of mediating between different value systems and experiences and constructing relationships of mutual respect (Hsieh; Waitzkin). The instruments that are purported to empower patients by providing scientific measurement of outcomes may miss some of the "outcomes" that are most important to patients or may fail to provide meaningful information when patients believe the intent of measurement is to deny rather than improve care (Pescosolido). Cultural differences may pose considerable barriers to care but the strategic and creative communication of translators, providers, and patients reveal the power of interpersonal interaction to overcome some of these constraints (Hsieh).

Showing *how social meanings and prejudices impact health behavior and access* is a third theme running through these chapters. That patients reach their own interpretations of health, illness, and care regimens has been well-documented. Likewise, we know that patients, providers, and the public at large sometimes hold prejudiced and stigmatizing beliefs about illness. In conversations between care providers and patients or between patients and members of their social network, we see how cognitions become actions or how schemas shape our reactions. Patient beliefs shape their decisions about treatment and medication adherence (Hsieh; Lambert et al.; Waitzkin). Spiritual beliefs may facilitate relationships that serve as important sources of social support (Peterson). Beliefs about stigma (and fear that one will be a victim) may prevent self-care and preventive behavior (Rintamaki). To our knowledge of social meanings and prejudices, these chapters add insight into the kinds of interaction patterns through which beliefs these may be transmitted, enacted, or combated.

Several authors address *how general interactional structures may facilitate or hinder delivery of health care*. We come to health-related interactions with established norms and practices. Some of those structures are the basic forms and sequences of conversation, patterns that we use efficiently and usually do not notice, but patterns that can also run at cross-purposes with health-related goals (Heritage). In addition to the basic structures of conversation, there are also relationship-specific patterns of power and nurturance (Duggan et al.) and culturally-distinctive patterns of communication (Hsieh) that may create tensions, misunderstandings, power struggles, and cross-purposes in health related talk.

A final theme concerns *how the impact of social structure on health access and outcomes may be mediated by communication processes.* With dramatic changes in the delivery and financing of health care has come scholarly interest in how organizational structures may result in health care that is unequally distributed or poorly delivered. The authors in this volume show how organizational structures manifest in conversations and patterns of interaction with consequences for equitable access and satisfactory outcomes. One way managed care affects physician and patient satisfaction and outcomes is by disrupting the continuity in the provider-patient relationship and by creating interactions in which physicians have conflicting loyalties and patients feel less trust (Real & Street). Yet, we also are reminded that the power of institutional contexts is not uniform: for example, the degree to which physicians are dissatisfied with managed care depends upon personal attitudes and their past history of interactions in a managed care system (Lammers & Barbour). Communication strategies and technologies employed by physicians and patients also may be a way of responding to institutional constraints (Haskard et al.; Real & Street).

Health scientists, health care providers, and public health professionals increasingly are recognizing the importance of health communication to improving individual and public health outcomes. For example, *Healthy People 2010* described health objectives for the United States developed through the collaboration of health scientists, national organizations, government agencies, and public input. In a chapter devoted to health communication, the report acknowledges that health communication is "a necessary element of efforts to improve personal and public health" (p. 11-1). The report further stated that leading health indicators (including physical activity, overweight and obesity, tobacco use, substance abuse, responsible sexual behavior, mental health, injury and violence, environmental quality, immunization, and access to health care) "all depend to some extent on effective health communication" (p. 11-5). The report elaborated: "For individuals, effective health communication can help raise awareness of health risks and solutions, provide the motivation and skills needed to reduce these risks, help them find support from other people in similar situations, and affect or reinforce attitudes" (p. 11-1). Initiatives such as *Healthy People 2010* look to health communication scholarship to contribute to efforts to improve length and quality of life and eliminate health disparities. We hope this volume will encourage attention to health communication practices in personal relationships and in health care organizations and serve as a source of questions, models, and directions for further research.

References

Albrecht, T. L., & Goldsmith, D. J. (2003). Social support, social networks, and health. In T. L. Thompson, A. M. Dorsey, K. I. Miller, & R. Parrott (Eds.), *Handbook of health communication* (pp. 263–284). Mahwah, NJ: Erlbaum.

Beck, C. S., Benitez, J. L., Edwards, A., Olson, A., Pai, A., & Torres, M. B. (2004). Enacting "health communication:" The field of health communication as constructed through publication in scholarly journals. *Health Communication, 16,* 475–492.

Brown, J. B, Stewart, M., & Ryan, B. L. (2003). Outcomes of patient-provider interaction. In T. L. Thompson, A. M. Dorsey, K. I. Miller, & R. Parrott (Eds.), *Handbook of health communication* (pp. 141–161). Mahwah, NJ: Erlbaum.

Cegala, D. J., & Broz, S. L. (2003). Provider and patient communication skills training. In T. L. Thompson, A. M. Dorsey, K. I. Miller, & R. Parrott (Eds.), *Handbook of health communication* (pp. 95–119). Mahwah, NJ: Erlbaum.

Cline, R. W. (2003). Everyday interpersonal communication and health. In T. L. Thompson, A. M. Dorsey, K. I. Miller, & R. Parrott (Eds.), *Handbook of health communication* (pp. 285–313). Mahwah, NJ: Erlbaum.

Cohen, S., Underwood, L. G., & Gottlieb, B. H. (2000). *Social support measurement and intervention: A guide for health and social scientists.* New York: Oxford University Press.

Duggan, A. (2006). Understanding interpersonal communication processes across health contexts: Advances in the last decade and challenges for the next decade. *Journal of Health Communication, 11,* 93–108.

Griffin, S. J., Kinmouth, A. L., Veltman, M. W. M., Gillard, S., Grant, J., & Stewart, M. (2004). Effect on health-related outcomes of interventions to alter the interaction between patients and practitioners: A systematic review of trials. *Annals of Family Medicine, 2,* 595–608.

Haywood, K., Marshall, S., & Fitzpatrick, R. (2006). Patient participation in the consultation process: A structured review of intervention strategies. *Patient Education and Counseling, 63,* 12–23.

Healthy People 2010: Volume 1 (2nd ed.). Retrieved August 22, 2008 from http://www.healthypeople.gov/document/pdf/volume1/11HealthCom.pdf

Kirmayer, L. J., & Sartorius, N. (2007). Cultural models and somatic syndromes. *Psychosomatic Medicine, 69,* 832–840.

Kline, K. N. (2003). Popular media and health: Images, effects, and institutions. In T. L. Thompson, A. M. Dorsey, K. I. Miller, & R. Parrott (Eds.), *Handbook of health communication* (pp. 557–581). Mahwah, NJ: Erlbaum.

Kline, K. N. (2006). A decade of research on health content in the media: The focus on health challenges and sociocultural context and attendant informational and ideological problems. *Journal of Health Communication, 11,* 43–59.

Lupton, D. (2003). The social construction of medicine and the body. In G. L. Albrecht, R. Fitzpatrick, & S. C. Scrimshaw (Eds.), *Handbook of social studies in health and medicine* (pp. 50–63). London: Sage.

McElroy, A., & Jezewski, M. A. (2003). Cultural variation in the experience of health and illness. In G. L. Albrecht, R. Fitzpatrick, & S. C. Scrimshaw (Eds.), *Handbook of social studies in health and medicine* (pp. 191–209). London: Sage.

Murray-Johnson, L., & Witte, K. (2003). Looking toward the future: Health message design strategies. In T. L. Thompson, A. M. Dorsey, K. I. Miller, & R. Parrott (Eds.), *Handbook of health communication* (pp. 473–495). Mahwah, NJ: Erlbaum.

Noar, S. M. (2006). A 10-year retrospective of research in health mass media campaigns: Where do we go from here? *Journal of Health Communication, 11,* 21–42.

Parrott, R. (2004). Emphasizing "communication" in health communication. *Journal of Communication, 54,* 751–787.

Roter, D. L., & Hall, J. A. (2006). *Doctors talking with patients/Patients talking with doctors: Improving communication in medical visits.* Westport, CT: Praeger.

Salmon, C., & Atkin, C. (2003). Using media campaigns for health promotion. In T. L. Thompson, A. M. Dorsey, K. I. Miller, & R. Parrott (Eds.), *Handbook of health communication* (pp. 449–472). Mahwah, NJ: Erlbaum.

Sans-Corrales, M., Pujol-Ribera, E., Gené-Badia, J., Pasarín-Rua, M. I., Iglesias-Pérez, B., & Casajuana-Bruent, J. (2006). Family medicine attributes related to satisfaction, health and costs. *Family Practice, 23,* 308–316.

Sarason, B. R., Sarason, I. G., & Gurung, R. A. R. (1997). Close personal relationships and health outcomes: A key to the role of social support. In S. Duck (Ed.), *Handbook of personal relationships* (2nd ed., pp. 547–573). New York: Wiley.

Suarez-Almazor, M. E. (2004). Patient-physician communication. *Current Opinion in Rheumatology, 16,* 91–95.

Walker, K. L., & Dickson, F. C. (2004). An exploration of illness-related narratives in marriage: The identification of illness-identity scripts. *Journal of Social and Personal Relationships, 21,* 527–544.

Whaley, B. B. (Ed.). (1999). *Explaining illness: Research, theory, and strategies.* New York: Routledge.

Chapter 1

Physician-Patient Communication

Psychosocial Care, Emotional Well-Being, and Health Outcomes

*Kelly B. Haskard, Summer L. Williams, and
M. Robin DiMatteo*

Effective physician-patient communication, including awareness of, and engagement with, patients' psychosocial needs, emotional well-being, and mental health challenges, is essential to physician-patient concordance and to outcomes including patient satisfaction, adherence, and treatment response. Although patient satisfaction is the most frequently studied outcome of communication (Ong, de Haes, Hoos, & Lammes, 1995), adherence and health care outcomes have also been related to physicians' interpersonal contact expressed through warmth, caring, and listening to the patients' concerns (Korsch, Gozzi, & Francis, 1968). Such interpersonal elements as affiliativeness (in contrast to dominance, for example) promote patient satisfaction with the medical visit (Buller & Buller, 1987). Partnership and social support from health professionals, as well as from friends and family, are essential to patients' adherence to recommended treatments (DiMatteo, 2004a; DiMatteo, Reiter, & Gambone, 1994). Research efforts increasingly are being directed toward understanding the role of the therapeutic relationship in fostering physician awareness and patient disclosure of the emotional challenges of illness (Meredith, Orlando, Humphrey, Camp, & Sherbourne, 2001). Appreciating the role of mental health issues, particularly depression and anxiety, in primary care is an essential, though challenging, aspect of everyday medical practice (Wells & Sherbourne, 1999).

The purpose of this chapter is to examine the dimensions of health care interaction that influence physician-patient communication. It is argued that primary care practice inherently requires both awareness and management of psychosocial, emotional, and often mental health challenges in the care of patients. This chapter will address the role of communication in meeting these challenges and improving health care outcomes, and will examine whether and how health professionals' skills can be improved to achieve effective communication.

The concepts and themes of this chapter will be illustrated with a composite patient vignette, and the most recent evidence will be presented from research on physician-patient communication and the value of care for patients' psychosocial needs, emotional well-being, and mental health in the primary care setting.

Effective Communication: A Key to Patient-Centered Care

Grace is 25 years old and has Type 1 diabetes. She recently graduated from college and is embarking on a career in public relations with a well-known New York firm. Her job is stressful with little control, and she usually works more than 60 hours a week. Grace is emotionally close to her family in California, but is not able to see them often. For the first time in her life, Grace is living at such a fast pace that she is failing to make her diabetes, and her overall health, top priorities. After many years of continuous care with the same physician, Grace must see a new doctor in New York. At her first visit, Grace experiences Dr. Carter as businesslike, somewhat cold and remote, and disinterested in discussing anything beyond the technical management of her diabetes.

Communication in the Physician-Patient Relationship

The extensive research literature on physician-patient communication has examined both verbal and nonverbal behavior in the therapeutic dyad. Although somewhat greater attention has been focused on verbal communication (Roter & Hall, 1992), nonverbal behavior has been shown to be essential to the interpersonal context of medical care (Hall, Harrigan, & Rosenthal, 1995). Medical interaction involves two communicative functions—instrumental (task-oriented) exchange and relational (or socioemotional) communication. Task-oriented exchange such as the focus of Dr. Carter in his care of Grace in the vignette above, is primarily verbal, and consists of information-seeking, information-giving, and information-verifying (Cegala, 1997). Such communication usually emphasizes the discussion of biomedical topics (Roter et al., 1997).

Relational communication, on the other hand, is more likely to occur in the context of nonverbal messages, although it also involves verbal communication concerning psychosocial topics. Relational communication includes both verbal and nonverbal expressions of empathy and concern through explicit discussion of emotional experience as well as eye contact, voice tone, facial expressions, and body language and orientation (Ambady & Rosenthal, 1992; DePaulo & Friedman, 1998; Waitzkin, 1984). Nonverbal behaviors play a particularly important role in the development of physician-patient rapport and patient satisfaction (Hall, Roter, & Katz, 1988). Patients tend to be more satisfied with physicians who are better at decoding and encoding nonverbal behavior, particularly those who are more sensitive to patients' body movement cues of emotion (DiMatteo, Taranta, Friedman, & Prince, 1980).

Socioemotional and Technical Communication

Socioemotional communication, also known as the "art of medicine," "bedside manner," humanism, and relational communication began to receive increased attention several decades ago when research evidence suggested that patients were as concerned with the interpersonal aspects of their care as they were with their physicians' technical competence and expertise (DiMatteo, Friedman, & Taranta, 1979; Friedman, Prince, Riggio, & DiMatteo, 1980). Physicians' affective and empathic communication is especially important in the opening and history-taking portion of the medical visit when agendas are being set that ultimately affect patients' health care outcomes (Haidet & Paterniti, 2003; Roter, 2000). Examples of relational and socioemotional communication include such behaviors as asking open-ended questions about the patient's history and current medical and psychological condition, allowing the patient to speak freely, and affirming the patient's emotional experience and concerns. Research has shown that when their physicians' verbal responses indicate disinterest or avoidance (as we see in the behavior of Dr. Carter toward Grace, below), patients limit their disclosure of and willingness to discuss both biomedical and emotional issues that are relevant to their care (Wissow et al., 2002). It is not a surprise, then, that physicians' socioemotional (interpersonal) behaviors are highly correlated with the technical quality of care that they deliver (DiMatteo & DiNicola, 1981).

The Achievement of Effective Physician-Patient Communication

> Grace is dissatisfied with Dr. Carter's care, but she does not have time to find another doctor who practices in her health insurance panel. Grace's visits to Dr. Carter often feel like a power struggle. She feels that he is condescending, critical, and insensitive about her management of her diabetes. His tone of voice is passive and disinterested, and he makes little eye contact with her. He interrupts her frequently when she is talking, and he does not seem to listen to what she is saying. When she tries to talk about the stress of her work and her personal life, and even her health habits, he changes the subject to strictly biomedical topics.

Physician-patient communication, both verbal and nonverbal behavior, has been studied in relation to a variety of outcomes. For example, physician voice tone and its interaction with verbal content predict patient satisfaction with care (Hall, Roter, & Rand, 1981). Negative voice tone combined with more positive speech tends to elicit the highest level of satisfaction from patients, perhaps because patients perceive anxious physician voices as demonstrating caring and concern. When physicians were more anxious and angry in their speech, their patients were found to have better compliance with appointment follow-up (Hall, Roter, & Rand, 1981), and alcoholic patients were more adherent to treatment recommendations when their physicians' voice tones conveyed greater worry and anxiety (Milmoe, Rosenthal, Blane, Chafetz, & Wolf, 1967). In research on verbal behavior, some of the most consistent impediments to effective health outcomes involve physicians' underestimation of their patients' level of understanding medicine and their continued use of medical jargon while withholding satisfactory conceptual explanations that would help patients help themselves (DiMatteo & Hays, 1980).

There are numerous reasons why effective communication may be difficult for physicians to implement. Providers may be more concerned with the technical, biomedical aspects of care, too pressed for time to consider psychosocial issues, and unconvinced of the value of effective communication despite its link to better health outcomes (Kreps & Kunimoto, 1994). Of course, reciprocity in physician-patient communication can influence the course of medical treatment and patients' own verbal and nonverbal cues can influence their physicians' behavior. For example, in one study the amount of information that physicians gave to patients was strongly influenced by patients' communicative styles (Street, 1991). The frequency with which patients asked questions strongly affected the degree to which their physicians provided medical information in general and diagnostic and treatment information in particular. Street (1991) found that patients' verbal responsiveness was influenced by their physicians' partnership-building behaviors, and the degree to which patients expressed concerns and opinions was positively related to their doctors' statements of agreement and solicitation of their questions, opinions, and feelings. Past research has shown that patients can be trained in communication skills that enable them to ask more effective questions and more competently seek information about their condition, facilitating and improving the process of information sharing (Cegala, McClure, Marinelli, & Post, 2000). A patient's behavior can affect how the physician communicates with him or her, and the patient's identity, health, and demographic characteristics can play a role in the physician-patient interchange. When patients and physicians are of the same racial background, visits last longer and patients show more positive affective behaviors, than when patients and physicians are of different racial backgrounds (Cooper et al., 2003). Lower education level, minority status, and both younger and older age and male gender of patients have been found to result in a less participatory physician approach (Kaplan, Gandek, Greenfield, Rogers, & Ware, 1995). Patients' education and socioeconomic status can influence their communication and health behaviors (Mechanic, 1992), and some patients may be too fearful or too sick to communicate and negotiate their treatment effectively (Kreps & Kunimoto, 1994). These findings have relevance for patient outcomes, particularly through adherence, which is enhanced when patients play an active role in their treatment. Both the advantages and the challenges of patients' experience of the sick role interface with physicians' own attempts to cope with and navigate the circumstances of their lives and pressures of medical practice (DeVoe, Fryer, Hargraves, Phillips, & Green, 2002; Mechanic, 1992; Thomas, 2004). Job-related cognitive and physical pressures may even prompt many physicians to rely unintentionally on stereotypical schemas about certain ethnic groups, affecting the quality of care they provide (Burgess, Fu, & van Ryn, 2004).

Indeed, patient involvement in medical decision making, and the collaborative mutual participation of physicians and patients, is typically negotiated in their communicative interchange. The degree of mutual respect between them can have a profound effect on the reciprocity of information exchange that ensues in the interaction. Such mutual participation is associated with greater patient satisfaction and ultimately more positive health care outcomes (Martin, DiMatteo, & Lepper, 2001; Martin, Jahng, Golin, & DiMatteo, 2003).

Participative decision making in physician-patient communication can be complex, however, as evidenced in a detailed scheme that involves various levels of patient-physician collaboration and patient autonomy, as well as options for patient or physician abdication of responsibility or even relationship termination (Ballard-Reisch, 1990). Some patients, of course, prefer their physician to have more control in the relationship, whereas others prefer a more consumerist approach in which the patient takes an active role in his or her health care decisions (Street, Krupat, Bell, Kravitz, & Haidet, 2003). Patients who want to be more involved tend to ask more questions and are more confident, and physicians who are willing to sustain collaborative relationships with these patients are able to support their patients' efforts and prompt them to be involved and active in their care (Street et al., 2003).

The concept of physician-patient *concordance* is relevant here. Concordance involves mutual understanding and trust in the therapeutic relationship, and is marked by open communication, collaboration, and agreement on how to manage a patient's health concerns. Concordance leads to shared decision-making, better adherence to medication, and better health care outcomes (Elwyn, Edwards, & Britten, 2003). In one study, patients who had high ratings of concordance with their physicians were one third more likely to follow their doctors' medical recommendations than those for whom concordance was low (Kerse et al., 2004). In a study of geriatric patients, physician-patient concordance (as rated by both parties) was a significant predictor of patient adherence (Maly, Leake, Frank, DiMatteo, & Reuben, 2002). In a relationship of concordance, patients understand the costs and benefits of their suggested regimens and through negotiation with their physicians arrive at mutually agreeable treatments and greater levels of satisfaction with care. Of course, how well such negotiation can work may depend upon the seriousness of the patient's illness. Some research has shown that even in the care of cancer, patients generally desire all possible information regarding their condition and treatment, even if that information is distressing (Chaitchik, Kreitler, Shaked, Schwartz, & Rosin, 1992; Hogbin & Fallowfield, 1989). Other studies, however, suggest that some individuals with serious illnesses may reject distressing information in an attempt to cope with uncertainty (Brashers, Goldsmith, & Hsieh, 2002). Mutual understanding and trust require that physician and patient communicate about the information that patients desire. Such communication is a critical goal of medical encounters that fosters positive patient outcomes.

Patient-Centered Communication in Psychosocial Care

Affective, patient-centered communication is critically important to the detection, understanding, and treatment of patients' psychosocial concerns and challenges. Although far more attention is typically paid to information exchange in the therapeutic interaction, it is *relational* communication that allows for effective psychosocial and emotional care of the patient (Cegala, 1997). An accepted notion among medical communication researchers is that "a good interpersonal relationship can be regarded as a prerequisite for optimal medical care" (Ong et al., 1995, p. 904).

The importance of patient-centeredness frequently has been supported in research on physician-patient communication (Stewart, 1984; Swenson et al., 2004). Stewart (1984) defined patient-centered interactions as "those in which the patient's point of view is actively sought by the physician" (p. 167). The patient-centered concept arose from the field of humanistic psychology and the work of Carl Rogers (1951, 1959), in which empathy, genuineness, and unconditional positive regard are the three key components of a successful therapeutic alliance. The patient-centered perspective also incorporates ideas from existential psychotherapy (May, 1983; Yalom, 1980), the goal of which is to understand the patient by understanding the patient's point of view. The four key experiences of struggle as conceptualized by existential psychotherapy are awareness of death, freedom, purpose/meaning, and aloneness (Yalom, 1980). These issues are as important in the physician-patient relationship as they are in psychotherapy. In medical practice, in which patients typically present with issues of limitation, pain, and mortality, the physician often is called upon to help patients struggle with challenges to their health and well-being as well as to their sense of meaning. Relatedly, Balint (1957) employed perspectives from psychiatry and psychotherapy to influence primary care medicine and focused particularly on the role of physician humanism and relational care in understanding and effectively treating medical patients (Scheingold, 1988).

The humanization of medical care requires recognition of the psychosocial issues important to patients as well as the physician's appropriate response to them. These issues include patient's mental health and diagnosis of emotional disorder. As Robinson and Roter (1999) have shown, patients are likely to respond to direct inquiry by their physicians about psychosocial distress, often resulting in physicians briefly counseling their patients in return.

Physician Empathy/Humanism and Patient-Centered Treatment

Grace has frequently dealt with physicians in the management of her diabetes, and has typically felt comfortable talking with them about her emotional and physical needs. One of her childhood physicians knew all about her school projects, best friends, and swim team triumphs. Grace believes that it would help to discuss personal and even emotional issues with her doctor, but Grace feels that Dr. Carter's communication style does not facilitate rapport and a sense of trust.

The quality of a physician's communication skill is directly connected to patient outcomes such as satisfaction and treatment adherence. When such communication is missing, as in the case of Grace and Dr. Carter, health outcomes may be in jeopardy. The American Board of Internal Medicine (ABIM, 1983) defined humanistic behavior as involving integrity, respect, and compassion; and holding high standards for moral behavior in professional life. The ABIM stresses the importance of humanistic qualities in physician-patient interaction throughout residency training (Linn, DiMatteo, Cope, & Robbins, 1987) and requires residency programs to evaluate trainees' humanistic behaviors, including qualities of integrity, respect, and compassion (Weaver, Ow, Walker, & Degenhardt, 1993).

There is much strong empirical evidence linking the many dimensions of physician humanism to patients' health care outcomes, including research demonstrating that patients who visited their physicians with a psychological problem (in addition to a medical or physical problem) had more positive experiences when their physicians were empathic and listened to them (Cape, 1996). Patient satisfaction has been associated with greater receptivity, immediacy, and similarity, all components of an empathic relationship. Receptivity, defined as "willingness to listen, openness to concerns, and interest," accounted for 51%–64% of the variance in satisfaction (Burgoon et al., 1987, p. 318). In addition, the authors found that increased adherence was related to increased affective satisfaction.

Psychosocial care of patients is an important aspect of physician humanism (Bensing, 1991). Using three independent sources of evaluation of physicians and hypertensive patients, Bensing (1991) found that visits rated high on psychosocial care were strongly predicted by affective behavior of physicians (especially nonverbal affective behavior such as eye contact and shown interest) as well as patient-centeredness and verbal empathy. Empathy is connected closely to humanism and in a clinical context has been defined as "the ability to understand the patient's situation, perspective, and feelings and to communicate that understanding to the patient" (Coulehan et al., 2001, p. 221). Empathic doctor-patient relationships consist of eliciting feelings, paraphrasing and reflecting, using silence, listening to what the patient is saying as well as unable to say, and includes encouragements and nonverbal behavior (Comstock, Hooper, Goodwin, & Goodwin, 1982; DiMatteo et al., 1980).

Trust and Open Communication Promotes Patients' Emotional Disclosure

Through narrative, a patient expresses the reason for the medical visit as well as the ways in which the health problem affects his or her life. A biopsychosocial perspective prepares the physician to understand the patient's narrative (Smith & Hoppe, 1991). Telling of the story is particularly relevant in the context of psychosocial concerns such as anxiety or depression (Haidet & Paterniti, 2003; Mishler, 1984; Roter & Hall, 1992; Smith & Hoppe, 1991). Patients can develop greater rapport with and trust in their physicians if they feel understood and free to communicate openly and honestly about negative or problematic emotional experience. Such emotional disclosure can be challenging, of course, because of the different perspectives of the physician, who speaks the "voice of medicine" and the patient who speaks the "voice of the lifeworld" (Mishler, 1984). In studies of primary care visits, these differences in perspective are apparent: Less than 35% of patients in one study reported a psychosocial problem as their reason for the visit, and only 17% of them did so in the opening of the visit. Many patients (34%) brought up the issue later in the visit, however, potentially disrupting its organization and plan. Further, in a study with standardized patients, Carney, Eliassen, et al. (1999) found that physicians who detected minor depression in patients, particularly at the beginning of the visit, were those who used more affective questioning and open-ended, psychosocial questions.

Trust is a necessary part of the patient-physician relationship and it promotes emotional disclosure (Branch, 2000). Trust involves demonstrating caring for the patient as well as keeping promises such as to follow up with test results or referral to a specialist. Advocacy for the patient contributes strongly to the perception of trustworthiness (Branch, 2000). Patients must believe that their physician is someone who can understand their unique experience, and who provides reliable and honest advice and necessary assistance (Branch, 2000).

Trust and open communication between physician and patient are essential components of patient-centered communication, particularly to the provision of effective mental health care in the primary care setting. Physicians can improve patients' well-being by using empathic communication. With such communication, depression and anxiety can be discussed with greater ease, leading to enhancement of patient outcomes.

Incidence and Prevalence of Depression and Anxiety in Primary Care Patients

Grace has lately been experiencing symptoms of both depression and anxiety, but she does not talk about her feelings with family and friends. She is frightened by these feelings, and she tries to manage them with uncontrolled spending. Her lunch hours often involve buying expensive clothes and shoes and skipping lunch, resulting in bills she cannot pay, unacceptable blood-sugar fluctuations, and feelings of guilt and self-recrimination. She wishes that she could mention these feelings to Dr. Carter, but she does not expect that he would be supportive.

Effective recognition, diagnosis, and management of mental health challenges, such as those facing Grace are essential in primary care. Primary care providers are the first and often only connection to care for more than 50% of the patients with mental illness in the United States (Bertakis, Roter, & Putnam, 1991). Major depression has a prevalence of 4.8%–8.6% in primary care practice (Bertakis et al., 2001), and in the United States alone, major depression is associated with more than 20,000 suicides and $47 billion in health care costs annually (Greenberg, Stiglin, Finkelstein, & Berndt, 1993). Up to 40% of primary care patients have a mental health problem of some sort (Goldman, Nielsen, & Champion, 1999), and 19% of outpatients report having significant emotional distress during the four weeks prior to their medical visit (Callahan et al., 1998).

Primary care practices are common sites for the diagnosis of depression and anxiety. Depressed patients visit primary health care facilities two to three times more frequently than those who are not depressed (Block, Schulberg, Coulehan, McClelland, & Gooding, 1988), and, although individuals with severe or incapacitating mental illnesses tend to refer themselves or be referred to the mental health sector, those with more subtle or somatic manifestations of depression and anxiety tend to be seen most often in primary care (Lemelin, Hotz, Swenson, & Elmslie, 1994; also see Waitzkin, this volume). Screening for depression and anxiety in primary care is therefore critically important. Meta-analytic research suggests that mental health screening has a positive relationship with the detection of depression, although further research is needed to assess the effects on patients' outcomes (Pignone et al., 2002). Physicians in managed care prepaid settings have been found to be less likely to recognize depression than those in fee-for-service settings (Wells, Hays, et al., 1989) and that time in the medical visit is essential to the discussion of patients' emotional experience.

Minor depression can occur with equal or greater frequency than major depression (Wagner et al., 2000) and even more patients suffer milder, but clinically significant subthreshold levels of depression (Wells, Stewart, et al., 1989). One study comparing patients in family practice found that patients with minor depression were significantly more debilitated in social health, self-esteem, physical health, perceived poor health, and perceived pain than patients with no depressive symptoms (Wagner et al., 2000). In addition, minor depression was found to be closer to major depression in levels of disability than had been previously believed; however, minor depression is not as easily recognized in primary care as major depression (Carney, Dietrich, et al., 1999). Adherence by physicians to treatment guidelines as well as greater physician awareness of the significance of minor depression in patients' lives are essential to the recognition of this critically important issue in the lives of many patients.

The effects of depression on physical and mental health related quality of life (HRQOL) can be substantial (Wells & Sherbourne, 1999), and these effects may be even more detrimental than common chronic medical conditions. Studies of depressed patients have described limitations in well-being, physical functioning, and role functioning such as work and school (Hays, Wells, Sherbourne, Rogers, & Spritzer, 1995; Sherbourne, Wells, & Sturm, 1997).

In examining depressed patients in primary care, it is important for physicians to consider the psychosocial factors that influence the course of depression. An active coping style has been found to be a strong predictor of change in mental health and depression status over time, and a decrease in depressive symptoms over time was related to less frequent chronic medical illnesses, and greater social support and physical activity (Sherbourne, Hays, & Wells, 1995). This study demonstrates the importance of problem-focused efforts, the management of mental health and stressful life events, and discussion with patients of individual lifestyle, available social support, and beliefs about depression (Sherbourne et al., 1995). Other psychosocial factors that might be important for providers to consider as they treat patients include early life traumatic experiences, family history of depression, and past history of depression (Nemeroff et al., 2003).

Recognition and Diagnosis by Primary Care Physicians

Depression can be difficult to recognize in primary care, particularly because it can be associated with comorbid medical conditions and a greater reporting of physical complaints (Callahan et al., 1997). Depression often coexists with physical illness, which physicians may find more comfortable to discuss (Lemelin et al., 1994) and patients may find more comfortable to present, especially when the patient also has significant chronic physical illness (Wright et al., 1980). Further, physicians often understand depression to be more of an acute illness rather than a recurrent or chronic one, assuming that the patients' symptoms will pass with time (Waldron, 1999). Patients who offer a psychiatric or psychosocial "presenting problem" to their doctors, and whose symptoms are of more recent origin, represent more than one psychiatric diagnosis, or reflect more severe mental illness have a greater likelihood of receiving a correct mental health diagnosis than those whose presentations are subtle (Ormel et al., 1990). Certain patient characteristics also are associated with the detection of depression, which is more likely if the physician is familiar with the patient, if the patient has certain suggestive clinical cues such as history of or treatment for depression, and distress and presence of vegetative symptoms (Klinkman, Coyne, Gallo, & Schwenk, 1998). Data from the Medical Outcomes Study found that mental health disorders such as depression occurred more frequently in patients who were older, female, White, unmarried, and of lower income and educational status and that physicians were less likely to detect depression in African American and Hispanic patients (Borowsky et al., 2000).

The PRIME-MD questionnaire is a valuable screening instrument to aid physicians in diagnosing mild to severe depression in primary care patients (Brody et al., 1998). It consists of nine core depressive symptoms and can be used to identify patients with milder levels of depression in contrast with those who have moderate to severe impairment. Even this simple instrument can be difficult to implement in practice, however. Brody and colleagues (1998) argued that it may be best for physicians to carry around with them the nine symptoms of depression in order to better recall the diagnostic criteria for depression. The development and strengthening of mental health care skills of physicians is critical, however, given the high prevalence of mental health challenges in primary care medicine.

Comorbidity of Depression with Other Medical Conditions

In 1988, the World Health Organization commissioned an international study to investigate the rates of psychiatric/mental disorders in primary care (Sartorius, Ustun, Lecrubier, & Wittchen, 1996). Depressive disorders were found to be most common among primary care patients (10.4%), followed by anxiety disorders (8% of patients). Nearly half of the cases of anxiety and depression co-occurred in the same patients at the same time. Subthreshold anxiety and depression were more common than major depression and severe anxiety (Sartorius et al., 1996). Further, the authors found depression that was comorbid with a physical health problem was less likely to be detected and sufficiently treated than depression that occurred alone, although depression occurring with another disorder caused more days of disability in a month than depression alone (Sartorius et al., 1996). Depression and anxiety are often comorbid with other physical health problems, and a truly biopsychosocial perspective and pursuit of a patient-centered rapport are essential to the provision of effective care. Rates of depression comorbidity vary in populations of pain sufferers but tend to be high (even up to 100%; Romano & Turner, 1985). Such an issue is of paramount importance for primary care physicians, who are likely to be the first line of care for patients in pain. A study of depressed patients with chronic pain assessed their patterns of service use and found that patients with comorbid pain and depression were more likely to use primary care than mental health specialty care (Bao, Sturm, & Croghan, 2003), pointing to the critical importance of primary care physicians' awareness of and training to deal with mental health issues.

Patients often provide information or clues that hint at emotional or psychosocial issues in their lives. One study found that clues about patients' worries and emotions are clearly present in over 50% of primary care interactions (Levinson, Gorawara-Bhat, & Lamb, 2000). This study also found that these clues often occurred in the context of presentation of a physical, biomedically-based problem. Indeed, given that clues to deeper problems and significant psychological challenges are often available in patients' communications, it is critically important that physicians recognize and respond to them. These instances in medical visits have also been termed "windows of opportunity" (Branch & Malik, 1993), and through the physicians' facilitative style, active listening, avoidance of blame, and sensitivity to patients' nonverbal expressions of emotion, detection of patients' depression and anxiety may be facilitated (Robbins, Kirmayer, Cathebras, Yaffe, & Dworkind, 1994).

Many physicians are concerned that their suggestion of patient depression may be taken by the patient as an accusation of malingering, and many may attribute patient distress to situational factors and remain unaware of the seriousness of depression (Lemelin et al., 1994). When symptoms are mild and patients have higher functioning and no comorbid anxiety, physicians' detection of depression tends to be limited, and they may ascribe patient depression to stress and dismiss it as a normal response to distressing diagnosis or treatment (Coyne, Schwenk, & Fechner-Bates, 1995). Many physicians feel that the identification of a "precipitating event" disqualifies a patient from a diagnosis of major depression, but such thinking reflects an outdated classification system that dichotomized depression into exogenous depression, which may be viewed as a response to an external circumstance, and endogenous depression, for which no obvious "cause" can be found. Exogenous (or reactive) depression was usually regarded as less serious and likely to resolve with time (Goldberg, 1993). A physician's inability to recognize depression also may be due to a lack of knowledge of the symptoms of depression and their management, a failure to consider the diagnosis of depression because of a preoccupation with organic illness, an underrating of the severity or treatability of depression, and the failure of effective communication to elicit symptoms needed to make the diagnosis (Schulberg & McClelland, 1987).

Of course, patients also play a role in the detection of depression and anxiety. Some reject or deny mental health conditions fearing stigma or attributions of weakness (Docherty, 1997), even when they experience decreased productivity, disruption in their overall functioning, and an increased likelihood of missing work (McQuaid, Stein, Laffaye, & McCahill, 1999). Some may have numerous physical complaints and increased somatization as well as increased visit frequency when depression exists alone or in combination with physical illness (Lemelin et al., 1994) but may respond only to their physicians' use of colloquial terms such as "discouragement" for leading into an inquiry about depression (Goldberg, 1993).

Practice Factors

The use of screening instruments for anxiety and depression would be helpful, but as Felker and colleagues (2003) suggested, issues such as time pressure and lack of skill with emotional health problems can limit physicians' use of these instruments (Williams et al., 1999). Further, as David Brody, M.D., commented "Depression is common in the patients [physicians] see, and if you don't ask about it, you won't pick it up. You can't just depend on [determining] that the patient looks depressed, and you can't depend on the patient coming in and telling you he's depressed" (Waldron, 1999, p. 33).

Issues in the medical care environment also can influence detection and treatment of mental health concerns. The fee schedule for primary care physicians rewards the treatment of physical illness and discourages taking the time to provide effective psychosocial care. Patients' insurance plans may have limited treatment options for mental health care (Williams et al., 1999) and special effort may be needed to care for psychological problems and psychosocial issues adequately (Lemelin et al., 1994).

Adherence/Response to Treatment

Grace has little time to relax or be with friends and often feels that she is missing out on a social life. Because of her hectic schedule, Grace often skips meals, eats high sugar snacks to soothe herself emotionally, and does not exercise. She does adequately test her blood sugar and take her insulin injections, however. Dr. Carter did stress the importance of her diabetes treatment regimen, but her depression is a risk factor for nonadherence to the full complement of diabetes treatments for poor long-term management of her chronic illness.

Adherence has been shown to be significantly and positively predictive of patients' health outcomes (DiMatteo, Giordani, Lepper, & Croghan, 2002) and is closely tied to communication and patient-centered care. Nonadherence is a serious problem in chronic illness sufferers. One meta-analysis has found that on average 25% of medical patients are nonadherent across all disease conditions, but that for some conditions including diabetes, nonadherence can be close to 40% (DiMatteo, 2004b). As illustrated in the case of Grace, physician-patient communication can strongly affect patient adherence. In HIV care, for example, in which nonadherence can be fatal, 6 of 7 measures of interpersonal care were found to be positively and significantly associated with patient adherence. These included physician trust, overall satisfaction, and general communication (Schneider, Kaplan, Greenfield, Li, & Wilson, 2004).

The process of medication taking is complex and affected by patient's beliefs, responsibilities, preferences, and relationships (Adams, Pill, & Jones, 1997; also see Lambert, Levy, & Winer, this volume). Furthermore, changes in the self brought about by illness, may result in social isolation and withdrawal, limits on life goals, changing ideas of the self, and even the feeling that one is a burden to others (Charmaz, 1983). Patient-centered medical care is one way to encourage the patient's progress toward adherence and healing. Through unrestricted communication, active listening, and the use of open-ended questions, a physician can better understand the ways in which a patient's identity is affected by illness. Physician understanding of patient health beliefs and lifestyle factors can be instrumental in designing a regimen that the patient will be able to follow. Such understanding influences the process of medical care and determines how the patient will experience the physician, the prescribed regimen, and the illness itself.

The issue of patient adherence is important to consider in the context of patient mental health. In a meta-analysis, depressed medical patients were found to be three times more likely to be nonadherent than nondepressed patients (DiMatteo, Lepper, & Croghan, 2000). Patients' hopelessness about their lives and conditions and their social distancing from sources of support and help can affect their ability to follow through with medical recommendations. Social support has been found to strongly influence adherence to medical treatments, and may be a powerful mediator of the depression-adherence relationship (DiMatteo, 2004a). Further, the relationship between social support and health may be mediated by both adherence and depression (DiMatteo, 2004a). Carney and colleagues (1998) studied depression and adherence in patients with coronary heart disease and found that depression may have influenced symptomatic patients to be nonadherent. Kulik and Mahler (1993) found that bypass patients with more emotional support were less depressed and anxious and more adherent to recommended behaviors. Depression tends to lead to nonadherence and associated negative health outcomes, and depression compels withdrawal from social interactions, leading to a decrease in social support and consequent detrimental effects on health (DiMatteo, 2004a; DiMatteo et al., 2000).

The prescription and use of antidepressants presents its own challenges to the physician-patient relationship. Antidepressant prescribing in primary care is an active process tied to the physician-patient relationship and requires considerable physician involvement in influencing patients' knowledge, beliefs, and behavior (Bultman & Svarstad, 2000). Collaborative style on the part of a physician can have a positive effect on patient outcomes, fostering increased patient knowledge of their medication regimen, improved initial beliefs about the medication, greater satisfaction, and higher overall adherence (Bultman & Svarstad, 2000). Patients who are more involved in their care and are supported through their medication use by their physicians are more likely to be adherent. Especially in the realm of antidepressant therapy, physician openness and participatory communication is beneficial for patients who may experience problems with side effects and other related concerns. The finding that psychotherapy is significantly related to adherence to antidepressant treatment (Tai-Seale, Croghan, & Obenchain, 2000) suggests the importance of the physician-patient relationship and social support received through the therapeutic relationship.

Research has shown that adherence to recommended behavior change is strongly associated with the strength of the physician-patient relationship (Safran et al., 1998). Nonadherence can increase physician and patient frustration, which may lead to incorrect diagnoses and unnecessary treatment (DiMatteo, et al., 2002). Physicians' ability to decode nonverbal cues was significantly correlated with their patients' adherence to keeping scheduled appointments (DiMatteo, Hays, & Prince, 1986). Physicians' job satisfaction has even been identified as a significant predictor of adherence at 2-year follow-up. This finding is particularly interesting considering the importance of psychosocial care and attention. If physicians themselves feel less stress and strain, it is likely that they would be more encouraging of their patients' well-being and mental health. Patients' quality of life is important and their treatments should be structured to fit their lives. Physicians who talk openly with their patients about side effects and problems with the regimen will likely have patients who are more adherent (Chewning & Sleath, 1996). Collaborative relationships require recognition of the need for effective communication, a conscious approach to the therapeutic relationship as a collaboration, awareness of the patient's beliefs and mental health status, and a recognition of the patient's right to choose his or her own course of action (DiMatteo et al., 1994; Schneider et al., 2004).

Patient Satisfaction

In addition to adherence, the relationship between a physician and patient can affect important outcomes such as patient satisfaction (Kaplan, Greenfield, & Ware, 1989; Roter & Hall, 1992). Recent meta-analytic study of verbal and nonverbal physician communication (Beck, Daughtridge, & Sloane, 2002) found that 50% of studies of physician verbal and nonverbal behaviors have measured satisfaction as the outcome variable, and in many of these studies the specific verbal behaviors linked to satisfaction included empathy, patient-centered behavior, courtesy, and friendliness. Patient satisfaction was heavily dependent upon empathic and relational communication.

In research on audiotaped medical visits for which patients filled out a patient satisfaction questionnaire, greater patient satisfaction occurred in visits in which more questions were asked of patients about psychosocial topics (Bertakis, Roter, & Putnam, 1991) and physicians used a more psychosocial communication style (Roter et al., 1997). The majority of visits (66%), however, tend to be physician-dominated and narrowly focused on biomedical topics, with cues of distress and opportunities to listen to patients' deeper concerns inadvertently missed. Related to this, patients who are more comfortable discussing their personal issues with their physicians and who perceive their physicians as more empathic are also more satisfied with their care (Sullivan, Stein, Savetsky, & Samet, 2000). Patients' trust in their physician is strongly, positively associated with satisfaction (Safran et al., 1998).

Patient satisfaction also is related to physicians' nonverbal behavior and skills. Larsen and Smith (1981) found that in the physician-patient interaction, higher satisfaction was associated with two components of physician immediacy, forward lean and body orientation. Ratings of the patient-provider relationship are also associated with better quality care for depression that meets recommended guidelines for the use of antidepressants or psychotherapy (Meredith et al., 2001). Patient ratings of satisfaction and the interpersonal relationship were found to be correlated with each other, but separate enough to raise the possibility that satisfaction may reflect technical competence as much as ratings of affective behavior (Meredith et al., 2001).

Communication Training: How to Achieve Better Patient Outcomes

Many health care outcomes can be improved by training both physicians and patients in communication skills, paving the way to more open and collaborative communication.

Physician Training

Dr. Carter was trained in an era when medicine had strictly defined gender and professional roles. Physician-patient communication was strictly biomedical, and the therapeutic relationship was hierarchical. Dr. Carter's training did not emphasize open communication, empathy, or psychosocial care. To better understand Grace's condition and provide appropriate care, it may be helpful for Dr. Carter to attend some communication skills training sessions. Future directions for Grace include focused mental health care, lifestyle changes and stress management, increased social support, and open, assertive communication with Dr. Carter. These changes would be a step toward improving her adherence and well-being.

An appreciable amount of research has focused on physician communication training (Post, Cegala, & Miser, 2002). In most cases, it has involved active listening, the promotion of patient-centered care, and feedback about performance (Millis et al., 2002; Smith et al., 1991).

Training can be especially beneficial in the area of psychosocial communication and empathy because improved communication between doctors and patients leads to better health outcomes for patients (Hall et al., 1988; Ong et al., 1995; Roter, 1989). An emphasis on narrative and artistic representations of the experience of illness is one way that medical students and physicians can develop and strengthen empathy. By viewing the history-taking as a time to learn the patient's story and better understand him or her, empathy is helpful in promoting physician-patient communication (Spiro, 1993). Suchman, Markakis, Beckman, and Frankel (1997) developed a model describing how physicians can learn to communicate empathically with patients. The authors identified "empathic opportunities" in which patients' expressions of emotion were subtle and the physician might either shut down this emotional expression in some way or reinforce its expression. Recognition of this emotional expression requires empathy and involves learning to detect emotional cues by the patient and providing a response that facilitates rather than dominates the interaction (Stewart, 1984). In another model, trained physicians who were videotaped after their training demonstrated increases in empathy, better responses to patient cues, and greater use of open-ended questioning (Jenkins & Fallowfield, 2002). These findings were supported by physicians' reports of changes in their attitudes and skills in communication. Intensive training in interviewing and psychosocial topics has been reported to both increase resident knowledge about psychosocial issues and improve interviewing of both real and standardized patients (Smith et al., 1998). A study specifically focused on "improving residents' confidence in psychosocial skills needed in primary care (i.e., psychological sensitivity, emotional sensitivity, managing somatization, and directive and nondirective facilitation of patient communication)" found that residents who were trained expressed significantly greater levels of confidence in all five areas of psychosocial skill (Smith et al., 1995, p. 315). Furthermore, studies have been undertaken to train practicing physicians. A randomized clinical trial of practicing primary care physicians trained physicians in either emotion-handling or problem-defining skills. Both groups were also trained in understanding psychosocial problems in primary care settings (Roter et al., 1995). Videotaped analyses of the patient visits demonstrated that physicians had learned and integrated the taught skills. These trained doctors showed better recognition of patient psychosocial problems and patients also reported benefit in terms of a reduction in their levels of emotional pain.

Patient Training

The past several years have seen an increase in patient involvement in health care, with research suggesting that patients can improve their skills at participating (Cegala, 2001). Post, Cegala, and Meiser (2002) reviewed 16 studies on patient training from 1975–2000 and described patient improvement in a number of areas: question-asking, adherence, patient control, disease-related outcomes, and functional status. Patient communication skills training also has been shown to enhance adherence with recommended treatments and/or follow-up appointments and referrals (Cegala, Marinelli, & Post, 2000; Roter, 1977).

Specific research has focused on teaching patients particular skills to improve communication. One system developed to increase patient's participation in their medical care is the PREPARED™ model (DiMatteo et al., 1994), which outlines eight steps in decision-making that enable patients to be more collaborative with their physicians. Other patient training approaches have also found positive effects (Cegala, 2001; Thompson, Nanni, & Schwankovsky, 1990), although some have found no effect or even a decrease in patient satisfaction (Greenfield, Kaplan, Ware, Yano, & Frank, 1988; Lewis et al., 1991; Thompson et al., 1990). Future research will be needed to address this area.

Conclusion

The goals of this chapter were to examine the outcomes of good communication and to understand the role of the physician and patient in achieving effective partnership. Psychosocial communication is critically important in the care of patients' mental health and well-being. Many primary care patients, such as Grace presented in the narrative, struggle with depression and anxiety, which affect their chronic disease management and outcomes. Thus, it is important for physicians to communicate empathically and openly in order to understand how psychosocial issues affect their patient's lives, health, and health habits. Various aspects of communication including nonverbal skill, affective talk, patient involvement, physician-patient rapport, and concordance all contribute to more positive patient outcomes, including patient satisfaction, adherence, and responses to treatment. Evidence is building that training in communication skills and increased empathic practice and sensitivity to mental health lead to enhanced physician-patient relationships and communication.

References

Adams, S., Pill, R., & Jones, A. (1997). Medication, chronic illness and identity: The perspective of people with asthma. *Social Science & Medicine, 45,* 189–201.

Ambady, N., & Rosenthal, R. (1992). Thin slices of expressive behavior as predictors of interpersonal consequences: A meta-analysis. *Psychological Bulletin, 111,* 256–274.

American Board of Internal Medicine. (1983). Evaluation of humanistic qualities in the internist. *Annals of Internal Medicine, 99,* 720–724.

Balint, M. (1957). *The doctor, his patient and the illness.* London: Pitman Medical.

Ballard-Reisch, D. (1990). A model of participative decision making for physician-patient interaction. *Health Communication, 2,* 91–104.

Bao, Y., Sturm, R., & Croghan, T. W. (2003). A national study of the effect of chronic pain on the use of health care by depressed persons. *Psychiatric Services, 54,* 693–697.

Beck, R. S., Daughtridge, R., & Sloane, P. D. (2002). Physician-patient communication in the primary care office: A systematic review. *Journal of the American Board of Family Practice, 15,* 25–38.

Bensing, J. (1991). Doctor-patient communication and the quality of care. *Social Science & Medicine, 32,* 1301–1310.

Bertakis, K. D., Helms, L. J., Callahan, E. J., Azari, R., Leigh, P., & Robbins, J. A. (2001). Patient gender differences in the diagnosis of depression in primary care. *Journal of Women's Health and Gender Based Medicine, 10,* 689–698.

Bertakis, K. D., Roter, D., & Putnam, S. M. (1991). The relationship of physician medical interview style to patient satisfaction. *The Journal of Family Practice, 32,* 175–181.

Block, M., Schulberg, H. C., Coulehan, J. C., McClelland, M., & Gooding, W. (1988). Diagnosing depression among new patients in ambulatory training settings. *Journal of the American Board of Family Practice, 1,* 91–97.

Borowsky, S. J., Rubenstein, L. V., Meredith, L. S., Camp, P., Jackson-Triche, M., & Wells, K. B. (2000). Who is at risk of nondetection of mental health problems in primary care? *Journal of General Internal Medicine, 15,* 381–388.

Branch, W. T., Jr. (2000). The ethics of caring and medical education. *Academic Medicine, 75,* 127–132.

Branch, W. T., & Malik, T. K. (1993). Using "windows of opportunities" in brief interviews to understand patients' concerns. *Journal of the American Medical Association, 269,* 1667–1668.

Brashers, D. E., Goldsmith, D. J., & Hsieh, E. (2002). Information seeking and avoiding in health contexts. *Human Communication Research, 28,* 258–271.

Brody, D. S., Hahn, S. R., Spitzer, R. L., Kroenke, K., Linzer, M., deGruy, F. V., III, et al. (1998). Identifying patients with depression in the primary care setting: a more efficient method. *Archives of Internal Medicine, 158,* 2469–2475.

Buller, M. K., & Buller, D. B. (1987). Physicians' communication style and patient satisfaction. *Journal of Health and Social Behavior, 28,* 375–388.

Bultman, D. C., & Svarstad, B. L. (2000). Effects of physician communication style on client medication beliefs and adherence with antidepressant treatment. *Patient Education and Counseling, 40,* 173–185.

Burgess, D. J., Fu, S. S., & van Ryn, M. (2004). Why do providers contribute to disparities and what can be done about it? *Journal of General Internal Medicine, 19,* 1154–1159.

Burgoon, J. K., Pfau, M., Parrott, R., Birk, T., Coker, R., & Burgoon, M. (1987). Relational communication, satisfaction, compliance-gaining strategies, and compliance in communication between physicians and patients. *Communication Monographs, 54,* 307–324.

Callahan, E. J., Bertakis, K. D., Azari, R., Helms, L. J., Robbins, J., & Miller, J. (1997). Depression in primary care: Patient factors that influence recognition. *Family Medicine, 29,* 172–176.

Callahan, E. J., Jaen, C. R., Crabtree, B. F., Zyzanski, S. J., Goodwin, M. A., & Stange, K. C. (1998). The impact of recent emotional distress and diagnosis of depression or anxiety on the physician-patient encounter in family practice. *The Journal of Family Practice, 46,* 410–418.

Cape, J. D. (1996). Psychological treatment of emotional problems by general practitioners. *British Journal of Medical Psychology, 69,* 85–99.

Carney, P. A., Dietrich, A. J., Eliassen, M. S., Owen, M., & Badger, L. W. (1999). Recognizing and managing depression in primary care: A standardized patient study. *The Journal of Family Practice, 48,* 965–972.

Carney, P. A., Eliassen, M. S., Wolford, G. L., Owen, M., Badger, L. W., & Dietrich, A. J. (1999). How physician communication influences recognition of depression in primary care. *The Journal of Family Practice, 48,* 958–964.

Carney, R. M., Freedland, K. E., Eisen, S. A., Rich, M. W., Skala, J. A., & Jaffe, A. S.

(1998). Adherence to a prophylactic medication regimen in patients with symptomatic versus asymptomatic ischemic heart disease. *Behavioral Medicine, 24,* 35–39.

Cegala, D. J. (1997). A study of doctors' and patients' communication during a primary care consultation: Implications for communication training. *Journal of Health Communication, 2,* 169–194.

Cegala, D. J. (2001, September). *Position paper: Patient communication skills training: Past, present, and future.* Paper presented at the Consumer-Provider Communication Symposium, Bethesda, MD.

Cegala, D. J., Marinelli, T., & Post, D. (2000). The effects of patient communication skills training on compliance. *Archives of Family Medicine, 9,* 57–64.

Cegala, D. J., McClure, L., Marinelli, T. M., & Post, D. M. (2000). The effects of communication skills training on patients' participation during medical interviews. *Patient Education and Counseling, 41,* 209–222.

Chaitchik, S., Kreitler, S., Shaked, S., Schwartz, I., & Rosin, R. (1992). Doctor-patient communication in a cancer ward. *Journal of Cancer Education, 7,* 41–54.

Charmaz, K. (1983). Loss of self: A fundamental form of suffering in the chronically ill. *Sociology of Health and Illness, 5,* 168–195.

Chewning, B., & Sleath, B. (1996). Medication decision-making and management: A client-centered model. *Social Science & Medicine, 42,* 389–398.

Comstock, L. M., Hooper, E. M., Goodwin, J. M., & Goodwin, J. S. (1982). Physician behaviors that correlate with patient satisfaction. *Journal of Medical Education, 57*(2), 105–112.

Cooper, L. A., Roter, D. L., Johnson, R. L., Ford, D. E., Steinwachs, D. M., & Powe, N. R. (2003). Patient-centered communication, ratings of care, and concordance of patient and physician race. *Annals of Internal Medicine, 139,* 907–915.

Coulehan, J. L., Platt, F. W., Egener, B., Frankel, R., Lin, C., Lown, B., et al. (2001). "Let me see if I have this right...": Words that help build empathy. *Annals of Internal Medicine, 135,* 221–227.

Coyne, J. C., Schwenk, T. L., & Fechner-Bates, S. (1995). Nondetection of depression by primary care physicians reconsidered. *General Hospital Psychiatry, 17,* 3–12.

DePaulo, B., & Friedman, H. S. (1998). Nonverbal communication. In D. T. Gilbert, S. T. Fiske, & G. Lindzey (Eds.), *Handbook of social psychology* (4th ed., Vol. 2, pp. 3–40). New York: Oxford University Press.

DeVoe, J., Fryer, G. E., Jr., Hargraves, J. L., Phillips, R. L., & Green, L. A. (2002). Does career dissatisfaction affect the ability of family physicians to deliver high-quality patient care? *The Journal of Family Practice, 51,* 223–228.

DiMatteo, M. R. (2004a). Social support and patient adherence to medical treatment: A meta-analysis. *Health Psychology, 23,* 207–218.

DiMatteo, M. R. (2004b). Variations in patients' adherence to medical recommendations: A quantitative review of 50 years of research. *Medical Care, 42,* 200–209.

DiMatteo, M. R., & DiNicola, D. D. (1981). Sources of assessment of physician performance: A study of comparative reliability and patterns of intercorrelation. *Medical Care, 19,* 829–842.

DiMatteo, M. R., Friedman, H. S., & Taranta, A. (1979). Sensitivity to body nonverbal communication as a factor in practitioner-patient rapport. *Journal of Nonverbal Behavior, 4,* 18–26.

DiMatteo, M. R., Giordani, P. J., Lepper, H. S., & Croghan, T. W. (2002). Patient adherence and medical treatment outcomes: A meta-analysis. *Medical Care, 40,* 794–811.

DiMatteo, M. R., & Hays, R. (1980). The significance of patients' perceptions of physician conduct: A study of patient satisfaction in a family practice center. *Journal of Community Health, 6,* 18–34.

DiMatteo, M. R., Hays, R. D., & Prince, L. M. (1986). Relationship of physicians' nonverbal communication skill to patient satisfaction, appointment noncompliance, and physician workload. *Health Psychology, 5,* 581–594.

DiMatteo, M. R., Lepper, H. S., & Croghan, T. W. (2000). Depression is a risk factor for noncompliance with medical treatment: Meta-analysis of the effects of anxiety and depression on patient adherence. *Archives of Internal Medicine, 160,* 2101–2107.

DiMatteo, M. R., Reiter, R. C., & Gambone, J. G. (1994). Enhancing medication adherence through communication and informed collaborative choice. *Health Communication, 6,* 253–265.

DiMatteo, M. R., Taranta, A., Friedman, H. S., & Prince, L. M. (1980). Predicting patient satisfaction from physicians' nonverbal communication skills. *Medical Care, 18,* 376–387.

Docherty, J. P. (1997). Barriers to the diagnosis of depression in primary care. *Journal of Clinical Psychiatry, 58*(Suppl. 1), 5–10.

Elwyn, G., Edwards, A., & Britten, N. (2003). "Doing prescribing": How might clinicians work differently for better, safer care. *Quality and Safety in Health Care, 12*(Suppl. 1), i33–i36.

Felker, B. L., Hedrick, S. C., Chaney, E. F., Liu, C. F., Heagerty, P., Caples, H., et al. (2003). Identifying depressed patients with a high risk of comorbid anxiety in primary care. *The Primary Care Companion to the Journal of Clinical Psychiatry, 5,* 104–110.

Friedman, H. S., Prince, L. M., Riggio, R. E., & DiMatteo, M. R. (1980). Understanding and assessing nonverbal expressiveness: The affective communication test. *Journal of Personality and Social Psychology, 39,* 333–351.

Goldberg, R. J. (1993). Depression in medical patients. *Rhode Island Medicine, 76,* 391–396.

Goldman, L. S., Nielsen, N. H., & Champion, H. C. (1999). Awareness, diagnosis, and treatment of depression. *Journal of General Internal Medicine, 14,* 569–580.

Greenberg, P. E., Stiglin, L. E., Finkelstein, S. N., & Berndt, E. R. (1993). Depression: A neglected major illness. *Journal of Clinical Psychiatry, 54,* 419–424.

Greenfield, S., Kaplan, S. H., Ware, J. E., Jr., Yano, E. M., & Frank, H. J. (1988). Patients' participation in medical care: Effects on blood sugar control and quality of life in diabetes. *Journal of General Internal Medicine, 3,* 448–457.

Haidet, P., & Paterniti, D. A. (2003). "Building" a history rather than "taking" one: A perspective on information sharing during the medical interview. *Archives of Internal Medicine, 163,* 1134–1140.

Hall, J. A., Harrigan, J. A., & Rosenthal, R. (1995). Nonverbal behavior in clinician-patient interaction. *Applied & Preventive Psychology, 4,* 21–37.

Hall, J. A., Roter, D. L., & Katz, N. R. (1988). Meta-analysis of correlates of provider behavior in medical encounters. *Medical Care, 26,* 657–675.

Hall, J. A., Roter, D. L., & Rand, C. S. (1981). Communication of affect between patient and physician. *Journal of Health and Social Behavior, 22,* 18–30.

Hays, R. D., Wells, K. B., Sherbourne, C. D., Rogers, W., & Spritzer, K. (1995).

Functioning and well-being outcomes of patients with depression compared with chronic general medical illnesses. *Archives of General Psychiatry, 52,* 11–19.

Hogbin, B., & Fallowfield, L. (1989). Getting it taped: The "bad news" consultation with cancer patients. *British Journal of Hospital Medicine, 41,* 330–333.

Jenkins, V., & Fallowfield, L. (2002). Can communication skills training alter physicians' beliefs and behavior in clinics? *Journal of Clinical Oncology, 20,* 765–769.

Kaplan, S. H., Greenfield, S., & Ware, J. E., Jr. (1989). Assessing the effects of physician-patient interactions on the outcomes of chronic disease. *Medical Care, 27*(Suppl. 3), S110–127.

Kaplan, S. H., Gandek, B., Greenfield, S., Rogers, W., & Ware, J. E. (1995). Patient and visit characteristics related to physicians' participatory decision-making style. Results from the Medical Outcomes Study. *Medical Care, 33,* 1176–1187.

Kerse, N., Buetow, S., Mainous, A. G., III, Young, G., Coster, G., & Arroll, B. (2004). Physician-patient relationship and medication compliance: a primary care investigation. *Annals of Family Medicine, 2,* 455–461.

Klinkman, M. S., Coyne, J. C., Gallo, S., & Schwenk, T. L. (1998). False positives, false negatives, and the validity of the diagnosis of major depression in primary care. *Archives of Family Medicine, 7,* 451–461.

Korsch, B. M., Gozzi, E. K., & Francis, V. (1968). Gaps in doctor-patient communication I: Doctor-patient interaction and patient satisfaction. *Pediatrics, 42,* 855–871.

Kreps, G. L., & Kunimoto, E. N. (1994). *Effective communication in multicultural health care settings.* Thousand Oaks, CA: Sage.

Kulik, J. A., & Mahler, H. I. (1993). Emotional support as a moderator of adjustment and compliance after coronary artery bypass surgery: A longitudinal study. *Journal of Behavioral Medicine, 16,* 45–63.

Larsen, K. M., & Smith, C. K. (1981). Assessment of nonverbal communication in the patient-physician interview. *The Journal of Family Practice, 12,* 481–488.

Lemelin, J., Hotz, S., Swenson, R., & Elmslie, T. (1994). Depression in primary care. Why do we miss the diagnosis? *Canadian Family Physician, 40,* 104–108.

Levinson, W., Gorawara-Bhat, R., & Lamb, J. (2000). A study of patient clues and physician responses in primary care and surgical settings. *Journal of the American Medical Association, 284,* 1021–1027.

Lewis, C. C., Pantell, R. H., & Sharp, L. (1991). Increasing patient knowledge, satisfaction, and involvement: Randomized trial of a communication intervention. *Pediatrics, 88,* 351–358.

Linn, L. S., DiMatteo, M. R., Cope, D. W., & Robbins, A. (1987). Measuring physicians' humanistic attitudes, values, and behaviors. *Medical Care, 25,* 504–515.

Maly, R. C., Leake, B., Frank, J. C., DiMatteo, M. R., & Reuben, D. B. (2002). Implementation of consultative geriatric recommendations: the role of patient-primary care physician concordance. *Journal of the American Geriatrics Society, 50,* 1372–1380.

Martin, L. R., DiMatteo, M. R., & Lepper, H. S. (2001). Facilitation of patient involvement in care: Development and validation of a scale. *Behavioral Medicine, 27,* 111–120.

Martin, L. R., Jahng, K. H., Golin, C. E., & DiMatteo, M. R. (2003). Physician facilitation of patient involvement in care: Correspondence between patient and observer reports. *Behavioral Medicine, 28,* 159–164.

May, R. (1983). *The discovery of being: Writings in existential psychology*. New York: Norton.

McQuaid, J. R., Stein, M. B., Laffaye, C., & McCahill, M. E. (1999). Depression in a primary care clinic: The prevalence and impact of an unrecognized disorder. *Journal of Affective Disorders, 55*, 1–10.

Mechanic, D. (1992). Health and illness behavior and patient-practitioner relationships. *Social Science & Medicine, 34*, 1345–1350.

Meredith, L. S., Orlando, M., Humphrey, N., Camp, P., & Sherbourne, C. D. (2001). Are better ratings of the patient-provider relationship associated with higher quality care for depression? *Medical Care, 39*, 349–360.

Millis, S. R., Jain, S. S., Eyles, M., Tulsky, D., Nadler, S. F., Foye, P. M., et al. (2002). Assessing physicians' interpersonal skills: Do patients and physicians see eye-to-eye? *American Journal of Physical Medicine and Rehabilitation, 81*, 946–951.

Milmoe, S., Rosenthal, R., Blane, H. T., Chafetz, M. E., & Wolf, I. (1967). The doctor's voice: Postdictor of successful referral of alcoholic patients. *Journal of Abnormal Psychology, 72*, 78–84.

Mishler, E. A. (1984). *The discourse of medicine: Dialectics of medical interviews*. Norwood, NJ: Ablex.

Nemeroff, C. B., Heim, C. M., Thase, M. E., Klein, D. N., Rush, A. J., Schatzberg, A. F., et al. (2003). Differential responses to psychotherapy versus pharmacotherapy in patients with chronic forms of major depression and childhood trauma. *Proceedings of the National Academy of Sciences, 100*, 14293–14296.

Ong, L. M., de Haes, J. C., Hoos, A. M., & Lammes, F. B. (1995). Doctor-patient communication: A review of the literature. *Social Science & Medicine, 40*, 903–918.

Ormel, J., Van Den Brink, W., Koeter, M. W., Giel, R., Van Der Meer, K., Van De Willige, G., et al. (1990). Recognition, management and outcome of psychological disorders in primary care: A naturalistic follow-up study. *Psychological Medicine, 20*, 909–923.

Pignone, M. P., Gaynes, B. N., Rushton, J. L., Burchell, C. M., Orleans, C. T., Mulrow, C. D., et al. (2002). Screening for depression in adults: A summary of the evidence for the U.S. Preventive Services Task Force. *Annals of Internal Medicine, 136*, 765–776.

Post, D. M., Cegala, D. J., & Meiser, W. F. (2002). The other half of the whole: Teaching patients to communicate with physicians. *Family Medicine, 34*, 344–352.

Robbins, J. M., Kirmayer, L. J., Cathebras, P., Yaffe, M. J., & Dworkind, M. (1994). Physician characteristics and the recognition of depression and anxiety in primary care. *Medical Care, 32*, 795–812.

Robinson, J. W., & Roter, D. L. (1999). Psychosocial problem disclosure by primary care patients. *Social Science & Medicine, 48*, 1353–1362.

Rogers, C. R. (1951). *Client-centered therapy: Its current practice, implications, and theory*. Boston: Houghton Mifflin.

Rogers, C. R. (1959). A theory of therapy, personality, and interpersonal relationships as developed in the client-centered framework. In S. Koch (Ed.), *Psychology: A study of science. Vol. 3: Formulations of the person and the social context* (pp. 184–256). New York: McGraw-Hill.

Romano, J. M., & Turner, J. A. (1985). Chronic pain and depression: Does the evidence support a relationship? *Psychological Bulletin, 97*, 18–34.

Roter, D. L. (1977). Patient participation in the patient-provider interaction: The effects of patient question asking on the quality of interaction, satisfaction and compliance. *Health Education Monographs, 5*, 281–315.

Roter, D. L. (1989). Which facets of communication have strong effects on outcome: A meta-analysis. In M. Stewart & D. Roter (Eds.), *Communication with medical patients* (pp. 183–196). Newbury Park, CA: Sage.

Roter, D. L. (2000). The enduring and evolving nature of the patient-physician relationship. *Patient Education and Counseling, 39*, 5–15.

Roter, D. L., & Hall, J. A. (1992). *Doctors talking with patients, patients talking with doctors: Improving communication in medical visits.* Westport, CT: Auburn House.

Roter, D. L., Hall, J. A., Kern, D. E., Barker, L. R., Cole, K. A., & Roca, R. P. (1995). Improving physicians' interviewing skills and reducing patients' emotional distress: A randomized clinical trial. *Archive of Internal Medicine, 155*, 1877–1884.

Roter, D. L., Stewart, M., Putnam, S. M., Lipkin, M., Jr., Stiles, W., & Inui, T. S. (1997). Communication patterns of primary care physicians. *Journal of the American Medical Association, 277*, 350–356.

Safran, D. G., Taira, D. A., Rogers, W. H., Kosinski, M., Ware, J. E., & Tarlov, A. R. (1998). Linking primary care performance to outcomes of care. *The Journal of Family Practice, 47*, 213–220.

Sartorius, N., Ustun, T. B., Lecrubier, Y., & Wittchen, H. U. (1996). Depression comorbid with anxiety: Results from the WHO study on psychological disorders in primary health care. *British Journal of Psychiatry, 30*(Suppl.), 38–43.

Scheingold, L. (1988). Balint work in England: Lessons for American family medicine. *The Journal of Family Practice, 26*, 315–320.

Schneider, J., Kaplan, S. H., Greenfield, S., Li, W., & Wilson, I. B. (2004). Better physician-patient relationships are associated with higher reported adherence to antiretroviral therapy in patients with HIV infection. *Journal of General Internal Medicine, 19*, 1096–1103.

Schulberg, H. C., & McClelland, M. (1987). A conceptual model for educating primary care providers in the diagnosis and treatment of depression. *General Hospital Psychiatry, 9*, 1–10.

Sherbourne, C. D., Hays, R. D., & Wells, K. B. (1995). Personal and psychosocial risk factors for physical and mental health outcomes and course of depression among depressed patients. *Journal of Consulting and Clinical Psychology, 63*, 345–355.

Sherbourne, C. D., Wells, K. B., & Sturm, R. (1997). Measuring health outcomes for depression. *Evaluation and the Health Professions, 20*, 47–64.

Smith, R. C., & Hoppe, R. B. (1991). The patient's story: Integrating the patient- and physician-centered approaches to interviewing. *Annals of Internal Medicine, 115*, 470–477.

Smith, R. C., Lyles, J. S., Mettler, J., Stoffelmayr, B. E., Van Egeren, L. F., Marshall, A. A., et al. (1998). The effectiveness of intensive training for residents in interviewing: A randomized, controlled study. *Annals of Internal Medicine, 128*, 118–126.

Smith, R. C., Mettler, J. A., Stoffelmayr, B. E., Lyles, J. S., Marshall, A. A., Van Egeren, L. F., et al. (1995). Improving residents' confidence in using psychosocial skills. *Journal of General Internal Medicine, 10*, 315–320.

Smith, R. C., Osborn, G., Hoppe, R. B., Lyles, J. S., Van Egeren, L., Henry, R., et al. (1991). Efficacy of a one-month training block in psychosocial medicine for residents: A controlled study. *Journal of General Internal Medicine, 6*, 535–543.

Spiro, H. (1993). Introduction. In H. M. Spiro, M. McCrea Curnen, E. Peschel, & D. St. James (Eds.), *Empathy and the practice of medicine: Beyond pills and the scalpel.* New Haven, CT: Yale University Press.

Stewart, M. A. (1984). What is a successful doctor-patient interview? A study of interactions and outcomes. *Social Science & Medicine, 19,* 167–175.

Street, R. L., Jr. (1991). Information-giving in medical consultations: The influence of patients' communicative styles and personal characteristics. *Social Science & Medicine, 32,* 541–548.

Street, R. L., Jr., Krupat, E., Bell, R. A., Kravitz, R. L., & Haidet, P. (2003). Beliefs about control in the physician-patient relationship: Effect on communication in medical encounters. *Journal of General Internal Medicine, 18,* 609–616.

Suchman, A. L., Markakis, K., Beckman, H. B., & Frankel, R. (1997). A model of empathic communication in the medical interview. *Journal of the American Medical Association, 277,* 678–682.

Sullivan, L. M., Stein, M. D., Savetsky, J. B., & Samet, J. H. (2000). The doctor-patient relationship and HIV-infected patients' satisfaction with primary care physicians. *Journal of General Internal Medicine, 15,* 462–469.

Swenson, S. L., Buell, S., Zettler, P., White, M., Ruston, D. C., & Lo, B. (2004). Patient-centered communication. Do patients really prefer it? *Journal of General Internal Medicine, 19,* 1069–1079.

Tai-Seale, M., Croghan, T. W., & Obenchain, R. (2000). Determinants of antidepressant treatment compliance: implications for policy. *Medical Care Research Review, 57,* 491–512.

Thomas, N. K. (2004). Resident burnout. *Journal of the American Medical Association, 292,* 2880–2889.

Thompson, S. C., Nanni, C., & Schwankovsky, L. (1990). Patient-oriented interventions to improve communication in a medical office visit. *Health Psychology, 9,* 390–404.

Wagner, H. R., Burns, B. J., Broadhead, W. E., Yarnall, K. S., Sigmon, A., & Gaynes, B. N. (2000). Minor depression in family practice: Functional morbidity, co-morbidity, service utilization and outcomes. *Psychological Medicine, 30,* 1377–1390.

Waitzkin, H. (1984). Doctor-patient communication. Clinical implications of social scientific research. *Journal of the American Medical Association, 252,* 2441–2446.

Waldron, T. (1999). "Low-grade" depression. Primary care physicians need a crash course in detection and treatment. *Behavioral Healthcare Tomorrow, 8*(2), 32–35.

Weaver, M. J., Ow, C. L., Walker, D. J., & Degenhardt, E. F. (1993). A questionnaire for patients' evaluations of their physicians' humanistic behaviors. *Journal of General Internal Medicine, 8,* 135–139.

Wells, K. B., Hays, R. D., Burnam, M. A., Rogers, W., Greenfield, S., & Ware, J. E., Jr. (1989). Detection of depressive disorder for patients receiving prepaid or fee-for-service care. Results from the Medical Outcomes Study. *Journal of the American Medical Association, 262,* 3298–3302.

Wells, K. B., Stewart, A., Hays, R. D., Burnam, M. A., Rogers, W., Daniels, M., et al. (1989). The functioning and well-being of depressed patients. Results from the Medical Outcomes Study. *Journal of the American Medical Association, 262,* 914–919.

Wells, K. B., & Sherbourne, C. D. (1999). Functioning and utility for current health of patients with depression or chronic medical conditions in managed, primary care practices. *Archives of General Psychiatry, 56,* 897–904.

Williams, J. W., Jr., Rost, K., Dietrich, A. J., Ciotti, M. C., Zyzanski, S. J., & Cornell, J. (1999). Primary care physicians' approach to depressive disorders. Effects of physician specialty and practice structure. *Archives of Family Medicine, 8,* 58–67.

Wissow, L. S., Roter, D., Larson, S. M., Wang, M. C., Hwang, W. T., Johnson, R., et al. (2002). Mechanisms behind the failure of residents' longitudinal primary care to promote disclosure and discussion of psychosocial issues. *Archives of Pediatric and Adolescent Medicine, 156,* 685–692.

Wright, J. H., Bell, R. A., Kuhn, C. C., Rush, E. A., Patel, N., & Redmon, J. E., Jr. (1980). Depression in family practice patients. *Southern Medical Journal, 73,* 1031–1034.

Yalom, I. D. (1980). *Existential psychotherapy.* New York: Basic Books.

Chapter 2

Unexamined Discourse

The Outcomes Movement as a Shift from Internal Medical Assessment to Health Communication

Bernice A. Pescosolido, Thomas W. Croghan, and Joel D. Howell

Major currents of health communication research look to the influence of physician-patient communication on health care outcomes, how features of health care shape physician-patient communication, and the way that health risk and programs are communicated to the public through media (see Haskard, Summer, & DiMatteo, this volume; also Thompson, Dorsey, Miller, & Parrott, 2003). Yet, despite its impressive accomplishments over the past 40 years (Parrott, 2004, also this volume), even a brief review of the burgeoning body of research on health communication seems to point to a gap and an opportunity. Although issues of change and innovation are not foreign to its research foci (e.g., telemedicine, Turner, 2003), it seems that little work directly addresses a major shift that has accompanied the health care reforms of the late 20th and early 21st century, specifically the large-scale collection and use of outcomes data designed to improve the quality of care. That is, pushed by concerns about escalating costs, increasing reports about health disparities, and the entry of new, managed forms of care, there has been a move toward accountability in medicine requiring data on the effects of care, be they reports of patient satisfaction, an assessment of costs, evaluations of whether procedural guidelines were followed, or tracking the impact of the provision of medical care. By any measure, outcomes data have become a major element of 21-century medicine shaping issues of access to health care, the medical encounter between "providers" and "consumers," and health policy initiatives, including the organization and financing of care.

Of course, physicians, policy makers, and the public always have been concerned with the outcomes of health care, trying to make sense of whatever patterns emerged from personal or clinical observations they made. But the key to its relevance to health communication research is the shift in the collection and intended use of data. Research on medical outcomes initially was internally focused—physicians informing physicians of what works, what side effects may be expected, and how to better organize practice. This is the traditional use of outcomes data and its relevance for health communication lies in the ability of these kinds of measures to provide feedback to physicians and researchers about how the physician-patient interactions may shape what happens after the medical encounter. For example, researchers have looked at how physician-patient interaction shapes satisfaction (Sullivan, Stein, Savetsky, & Samet, 2000) and follow-through with medical recommendations (Schneider, Kaplan, Greenfield, Li, & Wilson, 2004). In the language of the outcomes movement (Andersen, Rice, & Kominski, 1996), practice quality (i.e., "what occurs in the interaction between a patient and a provider," p. 151) influences outcomes (i.e., "the intermediate or ultimate results of efforts to prevent, diagnose, and treat various health problems encountered by the population," p. 161).

The 1960s and 1970s, however, represented an important tipping point when health services researchers, rather than physician researchers, began to systematically bring sophisticated methods and data to document the outcomes of health care. By the 1990s, the focus on accountability and choice under health care reform suggested that outcomes data could and should be disseminated to help the public make decisions about their own care, to allow policy makers to examine how public funds should be used, and to assist insurance companies in adjusting their policies on covering particular procedures, providers, and health care organizations. That is, outcomes data took on new forms and roles. In our various roles, we have been involved in the development of "report cards" that have been or are being designed by most state governments, theoretically, to make outcomes data available so that the public may make informed choices about which publicly-financed providers and health care organizations to use. In addition, we have been involved in the development of organization-based efforts to implement the outcomes movement and have interviewed senior health care managers about how they see the benefits of outcomes tools and requirements to use them.

In essence, health care reforms have shifted outcomes data from internal, expert discourse to health communication. It is this recent turn in the concern with health care outcomes—a turn accompanied by the idea that health information communicated to various "stakeholders" is a lynchpin of health care reform—that we refer to as the "contemporary" or "modern" health outcomes movement. It includes any systematic attempt to assess the effect of health care in a defined population, combined with the intent to produce health communications that may change health policy, medical practice, and health behaviors based on those findings. "Data-based decision-making," "utilization review," "report cards," and "outcomes research" (e.g., see Tanenbaum, 1999) all represent a shift in emphasis whereby information is to be provided back to health care providers and organizations, insurance companies and other payers, and the public.

Yet, it is this form of health communication that opens up new research possibilities in the research agenda of health communication. There are reasons why it has not yet moved to the center of health communication concerns. Much of health communication focuses on research that can humanize medicine and medical care (e.g., understanding and improving the medical encounter, moving toward patient-centered medical care; see Stewart, 1984).

Despite its best intention to empower stakeholders, health care reform seems to move in the other direction, interjecting more technical and financial issues into medical care, imposing access limits and introducing financial incentives for both providers and patients. Further, the outcomes movement may require stretching the kinds of typologies that help organize theories and investigations. Health communication researchers make the distinction between verbal and symbolic communication (Haskard et al., this volume). The process by which outcomes data are collected, understood, and used does not fit neatly here and is even outside of health communication research's focus on media. In staking out a claim that health communication research should target the outcomes movement, we will need to focus on all three types of discourse (societal, expert, and lay), how they have become intertwined over time, and how formal efforts to assess the outcomes of care have been understood and responded to by examining the informal communications of the lay public (see Thompson, 2003, for definitions).

In any case, our purpose in this chapter is to introduce the health outcomes movement and conceptualize it as an opportunity to understand a new form of contemporary health communication, one that purports to align with the emphasis on patient-centered care. In this sense, it fits squarely within the tradition of health communication research because we are interested in the underlying meaning and real effects of communication on health care. Here, we review the historical forms that discourse on measuring outcomes has taken, the progression in expert efforts to measure them, and the meaning the public attaches to these efforts and their participation in them. Specifically, we first trace the attempts, originally in medicine, and then in health services research to assess the outcomes of health care. We ask how and why specific types of outcomes measurement took shape when they did, particularly the shift to bringing in patients' "voice" and communicating back to public stakeholders. Second, we examine the scientific attention to the measurement of outcomes. We look at the nature of the major instruments being used, discuss their implications for health communication, and chart changes in scientific publication on outcomes. Finally, and most importantly, we explore the meanings that the lay public reads into the effort to measure what matters to them in the outcomes of health care. Here, we try to get "underneath" the written version of a "simple task-oriented exchange" (Cegala, 1997), assessing the match between the explicit goal of the outcomes movement, its most famous instrument (the SF-36), and the reality of what individuals think about the process, the targeted outcomes in the SF-36, and how they approach providing feedback. We also take up one of the challenges of health communication research's call to focus more on issues of culture and ethnicity (Kaplan, Gandek, Greenfield, Rogers, & Ware, 1995) by exploring how African Americans in Boston, Latinos in Los Angeles, and Whites in Indianapolis think about outcomes of care and the effort to get their feedback.

In sum, this chapter sets the historical context for the rise of the widespread use of patient communications on health care outcomes and provides a preliminary look at how individuals in three cities see the attempt to collect relevant outcomes data directly from patients. Our guiding purpose is to look at the contested meanings of "outcomes." For health care reform, outcomes measurement is supposed to bring science (i.e., a science of reliability and validity) to the empowerment of patients and payers. Our preliminary exploration into what individuals think about this effort reveals that, at minimum, the effort does not always tap into what matters to patients, and at its worst, is viewed by individuals as an attempt to deny them care, rather than empower them. Particularly to the African Americans we spoke with, outcomes measurement symbolizes the potential power to deny them health care and they respond accordingly to formal requests to fill out surveys. If outcomes data are only as useful as the information people bring to them, then our analysis suggests that the outcomes movement has missed its mark, tainted by lay suspicion of what *really* underlies the effort to ascertain their reaction to care. Our focus on contested meanings reveals a sharp contrast between the goals and intentions of the outcomes movement and the perceptions and practices of lay stakeholders. Importantly for health communication research, the limits of our exploration into the meaning and measurement of outcomes to patients opens up a range of questions that require the theories, insights, and methods of the field of health communication.

The Rise of Societal Discourse on Medical Care Outcomes, Data Collection, and Dissemination to Stakeholders

The Pre-Outcomes Era: Physicians Communicate Among Themselves

Outcomes research always has been implicit in the ideology of clinical care. As far back as the 1600s, researchers like John Graunt compiled data on births and deaths in London, noting the relative mortality rates of various diseases (Kreager, 2002). In the 1800s, Pierre Louis wondered if bleeding was an effective therapy for patients with pneumonia who were being treated in Parisian hospitals, asking if it was better to bleed early or late in the disease, and questioning if it was better to bleed a great deal or only a small amount. He concluded that bleeding simply did not lead to better outcomes, but—not for the last time—his numerical conclusions were generally disregarded by clinicians with whom he worked (Bollet, 1973; Davidoff, 1999; Massey, 1989; Matthews, 1995; Warner, 1986). In the mid-19th century, others like Austin Flint, Sr., best known for his work on heart murmurs, also analyzed statistical data on the outcome of bloodletting. His analysis on patients at Charity Hospital in New Orleans led him to abandon bloodletting as an appropriate treatment for pneumonia (Leslie, 2002).

Although this sort of work on outcomes was discussed among members of the medical community, the dissemination stopped there. There were no insurance providers to mediate care, nor was such work likely to be known to the mainly illiterate hospitalized patients treated by Louis and Flint. This is not to say that no patients had knowledge of outcomes or reacted to their own observations of outcomes. In one of the most famous medical studies of the 19th century, Ignaz Semmelweis demonstrated that if clinicians cleaned their hands with chlorine between doing autopsies and examining pregnant women in labor, it would prevent women from death due to childbed fever (Carter, 1983). He observed, and then studied, a striking difference in the outcomes on two wards in the Vienna General Hospital: Women on the physicians' ward were far more likely to die than women on the midwives' ward. In general, formal communication of these health outcomes were limited to the relatively closed world of the medical community. Nonetheless, informal communication processes were in operation: these differences in mortality rates were well known to women in Vienna, who went to great lengths not to be admitted to the physicians' ward.

By the turn of the 20th century, many Americans came to believe that science and technology held the key to all manner of betterment, including health care (Freidson, 1970; Pescosolido & Martin, 2004; Starr, 1982). In this new world, a Boston surgeon undertook one of the most important early attempts to do the sort of systematic, population-based data collection that has come to be seen as the sine qua non of the outcomes movement. Surgery was the bold, new medical method of the day, and E. A. Codman wanted to know which surgeons and surgical practices led to better outcomes. He proposed an "end result system," a set of ideas and methods not that different from what would later become the core elements of the late 20th-century outcomes movement. Codman proposed systematically tracking the results of operations amongst his surgical colleagues in order to make judgments about which procedures and which surgeons were better than others. His efforts, however, became bogged down in two ways. First, the political and social power of Boston surgeons eventually prohibited this sort of encroachment on their individual autonomy, hard-won as part of the initial social contract between scientific medicine and American society (Pescosolido & Boyer, 1999). Second, the technology needed for such large-scale information management simply did not exist. Codman's workspace was a large piece of lined paper. He started to write down the results of each operation by each surgeon. Eventually, the paper became so large and the handwriting so small that he could proceed no further (Davies, 2001; Donabedian, 1976, 1989, 1990; Kaska & Weinstein, 1998; Neuhauser, 1990; Reverby, 1981; see also Johnson, Vinh, & Sweet, 2000, on Codman's bone tumor registry).

Experts Take Over: Enter Health Services Research

Technological changes by mid-century improved researchers' ability to do outcomes research in very important ways. New survey techniques made it possible to acquire data directly from patients, whereas new computing devices made it possible to store and analyze large collections of data. The innovations were at first centered in a few specific places (e.g., University of Michigan's Survey Research Center, the Bureau of Applied Social Research at Columbia University, and the National Institutes of Health; see Bloom, 2002; Susser, 1985). These institutions are important, not only because they served as actual sites for data analysis and developed an important set of new technologies (i.e., surveys), but also because their creation served as a marker for increasing attention to research outside of medicine and for the training of a generation of researchers who would create health services research.

The early 1950s saw the creation of the first surveys that asked patients to self-report their health status. If this new technology could effectively measure the health of the public, it could be used to measure the health of different populations, some of whom had been exposed to one or another heath care intervention that could be contrasted. Surveys could then be considered as a tool to evaluate the impact of various interventions on health. Although initial efforts focused on understanding how the public evaluates health and health-care problems, their use of the medical care system became a major concern of those interested in issues of access, adherence, and effectiveness (e.g., Anderson, 1966; Howell, 1993).

But using surveys to assess outcomes requires a decision about what constitutes an "outcome." Shortly after surveys started to be widely used, health-services researcher Avedis Donabedian (1966, 1988b) made an important conceptual leap when he introduced what continues to be the dominant model for evaluating the quality of health care. His basic framework divided health care provision into the triad of structure, process, and outcome. At the same time that Donabedian was developing his theory of how to evaluate health care, new technology was making it possible to collect, share, and analyze data on a large scale. This new technology included not only computational devices but also data networks. Pen and paper gave way to large, room-size, punch-card-programmed computers of the 1950s and 1960s, which, in turn, gave way in the 1970s and 1980s to desktop, and soon laptop, devices with data management and analytic capabilities that outstripped even the wildest dreams of Codman and his contemporaries. These devices brought data management into offices and institutions all around the country (Donabedian, 1985, 1988a). By the mid-1980s, local data management was within reach of many academics and health professionals. In the 1980s and 1990s, a new network—the Internet—became available for data sharing. Since that time, the Internet has become part of everyday existence for Americans[1] and an essential element in the daily life of those who study health care.

Near the end of the 20th century, people who wanted to assess health outcomes had readily available new tools for acquiring data (such as surveys), tools for thinking about that data (the trio of structure, process, and outcome), and tools for manipulating that data (such as computers and the Internet).

More than Academic Research: The Modern Outcomes Movement Takes Shape

In this chapter, we assert that the development of new tools combined with changes in stakeholder response to the costs of and access to medical care gave birth to a new sort of "outcomes movement" (Andersen et al., 1996). Some historians suggest that modern outcomes assessment has its origins in the 1960s in studies by Robert H. Brook, a clinician at the Johns Hopkins University School of Medicine. Brook reviewed the process of care for patients with three common disorders: hypertension, urinary tract infections, and ulcers (e.g., Brook et al., 1983; Keeler, Brook, Goldberg, Kamberg, & Newhouse, 1985; Vickrey et al., 1994). Seeking to discover how patients felt about the outcomes of their care, he asked specialists and generalists to review the treatment of 300 patients with these conditions. Eight out of 10 times the physicians judged the treatment to be more effective than their patients judged it to be; specialists proved no better than generalists at matching the patients' assessments. Whatever definition of "effective" one chose to adopt, it became clear that there were very clear differences in perceived outcomes between those providing and those receiving the treatment.

Others date the contemporary outcomes movement to the work of John Wennberg, Alan Gittelsohn, and their colleagues in Codman Associates at Dartmouth University. In the 1970s, their geographically-based analysis showed wide regional variation in the use of services (e.g., hip replacement surgery, prostatectomy, CT scans, ultrasounds). More importantly, that variation was associated with little difference in health care outcomes (e.g., Wennberg & Gittelsohn, 1973). These findings led many to wonder about unnecessary surgery, inappropriate care, and rising costs, as well as to ask about the relationship (if any) between provision of health care and outcomes (see Paul-Shaheen, Clark, & Williams, 1987, for a review).

A third major effort credited with spearheading a new wave of outcome-focused research began in 1971 when the National Center for Health Services Research, now the Agency for Healthcare Research and Quality (AHRQ), awarded the Rand Corporation more than $80 million to conduct the Health Insurance Experiment (HIE), still one of the largest controlled experiments and health policy studies in history. Involving over 2,750 families and more than 7,700 individuals at six sites across the country, HIE families replaced their existing health insurance policies with one of 14 experimental policies that varied with respect to coverage and out-of-pocket costs (e.g., Newhouse & The Insurance Experiment Group, 1993).

HIE participants filed claims with the study, were given physical examinations, and completed questionnaires once a year to produce data on the state of their health. The HIE pioneered the criteria by which health status and quality of care could be measured, including the SF-36[2] (e.g., see Ware, 2000; Ware, Kosinski, & Keller, 1996; Ware & Kosinski, 2001). In the end, the HIE showed that free care is very costly and no more effective. Although the average family spent 50% more on health services in the free plan than families who had cost-sharing plans or were enrolled in an HMO, free care produced no better health outcomes for the average person than did cost-sharing plans or an HMO (Newhouse & The Insurance Experiment Group, 1993). Free care did have some slight positive effects for people who were sick when they enrolled in the experiment, but these effects were small compared with their costs.

As these pioneers and pioneering efforts proceeded, concern with costs was rapidly coming to be a prominent part of the national health care agenda. The 1990s saw an increasing chorus of concerns about the runaway levels of spending for health care in the United States (e.g., Browning, 1992; Buck & Klemm, 1992; Ginzberg, 1990; Jencks & Schieber, 1991; Sonnefeld, Waldo, Lemieux, & McKusick, 1991). Rapid increases in spending for health care were a concern for employers, who purchase most of the health care in the country, for policy makers concerned with Medicare spending, and for a public with increasingly high levels of co-payments or no health insurance at all (Helbing, Latta, & Keene, 1991). Further, cross-national analyses indicated that people living in countries spending far less had health outcomes at least as good (and usually better) than people living in America (Lassey, Lassey, & Jinks, 1997; Woolhandler & Himmelstein, 1991). In this context, more studies of health and health care adopted new ideas and approaches for measuring health outcomes (e.g., the Medical Outcomes Study, a large survey of four chronic illnesses, Haley, McHorney, & Ware, 1994; McHorney, Ware, & Raczek, 1993).

But what could be done to ensure that the data generated by studies of health outcomes would be applied to the benefit of people in the community? The outcomes movement took on new form and meaning that made health communication a centerpiece. The sentinel event in the consolidation of the outcomes movement may have been Paul Ellwood's Shattuck lecture to the Massachusetts Medical Society (later published in the *New England Journal of Medicine*, Ellwood, 1988). Ellwood, a long time advocate of health maintenance organizations and the budding managed-care industry, coined the term *outcomes management* in this lecture. He also offered a definition: *a process designed to help patients and doctors make more informed and rational choices about medical care*. This approach was picked up by the Clinton administration. That is, as concerns for costs and quality merged, the American medical system underwent a stunning national attempt at health care reform. Although it failed, the social currents that led to this federal effort, nonetheless, dramatically altered the private landscape of care (Mechanic, 2004; Pescosolido & Kronenfeld, 1995; Quadagno, 2004; Skocpol, 1996). Further, we might argue that the AHRQ began, in earnest, the shift to health communication with its Medical Treatment Effectiveness Program (MEDTEP; HS-94-002) and its most famous component, the Patient Outcomes and Research Team (PORT) Studies. In both the original PORT (1989) and PORT II (1994), AHRQ (at the time named AHCPR, the Agency for Health Care Policy Research) sought to fund "innovative and timely research that will provide convincing evidence for or against the effectiveness and/or cost effectiveness of alternative clinical intervention used to prevent, diagnose, treat and manage common clinical conditions" so as to "make substantial new contributions to improve patient outcomes, clinical practitioners, and health-care policy" (National Institutes of Health, 1994).[3]

Thus, by the 1990s, the outcomes movement took on full force and the shift from internal assessment to health communication was complete. In 1993, Medline first used the term *evidence-based medicine*. Government reports and NIH research "blueprints" moved from issues of access to focus on the outcomes of care and to dissemination of information to stakeholders, including the public (National Institutes of Health, 1993; Pellmar & Eisenberg, 2000; Shonkoff & Phillips, 2000; Singer & Ryff, 2001; U.S. Dept. of Health and Human Services, 1999, 2000). For example, *Caring for People with Severe Mental Disorders: A National Plan of Research to Improve Services* (National Institute of Mental Health, 1991) was clear: "without careful studies of what works, under what circumstances, and for which kinds of individuals, there is little factual guidance available to policymakers, system managers, care providers, and consumers." The notion of "data-based decision-making" also echoed in the halls of state governments and in the business community, altering the concerns of policymakers, forging new relationships with researchers, and embracing the need to provide data on outcomes to current and future consumers of health care (e.g., Hogan & Essock, 1991; Lerner, Galvin, & Buck, 1993).

Funding priorities in private and public sectors pushed researchers to outcomes research and to efforts to "translate" and "disseminate" their research findings to the public. Pharmaceutical companies sponsored such research, in part as a tool to influence formulary decisions (Lyles, Luce, & Rentz, 1997). Federal agencies issued Requests for Applications (RFAs) and Program Announcements (PAs) that not-so-subtly pushed grant applicants to focus on outcomes and include descriptions of dissemination efforts. Finally, the call for managed care as a solution to the fiscal crisis in health-care provision raised concerns about what would happen to patients, providers, and organizations, increasing the monitoring interest of public watchdogs as well as corporate managers (Mechanic, 2001). Figure 2.1 depicts the striking increase in the number of research articles classified under the keyword "outcomes assessment."[4] Even our blunt-force approach to information gathering attests to a dramatic change in research attention. For example, looking at the trend in the growth of articles using the more stringent, "focused search" criterion (in which the subject heading was considered the major point of the article), we find fewer than 10 articles before 1990, 98 in 1991, over 250 in 1992, over 400 by 1994, and more than 500 in every year since 1995 with a big jump to over 1,000 articles in 2002.[5]

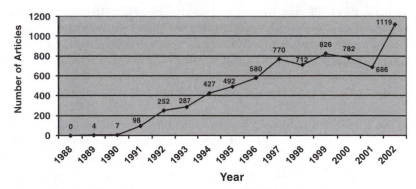

Figure 2.1   Outcome assessment (health care) articles by year, 1988–2002

This rise in attention represents more than academic or policy discourse. We spoke to senior level managers at large health care organizations to get a sense of whether and how the outcomes movement has taken shape at their workplaces.[6] These senior level managers echoed the ideas and importance of the outcomes movement and the research literature and policy efforts. All three indicated that the implementation of guidelines to measure outcomes was critical in "providing a voice for the payer." As the research literature indicates, in general (Tanenbaum, 1999), outcome measurement was both deeply and widely ingrained in their health care organizations, with health care managers seeing it as a "strategic process" to provide feedback to improve the organization of care. However, they reported a concern with how to do outcomes measurement, seeing "access to routine clinical data" as the "holy grail" and reported a wide variety of polices and measures used as they tried to figure out what offered the best fit between quality data and logistical problems for their organizations and their clients.

This accounting shows a remarkable research, policy, and organizational response to the ideas and the ideals of the outcomes movement. Given the magnitude of this reaction, it is unlikely that the interest in outcomes will disappear anytime soon. As a relatively recently introduced form of health communication, efforts to understand the impact on intended audiences become crucial. Below, we offer a brief and preliminary look at how the public understands, assesses, and gives meaning to the effort to collect outcomes data from them.

The Meaning of Outcomes Measures and the Measurement Process to the Public: A Preview

The focus on technology, scientific standards, and policy efforts belies the potential meaning of this form of health communication. Data are only as good as the understanding and intention of the people who provide them. What do members of the "public" in three U.S. cities think about the issues raised in outcome measurement tools and the methods of outcome assessment involving their direct participation? By the "public," we mean individuals who have used health care but are not connected to health care organizations or related industries such as pharmacies or health insurance companies. In other words, we are interested in what the average person thinks about the forms they are asked to fill out by their physicians, their HMOs, and their insurance companies to get at the outcomes of the care they received—how they feel about their health and their health care experience.

To do this, we used a series of 12 focus groups. Of course, any method has strengths and weaknesses; focus groups are no exception. As Morgan (1996) pointed out, the focus group has three essential components: a research purpose, an interactive or group discussion, and a discussion guided by the research/moderator. Research has indicated that focus groups, compared to surveys, are able to elicit more information about sensitive topics, especially on a topic for which there is little previous research (Ward, Bertrand, & Brown, 1991; Saint-Germain, Bassford, & Montano, 1993). Focus groups seemed to be the preferred, exploratory method because we had little idea of how sensitive the issue of health care outcome reporting was to patients, how much they had thought about the actual process of filling out patient surveys, and what kinds of questions would elicit responses to the topics of concern to us. Given the lack of public discourse on the issue of filling out these forms, we determined that the ability to interact with others might facilitate discussion and result in greater productivity than individual interviews (Fern, 1982). As Morgan and Krueger (1993) pointed out, focus groups are not only useful for new topics; group discussion can also facilitate our understanding of the sources of complex motivations.

Nevertheless, the focus group method has two limits that affect our findings. Focus groups, because of their very nature (e.g., recruitment through flyers and social networks) and the use of a guided script with a moderator explicitly charged with structuring discussion, have limited generalizability, compared to surveys with sampling designs targeted to represent the population of interest. Further, even with the guided script, the focus group moderator may facilitate some directions in discussion while hindering others. Our purpose here, however, was to see if individuals in the community have *any* reaction to the range of issues that are asked about in patient surveys, the way they are administered, and what they believe about the meaning and uses of these surveys. To that extent, we thought it essential to maximize variability in responses to our script. Given contemporary concerns with differential access, treatment, and outcomes (Alegría et al., 2002; Cooper-Patrick et al., 1999; Committee on Quality of Health Care in America—Institute of Medicine, 2001), we conducted focus groups in three cities (Boston, Indianapolis, and Los Angeles), raising questions about the meaning and usefulness of the outcomes forms they are now often asked, and sometimes required, to fill out.[7] As an exploratory study, we sought to maximize differences in race and ethnic response. Given that Indianapolis is often used by companies as a test market because of its representation of the U.S. population, we conducted focus groups of Whites there. Further, given a history of racially-charged events in Boston, we choose this city to conduct focus groups of African Americans. Finally, given the Hispanic population presence, we conducted our focus groups with Hispanics in Los Angeles. Respondents were recruited by a local coordinator in each city using flyers hung in public places (e.g., supermarkets, homeless shelters, YMCAs) and a recruitment script prepared by the first author. Respondents who called in were screened for a race/ethnic and income match for the two sets of focus groups in each city. We held a set of sessions with a lower-income ("below the poverty level") and a middle-income group ("above the poverty level"). In total, then, we had 6 focus groups and conducted 11 focus group sessions.[8] Groups ranged from 5 to 10 people for a total of 44 participants across the three cities and were fairly balanced on gender.

We used a two-session strategy. On the first day, we introduced our concern with understanding "how people think about health, what matters to them, and what areas of their life are impacted by health" (Focus group moderator, 6/24/02). On the second day, we used a survey form of outcomes assessment (the SF-36) as a pivotal reference point to elicit participants' perspectives. We asked for their views on how useful these measurement tools were in light of what was important to them. We also asked how they viewed the process of being requested to provide information that would be used to monitor (and hopefully, improve) quality in the health care system. In essence, we were asking them to assess the utility of this new emphasis on and approach to health communication.

Focus groups were attended by the moderator and a field coordinator who wrote up a summary of each session and debriefed the first author. All focus groups were tape recorded and transcribed. Analysis proceeded by identifying themes and cross-checking with coordinator notes and with the coordinator. For this analysis, we concentrate on the broad-brush themes regarding health care and outcomes measurement. Overall, two general themes appeared across all of the focus groups—lack of connection to participants' social worlds and issues of access to care and paperwork; however, the focus groups in Boston, with the African American participants, raised a particular concern about confidentiality and the intent of outcomes measurement. We end by discussing this issue and the need for more in-depth data to pursue this theme.

Resonance with Social Worlds

The first theme to emerge focused on the lack of connection, in one way or another, of the topics in the instruments to the participants' own concerns. That is, the focus group respondents in all cities found the concerns in the SF-36 to be superficial on issues of social relationships.

For example, both groups in Indianapolis thought that the issues raised in the SF-36 were "fine." The Indianapolis respondents reported that the categories covered (e.g., health status, change from 1 year ago, vigorous activities, moderate activities) and the examples given (e.g., pushing a vacuum cleaner, bowling, or playing golf) were "decent," "relevant," and "very clear." Their critiques generally were oriented to details ("you should make it [time frame] a little bit longer than four weeks"; how about "expected to accomplish" rather than just "accomplished less than you would like" because "I think everybody accomplishes a little less than they would like to do" or perhaps "Have you been less productive than normal?").

When their discussions turned to the impact of illness and the missing emphases in the outcomes instruments we asked them to review, they echoed a concern familiar to health communication research. That is, the overall theme of the response to our queries centered on the lack of emphasis on the social aspects of health care and health care outcomes. As Cline (2003) suggested, everyday interpersonal communication is critical to health and health behavior. In a broader frame, participant concerns resonated with the salience of lay social networks and social supports that has become central to social epidemiology, medical care utilization theories and studies of health care outcomes (Pescosolido & Levy, 2002).

Specifically, our respondents commented on the importance of social relationships and their absence in the outcome measures. They indicated, with regard to restrictions in daily activities resulting from illness, they "would be most concerned about how it affects my social relationships" (Dan, 6/25/2002). In particular, they suggested that too few of the questions focused on issues surrounding friends and family. More importantly, participants in the middle income focus group voiced concerns that doctors don't see these issues as important, and consequently, they feared bringing them up:

TOM: …You don't want to go to the doctor and go like "Yeah, man, I've just been so down lately. I can't go out to movies with my girlfriend. I just can't do it." You know. It sounds kind of corny to say something like that but I mean maybe that's something that really bothers you.
JANE: It sort of validates that// [interruption]
TOM: …yeah, it validates you have a social life and taking that into consideration. (6/26/2002)

Similarly, the lower-income focus group members commented on the relative lack of attention to social relationships and targeted family more directly:

CINDY: Parenting. You know, is it affecting your parenting skills? Is it affecting your relationship with your spouse? I think those are important questions.

JUNE: The way you feel around people is going to affect how you feel. (6/27/2002)

Further, both Boston groups questioned the cultural relevance of some of the wording for African Americans, particularly in the mental health section (e.g., "full of pep," "feel peaceful and calm"). The Hispanic focus group members in Los Angeles echoed some of the same concerns about out-of-date or colloquial language that had little resonance in their social world (i.e., "down in the dumps"). With specific regard to outcome measures and measurement, they, like the other groups, wanted to add sports and exercise, and more on social relationships, especially sex life ("Sex has got to be in there."). Like the African American groups, they focused on these relationships as family-based, concentrating on caretaking responsibilities and mentioning cooking specifically.

These groups provided a great deal of direction about regrouping items and rethinking the response categories that would allow them to get to needs in their lives (e.g., adding open-ended questions so people could provide explanations). Similarly, they wanted to add or change some examples that would make the topics covered more representative of their social worlds (e.g., add more on family, taking care of children, sports, exercise, sex life).

Issues of Access to Care: Restrictions and Paperwork

The second general comment offered by focus group participants surrounded access. Indianapolis respondents were more concerned about access issues (e.g., pre-approvals, limits on services) than about what was left out of the outcome instruments. They mentioned "So many meds—so hard to cover" (Susan, 6/24/2002), and when one participant noted that her insurance had been cancelled, other participants chimed in:

GINNY: Doesn't seem legal.
ROY: Causes mental anguish.
DEBBIE: Exactly. (6/24/2002)

Respondents in Los Angeles went further to suggest that the context of health care often is unwelcoming: "You just come in and you're getting pushed out already [unintelligible word] if you can even get in" (Carlos 6/26/2002). Juan expands on this theme later in the group's discussion by mentioning the role of resources in limiting care: "They probably thought, you know, that the parents couldn't afford it so they most likely didn't do the test, and so, she died, you know" (6/26/2002).

The Los Angeles participants, more than other groups, mentioned the role of education—people who are not educated enough, doctors who are not educated enough about mental health issues, and the desire to be "educated" in the physician-patient relationship about their health problem. Yet, by the simple mention, they are suggesting that this is not happening at present.

African American participants in Boston began by discussing some of the same insurance issues that had concerned the Indianapolis group. A good deal of the general discussion revolved around the lack of coverage for everything from eyeglasses to counseling for children. Unlike any other of the focus group sessions in other cities, race was spontaneously brought up by participants as playing a role: Said Laurie, "Another little Black boy who had a problem nobody cared about. Give him a drug and send him on his way" (7/23/2002).

CHERI: The whole thing is not to be treated like I'm an idiot just because I'm Black. I know what's going on with my health, my body. I don't know what causes diabetes or heart disease or cholesterol going crazy. Talk to me, talk to me, I know what's going on. Don't treat me like I'm an idiot. (7/23/2002)

A Point for Further Consideration: Skepticism about the Use of Outcome Data Among African Americans

Both Boston groups reported more concerns about the questions than had those in Indianapolis or Los Angeles. They noted, specifically, that some of the examples were "kind of vanilla" (e.g., golf) and others needed to be rephrased "to make this plain and simple."

A number of participants volunteered that they would not fill out such a questionnaire (e.g., "If I looked at this, I would have thrown it away," Mary, 7/24/2002) or that they would do it superficially (e.g., "I rush through it to get it over and done with and there could be something that's very important in this that I missed because I just wanted to get this out of my face," Lucy, 7/27/2002). Most importantly, members in both groups were skeptical about the real purpose. Marty, a respondent in the "below the poverty level group," commented: "This is a test that will trip you up" (7/24/2002). And, on a specific item, Lucy asked directly, "Is that a trick question?" (7/25/2002). Further, after asking the focus group leader to explain when and under what conditions the information would be collected, the "above the poverty level" group members questioned whether this type of health communication was designed to assist them or other stakeholders who do not share similar interests:

JOE: But you look at these questionnaires, the insurance companies use this questionnaire, they can use this to their advantage.
MULTIPLE VOICES: Yes.
JOE: They can make, they can make their own assumptions about what is right and wrong.

LUCY: Make your insurance go up higher.

JOE: Exactly.

IRIS: If you're at risk, it's going up higher.

JOE: Exactly.

CHERI: But who's to say? If I'm a diabetic, these questions could kill me and therefore, you won't be truthful.

JOE: Exactly. (7/25/2002)

In sum, the Boston group voiced skepticism about the intended use of these data and whether the utility of health communication would be thwarted by concerns about their use. In contrast, one of the Indianapolis groups spent a good deal of time discussing when the SF-36 would be most useful to a doctor if it was administered once, if there was no follow up, etc. However, never in this discussion did they question the intent of the instrument. In fact, Charles, in response to a discussion on the wording and question ordering explicitly says, "It's not a test." The only place where they indicated that people might not "tell the truth" is with regard to when doctors ask about smoking, drinking, and drug use because they indicated that the only advice or treatment they would receive would focus on quitting these behaviors (6/27/2002). One Indianapolis respondent exclaims: "I wish my doctor had a questionnaire like this" (Ginny), and, in response, others in the group complained that they have never seen this before. Roy agrees and also suggests, "I'd like to see more doctors have something like this" (6/26/2002). In the end, however, they raise the issue of insurance companies in jest: "It's none of the insurance company's business" (Debbie, 6/27/2002).

Summary

Our look at the public's view of outcome issues and outcome instrumentation suggested a good deal of concern with contemporary medical care. All the groups agreed on the importance of many of the issues addressed and the questions as asked in standard outcome survey forms; however, they also focused on whether the issues fit with contemporary life, in general, and with specific issues of concern to them. With the exception of the willingness of the African American group to express deep concerns about the real policy intent of and use of these measures, most participants concentrated on the assigned task of reshaping the questions. In the minds of many, the outcomes movement is associated with a proliferation of requests to fill out insurance and post-care survey forms and with issues of restricting access. This linkage ought not to be a surprise. Although both managed care and the outcomes movement had their roots in a much earlier historical period and both came of age in the 1960s and 1970s, it was their visibility in the 1980s and 1990s that made these organizations and approaches household words (Cutler, 2001; Donabedian, 1983; Ellwood & Enthoven, 1995; Skocpol, 1996; Wong & Hellinger, 2001).

Meaningful Health Communication from the Outcomes Movement?

Health communication research and the outcomes movement share two basic assumptions. First, medical care should be more patient-centered. Second, understanding what transpires in medical care encounters is important; can directly inform improvements in health and health care; and can be studied by examining the process and meaning of the experiences of individuals treated in the health care system. The explicit purpose of the outcomes movement was to introduce and standardize health communication back to various stakeholders, including but not limited to the public, so that they would use this information to make "more rational" decisions about health care. Individuals would be able to choose more wisely about medical treatment options, providers, and health care organizations; and, policy makers would be able to more wisely invest corporate or societal resources into the health care system.

Yet, these two important and relatively recent developments in the health care arena have not crossed paths to any significant degree. Although a great deal of effort in outcomes research has been devoted over the last 25 years in developing measures to assess the outcomes of health care, little research has focused on the meaning attached to the method of collecting outcomes data from patients, themselves, in the attempt to make the health care system more patient centered, effective, and efficient. Although health communication research has opened up the logistics, challenges, and meanings of the physician-patient relationship, it may have taken for granted measures of health care outcomes and not tracked the entry of reforms that widen the use of these measures as tools for researchers to inform the public, shape public policy, and hold health care providers and organizations accountable.

Here, we briefly traced the rise of the outcomes movement, examining the shift in measuring the results of heath care from an internal focus by physicians to a policy-oriented enterprise by health services research and now incorporated into the routines of government and private health care systems and organizations. Further, we took a preliminary look at how individuals understand and give meaning to their health care and to one of the most visible and respected outcomes tools, the SF-36, designed to improve their experiences.

We find that measures created for research and policy purposes may not capture what is important to individuals who receive care. Our focus group respondents expressed the usual complaints about filling out forms but also raised issues of access as critical. Further, and more importantly, there was a hint of skepticism attached to the "real" meaning of collecting these data. Particularly among African Americans, there is concern that these data are designed to impose greater restrictions on health care availability.

We see no slackening of the emphasis on outcomes assessment in the health care system. The changes that led to the outcomes movement—new data acquisition and management technology, a continued belief in the power of science and technology, the emphasis on patient voice, and societal concerns about the medical care system—show no signs of abating. Recent concerns about the rising cost of health care will only increase the desire to monitor the quality of what is being delivered, because outcome measurements are critical to "define accountability and provide a set of values that can both guide and monitor reform" (Lehman, 1995, p. 91).

As we have documented, however, exactly what different groups mean by the term *outcomes* varies widely, is often poorly defined, and is not well understood by the public or researchers. Can either direct feedback from patient or provider-based measurements provide "the answer" to a concern with an accurate assessment of outcomes? We suggest that this will be the case only if the process of health communication is studied directly. Defined by Ellwood (1988) as a "technology of patient experience" that estimates the relationship between medical interventions and outcomes, the goal for outcomes management is as glorious as it is ambitious. But, the reality is that we know little about patient experience with outcomes management. Simple instruments such as the SF-36 produced during the HIE were intended to be used routinely to monitor individual and population-based outcomes and to provide feedback to health plans and physicians about the well-being of their patients in a continuous quality improvement process. McDowell and Newell (1996) see the SF-36 as having a "meteoric rise to prominence." Their observation is undoubtedly correct; however, both the instrumentation and the process by which they have been administered for use in general population surveys and clinical trials may not fit with the outcome movement's intention to give patients a voice in improving health care.

Clearly, we stand at an important juncture in the history of health care systems. If the outcomes movement began with the intention of learning whether health care systems "work" for patients, even our brief look into what patients think about the effort and how they provide feedback suggests that the goal and current practice may stand far apart. If the outcomes movement does not address what is important to the actual users of health care or if its methods or goals are viewed with suspicion, the entire enterprise of outcomes assessments is called into question.

Schneider, Riehl, Courte-Wieecke, Eddy, and Sennett (1999) suggested that assessing the quality of health care delivery continues to represent "one of the most critical challenges of coming years" (p. 1184). If we conclude that patient-based data are required, then research on health outcomes may offer one avenue to improve health communication to individuals asked to provide data and to other stakeholders about the meaning that patients give to these tools. Health communication research stands in an optimal position to fill this gap.

Acknowledgment

We thank the Robert Wood Johnson Health Policy Scholar Program for support and the Indiana Consortium for Mental Health Services Research for their continued assistance.

Notes

1. By 2002 over 66% of Americans reported having access to a computer at home, work, or school (Davis, Smith, & Marsden, 2003; see also Shortliffe, 1998).
2. The SF-36 instrument is a "multi-purpose short-form health survey" that offers eight scale profiles of "functional health and well-being" scores, physical and mental health summaries (psychometrically-based), and a "preferences-based health utility index" (http://www.sf-36.org). The eight scales are (a) physical functioning, (b) ability to perform normal roles due to physical health, (c) bodily pain, (d) general health, (e) vitality, (f) social functioning, (g) ability to perform normal roles due to emotional health, and (h) mental health. Respondents are asked to fill out a form that uses a 4-week recall period and asks them questions such as how they rate their overall health; whether they feel tired and worn out all the time; whether they were limited in work or other daily activities as a result of their physical health, etc.
3. Somewhat earlier, in 1984, the DRG (Diagnostic Related Group) system, developed at Yale University, was implemented as an attempt to reduce health-care costs (see McGuire, 1991).
4. Specifically, we searched MEDLINE each year from 1988 to 2002 with keywords "Outcomes Assessment (Health Care)" using both a focused and expanded search strategy. Our focus is not on the absolute numbers, which would require a detailed content analysis not provided here. We are simply interested in the general pattern that, even in the face of a proliferation of journals over the same period, supports our contention of a dramatic increase in attention to issues surrounding the outcomes movement.
5. Further, in analyses not presented here, an expanded search reveals an even more dramatic and fairly monotonic increase from 19 articles in 1988 to almost 30,000 in 2002.
6. These comments are drawn from three interviews with senior health care executives who are "on the line" for making decisions about how to measure and use outcomes for their health care organization. We purposely selected managers at prominent health care organizations on the East and West Coasts and in the Midwest. The protocol for these interviews were reviewed and approved by the Institutional Review Board at Indiana University (#03-8207).
7. Conducted as part of the RWJF Investigator Awards in Health Policy Research Program for "Conceptualizing the Social, Economic and Cultural Issues Underlying Health Care Outcomes" (awarded to the first two authors). The protection of human subjects aspects of this research were reviewed and approved by the Institutional Review Board at Indiana University (Protocol Number: 02-7103).
8. One group in Los Angeles requested a combined session.

References

Alegría, M., Canino, G., Rios, R., Vera, M., Calderón, J., Rusch, D., et al. (2002). Mental health care for Latinos: Inequalities in use of specialty mental health services among Latinos, African Americans, and non-Latino Whites. *Psychiatric Services,* 53, 1547–1555.

Anderson, O. W. (1966). Influence of social and economic research on public policy in the health field. A review. *Milbank Memorial Fund Quarterly, 44,* 11–51.

Andersen, R., Rice, T., & Kominski, G. (1996). *Changing the U.S. health care system.* San Francisco: Jossey-Bass

Bloom, S. W. (2002). *The word as scalpel: A history of medical sociology.* New York: Oxford University Press.

Bollet, A. J. (1973). Pierre Louis: The numerical method and the foundation of quantitative medicine. *American Journal of the Medical Sciences, 266,* 92–101.

Brook, R. H., Ware, Jr., J. E., Rogers, W. H., Keeler, E. B., Davies, A. R., Donald, C. A., et al. (1983). Does free care improve adults' health? Results from a randomized controlled trial. *New England Journal of Medicine, 309,* 1426–1434.

Browning, S. M. (1992). Forces for reforming the U.S. health care system: A review of the cost and access issues. *Health Economics, 1,* 169–180.

Buck, J. A., & Klemm, J. (1992). Recent trends in Medicaid expenditures. *Health Care Financing Review, Annual Supplement,* 271–283.

Carter, C. C. (1983). *Ignaz Semmelweis: The etiology, concept, and prophylaxis of childbed fever* (I. Semmelweis, Trans., & K. C. Carter, Intro.). Madison: University of Wisconsin Press.

Cegala, D. J. (1997). A study of doctors' and patients' patterns of information exchange and relational communication during a primary care consultation: Implications for communication skills training. *Journal of Health Communication, 2,* 169–194.

Cline, R. J. (2003). Everyday interpersonal communication and health. In T. L. Thompson, A. M. Dorsey, K. I. Miller, & R. Parrish (Eds.), *Handbook of health communication* (pp. 285–317). Mahwah, NJ: Erlbaum.

Committee on Quality of Health Care in America, Institute of Medicine. (2001). *Crossing the quality chasm: A new health system for the 21st century.* Washington, DC: National Academies Press.

Cooper-Patrick, L., Gallo, J., Gonzales, J., Vu, H., Powe, N., Nelson, C., et al. (1999). Race, gender, and partnership in the patient-physician relationship. *Journal of the American Medical Association, 282,* 583–589.

Cutler, D. M. (2001). *Health policy in the Clinton era: Once bitten, twice shy.* Cambridge, MA: National Bureau of Economic Research.

Davidoff, F. (1999). In the teeth of the evidence: The curious case of evidence-based medicine. *Mount Sinai Journal of Medicine, 66,* 75–83.

Davies, H. T. (2001). Exploring the pathology of quality failings: Measuring quality is not the problem-changing it is. *Journal of Evaluation in Clinical Practice, 7,* 243–251.

Davis, J., Smith, T. W., & Marsden, P. (2003). *General Social Surveys, 1972–2002: Cumulative Codebook.* Chicago: University of Chicago: National Opinion Research Center.

Donabedian, A. (1966). Evaluating the quality of medical care. *Milbank Memorial Fund Quarterly, 44,* 166–206.

Donabedian, A. (1976). Effects of Medicare and Medicaid on access to and quality of health care. *Public Health Reports, 91,* 322–331.

Donabedian, A. (1983). The quality of care in a health maintenance organization: A personal view. *Inquiry, 20,* 218–222.

Donabedian, A. (1985). Twenty years of research on the quality of medical care. *Evaluation and the Health Professions, 8,* 243–265.

Donabedian, A. (1988a). The assessment of technology and quality. A comparative study of certainties and ambiguities. *International Journal of Technology Assessment in Health Care, 4,* 487–496.

Donabedian, A. (1988b). The quality of care: How can it be assessed? *Journal of the American Medical Association, 260,* 1743–1748.

Donabedian, A. (1989). The end results of health care: Ernest Codman's contribution to quality assessment and beyond. *Milbank Quarterly, 67,* 233–256.

Donabedian, A. (1990). Ernest A. Codman, M.D., the end result idea and the product of a hospital. A commentary. *Archives of Pathology & Laboratory Medicine, 114,* 1105.

Ellwood, P. M. (1988). Shattuck Lecture: Outcomes management. A technology of patient experience. *New England Journal of Medicine, 318,* 1549–1556.

Ellwood, P. M., & Enthoven, A. C. (1995). "Responsible Choices": The Jackson Hole Group Plan for health reform. *Health Affairs, 14,* 24–39.

Fern, E. F. (1982). The use of focus groups for idea generation: The effects of group size, acquaintanceship and moderator on response quantity and quality. *Journal of Marketing Research, 26,* 1–13.

Freidson, E. (1970). The emergence of medicine as a consulting profession. In E. Freidson (Ed.), *Profession of medicine* (pp. 3–22). New York: Dodd, Mead & Co.

Ginzberg, E. (1990). High-tech medicine and rising health care costs. *Journal of the American Medical Association, 263,* 1820–1822.

Haley, S. M., McHorney, C. A., & Ware, J. E., Jr. (1994). Evaluation of the MOS SF-36 Physical Functioning Scale (PF-10): I. Unidimensionality and reproducibility of the Rasch Item Scale. *Journal of Clinical Epidemiology, 47,* 671–684.

Helbing, C., Latta, V. B., & Keene, R. E. (1991). Medicare expenditures for physician and supplier services, 1970–88. *Health Care Financing Review, 12,* 109–120.

Hogan, M. F., & Essock, S. M. (1991). Data and decisions: Can mental health management be knowledge-based? *Journal of Mental Health Administration, 18,* 12–20.

Howell, J. D. (1993). The purchase of health care by selected American households in 1917–1919: A machine-readable source. *Bulletin of the History of Medicine, 67,* 696–702.

Jencks, S. F., & Schieber, G. J. (1991). Containing U.S. health care costs: What bullet to bite? *Health Care Financing Review (1991 Supplement), 13*(2), 1–12.

Johnson, L. C., Vinh, T. N., & Sweet, D. E. (2000). Bone tumor dynamics: An orthopedic pathology perspective. *Seminars in Musculoskeletal Radiology, 4,* 1–15.

Kaplan, S. H., Gandek, B., Greenfield, S., Rogers, S., & Ware, J. E. (1995). Patient and visit characteristics related to physicians' participatory decision-making style. *Medical Care, 33,* 1176–1187.

Kaska, S. C., & Weinstein, J. N. (1998). Historical perspective. Ernest Amory Codman, 1869–1940. A pioneer of evidence-based medicine: The end result idea. *Spine, 23,* 629–633.

Keeler, E. B., Brook, R. H., Goldberg, G. A., Kamberg, C. J., & Newhouse, J. P. (1985). How free care reduced hypertension in the health insurance experiment. *Journal of the American Medical Association, 254,* 1926–1931.

Kreager, P. (2002). Death and method: The rhetorical space of seventeenth-century vital measurement. In E. Magnello & A. Hardy (Eds.), *The road to medical statistics* (pp. 1–35). Amsterdam: Rodopi.

Lassey, M. L., Lassey, W. R., & Jinks, M. J. (1997). *Health care systems around the world: Characteristics, issues, reforms.* Upper Saddle River, NJ: Prentice Hall.

Lehman, A. F. (1995). Measuring quality of life in a reformed health system. *Health Affairs, 14*, 90–101.

Lerner, D. J., Galvin, R. S., & Buck, C. R. (1993). GE sheds light on managed care's impact on health. *Business and Health, 11*, 48–54.

Leslie, B. R. (2002). Austin Flint in New Orleans and the origins of evidence-based medicine. *Journal of the Louisiana State Medical Society, 154*, 144–148.

Lyles, A., Luce, B. R., & Rentz, A. M. (1997). Managed care pharmacy, socioeconomic assessments and drug adoption decisions. *Social Science & Medicine, 45*, 511–521.

Massey, R. U. (1989). Reflections on medicine. Pierre Louis and his numerical method. *Connecticut Medicine, 53*, 613.

Matthews, J. R. (1995). *Quantification and the quest for medical certainty.* Princeton, NJ: Princeton University Press.

McDowell, I., & Newell, C. (1996). *Measuring health: A guide to rating scales and questionnaires.* New York: Oxford University Press.

McGuire, T. E. (1991). DRGs: The state of the art, circa 1990. *Health Policy, 17*, 97–119.

McHorney, C. A., Ware, J. E., & Raczek, A. E. (1993). The MOS 36-Item Short-Form Health Survey (SF-36): II. Psychometric and clinical tests of validity in measuring physical and mental health constructs. *Medical Care, 31*, 247–263.

Mechanic, D. (2001). Lessons from the unexpected: The importance of data infrastructure, conceptual models, and serendipity in health services research. *Milbank Quarterly, 79*, 459–478.

Mechanic, D. (2004). The rise and fall of managed care. *Journal of Health and Social Behavior, 45*, 76–86.

Morgan, D. L. (1996). Focus groups. *Annual Review of Sociology, 22*, 129–152.

Morgan, D. L., & Krueger, R. (1993). When to use focus groups and why. In D. L. Morgan (Ed.), *Successful focus groups: Advancing the state of the art* (pp. 3–20). Newbury Park, CA: Sage.

National Institute of Mental Health. (1991). *Caring for people with severe mental disorders: A national plan of research to improve services.* Bethesda, MD: National Institute of Mental Health.

National Institutes of Health. (1993). MEDLINE/PubMed. U.S. National Library of Medicine.

National Institutes of Health. (1994). *Medical treatment effectiveness research — PORT-II.* (NIH Guide, Vol. 23, No. 18). Retrieved October 3, 2007, from http://grants2.nih.gov/grants/guide/pa-files/PA-94-066.html

Neuhauser, D. (1990). Ernest Amory Codman, M.D., and end results of medical care. *International Journal of Technology Assessment in Health Care, 6*, 307–325.

Newhouse, J. P., & The Insurance Experiment Group. (1993). *Free for all? Lessons from the RAND health insurance experiment.* Cambridge, MA: Harvard University Press.

Parrott, R. (2004). Emphasizing "communication" in health communication. *Journal of Communication, 54*, 751–787.

Paul-Shaheen, P., Clark, J. D., & Williams, D. (1987). Small area analysis: A review and analysis of the North American literature. *Journal of Health Politics, Policy and Law, 12,* 741–809.

Pellmar, T. C., & Eisenberg, L. (Eds.). (2000). *Bridging disciplines in the brain, behavioral, and clinical sciences.* Washington, DC: The National Academies Press.

Pescosolido, B. A., & Boyer, C. A. (1999). How do people come to use mental health services? Current knowledge and changing perspectives. In A. V. Horwitz & T. L. Scheid (Eds.), *A handbook for the study of mental health: Social contexts, theories, and systems* (pp. 392–411). New York: Cambridge University Press.

Pescosolido, B. A., & Kronenfeld, J. (1995). Health, illness, and healing in an uncertain era: Challenges from and for medical sociology. *Journal of Health and Social Behavior, 35(Extra Issue: Forty Years of Medical Sociology: The State of the Art and Directions for the Future),* 5–33.

Pescosolido, B. A., & Levy, J. A. (2002). The role of social networks in health, illness, disease and healing: The accepting present, the forgotten past, and the dangerous potential for a complacent future. *Social Networks and Health, 8,* 3–25.

Pescosolido, B. A., & Martin, J. K. (2004). Cultural authority and the sovereignty of American medicine: The role of networks, class and community. *Journal of Health Politics, Policy and Law, 29,* 735–756.

Quadagno, J. (2004). Why the United States has no national health insurance: Stakeholder mobilization against the Welfare State, 1945–1996. *Journal of Health and Social Behavior, 45,* 25–44.

Reverby, S. (1981). Stealing the golden eggs: Ernest Amory Codman and the science and management of medicine. *Bulletin of the History of Medicine, 55,* 156–171.

Saint-Germain, M. A., Bassford, T. L., & Montano, G. (1993). Surveys and focus groups in health research with older Hispanic women. *Qualitative Health Research, 3,* 341–367.

Schneider, E. C., Riehl, V., Courte-Wieecke, S., Eddy, D. M., & Sennett, C. (1999). Enhancing performance measurement: NCQA's road map for a health information framework. *Journal of the American Medical Association, 282,* 1184–1190.

Schneider, J., Kaplan, S. H., Greenfield, S., Li, W., & Wilson, I. B. (2004). Better physician-patient relationships are associated with higher reported adherence to antiretroviral therapy in patients with HIV infection. *Journal of General Internal Medicine, 19,* 1096–1103.

Shonkoff, J. P., & Phillips, D. A. (Eds.). (2000). *From neurons to neighborhoods: The science of early childhood development.* Washington, DC: The National Academies Press.

Shortliffe, E. H. (1998). Health care and the next generation internet. *Annals of Internal Medicine, 129,* 138–140.

Singer, B., & Ryff, C. (2001). *New horizons in health: An integrative approach.* Washington, DC: National Academy Press.

Skocpol, T. (1996). *Boomerang: Clinton's health security effort and the turn against government in U.S. Politics.* New York: W.W. Norton.

Sonnefeld, S. T., Waldo, D. R., Lemieux, J. A., & McKusick, D. R. (1991). Projections of national health expenditures through the year 2000. *Health Care Financing Review, 13,* 1–15.

Starr, P. (1982). *The social transformation of American medicine: The rise of a sovereign profession and the making of a vast industry.* New York: Basic Books.

Stewart, M. (1984). What is a successful doctor-patient interview? A study of interactions and outcomes. *Social Science & Medicine, 19*, 167–175.

Sullivan, L. M., Stein, M. D., Savetsky, J. B., & Samet, J. H. (2000). The doctor-patient relationship and HIV-infected patients' satisfaction with primary care physicians. *Journal of General Internal Medicine, 15*, 462–469.

Susser, M. (1985). Epidemiology in the United States after World War II: The evolution of technique. *Epidemiologic Reviews, 7*, 147–177.

Tanenbaum, S. (1999). Evidence and expertise: The challenge of the outcomes movement to medical professionalism. *Academic Medicine, 74*, 757–763.

Thompson, T. L. (2003). Introduction. In T. L. Thompson, A. M. Dorsey, K. I. Miller, & R. Parrott (Eds.), *Handbook of health communication* (pp. 1–5). Mahwah, NJ: Erlbaum.

Thompson, T. L., Dorsey, A. M., Miller, K. I., & Parrott, R. (Eds.). (2003). *Handbook of health communication.* Mahwah, NJ: Erlbaum.

Turner, J. W. (2003). Telemedicine: Expanding health care into virtual environments. In T. L. Thompson, A. M. Dorsey, K. I. Miller, & R. Parrot (Eds.), *Handbook of health communication* (pp. 515–536). Mahwah, NJ: Erlbaum.

U.S. Department of Health and Human Services (1999). *Mental health: A report of the Surgeon General.* Rockville, MD: U.S. Department of Health and Human Services.

U.S. Department of Health and Human Services (2000). *Healthy people 2010: Understanding and improving health.* Washington, DC: U.S. Department of Health and Human Services.

Vickrey, B. G., Hays, R. D., Rausch, R., Sutherling, W. W., Engel, Jr., J., & Brook, R. H. (1994). Quality of life of epilepsy surgery patients as compared with outpatients with hypertension, diabetes, heart disease, and/or depressive symptoms. *Epilipsia, 35*, 597–607.

Ward, V. M., Bertrand, J. T., & Brown, L. F. (1991). The comparability of focus group and survey results. *Evaluation Review, 15*, 266–283.

Ware, J. E., Jr. (2000). SF-36 Health survey update. *Spine, 25*, 3130–3139.

Ware, J. E., Jr., & Kosinski, M. (2001). Interpreting SF-36 summary health measures: A response. *Quality of Life Research: An International Journal of Quality of Life Aspects of Treatment, Care, and Rehabilitation, 10*, 405–413.

Ware, J. E., Jr., Kosinski, M., & Keller, S. (1996). A 12-item short-form health survey: Construction of scales and preliminary tests of reliability and validity. *Medical Care, 34*, 220–233.

Warner, J. H. (1986). *The therapeutic perspective: Medical practice, knowledge and identity in America 1820–1885.* Boston: Harvard University Press.

Wennberg, J. E., & Gittelsohn, A. M. (1973). Small area variations in health care delivery. *Science, 182*, 1102–1108.

Wong, H. S., & Hellinger, F. J. (2001). Conducting research on the Medicare market: The need for better data and methods. *Health Services Research, 36*, 291–308.

Woolhandler, S., & Himmelstein, D. U. (1991). The deteriorating administrative efficiency of the U.S. health care system. *New England Journal of Medicine, 324*, 1253–1258.

Chapter 3

Doctor-Patient Communication from an Organizational Perspective

Kevin Real and Richard L. Street, Jr.

Doctor-patient communication is a vital component of both patient health and physicians' professional lives. The quality of doctor-patient relationships can influence a number of factors (for reviews, see Roter & Hall, 1993; Stewart, 1995; Street, 2001; also see Haskard, Williams, & DiMatteo, this volume), including health outcomes (Kaplan, Greenfield, & Ware, 1989), patient adherence to medical treatment (DiMatteo, 1994), decisions to pursue malpractice litigation (Beckman, Markakis, Suchman, & Frankel, 1994; Levinson, Roter, Mullooly, Dull, & Frankel, 1997), pre-and-post-visit trust (Gallagher & Levinson, 2004), patient satisfaction (Stewart, 1995), and physician satisfaction (Gallagher & Levinson, 2004). An overlooked component of this relationship, however, is the organizational context in which these interactions occur. Hence, this chapter examines the question: In what way do health care organizations affect the process and outcomes of communication in medical consultations?

This is a very difficult question to answer for two reasons. First, there is no single organizational model of health care financing and delivery, especially with the increasing influence of third-party payers and various managed care forms of health care organizations. These exist in many forms, each of which may differentially affect the quality of care provided and the quantity and quality of doctor-patient communication. Second, theoretical models of provider-patient interaction try to explain what happens during the medical consultation in relation to individual and partner-level variables such as age, education, communicative style, relational history, and more. Although this work highlights the importance of communication in the medical encounter, it does little to account for the role of context in physician-patient communication. Street (2003) set forth an ecological perspective to propose that doctor-patient communication is situated within and affected by a variety of social contexts, including interpersonal, organizational, media, political, legal, and cultural. Although the interpersonal context is the fundamental one to this interaction, this chapter examines the organizational context surrounding doctor-patient communication.

Indeed, very little attention has been paid to the impact of the organization on the communication that occurs in these encounters. Although studies have examined physician and patient communication within medical encounters, only recently have researchers investigated how the clinical context influences these interactions (Street & Gordon, 2006). The organizational context is complex and can involve several factors that may affect doctor-patient communication, including policies for access to doctors, scheduling, how many patients are seen daily, how long MDs have to interact with patients, physician income, support staff for physicians, referral policies, organizational structures, technology, and much more. This chapter focuses on how health organizations are structured and financed and the impact of these features on the doctor-patient relationship. We also discuss how doctors (and to a lesser degree patients) work within and around these constraints during the medical consultation.

To address these issues, we first review the various organizational forms of health care delivery and how these continue to change over time. Second, we discuss how social and environmental changes have acted to reduce the autonomy of the medical profession and increase the influence of organizations. We then explore the impact of these organizational and social changes on specific aspects of the physician-patient relationship: conflicting loyalties, trust, and disruption of continuity. Finally, we examine how information and communication technology can mitigate these impacts on doctor-patient communication. Throughout this chapter, we examine the degree to which organizational context (e.g., solo vs. group practice setting; hospital vs. clinic) accounts for variation in doctor-patient communication.

Organizational Contexts of Health Care Delivery

Physicians work in many different organizational contexts, including hospitals, health maintenance organizations (HMO), staff or group model multispecialty clinics, large integrated delivery systems as well as traditional private practice group or solo settings (see Lammers & Barbour, this volume). Each of these contexts likely influences how physicians work and how they interact with patients. There are many forms of organized health care delivery but these can primarily be classified into office practices, medium-to-large sized clinics, and hospitals. Office practices include solo, partnership, and small group practice settings. Clinic settings can be comprised of large multispecialty groups, and then within this design are various strategies related in part to financing: the traditional indemnity model, the staff and group model health maintenance organizations (HMOs), and a set of hybrid practices, such as Independent Practice Associations (IPAs), Preferred Provider Organizations (PPOs), and Physician-Hospital Associations (PHAs). These newer hybrids are designs that combine a variety of models of health care delivery and financing, are typically responsive to changes in the health care marketplace, and contain a mixture of pre-paid plans, fee-for-service arrangements, and contracts for services.

Hospitals can be non-profit or for-profit and many now exist as part of networks or integrated systems of hospitals and other health care contexts (Lammers, Barbour, & Duggan, 2003). The important thing to understand in this whole array of organizational forms is that health care financing is not identical to health care organizational structures.

The most influential form of health care financing related to the organizational delivery of care in the United States involves third-party payers and what is most commonly known as managed care. In general, managed care refers to a system for delivering medical care that attempts to control costs and improve quality by monitoring how doctors treat illnesses, limiting referrals to specialists, and requiring authorization prior to hospitalization and other specialized treatments (Birenbaum, 1997; Kuttner, 1999). The term *managed care* is used to describe a variety of different financing and delivery plans, but at its core it describes the control of health care interactions and costs by third-party payers (insurers, employers, government). Although there has been some legitimate concern over the use of managed care terminology for its managerial overtones (Hacker & Marmor, 1999), as well as some who argue that health care has entered a "post managed care" era (Alexander & Lantos, 2006), this form of health care organizing and finance is still deeply embedded in the U.S. health care system. Because the focus of this chapter is an organizational perspective on doctor-patient communication, we use the term managed care despite its limitations. The development of managed care has led to changes in the relationship between health care financing (insurance) and health care organizations. Prior to the onset of managed care, the financing of health care was typically separate from organizational context. As managed care developed, financing became intertwined with health care organization design, structure, and logic.

Although managed care was (and still is) often synonymous with HMOs, any organizational context in which physicians practice can be financed through managed care policies. In some cases, managed care simply refers to a contractual arrangement between employers and/or insurance companies and physician groups. Plans can range from merely requiring third-party payer pre-certification of medical care to controlling and monitoring almost every aspect of the health care context (Wagner, 1997). At one end of the spectrum are HMOs, which are typically larger group and staff model clinics that provide care for a fixed amount per person per year, in which the health care organization and the insurer are one and the same. This is often the organizational context most associated with the term managed care in the minds of various health publics, including patients. In an HMO, the patients also are known as the insured and they usually come from a defined population (e.g., a company's employees)—and they receive care only from the providers employed by or contracted with the HMO, which assumes the risk involved in treating a population of patients. At the other end of the spectrum is fee-for-service, in which third-party payers pay the bills for physician and health care organization services. In between are hybrid organizational designs and networks (IPAs, PPOs, PHAs), which are a complex set of contractual arrangements designed to link providers with third-party payers. There are no defining organizational features for these new arrangements other than the contracts that connect them together and to payers. As such, physicians from solo, small group practices or large groups may belong to any of these vehicles and may even belong to more than one at the same time. These varied organizational contexts likely affect doctor-patient communication in particular ways, yet there is little research that links organizational context and structure to doctor-patient communication.

Examining doctor-patient communication within situated contexts can be particularly valuable when examining how physicians respond to organizational and institutional situations. Hoff (2003) argued that studying physicians in context requires a greater emphasis on particularistic research designs involving qualitative methods "as well as on comparative analysis that gathers data across a variety of organizational situations within the same study" (p. 94). Research that accounts for organizational context could examine the influence of specific organizational factors on doctor-patient communication. For example, the amount of time physicians have to talk with patients and the quality of this interaction likely influences the pattern of communication across health care organizational contexts (e.g., hospital, HMO, group or solo private practice setting). It may be that physicians who work on salary may have plenty of time to talk to patients. It could also be the case that their employer may require them to see a certain number of patients every hour. Much of this may depend on the amount of professional autonomy a particular organizational context provides for its physicians.

Increasing Organizational Influences on Physicians

The working life of a physician is significantly different in the first decade of the 21st century from what it was like in the middle of the 20th century, when physicians had a great deal of autonomy over their professional work. Freidson (1970) asserted that physicians maintained professional dominance in that they controlled the conditions of their work through political and legal authority. Starr (1982) argued that medicine was a "sovereign" profession because of the degree of control it had over its own work. This professional autonomy meant that physicians as a group were self-regulating, impervious to judgments from outside groups, free to practice without supervision from higher authorities, and maintained control over who entered the field (Abbott, 1988; Freidson, 1970; Starr, 1982). Physicians as individual practitioners had clinical autonomy and often were unquestioned by nurses, administrators, or even their own colleagues (Abrahamson, 1967). Abbott (1988) noted that, although medicine had been threatened by other occupations, it maintained authority over its body of work.

Those days are over in medicine as significant pressure has risen from numerous sources—insurers, employers, government, other professions, media, and so on—that has led to changes in the relationship between physicians and their patients. These structural and organizational changes may be partially reflected in the desire of younger physicians who no longer talk about trying to "establish a practice" but instead describe trying to "get a job" (Shortell, Gillies, Anderson, Erickson, & Mitchell, 2000). This also is suggested by the dramatic increase in the number of physician-employees. Many physicians, perhaps as much as 40%–50%, work as salaried employees in many different types of organizations, including for-profit and non-profit organizations, universities, and corporations (American Medical Association, 2000). This has led to charges by some that the reward structures of managed care have the potential to create conflicts of interests and lack of trust between physicians and patients when a doctor's income is linked to clinical decisions (Rodwin, 1993, 1995).

Research into communication and physicians in managed care organizations has been mixed. Lammers and Duggan (2002) reported that doctors involved in managed care contracts experienced reduced satisfaction, especially in regard to clinical autonomy. Real, Branson, and Poole (in press) found that physicians who practiced in private practice settings generally were dissatisfied with the state of affairs of medicine, primarily because of managed care and the perceived interference from third-party payers in clinical and financial matters. In contrast, salaried physicians working in a non-profit staff model HMO generally were satisfied in terms of their day-to-day experiences. Real surmised that the HMO was unique in that it was physician-led and the doctors believed they had clinical autonomy. Moreover, the HMO physicians in Real's study fit what Hoff (2001) argued is the proper lens in which to view physicians; instead of professional dominance, autonomy, and authority, physicians can be thought of as "workers" who have individual needs and goals that can sometimes be best met working as employees rather than independent practitioners. Other studies have found similar results: Physicians who work on salary in benevolent organizations feel unencumbered by administrative work and able to focus more on their patients and the practice of medicine (Gross & Budrys, 1991; Hoff, 2003; Hoff & McCaffrey, 1996). Seen in this light, some physicians may be less interested in the financial, entrepreneurial side of medicine and more interested in quality of life issues such as less on-call time, more time with their families, and less focus on the administrative aspects of running a practice.

Changes to physician autonomy in light of increasing organizational influence may impact doctor-patient communication in a number of ways, including control over time allotted for visit by the organization, physician attitudes toward communication, and more. In organizations in which patient visit time is limited, doctor-patient communication will be qualitatively different than in organizations in which there is less restriction. Shorter exams tend to limit information exchange and increase controlling communication behaviors by physicians (more directives, interruptions, less tolerance for questions), whereas longer visits allow patients more time to raise their concerns as well as physician responses to these issues (Bensing, Roter, & Hulsman, 2003; Street, 2003). Physician autonomy can affect communication preferences as well. Those physicians predisposed to engage in partnership-building, empathy, and encouragement will do this in contexts in which this is considered part of the organizational culture. On the other hand, in health care organizations that reduce physician autonomy over fundamental matters (such as visit length), individual physician predispositions are less salient. Although an individual doctor may want to develop rapport and allow patients time to talk in visits, there may simply not be enough time and resources for this to occur regularly. In these situations, patient attitudes toward doctor-patient communication become especially important, as patients who actively participate and are conversationally involved are more likely to have successful outcomes in their interactions with physicians than those who are less engaged (Street, 2003). Those patients who are more inclined to engage in information-seeking behaviors with physicians—asking questions and being assertive—are more likely to receive the answers they need to make informed health care decisions than other patients. As we summarize our findings thus far, on the one hand, there is increasing financial and organizational influence and, on the other, there is decreasing physician autonomy, some of which is voluntary in nature. This leads us to the following question: What has been the impact of these changes on the doctor-patient relationship?

Impact on Doctor-Patient Relationships

Organizations influence doctor-patient relationships in significant ways. For example, in an effort to control costs and quality, many health care organizations and third-party payers frequently monitor physician behavior, including the tests doctors order, any referrals they might make, drugs they may prescribe, the time they spend with patients, and decisions they make that involve the hospitalization of patients. This process, formally known as utilization review, is designed to rationalize the health care that organizations deliver by ensuring that physicians adhere to their organizational and contractual obligations. This can be accomplished in numerous ways, including preauthorization, immediate approval (usually over the telephone), and retrospectively, with reimbursement decided upon after the delivery of care (Wynia, Cummins, VanGeest, & Wilson, 2000). The organizational context of health care is complex, and doctor-patient relationships also can be affected by a number of other attributes, such as the overall goal of the organization (e.g., for-profit, non-profit); size and structure (e.g., solo practice, small group practice, multi-specialty staff model clinic, hospital); the extent to which the organization is independent or part of a national or multinational corporation; organizational policies; market-based competition; and the number and ratio of physicians and other providers on hand to treat patients. Organizations can guide and constrain the number of tests that physicians order, the time they spend with patients, the number of patients they see in a given day, the options for referrals to specialists, and the salary or reimbursement levels. Organizations also can provide technology and staff to support the administrative side of physician work, which can affect doctor-patient communication.

Organizational design and structure are a result of deliberate, conscious choices. Potter and McKinlay (2005) asserted that organizational policies and structures influence the quality of doctor-patient relationships in terms of the length of the relationship, the investment the organization is willing to make in patients, and the degree to which care will be ongoing or episodic. For example, acute care hospitals are structured so that attention is focused on the immediate needs of patient treatment—performing emergency surgery, taking X-rays, and post-operative recuperation. Physicians make rounds to check on the status and condition of patients, but rarely engage in lengthy bedside consults. On the other hand, traditional primary care practices are designed to allow physicians enough time and resources to understand each individual patient's overall (medical, family, and social) history in order to accomplish a number of aspects of patient care: diagnose and treat medical conditions, dispense medical advice, and develop an ongoing relationship with a patient (Potter & McKinlay, 2005). As these examples illustrate, the purpose, structure, history, and policies of medical organizations influences the nature of the provider-patient interaction. Doctor-patient communication in hospitals will be limited in most cases, whereas it will be comparatively greater in office-based practices in which physicians and patients have more time and inclination to communicate.

Accordingly, physicians practice medicine within organizations, such as hospitals, emergency rooms, and primary care offices that influence their relationships with patients. Moreover, external organizations in the form of third-party payers exert influence on the doctor-patient relationship. These new developments, falling under the rubric of managed care, have generated concern for the doctor-patient relationship. The rise of third-party payers in American medicine has had a major impact on doctor-patient relationships. Waitzkin (2001) argued that third-party payers often employ non-clinicians to monitor and challenge physician clinical decisions, determine patient load, and monitor the amount of time spent with individual patients. Furthermore, Potter and McKinlay (2005, p. 469) asserted,

> Because personnel from third-party payer organizations make decisions on whether or not they will reimburse a physician for a procedure performed or a recommended opinion, or pay for a patient's prescription (to name a few), these third parties are influential in the doctor—patient relationship.

A physician interviewed in Real (2002, pp. 140–141) described the relationship between his office and that of third-party payers:

> The second issue is dealing with managed care—whenever I do something, I have to have someone call them before I can do it. I have to have the employee in my office, who is not a trained physician, call an insurance company employee, who is not a trained physician and if that's not absurd, I don't know what is. Sometimes, the individual in my office, because she's not a trained physician, will use common language and it creates problems. For example, if the person in my office calls in and uses the word heart attack, it will be denied because those are not the words that are on the computer list that is in front of the person at the insurance company. The word that the person sitting at the computer at the insurance company needs to hear is myocardial infarction. Now they don't know what that means, but that is what they need because that is the word that matches what they have on their computer list. I waste time every day talking to these people. I am board-certified..., I've been the Chief of Staff at a major hospital, I've taught in medical schools so you'd think I know what I'm doing yet I have to talk to these people a dozen times a day. It is a lot of stress dealing with the insurance companies to do what needs to be done. Even when we include the diagnosis they turn it down.

On the other hand, some observers argue that there is a positive side to the influence of managed care organizations, at least at the population level. Minogue (2000), for example, argued that managed care is good for society in that physicians will practice medicine with an eye on the cost of care so that resources may be conserved for future patients.

Gray (1997) argued that managed care has shifted the focus of health care from interpersonal patient–physician relationships to cost containment measures enacted and enforced by large organizations. Other studies have found supporting evidence. For example, Shapiro, Tym, Eastwood, Derse, and Klein (2003) surveyed both patients and physicians in a number of different health care plans and found both physicians and patients reported that managed care plans imposed greater restrictions on treatment options and access to care. Moreover, they found that patients who belonged to HMOs reported greater restrictions in terms of access to specialists, emergency care, and the time they could spend with their physician than did those who received fee-for-service care. Kroll, Beatty, and Bingham (2003) found that people with physical disabilities in managed care plans were less satisfied with doctor-patient communication relative to those in fee-for-service plans. Rubin et al. (1993) reported that patients seeing physicians in HMO settings tended to rate their interactions with physicians significantly lower than did patients seeing physicians in solo fee-for-service practices. Murphy, Chang, Montgomery, Rogers, and

Safran (2001) found deteriorating trends in doctor-patient relationships in a longitudinal study of 2,400 insured adults; specifically, they found significant declines in the quality of communication, trust, interpersonal treatment, and organizational access over a 3-year period. In a qualitative study of general physician satisfaction, McMurray et al. (1997) found that doctors were concerned about the quality of their relationships with patients and colleagues in light of changes in the organizing and financing of medical care. A qualitative and comparative field study of physicians across three organizational contexts revealed that physicians in private practice settings were less satisfied with their relationships with patients than were physicians in a physician-led staff model managed care organization (Real, 2002). Prominent public health scholars (Emmanuel & Dubler, 1995; Mechanic & Schlesinger, 1996) long have asserted that managed care has threatened the physician-patient relationship. Taken together, this research indicates that health care organizations, particularly managed care organizations, are associated with changes to the physician-patient relationship.

As changes in the organization and financing of health care have unfolded over the past several years, there have been corresponding implications for doctor-patient communication. In this next section, we argue that organizations, third-party payers, and managed care have negatively affected the doctor-patient relationship in specific ways: conflicting loyalties, trust, and the disruption of the doctor-patient relationship. We then offer ways in which the use of communication technology in health care organizations can offset the otherwise negative impacts on doctor-patient communication by facilitating innovative uses of technology and interaction. These factors are possible explanations for the link that has been observed between managed care implementation and the dynamics of physician-patient communication.

Effects of Organizational Structure on the Doctor-Patient Relationship

Conflicting Loyalties   One result of the rise of organizations, third-party payers, and managed care has been the conflicting loyalties that physicians experience between meeting the needs of their patient and the needs of their organization (Carson, 2000). Critics have charged that doctors in managed care settings act as "double agents" in that they must attempt to simultaneously act in the interests of the patient and the managed care organization (Quaye, 2001; Waitzkin & Fishman, 1997). Sulmasy, Bloche, Mitchell, and Hadley (2000) found that more than 80% of physicians in their study believed that changes in the health care system had reduced physicians' commitment to an ethic of loyalty to their patients. This was especially true in regards to physicians who received financial incentives to limit tests, restrict treatment options, and reduce the range of referrals for their patients (Sulmasy et al., 2000). Those physicians who take increased financial incentives may feel the need to take greater control of the medical consultation as a way of heading off any troublesome questions from patients. On the other hand, some physicians in the Sulmasy et al. study were troubled that they faced such dilemmas. Physicians who find themselves in such situations may need to decide how they would work within and around these constraints during the medical consultation. Although few doctors would tell a patient upfront that they face conflicting professional and financial dilemmas (or that they stood to make more by doing less), there are cases in which physicians have engaged in deception and manipulation of the rules on behalf of their patients.

Using vignettes, Freeman, Rathore, Weinfurt, Schulman, and Sulmasy (1999) found that many physicians sanctioned the use of deception to third-party payers in order to obtain medical care for a patient when denied authorization, especially in high managed care penetration markets. There was no mention in the Freeman et al. study of physicians communicating these actions to their patients, so it can be assumed that many doctors may do this without telling their patients. Physicians may also deal with conflicting loyalties by manipulating the rules in order to get around the guidelines created by utilization review and third-party payers. Wynia et al. (2000) found that a sizable minority (39%) of physicians self-reported that they manipulated reimbursement rules so that patients could obtain coverage for services the physician deemed necessary. In some cases, physicians would do this because they believed it necessary, but in other cases, physicians reported having patients request that they deceive their third-party payer (on the patient's behalf). Moreover, physicians who spent less time with individual patients were more likely to manipulate the system; the reduced time was related to reduced levels of per patient reimbursement. Werner, Alexander, Fagerlin, and Ubel (2002) found physicians were more willing to engage in manipulation of third-party payer reimbursement rules in order to reduce the "hassle factor" of appealing denial of service claims. It could be that communication between patients and physicians who adhere to the rules of managed care organizations will be more formal and adversarial than for those physicians who try to bend the rules on behalf of their patients. At the same time, physicians who deceive or manipulate third-party payers may engage in conspiratorial communication (Lammers & Geist, 1997) with patients. This would involve both the patient and the physician being of like mind when it comes to treatment plans and insurance matters.

There is a legal aspect to the conflicting demands physicians face: contractual obligations to organizational rules and third-party payer reimbursement policies ,on the one hand, and legal liability related to the quality of care provided to the patient on the other (Freeman et al., 1999; Wynia et al., 2000). Following the rules of managed care organizations does not reduce physician exposure to malpractice claims or legal liability (Freeman et al., 1999; Hall, 1994). As such, physicians may be motivated to engage in greater control of communication in the medical consultation in order to reduce liability. On the other hand, they may be motivated to conspire with patients in order to gain their favor and reduce future legal problems. A third strategy may be to engage in ambiguous communication in order to allow the patient to make decisions they believe is in their best interests. Rather than being vague, ambiguity provides for multiple interpretations (Eisenberg, 1984) that could increase patient participation in the medical consultation. It could also increase patient acquiescence should a patient not desire to be involved in their own health care decision making.

Trust   Mechanic and Schlesinger (1996) argued that managed care has reduced both public and patient trust in physicians and there is ongoing empirical support for their assertions. Haas, Phillips, Baker, Sonneborn, and McCulloch (2003) found that individuals from communities with a higher prevalence of gatekeeping activities reported less trust in their physician than individuals from areas with lower prevalence of gatekeeping activity. Gatekeeping involves physician control of referrals within a network or system in order to reduce costs and limit out-of-network referrals. Haas et al. noted that individuals from high gatekeeping areas were more likely to believe that their physician was influenced by insurance company rules when making decisions about medical care. Ahern and Hendryx (2003) found significant variation in physician trust across communities that was correlated with levels of social capital, or the quality of community relationships that facilitate trust, civic engagement, shared norms, and norms of reciprocity (Mechanic, 2000; Putnam, 1993). Ahern and Hendryx found HMO enrollment to be negatively related to physician trust, but this effect was not uniform across all communities; cities with lower levels of social capital also had significantly lower levels of trust in physicians. These findings suggest that social capital might be a third variable driving both managed care market penetration and trust in physicians. Those communities in which trust, civic engagement, and norms of reciprocity were low may be less likely to have the civic infrastructure that supports trust in organizations and physicians.

Patient suspicions about physicians and third-party payers exist in part because of their own experiences but also as a result of media publicity about managed care, hidden financial incentives, referral restrictions, and lack of disclosure of conflict of interests. Physician conflict of interest can be related to both under- and overutilization. For instance, physicians in fee-for-service arrangements could order extra tests or procedures and send patients to labs or other facilities in which they own or have a financial interest, thus benefiting financially from this arrangement. Conversely, physicians could be required to manage costs while providing patient care (Pearson, Sabin, & Hyams, 2002). In the latter case, physicians may experience tensions between the directives of their organization and the needs of their patients. It is likely that in either scenario, communication transparency would make for awkwardness. It is hard to imagine a doctor feeling at ease telling a patient, "I own a piece of the lab I am sending you to for these tests." It is just as difficult to imagine a physician telling a patient, "I want to conserve costs for my health care organization so I will run only a limited number of tests on you." So, it is likely that transparency will not be the first option chosen by physicians in these organizational contexts.

This is an interesting case of how trust relates to particular communication features. If patients know these conflicting loyalties exist and they have low trust, then it seems unlikely that what a physician says or does will change their perceptions. For example, if the physician orders tests, the skeptical patient may assume this is merely engaging in defensive medicine and the doctor is protecting himself or herself, or he or she is getting a cut from the lab. If a physician does not order tests, the suspicious patient may assume this is cost-cutting. The question from a communication perspective is how can physicians who are trying to provide genuine and proper care work within and around these issues during the medical consultation? Are there ways physicians can actually build trust in this environment? One strategy may be the adoption of an "us and them" frame in the rapport with the patient. This does necessarily entail deception or manipulation of the system alone but may be just an expression of frustration with the HMO or particular health care organization. Physicians can explain to patients that what they are doing is helping them in light of the constraints placed upon them both by the third-party payer. In this case, communication can build trust between individual patients and physicians and help them to work together to find appropriate solutions to the problems they face within their particular structural and institutional constraints.

Disruption in Continuity   Continuity of care was a hallmark of the traditional model of patient care. Patients would see the same physician over time, and this physician would stay involved in the care even as the patient was seen by specialists. This central construct of medical care has changed, as continuity of care can be disrupted in the case in which patients, or more likely, their employer has changed health plans (Emmanuel & Dubler, 1995; Feldman, Novack, & Gracely, 1998). As Lammers and Geist (1997) asked, what difference does it make that a physician sees a patient every 10–15 minutes, that a patient may see a different provider every time, or that a physician is, in fact, never seen or replaced by physician extenders such as nurse practitioners or physician assistants? Changes in continuity of care can affect trust because of the disruption of an established health care provider-patient relationship (Flocke, Stange, & Zyzanski, 1997). Anecdotal information points to serious problems for patients brought about by changes in the doctor-patient relationship. Larson (2003) reported of patient suicide attempts—one successful—following the abrupt dismissal of their physicians by their organization. Communication between patients and doctors is different when there is physician turnover or when patients see the first available provider rather than the same physician over time. Communication is likely functional and limited to the encounter rather than relational in orientation.

One indicator or symptom of the disruption of the doctor-patient relationship may be increased use of emergency rooms and other clinics. For some patients, alternative organizational arrangements have supplanted the primary care office visit, including outpatient walk-in clinics where patients can usually get same-day treatment. Rosenblatt et al. (2000) found increased emergency room use by the elderly to be an indicator of disruption in the doctor-patient relationship, noting that those elderly with primary care physicians were less likely to use emergency rooms. Emergency room use by the poor, the elderly, and the uninsured for primary care is well documented. For these individuals, there is no ongoing care, no extensive taking of patient history, no development of rapport necessary for increased adherence to medication by their primary care physician. As a result, Potter and McKinlay (2005) argued that, instead of a relationship, there is an encounter, and instead of caring for patients, doctors treat symptoms. Communication in these encounters is likely marked by brevity and urgency related to the nature of the case and the pressure to see a higher number of patients. It would be nearly impossible for the provider to establish a visit-to-visit continuity of care history for the number and variety of patients he or she would see over time.

There are other ways in which continuity of care has been affected. Many health care organizations have become clinics in which patients do not necessarily see the same primary care physician all the time. Patients instead see whoever will take them, is working that day, or is available. In busy managed care clinics, even physicians who see the same patients may be constrained by patient load or time-per-patient limits that prevent them from developing meaningful doctor-patient relationships. Likewise, policies that discourage prevention or holistic care detract from the principle of continuity in that a physician knows the patient as more than just a case file. On the other hand, managed care plans could increase continuity by requiring that all care go through the primary care physician. The primary care physician would manage referrals, stay in touch with specialists, and keep track of the patient as they are cared for over time. There are other structural issues that involve organizations and physicians in terms of continuity of care. For example, there are now physicians who practice only in hospitals or in intensive care, and these physicians are unlikely to ever see patients anywhere else. If the primary care physician is involved at every stage, then this is less of an issue; however, if that physician is not involved, and this could be a function of organizational policies, then continuity is affected by structural and procedural issues.

Information and Communication Technology

One way in which health care organizations and managed care plans can offset the otherwise negative impacts on doctor-patient communication is by facilitating innovative uses of information and communication technology (ICT). There are undoubtedly multiple ways in which health care organizations could work to improve physician-patient relationships, and the use of ICT is but one. Technology has the potential to improve trust, continuity of care and communication between patients and their physicians. For example, health care organizations could address conflict of interest and trust issues by providing information to patients on secure web sites about provider compensation models. Critics of the disclosure of physician financial incentives assert that it would not help patients make informed choices about their medical care and that it could undermine trust between physicians and patients (T. E. Miller & Horowitz, 2000; Noone & Ubel, 1997; Ubel, 2001); however, Pearson, Kleinman, Rusinak, and Levinson (2006) found that actual disclosure tended to increase trust and loyalty by patients toward their physician and the health care organization. Continuity of care could be addressed using technology by providing information about the extent to which electronic medical records are available to providers that can assist in the transition from provider to provider. Of course, these suggestions are not replacements for seeing the same trusted physician every visit but they are ways in which health care organizations can use technology to mitigate some of the market-based issues facing the doctor-patient relationship.

Much of the impetus for this is the continued rise of the use of the Internet, as it is estimated that between 40%–70% of Internet users go online for health information, support, and services (Aspden & Katz, 2001; Mittman & Cain, 2001). Aspden, Katz, and Bemis (2001) reported that most of the doctors they surveyed recently had talked with patients who wanted to discuss information gathered from the Internet. Use of the Internet brings its share of issues: Patients have concerns related to privacy, response time, and routing the message to the appropriate party in the practice setting (Moyer, Stern, Dobias, Cox, & Katz, 2002), whereas doctors have concerns about legal liability, increased workload, inappropriate communication channel use (such as using e-mail in acute cases instead of face-to-face), as well as privacy and security (Leong, Gingrich, Lewis, Mauger, & George, 2005).

Health care organizations could use Web-based materials to help patients find reliable information and facilitate the sharing of it with their physician. Information and information seeking is an important dimension to both doctor-patient communication and the use of technology. There is plenty of evidence that health-related information seeking and retention of knowledge can lead to positive health outcomes (Viswanath & Finnegan, 1996; Winkleby, Flora, & Kraemer, 1994), however, not all individuals are motivated to seek out information on their own and people often avoid seeking information when it differs from their own beliefs (Babrow, 2001) or the topic is distressing (Brashers, Goldsmith, & Hsieh, 2002). In the medical consultation, this is a particularly interesting dynamic. Beisecker and Beisecker (1990) found that, although patients desired information about a number of medical topics, they did not engage in many information-seeking behaviors in the medical exam because they believed the doctor had the responsibility to make medical decisions. Patients, however, still had a desire for information, and one way in which health care organizations could address this would be to provide medical information using technology. The willingness of patients to seek information within the constraints of the health care organization and the doctor-patient relationship is influenced by the availability of that information, their perceived need for information, and the context in which this process takes place (Johnson, 1997). Access to information is fundamental to how likely it is that individuals will then seek information and availability shapes the extent to which patients can obtain medical information (Johnson, 1997).

Although information and communication technology use has been the norm in many industries for decades now, health care as a whole has been slow to implement standardized systems that connect physicians to patients, electronic medical records, and other forms of information technology. Physicians in particular have been slow to adopt information and communication technology (ICT), despite studies demonstrating their clinical benefits (Audet et al., 2004). Health care organizations have begun to adopt and implement technologies such as electronic medical records, clinical decision support systems, computerized prescribing, and order entry (Audet et al., 2004). Communication technology has the potential to significantly alter doctor-patient relationships because it can increase patient participation, reduce the amount of non-urgent telephone calls to physician offices, and improve patient access to health education materials (Leong et al., 2005; Street, 2003).

There are many ways in which the health care organization can influence the adoption, implementation, and appropriate use of technology by providers and patients to supplement and enhance the doctor-patient relationship. Whether the acquisition and use of technology is primarily market-driven, quality-driven, cost-driven, or influenced by a combination of these factors, medium-to-large-sized health care organizations typically have more resources to devote to ICT than do smaller physician practice settings. Indeed, Audet et al. (2004) found that physicians in larger groups (50 or more) are more likely to use communication technologies compared to physicians in solo practices. Audet et al. identified the top three barriers to adoption of ICT as start-up costs, lack of uniform standards, and lack of time. Physicians who practice in larger organizations are more likely to have access to technology for their use and their patients' use due to the organizational support and financing required to overcome these barriers.

The use of communication technology has many routine benefits, as connecting patients and physicians through email can increase patient involvement in supervising and documenting their own health care. Patients can use ICTs to schedule appointments, request information, and participate in prevention-oriented interactive web sites. Such technology could include filling out lifestyle-based surveys and receiving immediate feedback guiding health behavior.

As a result, the organizational context cannot be ignored when it comes to the use of communication technology in the doctor-patient relationship. In fact, it is probably far more accurate to say that ICT use is guided and constrained by organizations in terms of the choices that have been made by organizations about the type of technology to use and who has access to it.

Electronic mail is one form of ICT that may be particularly useful in facilitating doctor-patient communication. Although physicians may be guarded in their use of e-mail, a growing number use it to answer patient questions, offer advice, schedule appointments, and follow-up on treatment (Borowitz & Wyatt, 1998; Rice, 2001). Recent research has found that even though only 10% of the patients in two primary care centers ever used email to contact a physician, 70% of the patients indicated a willingness to use email with their physician (Moyer et al., 2002). Hobbs et al. (2003) discovered that close to 75% of physicians use e-mail with their patients, but the vast majority did so with only 1% to 5% of those patients. Barriers to physician-patient email were related to workload, security and physician reimbursements; researchers speculate that with adequate pre-screening, triage, and reimbursement mechanisms, physicians would accept increasing email communication with patients (Hobbs et al., 2003). Prescreening, triage, and reimbursement issues are all organizational issues and organizations can be designed to support physician use of technology.

Physicians (or their support staff) could initiate email contact to conduct routine guidance and education (e.g., to support lifestyle changes for newly diagnosed diabetic patients), to remind patients of scheduled appointments, or to check on a patient's progress (e.g., in a behavior change program). Research indicates that most email contact begins with patients, who provide information about their health or are requesting information about a diagnosis or treatment (Borowitz & Wyatt, 1998; Widman & Tong, 1997). E-mail has the potential to provide more egalitarian interactions in that on-line patients tend to be more assertive on the whole than do face-to-face patients and are more willing to use email to seek second opinions (Rice, 2001). For patients, email provides them with a way of accomplishing mundane tasks, such as ordering prescription refills, obtaining lab test, or getting feedback on less urgent problems (Couchman, Forjuoh, & Roscoe, 2001). Physician responses to email range from no reply at all to providing detailed information or diagnosis (Eysenbach & Diepgen, 1998); however, there are situations and issues in which ICT use may be inappropriate and create harm. Patients in need of urgent care who use email instead of other communication channels, such as face-to-face visits, could suffer consequences if their problems are not addressed quickly enough. It may be inappropriate for physicians to use e-mail to convey ambiguous test results or discuss complex health issues. Those individuals who receive new diagnoses or learn of serious medical conditions through electronic communication may be placed in unnecessarily vulnerable positions as a result.

Other uses of information and communication technology besides email have the potential to enhance the doctor-patient relationship as well. For example, electronic medical records could facilitate continuity by making sure that whenever a patient is seen, his or her full record is available for the physician to view and not housed in a central filing location that requires a day or two to shuttle files between offices. Electronic medical records have been implemented in health care organizations in an attempt to provide higher quality care, reduce medical errors, improve efficiency, and increase adherence to evidence-based guidelines (Hunt, Haynes, Hanna, & Smith, 1998; Kaushal, Shojania, & Bates, 2003; Rollman et al., 2002). Although use of electronic medical records within the medical consultation is not widespread, this technology is expected to become increasingly common over the next several years (Rouf, Whittle, Lu, & Schwartz, 2007). Doctor-patient communication is likely influenced by additional technology-related tasks in the exam room. For example, Rouf et al. (2007) found that patients in a VA primary care clinic believed that computers in the exam room affected the amount of time physicians talked to them and examined them but this was moderated by levels of physician experience: Attending physicians were perceived to focus on the patients more than did the residents.

Electronic records can be time-consuming when physicians are required to enter too much of the data manually. It is also not clear whether the physician and patient benefit most or the health care organization, with its need to maintain medical and financial records (Weiner & Biondich, 2006). Spending time managing data can detract from managing patients, given a physician's finite resources. Well-designed ICT can support and enhance interpersonal relationships in health care but often, the initial learning curve for physicians and new ICT is time consuming (R. H. Miller & Sim, 2004). Some scholars suggest the use of performance incentives and mandates to increase the use of electronic medical records (R. H. Miller & Sim, 2004). Seeking technological solutions to problems is attractive to many. It is important to remember that technology can complement the physician-patient relationship if it is designed and implemented appropriately. There are many communication and interpersonal factors (nonverbal, communication, empathy, compassion) inherent in the relationship that aid in the diagnosis and treatment of disease that cannot be replaced by technology.

Implications for Doctor-Patient Communication

There are implications for doctor-patient communication related to the use of information and communication technology for patients, physicians, and health care organizations. From the patient perspective, there are many reasons to be optimistic about ICT use in health care. One has the ability to gain a greater sense of control over one's health by gathering information through Internet searches and email communication with providers. The use of e-mail has the potential to transform the doctor-patient relationship from one of paternalism to one characterized by shared decision making and partnership (Bauer, 2000). Aspden, Katz, and Bemis (2001) reported that most of the doctors in their study had patients who wanted to discuss information gathered from the Internet; however, patients are not always willing to discuss what they find with their personal physician, for reasons related to the asymmetric nature of the doctor-patient relationship. For instance, a national survey of over 2000 respondents, revealed that only 37% of patients who seek health information online discussed what they found with their doctors (Aspden & Katz, 2001).

From a clinician perspective, the use of communication technology by patients is viewed unevenly by physicians. Some may feel threatened by patients who use the Internet to gather information (Beck, 2001), whereas others may be concerned with the quality of information gathered. Alternatively, other physicians may see the Internet as having a positive effect on patient relationships. Aspden et al. (2001) reported that one third of the doctors in their survey believed the patient's use of the Internet had led to a more productive consultation whereas only 14% thought it had a negative influence. Even though a number of physicians are cautious in their use of the technology, e-mail has the advantage for clinicians and patients in that it provides opportunities for more frequent and efficient communication because it can occur asynchronously (Mandl, Kohane, & Brandt, 1998). It seems reasonable to suggest that consultations of the virtual sort will expand the opportunities for doctor-patient communication *assuming* there is sufficient organizational support. Organizations can support physicians not only in providing IT support in the event of problems, but in dealing with the inevitable medical, legal, social, and attitudinal concerns that must be addressed (Mandl et al., 1998; Street, 2003).

From an organizational perspective, appropriate information requirements and choice of communication media (e-mail, Internet, telephone, face-to-face) may be determined by the complexity of the task at hand and the degree of ambiguity involved in the message (Daft & Lengel, 1986). Organizations can institute policies that guide the use of email (e.g., appointment confirmations but not rescheduling) that match the appropriateness of the task and message. If implemented properly, this could prevent any complex diagnoses or the breaking of bad news from being done electronically; instead, these would be face-to-face interactions. Of course, there are reasons beyond reducing uncertainty and increasing clarity in terms of communication media choice. Other perspectives assert that media use will be a complex function of social information (what communication channels do others use in the organization), perceived media characteristics, perceived task requirements, and attitudes toward communication media such as individual differences and prior communication technology experience (Salancik & Pfeffer, 1978). By guiding and constraining technology choices, organizations can influence the amount of ICT use and the degree to which physicians and, to a lesser extent, patients utilize technology.

One problem is that use of communication technology presumes rational patients and rational physicians interacting in dyadic mode, thus leaving out such multiple and complex communication issues as emotion, prior medical and communicative history, the inclusion of other providers (such as specialists and multidisciplinary teams), and given the asynchronous nature of e-mail, the extent to which the sender can know whether the other has received a critical message. Of course, there are ways to resolve this last issue by building solutions into the technology, but it remains to be seen as to whether this will be widely implemented across health care contexts. It will also be important for health care professionals, organizations, and society to ensure that the use of communication technology in health care does not deepen the digital divide. Issues such as access to technology, information literacy, and accessible, user-friendly technology interfaces can either create barriers that widen social disparities in health care access and outcomes or reduce disparities by generating greater access to health care. The lone physician toiling away in solo practice can hardly affect this process at a social level. Health care organizations, in tandem with other social structures (universities, legislatures, media), have the resources and power to shape the outcome of this debate.

Health care organizations can provide physicians access to ICT systems that contain results of diagnostic tests, updated literature, medical alerts, email, reminders and more from terminals located throughout the hospital, private offices, ambulatory clinics, and even from their homes (Slack, 2004). In the future, patients could access their test results, view upcoming appointments, review medications, request appointments, e-mail physicians, and laboratory and radiology tests through secure Web sites run by health care organizations (Sands & Halamka, 2004). Patients and physicians using a secure Web messaging system in a primary care clinic reported being satisfied with the use of this system, and physicians even received $25 from an insurer (on a trial basis) for each online communication with a patient (Liederman & Morefield, 2003); however, Houston, Sands, Jenckes, and Ford (2004) found similarly high rates of satisfaction mixed with inappropriate use of e-mail (chest pains, suicidal tendencies, etc.) in a study of early adopters of physician-patient e-mail. In many of these more sophisticated web-based email systems, enrollees were younger, more educated, and healthier than nonparticipants (Weingart, Rind, Tofias, & Sands, 2006). Other researchers have found that use of email has improved patient and physician satisfaction while increasing the potential for better communication (Leong et al., 2005). It is important to note that the future of technology use as an important part of the doctor-patient relationship is still up in the air.

Conclusion

The impact of organizational context on doctor-patient relationships and communication has been the central thesis of this chapter. We specifically focused on how health organizations are structured and financed and the impact of these features on doctor-patient communication. In our view, organizations are the sites where interpersonal health communication takes place and the contexts of peri-consultative communication. Doctor-patient communication does not occur in a vacuum, and it is critical to sort out the specific contextual influences that affect this phenomena. For example, in some cases, it may be related to the third-party payer effect, that is, the extent to which third-party payers influence or control the relationship between patients and their physicians. In other cases, the extent to which social, financial, legal and organizational forces have acted to reduce physician autonomy and the desire on the part of some physicians to be less engaged in the entrepreneurial side of medicine. In this chapter, we have described some of the outcomes of third-party payer effect and reduced autonomy on the doctor-patient relationship: the conflicting loyalties that physicians experience between the needs of the patients and the needs of the organization; reduced trust between patients and physicians; and disruption in the doctor-patient relationship due to third-party payers and organizational factors. We also examined how information and communication technology can mitigate these effects on doctor-patient communication.

Research into doctor-patient communication would be enriched by attention to the institutional context of patient care (see Lammers & Barbour, this volume). Health communication research can make a contribution to the study of doctor-patient communication by understanding how the organizational context plays a role in physician-patient communication. Empirical research focusing on doctor-patient communication could at the very least describe the organizational context in which these interactions occur. More ambitious studies (see Street & Gordon, 2006) could compare clinical and organizational contexts for any organizational effects on doctor-patient communication.

The change in the relationship between physicians and patients is complex and in part a response to social, cultural, and economic change. Organizations are an important part of this milieu and impinge on the relationship between patients and doctors. Where physicians work, how they are reimbursed, how much time they have to spend with patients, available treatment options, support staff, and technology use are among the many organizational factors that influence the medical consultation. It is important to consider that doctor-patient communication does not occur in isolation. It takes place in situated contexts that frame the very nature of the relationship.

References

Abbott, A. D. (1988). *The system of professions: An essay on the division of expert labor.* Chicago: University of Chicago Press.

Abrahamson, M. (1967). *The professional in the organization.* Chicago: Rand McNally.

Ahern, M. M., & Hendryx, M. S. (2003). Social capital and trust in providers. *Social Science & Medicine, 57*, 1195–1203.

Alexander, G. C., & Lantos, J. D. (2006). The doctor-patient relationship in the post-managed care era. *The American Journal of Bioethics, 6*, 29–32.

American Medical Association. (2000). *Socioeconomic characteristics of medical practice*. Chicago: Center for Health Policy Research.

Aspden, P., & Katz, J. E. (2001). Assessments of quality of health care information and referrals to physicians: A nationwide study. In R. E. Rice & J. E. Katz (Eds.), *The Internet and health communication: Experiences and expectations* (pp. 99–106). Thousand Oaks, CA: Sage.

Aspden, P., Katz, J. E., & Bemis, A. E. (2001). Use of the internet for professional purposes. In R. E. Rice & J. E. Katz (Eds.), *The internet and health communication: Experiences and expectations* (pp. 107–120). Thousand Oaks, CA: Sage.

Audet, A., Doty, M. M., Peugh, J., Shamasdin, J., Zapert, K., & Schoenbaum, S. (2004). Information technologies: When will they make it into physicians' black bags? *Medscape General Medicine, 6*. Retrieved February 19, 2006, from http://www.medscape.com/viewarticle/493210

Babrow, A. S. (2001). Uncertainty, value, communication, and problematic integration. *Journal of Communication, 51*, 553–573.

Bauer, C. (2000). Limiting factors on the transformative powers of email in patient-physician relationships: A critical analysis. *Health Communication, 12*, 239–259.

Beck, C. S. (2001). *Communicating for better health: A guide through medical mazes*. Boston: Allyn and Bacon.

Beckman, H. B., Markakis, K. M., Suchman, A. L., & Frankel, R. M. (1994). The doctor-patient relationship and malpractice: Lessons from plaintiff depositions. *Archives of Internal Medicine, 154*, 1365–70.

Beisecker, A. E., & Beisecker, T. D. (1990) Patient information-seeking behaviors when communicating with doctors. *Medical Care, 28*, 19–28.

Bensing, J., Roter, D. L., & Hulsman, R. L. (2003). Communication patterns of primary care physicians in the United States and the Netherlands. *Journal of General Internal Medicine, 18*, 335–342.

Birenbaum, A. (1997). *Managed care: Made in America*. Westport, CT: Praeger.

Borowitz, S. M., & Wyatt, J. C. (1998). The origin, content, and workload of email consultations. *Journal of the American Medical Association, 280*, 1321–1324.

Brashers, D. E., Goldsmith, D. J., & Hsieh, E. (2002). Information seeking and avoiding in health contexts. *Human Communication Research, 28*, 258–271.

Carson, R. A. (2000). Balancing loyalties or splitting the difference? *Academic Medicine, 75*, 443–444.

Couchman, G. R., Forjuoh, S. N., & Roscoe, T. G. (2001). E-mail communications in family practice: What do patients expect? *The Journal of Family Practice, 50*, 414–418.

Daft, R. L., & Lengel, R. H. (1986). Organizational information requirements, media richness and structural design. *Management Science, 32*, 554–571.

DiMatteo, M. R., (1994) Enhancing patient adherence to medical recommendations. *Journal of the American Medical Association, 271*, 79–83.

Eisenberg, E. M. (1984). Ambiguity as strategy in organizational communication. *Communication Monographs, 51*, 227–242.

Emmanuel, E. J., & Dubler, N. N. (1995). Preserving the physician-patient relationship in the era of managed care. *Journal of the American Medical Association, 273,* 323–329.

Eysenbach, G., & Diepgen, D. L. (1998). Responses to unsolicited patient email requests for medical advice on the World Wide Web. *Journal of the American Medical Association, 280,* 1333–1335.

Feldman, D. S., Novack, D. H., & Gracely, E. (1998). Effects of managed care on physician-patient relationships, quality of care, and the ethical practice of medicine. *Archives of Internal Medicine, 158,* 1626–1632.

Flocke, S. A., Stange, K. C., & Zyzanski, S. J. (1997). The impact of insurance type and forced discontinuity on the delivery of primary care. *The Journal of Family Practice, 45,* 125–126.

Freeman, V. G., Rathore, S. S., Weinfurt, K. P., Schulman, K. A., & Sulmasy, D. P. (1999). Lying for patients: Physician deception of third-party payers. *Archives of Internal Medicine, 159,* 2263–2270.

Freidson, E. (1970). *Professional dominance: The social structure of medical care.* New York: Atherton.

Gallagher, T. H., & Levinson, W. (2004). A prescription for protecting the doctor-patient relationship. *The American Journal of Managed Care, 10,* 61–68.

Gray, B. H. (1997). Trust and trustworthy care in the managed care era. *Health Affairs, 16,* 34–49.

Gross, H., & Budrys, G. (1991). Control over work in a prepaid group practice. In H. Z. Lopata & J. A. Levy (Eds.), *Current research on occupations and professions* (Vol. 6, pp. 279–96). Greenwich, CT: JAI.

Hall, R. C. W. (1994). Legal precedents affecting managed care: The physician's responsibilities to patients. *Psychosomatics, 35,* 105–117.

Haas, J. S., Phillips, K. A., Baker, L. C., Sonneborn, D., & McCulloch, C. E. (2003). Is the prevalence of gatekeeping in a community associated with individual trust in medical care? *Medical Care, 5,* 660–668.

Hacker, J. S., & Marmor, T. R. (1999). The misleading language of managed care. *Journal of Health Politics, Policy and Law, 24,* 1033–1043.

Hobbs, J., Wald, J., Jagannath, Y. S., Kittler, A., Pizziferri, L., Volk, L. A., et al. (2003). Opportunities to enhance patient and physician email contact. *International Journal of Medical Informatics, 70,* 1–9.

Hoff, T. J. (2001). The physician as worker: What it means and why now? *Health Care Management Review, 26,* 53–70.

Hoff, T. J. (2003). How physician-employees experience their work lives in a changing HMO. *Journal of Health and Social Behavior, 44,* 75–96.

Hoff, T. J., & McCaffrey, D. P. (1996). Adapting, resisting, and negotiating. *Work & Occupations, 23,* 165–90.

Houston, T. K., Sands, D. Z., Jenckes, M. W., & Ford, D. E. (2004). Experiences of patients who were early adopters of electronic communication with their physician: Satisfaction, benefits, and concerns. *The American Journal of Managed Care, 10,* 601–608.

Hunt, D. L., Haynes, R. B., Hanna, S. E., & Smith, K. (1998). Effects of computer-based clinical decision support systems on physician performance and patient outcomes: A systematic review. *Journal of the American Medical Association, 280,* 1339–1346.

Johnson, J. D. (1997). *Cancer-related information seeking*. Cresskill, NJ: Hampton.

Kaplan, S. H., Greenfield, S., & Ware, J. E. (1989). Assessing the effects of physician-patient interactions on the outcomes of chronic disease. *Medical Care, 27,* S110–27.

Kaushal, R., Shojania, K. G., & Bates, D. W. (2003). Effects of computerized physician order entry and clinical decision support systems on medication safety: A systematic review. *Archives of Internal Medicine, 163,* 1409–1416.

Kroll, T., Beatty, P., & Bingham, S. (2003). Primary care satisfaction among adults with physical disabilities: The role of patient-provider communication. *Managed Care Quarterly, 11,* 11–19.

Kuttner, R. (1999). The American health care system: Employer-sponsored health coverage. *New England Journal of Medicine, 340,* 248–252.

Lammers, J. C., Barbour, J., & Duggan, A. (2003). Organizational forms of the provision of health care: An institutional perspective. In T. Thompson, A. Dorsey, K. Miller, & R. Parrot (Eds.). *Handbook of health communication* (pp. 319–345). Mahwah, NJ: Erlbaum.

Lammers, J. C., & Duggan, A. (2002). Bringing physicians back in: Communication predictors of physicians' satisfaction with managed care. *Health Communication, 14,* 493–514.

Lammers, J., & Geist, P. (1997). The transformation of caring in the light and shadow of managed care. *Health Communication, 9,* 45–60.

Larson, E. B. (2003). Medicine as profession – back to basics: Preserving the physician-patient relationship in a challenging medical marketplace. *The American Journal of Medicine, 114,* 168–172.

Leong, S. L., Gingrich, D., Lewis, P. R. Mauger, D. T., & George, J. H. (2005). Enhancing doctor-patient communication using email: A pilot study. *Journal of the American Board of Family Medicine, 18,* 180–188.

Levinson, W., Roter, D. L., Mullooly, J. P., Dull, V. T., & Frankel, R. M. (1997). Physician-patient communication: The relationship with malpractice claims among primary care physicians and surgeons. *Journal of the American Medical Association, 277,* 553–559.

Liederman, E. M., & Morefield, C. S. (2003). Web messaging: A new tool for patient-physician communication. *Journal of the American Medical Informatics Association, 10,* 260–270.

Mandl, K. D., Kohane, I. S., & Brandt, A. M. (1998). Electronic patient-physician communication: Problems and promise. *Annals of Internal Medicine, 129,* 495–500.

McMurray, J. E., Williams, E., Schwartz, M. D., Douglas, J., Van Kirk, J., Konrad, R., et al. (1997). Physician job satisfaction: Developing a model using qualitative data. *Journal of General Internal Medicine, 12,* 711–714.

Mechanic, D. (2000). Rediscovering the social determinants of health. *Health Affairs, 19,* 269–276.

Mechanic, D., & Schlesinger, M. (1996). The impact of managed care on patients' trust in medical care and their physicians. *Journal of the American Medical Association, 275,* 1693–1697.

Miller, R. H., & Sim, I. (2004). Physicians' use of electronic medical records: Barriers and solutions. *Health Affairs, 23,* 116–126.

Miller, T. E., & Horowitz, C. R. (2000). Disclosing doctors' incentives: Will consumers understand and value the information? *Health Affairs, 19,* 149–155.

Minogue, B. (2000). The two fundamental duties of the physician. *Academic Medicine,* *75,* 431–42.

Mittman, R., & Cain, M. (2001). The future of the internet in health care: A five year forecast. In R. E. Rice & J. E. Katz (Eds.), *The internet and health communication: Experiences and expectations* (pp. 47–73). Thousand Oaks, CA: Sage.

Moyer, C. A., Stern, D. T., Dobias, K. S., Cox, D. T., & Katz, S. J. (2002). Bridging the electronic divide: Patient and provider perspectives on email communication in primary care. *American Journal of Managed Care, 8,* 427–433.

Murphy, J., Chang, H., Montgomery, J. E., Rogers, W. H., & Safran, D. G. (2001). The quality of physician-patient relationships: Patients' experiences 1996–1999. *The Journal of Family Practice, 50,* 123–129.

Noone, G. C., & Ubel, P. A. (1997). Managed care organizations should not disclose their physicians' financial incentives. *American Journal of Managed Care, 3,* 159–160.

Pearson, S. D., Sabin, J. E., & Hyams, T. (2002). Caring for patients within a budget: Physicians' tales from the front lines of managed care. *Journal of Clinical Ethics, 13,* 115–123.

Pearson, S. D., Kleinman, K., Rusinak, D., & Levinson, W. (2006). A trial of disclosing physicians' financial incentives to patients. *Archives of Internal Medicine, 166,* 623–628.

Potter, S. J., & McKinlay, J. B., (2005). From a relationship to encounter: An examination of longitudinal and lateral dimensions in the doctor-patient relationship. *Social Science & Medicine, 61,* 465–479.

Putnam, R. (1993). *Making democracy work: Civic traditions in modern Italy.* Princeton, NJ: Princeton University Press.

Quaye, R. (2001). Professional integrity in the age of managed care: Views of physicians. *International Journal of Health Care Quality Assurance Incorporating Leadership in Health Services, 14,* 82–86.

Real, K. (2002). *Communication and identification: Physicians and organizations.* Unpublished doctoral dissertation, Texas A & M University, College Station, TX.

Real, K., Bransom, R., & Poole, M. S. (in press). The symbolic and material nature of physician identity: Implications for physician-patient communication. *Health Communication.*

Rice, R. E. (2001). The internet and health communication: A framework of experiences. In R. E. Rice & J. E. Katz (Eds.), *The Internet and health communication: Experiences and expectations* (pp. 5–46). Thousand Oaks, CA: Sage.

Rodwin, M. A. (1993). *Medicine, money, and morals: Physicians' conflicts of interest.* New York: Oxford University Press.

Rodwin, M. A. (1995). Conflicts in managed care. *The New England Journal of Medicine, 332,* 604–607.

Rollman, B. L., Hanusa, B. H., Lowe, H. J., Gilbert, T., Kapoor, W. N., & Schulberg, H. C. (2002). A randomized trial using computerized decision support to improve treatment of major depression in primary care. *Journal of General Internal Medicine, 17,* 493–503.

Rosenblatt, R. A., Wright, G. E., Baldwin, L. M., Chan, L., Clitherow, P., Chen, F. M., et al. (2000). The effect of the doctor-patient relationship on emergency department use among the elderly. *American Journal of Public Health. 90,* 97–102.

Roter, D. L., & Hall, J. A. (1993). *Doctors talking to patients/Patients talking to doctors*. Westport, CT: Auburn House.

Rouf, E., Whittle, J., Lu, N., & Schwartz, M. D. (2007). Computers in the exam room: Differences in physician–patient interaction may be due to physician experience. *Journal of General Internal Medicine, 22*, 43–48.

Rubin, H. R., Gandek, B., Rogers, W. H., Kosinski, M., McHorney, C. A., & Ware, J. E., Jr. (1993). Patients' rating of outpatient visits in different practice settings: Results from the Medical Outcomes Study. *Journal of the American Medical Association, 270*, 835–840.

Salancik, G. R., & Pfeffer, J. (1978). A social information processing approach to job attitudes and task design. *Administrative Science Quarterly, 23*, 224–253.

Sands, D. Z., & Halamka, J. D. (2004). PatientSite: Patient centered communication, services, and access to information. In R. Nelson & M. J. Ball (Eds.), *Consumer informatics: Applications and strategies in cyber health care* (pp. 20–32). New York: Springer-Verlag.

Shapiro, R. S., Tym, K. A., Eastwood, D., Derse, A. R., & Klein, J. P. (2003). Managed care, doctors, and patients: Focusing on relationships, not rights. *Cambridge Quarterly of Healthcare Ethics, 12*, 300–307.

Shortell, S. M., Gillies, R. B., Anderson, D. A., Erickson, K. M., & Mitchell, J. B. (2000). *Remaking health care in America: The evolution of organized delivery systems* (2nd ed.). San Francisco: Jossey-Bass.

Slack, W. V. (2004). A 67-year-old man who emails his physician. *Journal of the American Medical Association, 292*, 2255–2261.

Starr, P. (1982). *The social transformation of American medicine*. New York: Basic Books.

Stewart, M. (1995). Effective physician-patient communication and health outcomes: A review. *Canadian Medical Association Journal, 152*, 1423–1433.

Street, R. L., Jr. (2001). Active patients as powerful communicators. In W. P. Robinson & H. Giles (Eds.), *The new handbook of language and social psychology* (pp. 541–560). Chichester, England: Wiley.

Street, R. L. (2003). Communication in medical encounters: An ecological perspective. In T. Thompson, A. Dorsey, K. Miller, & R. Parrott (Eds.), *The handbook of health communication* (pp. 63–89). Mahwah, NJ: Erlbaum.

Street, R. L., & Gordon, H. S. (2006). The clinical context and patient participation in post-diagnostic consultations. *Patient Education and Counseling, 64*, 217–224.

Sulmasy, D., Bloche, G., Mitchell, J., & Hadley, J. (2000). Physicians' ethical beliefs about cost-control arrangements. *Archives of Internal Medicine, 160*, 649–657.

Ubel, P. A. (2001). Money talks, patients walk? *Journal of General Internal Medicine, 16*, 204–205.

Viswanath, K., & Finnegan, J. R., Jr. (1996). The knowledge gap hypothesis: Twenty-five years later. In B. Burleson (Ed.), *Communication yearbook 19* (pp. 187–227) Thousand Oaks, CA: Sage.

Wagner, E. R. (1997). Types of managed care organizations. In P. R. Kongstvedt (Ed.), *Essentials of managed health care* (2nd ed., pp. 36–48). Gaithersburg, MD: Aspen.

Waitzkin, H. (2001). *At the front lines of medicine*. New York: Rowman & Littlefield.

Waitzkin, H., & Fishman, J. (1997). The patient-physician relationship in the era of managed care. In J. D. Wilkerson, K. J. Devers, & R. S. Givens (Eds.), *Competitive managed care: The emerging health care system* (pp. 136–161). San Francisco: Jossey-Bass.

Weiner, M., & Biondich, P. (2006). The influence of information technology on patient-physician relationships. *Journal of General Internal Medicine, 21*(Suppl. 1), S35–S39.

Weingart, S. N., Rind, D., Tofias, Z., & Sands, D. Z. (2006). Who uses the patient internet portal? The PatientSite experience. *Journal of the American Medical Informatics Association, 13*, 91–95.

Werner, R. M., Alexander, G. C., Fagerlin, A., & Ubel, P. A. (2002). Lying to insurance companies: The desire to deceive among physicians and the public. *American Journal of Bioethics, 4*, 53–59.

Widman, L. E., & Tong, D. A. (1997). Requests for medical advice from patients and families to health care providers who publish on the World Wide Web. *Archives of Internal Medicine, 157*, 209–212.

Winkleby, M. A., Flora, J. A., & Kraemer, H. C. (1994). A community-based heart disease intervention: Predictors of change. *American Journal of Public Health, 84*, 767–772.

Wynia, M. K., Cummins, D. S., VanGeest, J. B., & Wilson, I. B. (2000). Physician manipulation of reimbursement rules for patients: Between a rock and a hard place. *Journal of the American Medical Association, 283*, 1858–1865.

Chapter 4

Exploring the Institutional Context of Physicians' Work

Professional and Organizational Differences in Physician Satisfaction

John C. Lammers and Joshua B. Barbour

The health care system in the United States has changed dramatically in the last 30 years. Health organizations are under pressure from patients for access to high quality, affordable care. Employers, insurance companies, and federal agencies want lower costs, accountability, and safety. Hospitals and medical groups, as well as insurance companies and government agencies, are adopting management methods that emphasize efficiency, predictability, calculability, and control (Ritzer, 2004). Despite the efforts to more tightly manage health care in the United States, however, medical expenses continue to rise (Strunk, Ginsburg, & Gabel, 2002), and patients and payers are not alone in their expressions of dissatisfaction. Both nurses and physicians also have expressed concern about working conditions and quality of care in managed care arrangements (Harvard School of Public Health, 2000). The concerns of so many involved in the health care system at multiple levels (patients as well as providers, organizations as well as government agencies) present an opportunity to health services researchers in the form of research of keen interest to a broad audience. The changes in health care also present a mandate to address our field's lack of theoretical models that explain developments at both personal and organizational levels in health services.

The widely-used term *managed care* (see Real & Street, this volume) is the catch-all that describes developments in health care over the last 30 years. Managed care commonly refers to health services arrangements that employ prepayment for services, require pre-authorization from officials for services, and involve contracts among patients, providers, and administrators (Lammers, Barbour, & Duggan, 2003). The broadest definition includes

> Health insurance plans intended to reduce unnecessary health care costs through a variety of mechanisms, including: economic incentives for physicians and patients to select less costly forms of care; programs for reviewing the medical necessity of specific services; increased beneficiary cost sharing; controls on inpatient admissions and lengths of stay; the establishment of cost-sharing incentives for outpatient surgery; selective contracting with health care providers; and the intensive management of

high-cost health care cases. The programs may be provided in a variety of settings, such as health maintenance organizations and preferred provider organizations. (National Library of Medicine, 2008)

These types of arrangements now dominate health care in the United States (Barbour & Lammers, 2007; Lammers et al., 2003; Lammers & Duggan, 2002). The administrative context or "peri-consultation interaction" (see Real & Street, this volume) of patient-provider communication now has changed. Administrative policies for care delivery and payment form important new organizational structures (McPhee, 1985) in which communication between physicians and patients takes place. These structures also contextualize the relationships between physicians and managers, and among managers of the health care systems, which tends to bureaucratize health care (Lammers & Geist, 1997).

Managed care itself is not a unified entity, however, as a number of writers have observed (Hacker & Marmor, 1999; Real & Street, this volume). The term loosely covers many arrangements from highly corporate approaches to cost controls, to loose confederations of cooperating providers. From its least organized manifestation (independent practitioner associations) to its most comprehensive arrangements (staff model health maintenance organizations), the meaning of managed care involves the establishment of written guidelines for the provision of medical services (Mechanic, 2000, p. 103). The formal rules and guidelines of managed care have been the subject of considerable dissent in the medical community (Bloche, 1999; Feldman, Novack, & Gracely, 1998; Gonsoulin, 1997; Mechanic, 2000; Potter, 1999; Rodwin, 1998). For example, Sullivan (1999) worried that managed care and its financial imperatives threaten the professionalism of medicine.

For the most part, these changes in the context of the physician-patient relationship have not been linked to physicians' work by theoretically guided systematic research. Researchers concerned with the medical care setting of physician-patient communication, for example, have understood its context in terms of the privilege and authority of the physician and the privacy of the physician-patient encounter (Ray & Donohew, 1990, p. 29). Real and Street (this volume) pointed out that the specific formal organizational context, however, is rarely distinguished. Moreover, specific types of providers—such as primary care providers or specialists—are rarely distinguished in research on physicians' work (although they are distinguished in health policy research; see Robinson, 2001).

Nonetheless, managed care alters both professional roles as well as the organizational contexts of physicians' work (Barbour & Lammers, 2007; Lammers & Geist, 1997). As physicians are drawn into ever more rational social structures (Scott, 2003), principles and theories of organizations are likely to apply to their work. McPhee (1985) labeled organizational structure as "explicit, authoritative, metacommunication" (p. 162). This view of structure is especially congruent with the circumstances of managed care, because now, in contrast to their traditional autonomous roles as professional healers, physicians work by fixed routines (Weber, 1946, 1947), subject to organizational rules (Euske & Roberts, 1987). Thus, the case of physicians' roles in managed care provides an opportunity to study specific roles and the structural context of health services.

Role configurations, such as physicians' specialization (a socially micro-level phenomenon), and structures, such as practice settings (a socially macro-level phenomenon), can be understood together through the application of the institutional theory of organizational communication (ITOC) (Lammers & Barbour, 2006). An institutional approach considers "established and enduring patterns of beliefs and practices that apply at both the microlevel within organizations and at the macrolevel across organizations" (p. 262). ITOC thus provides a vehicle for examining how medical professionals' institutionalized beliefs and practices in particular organizational settings may result in greater or lesser satisfaction and effectiveness. Moreover, a hallmark of institutions, and a guiding aspect of ITOC, is the role of formal, written rules, contracts, and regulations that cut across organizational boundaries. From the regulations that govern Medicare reimbursement to the contracts the bind providers to patients in health plans, managed care represents an institutional structure of influence on health organizations and the providers who work in them.

This study identifies institutional contexts and role configurations in the provision of medical care. To study institutional contexts, we surveyed physicians in a community dominated by three organizations: a specialty clinic established as a treatment center for medical problems, a community clinic established with a public interest philosophy, and a loose federation of solo physicians known as an independent practitioner association (IPA). Physicians' role configurations in this study include their perceptions of satisfaction, autonomy, and ability to make clinical decisions, their attitudes toward medical practice, and their reports of communication with patients and managed care organizations. This characterization of role configuration is defined by individuals' perceptions of their roles. In other words, our analysis focuses on the relationship between individual physicians' perceptions and their institutional situations.

To this end, we first review physicians' administrative contexts and their professional medical roles as primary care or specialists providers. We suggest that both the administrative context and professional roles can be understood using an institutional perspective, which we also outline below in more detail. Next, we provide background on the community and the three organizations we studied, and we hypothesize the likelihood of satisfaction or dissatisfaction for physicians in the practices. Survey data of physician satisfaction is then presented and compared for specialist and generalist physicians practicing in each of the three organizations. Results suggest that the histories of the organizations, as well as specialty and practice arrangements, affect physicians' attitudes toward medical practice both in terms of satisfaction and clinical autonomy. Implications for health services research bridging organizational structures with physicians' work are discussed.

Assumptions about Professions and Organizations: Toward an Institutional Perspective

Although professional powers may transcend administrative or organizational arrangements (Freidson, 1986), many medical care providers today view managed care as a challenge to their professional discretion (Feldman, Novack, & Gracely, 1998; Real & Street, this volume; Rodwin, 1998). Perhaps the autonomy of physicians could be taken for granted before 1980, when the majority of practitioners saw their patients under fee-for-service reimbursement arrangements, and the number of physicians in group practice was smaller than it is today (Scott & Lammers, 1985). Many medical groups today depend on prepaid contracts or membership in preferred provider organizations to sustain revenues (Bodenheimer & Grumbach, 2002, p. 197); however, the administrative arrangements that accompany group practices intervene in physicians' conduct (Gross & Budrys, 1986). Physicians themselves have called into question managed care rules as they relate to their decision-making powers as well as their ethical responsibilities (Feldman, Novack, & Gracely, 1998; Friedman & Savage, 1998; Kralewski et al., 1998; Minogue, 2000). In this section, we review the role configurations and the organizational context of physicians as understood by past health services research. We make the case that the advent of managed care significantly affects these configurations and contexts, and we suggest that an institutional perspective is an appropriate lens for the study of these changes.

There are at least two directions in which professional medical roles have developed (Thomas, 1983). The literature on medical professional socialization has for many years highlighted the tension between the humanistic and scientific requirements of the role (Becker, Geer, Hughes, & Strauss, 1961; Conrad, 1988; Miller, 1993). This tension has been characterized in terms of caring versus curing (Conrad, 1988); holistic versus biomedical approaches (Longino, 1997); and the healer versus the scientist (Laine & Davidoff, 1996). A number of writers have laid these developments at the feet of the medical school training experience (Becker et al., 1961; Conrad, 1988; Miller, 1993).

One could argue, on the basis of this literature, that the longer a physician in training is exposed to the training environment, the more likely that she or he will adopt a scientific outlook. The scientific professional outlook is cultivated in the recruitment and selection process for medical schools. Candidates are selected on the basis of scientific acumen and an orientation toward systematic knowledge. Faculty members employed in careers of research rather than treatment reinforce the professional scientific outlook throughout graduate and postgraduate education (Bloom, 1989; Jefferys & Elston, 1989). The scientific outlook is further reinforced by the drive toward specialization in medicine that began during the middle part of the 20th century. Specialists became even more closely tied to academic medical centers to remain well informed and to have access to sophisticated technologies, facilities, and colleagues (Simmonds, Robbins, Brinker, Rice, & Kerstein, 1990).

In contrast, the American Academy of Family Physicians (2001) defined the primary care physician as "a generalist physician who provides definitive care to the *undifferentiated* patient at the point of first contact and takes continuing responsibility for providing the patient's care" (p. 2, emphasis added). The generalist outlook is an older, more traditional configuration of the health professional's role. Starr (1982) discussed the conflict early in this century between specialists, who sought control over particular types of procedures and practices, and their generalist forebears. In the United States, this eventually resulted in higher barriers to entry into medical practice by nonphysicians (such as technologists and midwives), but "fluid boundaries within the profession" (p. 325). Nonetheless, as in other fields, because of the cultural value placed on technical knowledge, physicians have found it difficult to remain generalists (Vanselow, 1998).

These two strands of professional roles in medicine are not exclusive. It would be inappropriate to say that some physicians are healers whereas others are scientists, but the emphasis on science in medical training is well-documented, and the differences in distribution, prestige, and earnings of generalists (including internists, family practitioners, and pediatricians) versus specialists (such as dermatologists or surgeons) is also well-documented (Bureau of Labor Statistics, 2000; Donabedian, 1986). Perhaps most important for our purposes, the undifferentiated nature of generalists' work compared to the specialist would lead us to expect different communication patterns, behaviors, and attitudes. For example, as gatekeepers in a managed care regime, generalists make initial diagnoses and referrals to specialists, whose narrow range of practice and expertise allows them to focus on treatment options. Indeed, Smetana et al. (2007) found a bias toward efficacy in research evaluating specialists, who typically focused on a single condition, in contrast to generalists, who concerned themselves with a wider spectrum of patient diseases and ailments. Stille, Primack, and Savageau (2003) found that the practice styles and communication habits of pediatric generalists and pediatric subspecialists made coordination of care difficult.

Managed care may be expected to affect these role configurations in various ways. As a program driven by cost-conscious insurance companies, employers, and governments, managed care does not reimburse physicians for training, research, or education. It favors the healing role in this respect. But managed care also involves practice guidelines, review panels, credentialing, scheduling, and other mechanisms that create efficiencies in the provision of care. We should, therefore, be able to observe managed care arrangements frustrating physicians in their ability to serve patients. In general, we suspect that

managed care is likely to frustrate patient care efforts of physicians by raising questions about their autonomy over care decisions and by raising ethical
issues with respect to the physicians' obligations to patients.

The organizational context of the provision of care often is regarded as
undifferentiated, even when understanding the context might have been
theoretically informative (Sharf, 1993). In a departure from studies of consultations in examining rooms, Wissow et al. (1998) studied physician-patient
communication in emergency departments, but did not compare these data
to nonemergency consultations. Suchman, Roter, Green, and Lipkin (1993)
studied physicians' satisfaction in patient interviews, including a wide range of
patient characteristics and circumstances in their analysis, but they included
no organizational variables. Key variables in the study, respondents' perceptions of the patient physician relationship, the data collection process, the
appropriateness of the use of time, and the absence of excessive demands on
the part of the patient all were likely linked to (noncontrolled) organizational
issues. Research in technologically mediated communication also suggests that
organizational and institutional forces must be taken into account in order to
understand their application to the physician-patient relationship (Baur, 2000;
Lehoux, Sicotte, Denis, Berg, & Lacroix, 2002).

It seems false, therefore, to assume uniformity across all administrative
arrangements in which physician-patient relationships occur. Public or private auspices; the volume of resources; the reimbursement methods; the rural
or urban location of the facility; whether the encounter occurs in a hospital,
clinic, or private office; and the size, history, climate, and culture of the organization may all contribute to differences in the communicative encounter
(Kralewski et al., 1998). Moreover, many of these factors have been changing
rapidly in recent years as managed care arrangements have developed.

In the administration of managed care, patients are seen as members of
populations, and administrative arrangements are based in part on the wealth
of those populations (Lammers et al., 2003). For example, physicians' revenues per member per month for commercial HMOs in 2000 averaged $167.32,
whereas Medicare revenues per member per month averaged $53.18 (Managed
Care Online, 2001), and the disparity was even greater for hospitals ($198.51
and $40.23, respectively). It is difficult to imagine that the disparity in reve-
nues between these two populations would not influence the medical encounter. Indeed, wealthier, more intensively managed health plans are more likely
to use pay-for performance schemes to reward physicians (Rosenthal, Landon,
Normand, Frank, & Epstein, 2006); yet Medicare patients report higher satisfaction with traditional plans versus managed care plans (Landon, Zaslavsky,
Bernard, Cioffi, & Cleary, 2004).

Financial pressures on medical care administrators, and, in turn, on physicians, are expected to continue to grow (Van de Ven, Engleman, & Rogers,
2001). The percent of employees of medium and large establishments who use
traditional indemnity insurance has been shrinking since 1980, whereas the

percent of such employees who use various forms of managed care has been growing (Ellis, 2001). As the funding environment becomes more constrained, administrative constraints also may be expected to grow.

Managed Care in an Institutional Perspective

These changes in professional roles and administrative context can be understood using an institutional perspective (Lammers & Barbour, 2006; Scott, Meyer, & Associates, 1994). The institutional perspective emphasizes the historical context and the extra-organizational environment of organizations (Lammers et al., 2003). Although particular organizations may be thought of as institutions, the concept more usefully applies to "clusters of conventions" (Barley, 2008, p. 496) that form the foundation upon which organizing occurs. Thus, the use of intensive management practices in medical care, the professional autonomy of physicians, the tendency for physicians to work as generalists or specialists, and the establishment of specialized or primary care medical clinics, together represent the institutions of medical care in the United States today.

The institutional roots of managed care may be found in the oldest prepaid medical practices like Kaiser Permanente, but the movement really gained momentum in the mid-1960s. Since the advent of Medicare and Medicaid in 1964, the vast majority of physicians' offices, medical groups, and hospitals have elected to comply with the regulations that authorize reimbursement for services through these programs. A few sustained standards but elected not to participate. Later, as private managed care efforts mounted throughout the 1980s, some hospitals and clinics resisted the changes, retaining niche services or patients. As the regulatory environment became more complex, with the advent of prepayment using the Diagnosis Related Groups (DRG) system (Geist & Hardesty, 1992) and eventually the Resource-Based Relative Value Scale (Harris-Shapiro, 1998), more experienced organizations and providers developed an advantage over inexperienced organizations and providers who had earlier resisted the trend toward fixed prepayment and pre-authorization, and other contractual guidelines. Therefore we are led to expect that providers who work in organizations with longer exposure to the regulatory environment (that is, the institutions) of managed care would be less inclined to complain about its pressures.

Barbour and Lammers (2007) explored physicians' satisfaction and dissatisfaction with managed care using an institutional perspective. Like others, Barbour and Lammers found that exposure to managed care—in terms of number of contracts and frequency of communication with managed care representatives—as a dissatisfier for physicians in general. But they also found that physicians' institutional beliefs about autonomy and their commitment to the profession acted as moderators on their feelings of dissatisfaction associated with managed care (p. 225). Paradoxically, however, Barbour and Lammers found that physicians who expressed strong belief in autonomy and also had more managed care contracts expressed higher, not lower, satisfaction with managed care. They speculated that having multiple contracts (as is the case in large multispecialty groups or IPAs) may insulate physicians from frequent communication with managed care representatives (p. 226). The roles of practice history and culture and the generalist-specialist distinction as correlates of physicians' satisfaction remains to be investigated.

In the next section, we describe three organizations (two multispecialty groups and an independent practitioner association) in a West Coast city that offer an opportunity to study the relationship of managed care to perceptions of professional autonomy and organizational contexts.

Medical Practice in Southcoast City

Southcoast City's (population 175,000) two dominant medical groups were both established in the mid-1920s, but developed different cultures (to protect the confidentiality of our respondents, we have used pseudonyms to describe the city and the clinics). The Community Clinic, one of the first group practices on the West Coast, was established with a public interest philosophy to serve people from every sector of the community. The Doctors' Clinic, also a pioneer group practice, was first established as a treatment center for particular diseases. Its founder also established a nearby research facility. Both clinics grew serving the community, though Doctors' Clinic built its reputation on specialty services, eventually drawing patients nationally and internationally, while Community became the city's resource for general health care. Doctors' Clinic made its reputation as a pioneer in the treatment of metabolic diseases, while Community boasted of the number of babies born in its facility. Both clinics became highly regarded in the community, state, and region as excellent multispecialty group practices.

In the late 1970s, Community Clinic began to accept managed care and HMO contracts to provide care to employees and Medicaid patients in the city, thereby giving it a strategic advantage over Doctors' Clinic when managed care contracts began to dominate the medical market place. In the late 1990s, the Doctors' Clinic had grown to include over 50 practitioners, about 20% of whom were primary care physicians (in family practice, internal medicine, and urgent care). The Community Clinic included over 80 physicians in its main location and several branch offices, of whom nearly 50% were in primary care. The Doctor's Clinic continued to thrive in specialty services.

As Southcoast City grew, so did the medical practice community, and a number of solo practitioners and small groups developed, independent of the Doctors' and Community Clinics. By the 1980s, these physicians too began to recognize the pressure for contracted care, and a third confederation of physicians arose to form Sovereign Health System, an independent practice association (IPA). At the end of 1998, the Sovereign IPA linked 125 physicians in a group of providers under an administrative structure that would seek contracts and coordinate payments for the group. By 2000, about two thirds of the Sovereign Health System physicians were specialists, none of whom were associated with the Doctor's Clinic or the Community Clinic.

Although Sovereign IPA included a range of physicians' and small groups' offices, the two clinics presented a sharply contrasting milieu to the visitor. The lobby of Doctor's Clinic resembled a luxurious hotel with bouquets of fresh flowers, dark hardwood furnishings, and refined decor. The clinic's glossy brochures described executive and "VIP" health physical examinations complete with luxury accommodations in nearby seaside hotels. In contrast, Community Clinic was the picture of efficiency; the crowded lobby was clean but utilitarian. Although its decor was not sparse, neither was it luxurious. Well-placed signs directed visitors to the appropriate wings of a sprawling complex. Doctors Clinic was located across the street from the largest local hospital, whereas Community Clinic was located on less expensive property about two miles away. The administrative offices of Sovereign IPA were located in the business district of the city, but the offices of the practitioners were scattered throughout the city in small office buildings.

Because of the different ways the two clinics and the independent group developed, one would expect continued differences in the ways providers respond to changes due to managed care arrangements. In particular, physicians in the Sovereign IPA are likely to treat more fee-for-service patients, because they were organized to seek group contracts and coordinate payments as part of their formal structure, which its members had been unable to do on their own. Community Clinic began accepting Medicaid and other managed care arrangements earliest in the organizational shift to such payment structures. Physicians there are likely to associate themselves with the ideology of managed care and hence be less dissatisfied with the limits and guidelines of these structures. They should feel they have greater authority to make clinical decisions and be more satisfied with their practices than physicians who are part of the Doctors' Clinic or Sovereign IPA. Similarly, physicians at the Doctors' Clinic or Sovereign IPA may have more extreme views that managed care arrangements compromise their integrity and that the rewards (both financial and personal) of practicing medicine under managed care arrangements are less satisfying. Physicians who are part of the Sovereign IPA are likely to be more closely aligned with traditional ideology and prefer to work in solo practices.

Based on the foregoing review of literature on generalists and specialist physicians, organizations, and reactions to managed care, as well as our observation about the three organizations, we hypothesize the following:

Hypothesis 1a: Sovereign IPA physicians will report more fee-for-service patients than either Doctors' Clinic physicians or Community Clinic physicians.

Hypothesis 1b: Community Clinic physicians will have had the longest experience with managed care, followed by Sovereign IPA physicians, and followed by Doctor's Clinic physicians.

Hypothesis 1c: Specialist physicians across all three groups will report more fee-for-service patients than primary care physicians.

Hypothesis 1d: Specialist physicians across all three groups will have had shorter experience with managed care than primary care physicians.

These hypotheses are checks that our expectations about physicians' experience with managed care are actually born out. Sovereign IPA, as a loose confederation of physicians will have more flexibility and thus more fee-for-service patients; however, we expect Doctor's Clinic's physicians to have remained in pre-managed care reimbursement arrangements longest, because the Doctor's Clinic is a single organization, internationally recognized for providing services to a wealthy elite who can afford high fees for services. Additionally, specialist physicians in general should see more fee-for-service patients and have less experience with managed care given that managed care arrangements have favored the primary care doctor as the gatekeeper and main manager of medical services (Robinson, 1999).

Hypothesis 2a: Physicians at Community Clinic will be more satisfied with the limits placed on their clinical autonomy than physicians at Sovereign IPA or Doctors' Clinic.

Hypothesis 2b: Primary care physicians will be more satisfied with limits placed on their clinical autonomy than specialists.

Again, as those most experienced with and/or favored by managed care, Community Clinic physicians and primary care physicians should report less dissatisfaction with administrative limits.

Hypothesis 3a: Sovereign IPA physicians will be most likely to believe that physicians work best as solo practitioners.

Hypothesis 3b: Physicians at Community Clinic will be least likely to believe that physicians work best as solo practitioners.

Hypothesis 3c: Specialists will be more likely than primary care physicians to believe that physicians work best as solo practitioners.

Specialists and the doctors at Sovereign IPA, with longer socialization as experts, are more likely to subscribe to the idea that solo practice is better form of medical practice. Also, as the most recent to subscribe to managed care reimbursement and care arrangements, they seem the most likely to favor solo practice. On the other hand, Community Clinic physicians should report the lowest levels of agreement that physicians should work best as solo practitioners, given their more extensive experience with managed care. Hypotheses 4 through 7 make similar arguments:

Hypothesis 4a: Physicians at the Community Clinic are least likely to believe that large managed care organizations compromise physicians' integrity.

Hypothesis 4b: Specialists are more likely than primary care physicians to believe that large managed care organizations compromise physicians' integrity.

Hypothesis 5a: Physicians in the Community Clinic are more likely than Sovereign IPA and Doctors' Clinic providers to believe their earnings are appropriate.

Hypothesis 5b: Primary care physicians are more likely than specialists to believe their earnings are appropriate.

Hypothesis 6a: Physicians in the Community Clinic are more likely to report that they have the authority to make clinical decisions.

Hypothesis 6b: Primary care physicians are more likely than specialists to report that they have the authority to make clinical decisions.

Hypothesis 7a: Physicians in the Community Clinic will report the highest level of satisfaction with practicing medicine.

Hypothesis 7b: Primary care physicians will report higher levels of satisfaction with practicing medicine than specialists.

These hypotheses summarize the specialist and organizational arguments we made above. Because of the lower level of scientific socialization experienced by generalists and because of greater experience with managed care at the Community Clinic, attitudes toward integrity, earnings, authority, and overall satisfaction with managed care should be greater there than in the other practice arrangements.

Survey Data

As part of a larger study (Lammers & Duggan, 2002), a 43-item questionnaire was mailed to all physicians ($N = 644$) practicing medicine in Southcoast City. The questionnaire was mailed to a saturation sample of doctors obtained from the rosters of the medical groups in the city and the membership list of the county medical society. Of the sample total, 14.1% were female, and 85.9% were male. The final response rate totaled 63.1% ($n = 406$). For more information on the survey, please see Lammers and Duggan (2002). For the current study, physicians affiliated with Community Clinic, Doctor's Clinic, or Sovereign IPA were identified. This limited our sample to 145 physicians, including 68 physicians (47%) practicing in the Community Clinic, 54 physicians (37%) practicing in the Doctors' Clinic, and 23 physicians (16%) practicing with the Sovereign IPA. The remaining 261 nonaligned physicians are considered in the second step of our analysis (see below).

Measures of Independent and Dependent Variables

There are two independent variables in this study: organizational context (Sovereign IPA, Community Clinic, and Doctors' Clinic) and practice type (primary care and specialist physicians). These were identified using the medical society's membership list. There are five dependent variables each measured using by Likert-type items. Responses to four single-item attitude statements form our first four dependent variables, rated on a five-point Likert scale on which 1 = strongly disagree and 5 = strongly agree (see Table 4.1). Three items were combined to create the fifth dependent variable, satisfaction.[1] Cronbach's α reliability for the satisfaction scale was .66.

As a manipulation check we included measures of the extent to which physicians were involved in fee-for-service and managed care arrangements. Involvement in fee-for-service arrangements was measured by asking physicians to report the percentage of their total patients that pay fee-for-service. Length of time working with managed care was measured by asking the year in which the physician first signed a managed care contract.

Analysis

One-way analyses-of-variance (ANOVAs) were conducted to assess the level of statistical difference between physicians associated with particular medical groups. Comparisons were run to test hypotheses for which the omnibus test was significant. Results for each ANOVA are reported in Table 4.1. Table 4.2 reports the means and confidence intervals for organizational context (Sovereign IPA, Community Clinic, and Doctors' Clinic), and significance tests are reported were appropriate for hypothesis testing. We ran t-tests to measure the differences between primary care and specialist physicians. The results of these tests are reported in Table 4.3.

Results

Comparing physicians in the three organizations, those hypotheses associated with the organizational context (Sovereign IPA, Community Clinic and Doctor's Clinic) were supported, and those hypotheses that tested the differences between primary care physicians and specialist physicians were not. The following section will review the results of the hypothesis testing by looking first at the differences between organizational contexts and then the differences between primary care and specialist physicians. Additional post hoc analyses of the difference between primary care and specialist physicians are reported to understand the lack of significant findings on this variable.

First, the hypotheses that tested differences between the physician groups were supported (see Table 4.1). The omnibus ANOVAs revealed significant overall differences between the groups (see Table 4.2). We followed the sig-

Table 4.1 Mean Comparisons for Practice Setting: Community Clinic, Doctors Clinic, and the Sovereign IPA

Source/Item	Sovereign IPA			Community Clinic			Doctor's Clinic		
	N	Mean	95% CI	N	Mean	95% CI	N	Mean	95% CI
What percentage of your patients use the fee-for-service method of payment?	67	39.51	32.43–46.58	54	20.74	15.21–26.26	21	27.43	17.98–36.87
How long have you been working with managed care contracts?	64	10.61	9.69–11.53	53	13.79	12.28–15.30	20	8.05	6.66–9.44
I am satisfied with the limitations on my clinical autonomy.	67	2.30	2.02–2.57	54	2.90	2.53–3.29	22	2.18	1.69–2.67
Physicians can do better work as solo practitioners.	67	3.10	2.85–3.36	54	1.98	1.70–2.26	23	2.30	1.72–2.90
Practicing in a large managed care organization compromises physician's integrity.	67	3.72	3.44–3.99	54	2.54	2.15–2.93	23	3.35	2.77–3.92
My earnings (relative to other occupations) are an appropriate amount.	67	2.19	1.90–2.49	54	2.70	2.34–3.07	23	1.78	1.41–2.15
I have the authority to make clinical decisions.	67	3.76	3.47–4.05	54	4.18	3.93–4.44	23	3.48	2.96–3.99
I am satisfied with practicing medicine.	68	3.14	2.88–3.40	54	3.59	3.30–3.90	23	2.90	2.48–3.32

Table 4.2 Analysis of Variance for Practice Setting: Community Clinic, Doctors Clinic, and the Sovereign IPA

Source/Item	N	df	F	η	p
What percentage of your patients uses the fee-for-service method of payment?	142[a]	2, 139	8.731	.334	.000
How long have you been working with managed care contracts?	137[a]	2, 134	14.70	.424	.000
I am satisfied with the limitations on my clinical autonomy.	143[a]	2, 140	4.591	.248	.012
Physicians can do better work as solo practitioners.	144[a]	2, 141	16.343	.434	.000
Practicing in a large managed care organization compromises physician's integrity.	144[a]	2, 141	12.770	.392	.000
My earnings (relative to other occupations) are an appropriate amount.	144[a]	2, 141	5.315	.265	.006
I have the authority to make clinical decisions.	144[a]	2, 141	4.014	.232	.020
I am satisfied with practicing medicine.	145	2, 142	4.366	.241	.014

Note. [a]The reduced n is due to missing data.

nificant omnibus test with multiple comparisons to investigate the specific differences between the groups. Hypotheses 1a and 1b, checks of our understanding of the case, were supported. Sovereign IPA physicians (Hypothesis 1a) reported a larger percentage of fee-for-service patients ($\bar{X}$ = 39.51%) than Community Clinic physicians ($\bar{X}$ = 20.74%) or Doctors' Clinic physicians ($\bar{X}$ = 27.43%); although, there was so statistical difference between Doctors' Clinic and either of the other settings. Community Clinic physicians reported the longest experience with managed care ($\bar{X}$ = 13.79 years) (Hypothesis 1b) followed by Sovereign IPA ($\bar{X}$ = 10.61 years) and Doctors' Clinic ($\bar{X}$ = 8.05 years), although Sovereign IPA and Doctors' Clinic were not statistically different.

Hypotheses 2 through 7 were tested using t-test comparisons of the focal practice group to the other two groups combined. Hypothesis 2a (physicians at Community Clinic will be most satisfied with limits placed on their clinical autonomy) was supported [t (140) = 2.959; SE = .225; p = .004]. Hypothesis 3a (Sovereign IPA physicians will be most likely to believe that physicians work best as solo-practitioners) was supported [t (141) = 5.019; SE = .192; p < .000]. Hypothesis 3b (physicians at Community Clinic will be least likely to believe that physicians work best as solo-practitioners) was supported [t (141) = –3.616; SE = .200; p < .001]. Hypothesis 4a (physicians at Community Clinic will be least likely to believe that large managed care organizations compromise

Table 4.3 Mean Comparisons for Practice Type for only those Physicians Affiliated with the Sovereign IPA, Community Clinic, and Doctor's Clinic: Primary Care Physicians and Specialist Physicians

Item	Primary Care Physicians			Specialist Physicians		
	N	Mean	95% CI	N	Mean	95% CI
What percentage of your patients uses the fee-for-service method of payment?	71	27.31	21.73–32.89	71	33.86	27.15–40.56
How long have you been working with managed care contracts?	69	12.03	10.93–13.12	68	10.90	9.68–12.11
I am satisfied with the limitations on my clinical autonomy.	72	2.50	2.24–2.76	71	2.52	2.19–2.85
Physicians can do better work as solo practitioners.	72	2.57	2.27–2.87	72	2.54	2.27–2.81
Practicing in a large managed care organization compromises physician's integrity.	72	3.03	2.71–3.35	72	3.40	3.07–3.72
My earnings (relative to other occupations) are an appropriate amount.	72	2.50	2.20–2.80	72	2.14	1.86–2.42
I have the authority to make clinical decisions.	72	3.93	3.70–4.16	72	3.82	3.52–4.11
I am satisfied with practicing medicine.	73	3.42	3.18–3.65	72	3.12	2.85–3.40

physicians' integrity) was supported [t (141) = −4.260; SE = .234; p < .000]. Hypothesis 5a (physicians at Community Clinic are more likely to believe their earnings are appropriate) was supported [t (141) = 3.239; SE = .221; p = .001]. Hypothesis 6a (physicians at the Community Clinic are more likely to report they have the authority to make clinical decisions) was supported [t (141) = 2.829; SE = .200; p = .005]. Finally, Hypothesis 7a (physicians at the Community Clinic will report the highest levels of satisfaction) was also supported [t (142) = 2.954; SE = .195; p = .004].

Although the hypotheses associated with organizational context were all supported, the differences between primary care and specialist physicians were not significant (see Table 4.3). The effect sizes that were found, however, were small (between r = .10 and .20) across the dependent variables. Given the number of subjects and our probability level, we would not have enough power to be able to detect small effect sizes. In fact, for a two-tailed test, alpha = .05, with 140 subjects' power would have ranged from .22 (for r =.10) to .66 (for r = .20) (Cohen, 1988). Because it would stand to reason that differences between primary care and specialist physicians could hold true regardless of organizational context, we retested these hypotheses using the entire sample of Southcoast City physicians.

An additional analysis of all of the subjects available (including subjects not affiliated with either clinic or the IPA) yielded the expected direction in each of the comparisons. The tests of the relationship of practice type and the length of time since entering into one's first managed care contract, the percentage of patients paying fee-for-service, and attitudes toward limitations on clinical autonomy, solo-practice, earnings, and authority to make clinical decisions did not yield significant results. However, specialist physicians ($\bar{X}$ = 3.85, n = 210, SD = 1.21) were more likely than primary care physicians ($\bar{X}$ = 3.39, n = 142, SD = 1.32) to report that they believe that large managed care organizations compromise physicians' integrity [t (350) = −3.362; SE = .136; p = .001]. Additionally, primary care physicians ($\bar{X}$ = 3.43, n = 143, SD = .99) reported higher levels of satisfaction than specialist physicians ($\bar{X}$ = 3.08, n = 213, SD = 1.14) [t (354) = 2.313; SE = .067; p = .021].

Discussion

This chapter has presented an empirical test of the differences between professional and organizational circumstances that contextualize the relationship between health care providers and their patients, and among health care providers in managed care arrangements. We have argued that past research, with its rigorous focus on the patient-provider dyad, has assumed homogenous professional identities and undifferentiated organizational arrangements' when differences in those identities and arrangements might actually make a difference in health outcomes. Our data suggest that different practice arrangements, and to some extent professional identities (Lammers & Garcia, in press), are predictive of attitudes toward medical practice and managed care.

There are, of course, limitations to this study. First, we have only considered practitioners in a single community, which is likely to be more affluent than the average American community and to have a higher penetration of managed care, possibly making our data less generalizable to a national population. Also, the differences between the Doctors' Clinic, the Community Clinic, and the Sovereign IPA may be exaggerated given their organizational histories. Perhaps more importantly, our data are only about physicians' reaction to managed care given their organizational arrangements. We have not presented data on patients or on physicians controlling for patient differences. Another important limitation of this study is that we have not controlled for the kinds of contract or practice arrangements under which the physicians at Doctors', Community, or the Sovereign IPA practice. We would expect that more accurate and discriminating definitions of these differences would yield more insight into the influence of managed care on practice satisfaction and attitudes, and thus on patient outcomes.

Our study could also be criticized for a lack of statistical independence between subjects (physicians). Because we studied groups of physicians, it could be argued that our subjects influenced each other. While acknowledging this argument, we would respond that medical practice on the one hand has always been one in which professional autonomy and independence has been highly valued. Moreover, we contacted our subjects independently and did not ask them about their views of each other. But the general problem of the lack of independence among subjects is also part of our research problem: To what extent do organizational and institutional forces beyond their direct control influence our subjects? We feel that these data shed some light on that topic.

The data in this study do, however, give credence to our arguments that practice arrangements and physician differences make a difference in physician attitudes toward their practices. We believe these "peri-consultative" (Real & Street, this volume) communications warrant further investigation by health services researchers. Although the motives of practitioners should not be questioned on moral grounds, their degree of specialization and the financial incentives under which they practice do vary and could be sources of variation in health outcomes. Moreover, managed care is still spreading in North America as excess hospital beds, physicians, and technology are exploited by management firms in search of operational efficiencies and profits (Kuttner, 1999). Thus, the experience of the community we studied may be predictive of the experience of other communities.

This study supports application of an institutional approach, as well. Specifically, our findings of differences among physicians who practice in different organizations, and those organizations' differences in managed care experience, provide a glimpse of observable links between individuals, organizations, and institutions. An advantage of an institutional approach is to demonstrate the ties between action and structure—at the individual, organizational and institutional levels. Physicians' own preferences and qualifications might influence self-selection into different kinds of practices; at the same time, however, different types of practices shape experience, attitudes, and perception. And all is occurring within the broader institutions (medical school training tension between science and humanism, changes in health care economics) that constrain and enable both individuals and organizations. We hope that this study takes research a step in that direction, but considerable specification remains. In particular, a complete picture of the institutions of medical care today would link professional identity and attitudes, as well as organizational and institutional variables (see Barbour & Lammers, 2007, for an example).

Health services researchers are known to claim that the health system in the United States was never consciously designed, but rather it evolved (Williams & Torrens, 1998). Our failure to understand its evolution has resulted in the world's most expensive system that fails to serve the U.S. population adequately. Applying institutional theory may provide keys to the design of a more satisfying system.

From a strictly organizational point of view, we agree with Real and Street (this volume) that the tacit boundary previous researchers have drawn around the patient-provider relationship seems outdated. Researchers could more carefully specify the circumstances under which medical (and other health-related) care episodes take place. Students of organizations have for a number of years been attempting to identify the salient and relevant contextual features of behavior within organizations (cf. Putnam & Stohl, 1996; Frey, 1994, 1995). Intensively managed medical care, as it spreads unevenly throughout the country (Eisenberg et al., 1999), offers researchers an opportunity to study the role of formal communication (that is written and contractual) in health care. Indeed, contracts in managed care are only one example of formalized communication in health care. As researchers, we should also apply ourselves to questions regarding practice guidelines, physician unionization, and binding arbitration clauses, as well. Each of these offers us an opportunity to more carefully specify just what we mean by health services, and to learn more about the intersection of the informal and intimate communication between patient and provider, and the formal, increasingly legal communication that constrains it.

Note

1. Items included were: "If I had to decide today, I would be likely to choose to become a physician again." "All in all, how satisfied are you with the contracted managed care organizations?" "All in all, how satisfied are you with your present position?" Interpretation of this scale follows a similar five-point scale (1 = very dissatisfied; 5 = very satisfied).

References

American Academy of Family Physicians. (2001). *Primary care.* Retrieved October 26, 2002, from http://www.aafp.org/x6988.xml

Barbour, J. B., & Lammers, J. C. (2007). Health care institutions, medical organizing, and physicians: A multilevel analysis. *Management Communication Quarterly, 21,* 201–231.

Barley, S. (2008). Coalface institutionalism. In R. Greenwood, C. Oliver, K. Sahlin, & R. Suddaby (Eds.), *The Sage handbook of organizational institutionalism* (pp. 491–518). London: Sage.

Baur, C. (2000). Limiting factors on the transformative powers of e-mail in patient–physician relationships: A critical analysis. *Health Communication, 12,* 239–260.

Becker, H., Geer, B., Hughes, E., & Strauss, A. (1961). *Boys in white: Student culture in medical school*. Chicago: University of Chicago Press.

Bloche, G. (1999). Clinical loyalties and the social purposes of medicine. *JAMA, 281*, 268–274.

Bloom, S. W. (1989). The medical school as a social organization: The sources of resistance to change. *Medical Education, 23*, 228–241.

Bodenheimer, T., & Grumbach, K. (2002). *Understanding health policy*. New York: Lange Medical Books.

Bureau of Labor Statistics. (2000). *Occupational outlook handbook*. Retrieved October 26, 2002, from http://stats.bls.gov/oco/ocos074.htm#earnings

Cohen, J. (1988). *Statistical power analysis for the behavioral sciences* (2nd ed.). Mahwah, NJ: Erlbaum.

Conrad, P. (1988). Learning to doctor: Reflections on recent accounts of the medical school years. *Journal of Health and Social Behavior, 29*, 323–332.

Donabedian, A. (1986). *Medical care chartbook* (8th ed.). Ann Arbor, MI: Health Administration Press.

Eisenberg, J. M., LeTourneau, B., McGinn, T. G., Nishikawa, J., Reinhardt, U., & Wilson, M. C. (1999). Health care trends, Part I: The promise and perils of evidence-based medicine. *Physician Executive, 25*(3), 43–52.

Ellis, R. P. (2001). Formal risk adjustment by private employers. *Inquiry, 38*, 299–309.

Euske, N. A., & Roberts, K. H. (1987). Evolving perspectives in organizational theory: Communication implications. In F. M. Jablin, L. L. Putnam, K. H. Roberts, & L. W. Porter (Eds.), *Handbook of organizational communication: An interdisciplinary perspective* (pp. 41–69). Thousand Oaks, CA: Sage.

Feldman, D. S., Novack, D. H., & Gracely, E. (1998). Effects of managed care on physician-patient relationships, quality of care, and the ethical practice of medicine. *Archives of Internal Medicine, 158*, 1626–1632.

Freidson, E. (1986). *Professional powers: A study of institutionalization of formal knowledge*. Chicago: The University of Chicago Press.

Frey, L. R. (Ed.). (1994). *Group communication in context: Studies of natural groups*. Mahwah, NJ: Erlbaum.

Frey, L. R. (Ed.). (1995). *Innovations in group facilitation: Applications in natural settings*. Cresskill, NJ: Hampton.

Friedman, L. H., & Savage, G. T. (1998). Can ethical management and managed care coexist? *Health Care Management Review, 23*(2), 56–62.

Geist, P., & Hardesty, M. (1992). *Negotiating the crisis: DRGs and the transformation of hospitals*. Mahwah, NJ: Erlbaum.

Gonsoulin, T. P. (1997). Ethical issues raised by managed care. *The Laryngoscope, 107*, 1425–1428.

Gross, H., & Budrys, G. (1986). Control over work in a pre-paid group practice. In J. Levy & H. Lopata (Eds.), *Current research in occupations and professions, Volume VI* (pp. 147–183). Greenwich, CT: JAI.

Hacker, J. S., & Marmor, T. R. (1999). The misleading language of managed care. *Journal of Health Politics, Policy & Law, 24*, 1033–1043.

Harris-Shapiro, J. (1998). RBRVS (Medicare Resource-Based Relative Value Scale) revisited. *Journal of Health Care Finance, 25*(2), 49–54.

Harvard School of Public Health. (2000). Doctors in five countries see decline in quality of care: New international survey reveals physician concerns with medical errors, a shortage of nurses, and inadequate facilities. Retrieved October 26, 2002, from http://www.hsph.harvard.edu/press/releases/press10122000.html

Jefferys, M., & Elston, M. (1989). The medical school as a social organization. *Medical Education, 23*, 242–251.

Kralewski, J. E., Rich, E. C., Bernhardt, T., Dowd, B., Feldman, R., & Johnson, C. (1998). The organizational structure of medical group practices in a managed care environment. *Health Care Management Review, 23*(2), 76–96.

Kuttner, R. (1999). The American health care system: Wall Street and health care. *The New England Journal of Medicine, 340*, 664–668.

Laine, C., & Davidoff, F. (1996). Patient-centered medicine: A professional evolution. *Journal of the American Medical Association, 275*, 152–155.

Lammers, J., & Garcia, M. (in press). Exploring the concept of "profession" for organizational communication research: Institutional influences in a veterinary organization. *Management Communication Quarterly.*

Lammers, J. C., & Barbour, J. B. (2006). An institutional theory of organizational communication. *Communication Theory, 16*, 356–377.

Lammers, J. C., Barbour, J., & Duggan, A. (2003). Organizational forms of the provision of health care: An institutional perspective. In T. Thompson, A. Dorsey, K. Miller, & R. Parrott (Eds.), *Handbook of health communication* (pp. 319–345). Mahwah, NJ: Erlbaum.

Lammers, J. C., & Duggan, A. P. (2002). Bringing the physician back in: Physician satisfaction with managed care arrangements. *Health Communication, 14*, 493–514.

Lammers, J. C., & Geist, P. (1997). The transformation of caring in the light and shadow of managed care. *Health Communication, 9*, 45–60.

Landon, B. E., Zaslavsky, A. M., Bernard, S. L., Cioffi, M. J., & Cleary, P. D. (2004). Comparison of performance of traditional Medicare vs Medicare managed care. *JAMA, 291*, 1744–1752.

Lehoux, P., Sicotte, C., Denis, J. L., Berg, M., & Lacroix, A. (2002). The theory of use behind telemedicine: How compatible with physicians' clinical routines? *Social Science & Medicine, 54*, 889–904.

Longino, C. F. (1997). Pressure from our aging population will broaden our understanding of medicine. *Academic Medicine, 72*, 841–847.

Managed Care Online (MCOL). (2001). Managed care fact sheets. Retrieved October 26, 2002, from http://www.mcareol.com/factshts/mcolfact.htm

McPhee, R. (1985). Formal structure in organizational communication. In R. McPhee & P. K. Tompkins (Eds.), *Organizational communication: Traditional themes and new directions* (pp. 149–178). Thousand Oaks, CA: Sage.

Mechanic, D. (2000). Managed care and the imperative for a new professional ethic. *Health Affairs, 19*, 100–111.

Miller, K. (1993). Learning to care for others and self: The experience of medical education. In E. B. Ray (Ed.), *Case studies in health communication* (pp. 3–14). Mahwah, NJ: Erlbaum.

Minogue, B. (2000). The two fundamental duties of the physician. *Academic Medicine, 75*, 431–442.

National Library of Medicine. (2008). *Managed care.* National Library of Medicine Medical Subject Headings. Retrieved August 14, 2008, from http://www.nlm.nih.gov/cgi/mesh/2008/MB_cgi

Potter, L. (1999). The managed care contract: Survival or closure? A lexicon of the financial environment. *Nursing Administration Quarterly, 23*(4), 58–62.

Putnam, L. L., & Stohl, C. (1996). Bona fide groups: An alternative perspective for communication and small group decision making. In R. Y. Hirokawa & M. S. Poole, (Eds.), *Communication and group decision making* (2nd ed., pp. 147–178). Thousand Oaks, CA: Sage.

Ray, E. B., & Donohew, L. (Eds.). (1990). *Communication and health: Systems and applications.* Mahwah, NJ: Erlbaum.

Ritzer, G. (2004). *The McDonaldization of society* (rev. ed.). Thousand Oaks, CA: Pine Forge Press.

Robinson, J. C. (2001). Theory and practice in the design of physician payment incentives. *Milibank Quarterly, 79,* 149–177.

Robinson, J. C. (1999). Blended payment methods in physician organizations under managed care. *JAMA, 282,* 1258–1263.

Rodwin, M. A. (1998). Conflicts of interest and accountability in managed care: The aging of medical ethics. *Journal of the American Geriatric Society, 46,* 338–341.

Rosenthal, M. B., Landon, B. E., Normand, S. T., Frank, R. G., & Epstein A. M. (2006). Pay for performance in commercial HMOs. *New England Journal of Medicine, 355,* 1895–1902.

Scott, W. R. (2003). *Organizations: Rational, natural, and open systems* (5th ed.). Englewood Cliffs, NJ: Prentice-Hall.

Scott, W. R., & Lammers, J. C. (1985). Trends in occupations and organizations in the medical care and mental health sectors. *Medical Care Review, 42,* 37–76.

Scott, W. R., Meyer, J. W., & Associates. (1994). *Institutional environments and organizations: Structural complexity and individualism.* Thousand Oaks, CA: Sage.

Sharf, B. (1993). Reading the vital signs: Research in health care communication. *Communication Monographs, 60,* 35–41.

Simmonds, A. C., Robbins, J. M., Brinker, M. R., Rice, J. C., & Kerstein, M. D. (1990). Factors important to students in selecting a residency program. *Academic Medicine, 65,* 640–643.

Smetana, G. W., Landon, B. E., Bindman, A. B., Burstin, H., Davis, R. B., Tjia, J., & Rich, C. E. (2007). A comparison of outcomes resulting from generalist vs. specialist care for a single discrete medical condition: A systematic review and methodologic critique. *Archives of Internal Medicine, 167,* 10–20.

Starr, P. (1982). *The social transformation of American medicine.* New York: Basic Books.

Stille, C. J., Primack W. A., & Savageau, J. A. (2003). Generalist-subspecialist communication for children with chronic conditions: A regional physician survey. *Pediatrics, 112,* 1314–1320.

Strunk, B., Ginsburg, P., & Gabel, J. (2002). Tracking health care costs: Hospital spending spurs double-digit increase in 2001. Data Bulletin No. 22. Retrieved October 26, 2002, from http://www.hschange.com/CONTENT/472/

Suchman, A., Roter, D., Green, M., & Lipkin, M. (1993). Physician satisfaction with primary care office visits. *Medical Care, 31,* 1083–1092.

Sullivan, W. M. (1999). What is left of professionalism after managed care? *Hastings Center Report, 29*(2), 7–23.

Thomas, L. (1983). *The youngest science: Notes of a medicine-watcher.* New York: The Viking Press.

Van de Ven, A., Engleman, R., & Rogers, R. (2001). *Integrating physician clinics into a large medical practice.* Paper presented at the 2001 Minnesota Health Services Research Conference.

Vanselow, N. A. (1998). Primary care and the specialist. *JAMA, 279*, 1394–1395.

Weber, M. (1946). *From Max Weber: Essays in sociology* (H. H. Gerth, & C. Wright Mills, Trans. and Eds.). New York: Oxford University Press.

Weber, M. (1947). *Max Weber: The theory of social and economic organization* (H. H. Gerth & C. Wright Mills, Trans. and Eds.). New York: Free Press.

Williams, S., & Torrens, P. (Eds.). (1998). *Introduction to health services*. Albany, NY: Delmar.

Wissow, L., Roter, D., Bauman, L., Crain, E., Kercsmar, C., Weiss, K., et al. (1998). Patient-provider communication during the emergency department care of children with asthma. *Medical Care, 36*, 1439–1450.

Chapter 5

Culture, Communication, and Somatization in Health Care

Howard Waitzkin

Mental health problems enter into many primary care encounters—25 to 60%, by most estimates—and about one half of all patients with mental health disorders initially present to primary care practitioners. Common problems include depression; spousal, child, and senior abuse; situational reactions to such events as job loss, homelessness, and financial stress; severe psychosocial trauma associated with violence and migration; and psychosis, especially among homeless people. National data illustrate the vast scope of these mental health problems in primary care (for illustrative studies of mental health problems presenting in primary care, see Holman, Silver, & Waitzkin, 2000; Jackson & Kroenke, 2008; Smith et al., 2005; for overall prevalence, see the National Comorbidity Study, Kessler et al., 2005).

Many initiatives have been organized to address these problems. Some of these initiatives appear to medicalize the underlying social problems by treating them as problems at the level of the individual. Few initiatives try to address the root causes of psychological distress that persist at the level of society. That is, the medical model of psychological suffering tends to frame suffering as a process experienced by the individual patient. With a reductionist vision, this model tends to exclude broader interventions that would aim to affect causes such as poverty, job insecurity, financial stressors, urban violence, migration, homelessness, and other social issues that remain beyond what we usually envision as tasks of medical or mental health care.

In this chapter, I focus on the relationships among trauma, mental health, and physical symptoms in patients who present to primary care practitioners. Some of these patients are refugees who have experienced severe trauma in their home countries; others are people born and raised in the United States. Such patients often present with "somatoform" symptoms—symptoms for which no organic pathology can be found (for a discussion of the relationship between somatoform symptoms and medically unexplained symptoms, see Smith et al., 2005). Patients with other psychological problems, such as depression and anxiety, also often present first to primary care practitioners rather than mental health practitioners; yet patients with somatoform symptoms, which can be difficult to distinguish from symptoms actually caused by organic pathology, can present major challenges. Such challenges are becoming an important part of primary care practice throughout the United States, especially as practitioners become more sensitized to the prevalence of mental health problems among their patients.

Two Case Summaries

The following case summaries of patients presenting for primary care illustrate such problems (Castillo, Waitzkin, Villasenor, & Escobar, 1995).

Case One: R. L.

R. L. is a 27-year-old male from El Salvador. He fled his native country after finding out that his name was on a death squad list for immediate execution. A white handprint with the initials E. M. (for "Escuadrones de la Muerte" or "Death Squads") also had appeared on the front door of his house. Nine months after his arrival in the United States, he learned that his wife had been assaulted and abducted by paramilitary forces. His two children witnessed their mother being raped and killed by a group of unidentified men during an attempt to extract information about R. L.'s whereabouts.

Shortly thereafter, R. L. presented to a primary care physician at a community clinic, where he was referred from the emergency room of a local hospital. During previous weeks, he had experienced multiple symptoms, including weakness (which caused him to be terminated from his temporary job), changes in sensation, abdominal pain, chest pain, insomnia, and weight loss. R. L.'s primary care physician pursued several possible organic diagnoses by ordering diagnostic studies. He also prescribed analgesics and other medications. After extensive evaluation, no physical cause was found for his somatic symptoms.

Psychiatric consultation was then sought. Somatization was diagnosed. Low-dose antidepressant medication was instituted as individual therapy continued. The psychiatrist coordinated follow-up with the primary care internist. R. L. grew more aware of emotional factors exacerbating his symptoms and developed new coping strategies. He joined a group of local Central American refugees, where he was encouraged to write and to recite poetry as a therapeutic tool. During the following months, his somatic symptoms gradually decreased.

Case Two: X. O.

X. O., a 19-year-old female from a rural area in Guatemala, migrated to the United States after witnessing the deaths of several family members and friends during military combat in her native country. Since her mother had left for the United States with her two younger children 2 years earlier, X. O. had been afflicted by intermittent anxiety and physical manifestations, such as tremors, restlessness, palpitations, diaphoresis, and hyperventilation. After she arrived in the United States, her symptoms continued and were further exacerbated when she discovered that her mother's new husband was an alcoholic who initiated domestic violence within the family, and the patient herself was battered several times. X. O.'s native language was Quiché, and even though she was orally proficient in Spanish, she was illiterate. Her limited language skills and education, as well as the fact that her working skills were nontransferable in the North American economy, created additional stress.

X. O. presented to a primary care resident physician at a community clinic with multiple somatic complaints, including chest pain, abdominal discomfort, pelvic pressure, headaches, numbness of her hands, nightmares, insomnia, and agitation. Her anxiety level had escalated to weekly panic attacks associated with agoraphobia. A thorough medical history, physical, and laboratory evaluation excluded organic causes. In addition, the resident obtained a psychosocial history that revealed her extremely stressful premigration experiences. Posttraumatic stress disorder (PTSD) and somatization were diagnosed as coexisting problems. Psychiatric treatment was obtained; the psychiatrist concluded that her somatoform symptoms were more severe than those typically seen among nonrefugees who experience domestic violence in the United States. The primary care physician and the patient's family cooperated in therapy and as a support system. Initially, she was seen two times a week in individual and family therapy. A tricyclic antidepressant was used on a short-term basis. Her emotional and physical symptoms declined, although terms such as stress, anxiety, and mental health did not seem to exist in her native linguistic repertoire.

These patients (R. L. and X. O.) and others like them have raised substantial questions. First, how frequently does somatization rooted in trauma occur among people who seek primary care? Second, what are the implications of these issues for primary care practice?

Cross-Cultural Issues in Primary Care Practice

Immigrants and refugees, as well as patients from ethnic and racial minorities, present a challenging spectrum of physical and psychological symptoms that is best understood in the context of cultural differences. A cross-cultural approach provides a framework for understanding somatoform symptoms in the primary care context.

First, *language barriers and cultural differences in communication patterns* create obstacles in patient-practitioner interaction that lead to a misunderstanding of somatoform symptoms (see Willging, Waitzkin, & Nicdao, 2008). Regarding verbal communication, interpreting spoken language poses a challenge in primary care encounters. Lay interpreters who accompany monolingual patients often are family members or friends who lack training in procedures of accurate interpretation. In addition to limited knowledge of medical terminology, lay interpreters may experience cultural inhibition or embarrassment at explaining patients' symptoms or conveying practitioners' requests for information. Because of these difficulties, the participation of trained, professional interpreters is highly desirable but frequently is not feasible to obtain in primary care settings (see Flores, 2005 for a review, also Hsieh, 2006, this volume; Sarver & Baker, 2000).

Cultural differences in medical roles and responsibilities create a second broad barrier to the recognition of somatoform symptoms in primary care encounters. For instance, a "lay referral system" for alternative forms of healing usually constitutes an important part of a culture's approach to illness. Thus, medical practitioners treating Southeast Asian or Latino immigrants may remain unaware of or insensitive to somatizing patients' use of herbal remedies, traditional healers, special foods, or other forms of alternative healing (Eisenberg et al., 1993; Eisenberg et al., 1998; Hoang & Erickson, 1982; Mull & Mull, 1983; Nguyen, 1985). A lay referral system, imported from the country of origin, may continue to provide alternative therapies in the United States alongside the techniques of scientifically oriented medicine. Even if practitioners become aware of these parallel healing practices, integration of alternative medical roles and responsibilities into the primary care setting may prove quite challenging.

A third cultural barrier in primary care involves *explanatory models of disease*. Medical anthropologists have described cross-cultural differences in explanatory models for physical symptoms and signs (Kleinman, 1988; Kleinman & Becker, 1998; also see the Latin American model of social medicine, Waitzkin et al., 2008). Attempts by professionals practicing modern medicine to explain patients' physical problems may lead to explanations that have little meaning in the context of a patient's culture. In particular, the divergence of scientific and "ethnomedical" or cultural explanatory models (Kirmayer & Sartorius, 2007) often creates tension as practitioners fail to take into account patients' understanding of illness as rooted in spiritual forces, supernatural processes, or other culturally shaped events. Cultures also differ markedly in the acceptability of psychological disturbance as an explanation for the experience of distress. As discussed further below, such cultural differences may help account for somatoform symptoms as a response to extreme stress.

Fourth, *contextual factors* that are culturally patterned may create further barriers to professional-client interaction. These contextual factors comprise social conditions in the family, the workplace, and other institutions, including the religious, educational, and legal systems that shape patients' and doctors' behavior in the medical encounter (Waitzkin, 1991). Patients and physicians at times may discuss such contextual conditions explicitly, but most often they appear as marginal features of communication, manifested indirectly if at all. When doctors do not recognize contextual factors, substantial tension and miscommunication can occur. The pertinent social context may include dietary customs, socialization of children, sexual activities, exercise, work habits, rituals, and other cultural traditions that impact on health and illness. Contextual factors, such as culturally prescribed responses to the experience of physical threats to survival during war or civil unrest, may determine the patterning of somatoform symptoms that patients present to primary care practitioners. As an example, for a refugee experiencing the extreme stress of war, inability to protect or to grieve for loved ones who die can create a difficult gap between reality and cultural expectations. When practitioners are unaware of such contextual issues, misunderstandings of patients' somatoform symptoms may result.

A fifth barrier to interaction involves cultural differences in the *emotional impact and stigma of illness*. Whereas many cultures attach stigma to certain diseases, such as cancer or tuberculosis, in other instances emotional disturbance becomes particularly stigmatized. For example, partly because of stigma, Southeast Asian and Latino cultures tend to interpret psychological or psychophysiological symptoms as manifestations of physical disorder and therefore present with somatoform symptoms. Likewise, in some Latino subcultures, emotional disturbances are viewed as both precursors to and consequences of physical disease (Escobar, 1987; Escobar, Waitzkin, Silver, Gara, & Holman, 1998). Such cultural interpretations of a close relationship between psychic and somatic experiences may prove difficult to comprehend for practitioners grounded in Anglo American cultural patterns.

Thus, a series of barriers can affect primary care encounters that involve participants from different cultural backgrounds. This model of cultural barriers places into a more general context the specific problem of somatization among patients who experience severe stress, for example, immigrants and refugees.

Immigrants, Refugees, and Trauma

How do immigrants differ from refugees? Generally, the following operational definitions prove helpful. *Immigrants* are individuals who have migrated from their home country because of perceived economic advantages, professional advancement, desire to join other family members, or other reasons that do not involve extreme threats to safety or survival. *Refugees* are individuals who have migrated from their home country because of severely stressful circumstances, including but not limited to war, torture, forced relocation, or similar changes that constitute extreme threats to safety or survival.[1]

Traumatic experiences in countries of origin may predispose refugees to heightened help-seeking behavior and somatization. Central Americans coming to the United States may face substantial psychosocial trauma. Many of them previously have experienced warfare, political persecution, economic hardship, incarceration, or injury, and they have been at risk of experiencing adjustment difficulties following their arrival in the United States (Cervantes, Salgado de Snyder, & Padilla, 1989). For refugees from Southeast Asia and the former Soviet Union with limited prior exposure to Western culture, immersion into new social, political, and economic structures may exacerbate their pre-migration trauma (Fazel, Wheeler, & Danesh, 2005; Hsu, 1999; O'Hare & Van Tran, 1998), which includes PTSD, depression, and other psychiatric disorders. This experience may result in psychosocial distress manifested through somatization, which is an important clinical feature in many Southeast Asian refugees' presentation to primary care practitioners (Lin, Carter, & Kleinman, 1985; Mollica, 2000; Moore & Boehnlein, 1991).

Experiences in the country of origin may precede stressful experiences in the country of refuge, such as attempts to find political asylum, refugee camps, new family relations, different language, lack of relevant work skills, and elimination of social support systems. Such experiences may result in emotional disturbances and also somatoform symptoms that prove to have no organic basis. Anxiety, depression, delayed grief, and PTSD may emerge as specific emotional reactions to refugee trauma. The development of both emotional and somatoform responses to traumatic experiences may be delayed until a refugee reaches the country of resettlement.

Somatization occurs across cultural boundaries and clearly is not a clinical feature exhibited only by the immigrant and refugee population (e.g., Duran et al., 2004; Escalona, Achilles, Waitzkin, & Yager, 2004). Cross-cultural research in the primary care setting remains limited; however recent efforts have included culture as a consideration in somatization (e.g., Bhugra & Mastrogianni, 2004; Kirmayer, Groleau, Looper, & Dao, 2004; Kirmayer & Young, 1998; Kung & Pei-Chun, 2008).

Somatoform Symptoms, Culture, and Primary Care Utilization

The diagnosis of the somatoform disorders is not straightforward, in either psychiatric or primary care settings. Because of such ambiguities, the primary care practitioner faces considerable difficulty in reaching an appropriate diagnosis. The *Diagnostic and Statistical Manual of Mental Disorders* (*DSM-IV*; American Psychiatric Association, 1994), the official diagnostic reference of the American Psychiatric Association, contains rather severe limitations. The *DSM* has defined six types of somatoform disorders that presume no other primary psychiatric disorder but may manifest clinical features that overlap with anxiety and depression; several changes in definitions occurred between *DSM-IV* and the prior edition, *DSM-III-R*. The *DSM* indicates that somatization is a long-standing pattern of illness behavior—a way of life dominated by medical experiences and possibly disturbed personal relationships.

There is little indication in the *DSM* of the possibility that physical symptoms may be at least partly sociosomatic in nature—that is, manifestations of socioeconomic, environmental, or political stress, particularly in relation to war. In addition, PTSD is regarded as a disorder resulting from exposure to a traumatic event that is *outside* the range of normal experience. Such events include combat, torture, natural disasters such as floods or earthquakes, and accidental disasters such as airplane crashes. Contrary to these clinical assumptions, in countries such as El Salvador, Guatemala, Nicaragua, and several Southeast Asian nations, war became a practice *within* the range of normal daily experience, including both combat and torture. Across countries and cultures, PTSD can be associated a variety of traumatic experiences, including accidents, fires or floods, rape, molestation, attacks, and can lead to somatization (Escalona et al., 2004).

Partly because patients with somatization use medical services more frequently than nonsomatizers, management of somatization can prove difficult and expensive (Barsky, Orav, & Bates, 2005). Even though access to care is not always available to minorities, it may be expected that somatization among at-risk cultural groups also would lead to greater health-care utilization and costs. Some studies have indicated that per-capita expenditures for hospital services among patients with somatization greatly exceed the average per-capita amount in the United States (Barsky et al., 2005; DeGruy, 2000).

It often is presumed that patients who somatize use services differently and in more costly ways than patients who do not. Relatively little information is available about these problems in primary care settings, however, especially those that attract patients from culturally diverse and minority backgrounds. Such patients are at a higher risk of misdiagnosis as well as inappropriate diagnostic or therapeutic interventions by physicians who are not sensitized to culturally based somatoform symptoms.

Trauma, Narrative, and Somatoform Symptoms

Perhaps more than in other clinical conditions, recognition and treatment of somatization require attention to the cross-cultural issues in primary care practice. Language and cultural differences in communication patterns lead to cross-cultural variations in the prevalence of somatoform symptoms, which make their recognition more difficult for primary care practitioners. To the extent that cultures differ in medical roles and responsibilities, patients who have experienced alternative healing practices may encounter disappointments when practitioners trained in Western medical traditions respond with technical studies and treatments for somatoform symptoms with major cultural or psychosocial components (Lee, Rodin, Devins, & Weiss, 2001). Likewise, when patients hold culturally determined explanatory models of disease, their expectations for medical intervention in somatoform conditions may conflict markedly with those of practitioners who are unaware of cultural differences in explanatory models. Contextual factors, especially traumas such as those provoked by war, civil unrest, and difficulties in migration, also affect the development of somatoform symptoms. In addition, reflecting cultural variation in the emotional impact and stigma of symptoms, several immigrant cultures encourage the interpretation of psychological symptoms as manifestations of somatic disorders.

How is extreme stress processed psychologically, and how is this process mediated by culture? Narrative is a useful conceptual focus in trying to answer this question. As a start, one might postulate that extreme stress (such as torture, rape, witnessing deaths of relatives, forced migration, and sexual abuse) is processed psychologically as a terrible narrative, a narrative of events too awful to hold in conscious memory, a narrative that cannot be told coherently in the internal story-telling of everyday consciousness, a narrative so terrifying that it must somehow be transformed. Within traditional psychoanalysis, "repression," "displacement," and "dissociation" are psychological defenses against the terrible narrative, and "hysteria" the predictable result. Yet such terms scarcely appear adequate to describe the psychic processing of overwhelming stress and the appearance of somatoform symptoms in persons who otherwise show little or no evidence of the usual "neurotic" features evoked by these terms.

Another case history illustrates the process of how incomplete narratives provide a linkage between severe trauma and somatoform symptoms. The patient here is a young woman from Native American and Latino cultural traditions. Similar psychosocial processes, however, occur among refugees from other countries and among many nonminority patients in the United States who have suffered severe trauma. The patient agreed to cooperate in a large study of mental health issues in primary care. In this study, subjects who sought primary care services participated in a structured psychiatric interview (the Composite International Diagnostic Interview, CIDI, an instrument developed by the World Health Organization to be used across cultures and languages), as well as a clinical interview conducted by a psychologist. The patient, a 34-year-old Chicana woman born in the United States of Latino and Native American descent, came to the clinic for treatment of vaginal itching and discharge and pelvic pain.

During the encounter with her physician, she makes no reference to symptoms outside the pelvis. Although the physician does not elicit further somatic symptoms during the first encounter, the CIDI, given by a research assistant, identifies five symptoms in four organ systems that remain unexplained. In the structured instrument, however, little information emerges about the details of the traumatic experiences in her life or about how these experiences might be related to her unexplained somatic complaints.

Not until the in-depth, clinical interview, given by a trained psychologist, does the patient's narrative of trauma and somatic symptoms emerge in a clear way, although even here the narrative remains fragmented and incomplete. The incoherence of the narrative combines with explicit references to cultural beliefs, including an "Indian voice" that protects her from emotional and physical harm. The following notes, prepared by the psychologist, summarize pertinent parts of the clinical interview:

In brief, this patient has experienced a long series of psychosocial traumas, which included sexual and physical abuse during childhood and two marriages. When the patient was six years old, her mother went to prison. During the mother's absence, she lived with various relatives and was physically abused in one home and sexually molested in another. She was in a serious car accident at age 16, the same year that she married and had a child. Her husband was physically abusive, and she left him, only to marry another abusive man. She left the second husband when he pulled a gun on her and threatened to kill her. At the time of the interview, she was keeping her whereabouts a secret, as his threats to kill her had continued after the separation.

This patient has suffered from multiple illnesses and somatic complaints since early childhood and has undergone 10 surgeries. Currently she complains of eight symptoms and suffers from six physical illnesses. In particular, she describes having had severe headaches since childhood. When she was young, they were so bad that they caused her to lose memory and to remain fatigued for several days. She vehemently denies, however, that there is any connection between her health problems and the stresses that she has experienced.

Since childhood, the patient has heard voices. When the voices talk to her, sometimes it feels as if she is in a trance. If too many of them are talking, they make her head hurt. She often writes down what the voices say and she has noticed that the handwriting she uses has several distinct styles. Some of the voices are able to spell perfectly, although ordinarily she is a poor speller. She describes an "Indian" voice that protects her and explains this in the context of information that her grandmother has shared with her about good spirits that "don't try to get in your body, but only talk to your mind." The Indian voice has protected her throughout her life.

Although the patient draws a link between headaches and the voices (she states that her head hurts when too many of the voices are talking to her), she does not draw a causal link between the headaches and any of the abuses that she has experienced. She describes her symptoms and experiences in a disjointed and dream-like fashion. Later during the interview, the psychologist (interviewer, I) elicits eight symptoms that remain unexplained, including severe headaches. At this point, the patient (P) describes the onset of the headaches during childhood, as well as the technical diagnostic measures that were initiated, leading to the diagnosis of migraine. Although the headaches do manifest some characteristics of classic migraine, which include vomiting, they also are associated with evidence of dissociation, such as memory loss and exhaustion, which split off the painful memories from consciousness. For this patient, the presence of voices, and especially a culturally patterned Indian voice, shapes the interrelationships among trauma, culture, and somatoform symptoms. At a conscious level, the patient does not connect the headaches, voices, and sexual abuse that she was experiencing at that time:

I: How was your health in childhood? Did you have any...

P: Yeah.

I: You were sick a lot, what kinds of problems?

P: I had hepatitis and [words unclear] in '68, I was in the hospital for a month, I had epilepsy attacks, they were giving me medication three times a day but then they stopped because [words unclear]...

I: [words unclear]...

P: I was feeling migraines or pressure, 'cause you know I was little I fell off the seesaw and I had like a little pebble, a little piece of rock or a little pebble there, you know, [words unclear] so I had those [words unclear] where they put the needles, not needles uh... CAT scan, [words unclear] all different stuff, because they thought it was a tumor.

I: Okay.

P: And I'd get real bad headaches, I mean super! And they I'd just vomit...

I: Is this when you were little?

P: Uh-huh. I'd vomit and I don't remember anything and uh... it was like an epilepsy attack.

I: So your headaches caused you to vomit and lose memory?

P: Yes, like tired for three days, now I can control it 'cause I'm older but for three days I'm like exhausted, pressure under the eyes, the cheekbones and then I have a real bad sinus.

The patient's narrative is fragmented and incomplete. She has experienced numerous stressful and traumatic events throughout her life. These events come to light during different phases of the in-depth interview with a psychologist and receive no mention at all during the encounter with her primary care physician. The traumatic events and the physical symptoms remain unconnected in the patient's and in the physician's consciousness.

Culture does, however, influence the coping mechanisms that this patient uses, in the form of the "Indian voice" that the patient feels protects her, a voice originating for the patient in Native American beliefs about good and bad spirits. Here, the processing of trauma and culture involves an incomplete or incoherent narrative of childhood experiences and traditional teachings. The culturally influenced narrative does not completely incorporate the extent of this patient's traumatic experiences. Yet, the protective voice can be thought of as a culturally influenced narrative that has helped this patient function on a daily basis, even though it may not have been capable of helping her process the trauma sufficiently to alleviate the multiple physical and psychological symptoms that she experiences. This narrative remains an unspoken link to physical symptoms that continue to trouble the patient in ways inaccessible to medical intervention, despite her many attempts to seek solutions in the medical sphere. Eliciting the narrative requires a method that permits in-depth probing, well beyond that of the standard medical or research interview.

Culture patterns the characteristic psychological and somatic processing of the terrible narrative. In some cultures, overt psychological breakdown and the stopping of participation in customary social roles may be a preferred "way of knowing" a narrative too terrible to tell. In other cultures, such psychological symptoms may be discouraged, and maintenance of customary social roles may be encouraged normatively even in the face of overwhelming stress. In the latter cultural context, the terrible narrative then may be transformed into somatic symptoms.

I would argue that the mechanism by which trauma is transformed into somatic symptoms often involves an incoherence in narrative structure, because of which the traumatic experience cannot be told as a coherent whole. This argument recognizes the substantial variability that manifests itself in the connections among trauma, culture, and somatization. Patients who have experienced trauma constitute only a subset of somatizing patients. Further, somatization often may occur as a comorbid condition along with such disorders as depression or anxiety, even though cultural norms may predispose to the appearance of somatic as opposed to psychological symptoms for most members of the culture who experience severe trauma (Castillo et al., 1995). Yet, the narrative structure and its coherence versus incoherence may provide a link among trauma, culture, and somatization in many patients whose physical symptoms cannot be explained by physical disease.

How specific symptoms present themselves also depends partly on how culture patterns their expression. For instance, in Southeast Asian cultures, which place high esteem and positive evaluation on the head, traumatic experiences associated with war and imprisonment predictably would manifest themselves as symptoms of headache, especially when the trauma has involved blows to the head (Hoang & Erickson, 1982; Mollica et al., 1992). On the other hand, in Latino cultures, in which conceptions of "nerves" and the impact of nervous conditions on physical symptoms are commonplace, complaints referable to the nervous system—such "pseudoneurologic" problems as dizziness, numbness, weakness of extremities, and so forth—predictably would appear more frequently (Alejandro et al., 2005; Escobar, Canino, Rubio-Stipec, & Bravo, 1992). Cultural patterning of somatic symptoms also has become clear in ethnic groups such as Italians, Jews, Irish Catholics, and upper-middle-class White Europeans (Shorter, 1992, 1994). In these groups, culture appears to mediate severe trauma in producing somatic complaints of characteristic forms, rather than permitting a more frank breakdown in day-to-day psychosocial functioning.

In short, the mechanisms connecting trauma, culture, and somatoform symptoms appear to include several key elements. First, a narrative of terrible trauma is processed psychologically in different ways, depending on the sociocultural context. The coherence versus incoherence of this narrative becomes a crucial feature in the transformation of traumatic events into somatoform symptoms. The sociocultural context patterns personal narrative at the psychological level, as well as the expression of narrative in social interactions, including those between patients and health care professionals. Although the experience of overt psychological disturbance and breaking with customary roles may emerge as the patterned reaction to extreme stress in some cultures, elsewhere the transformation of terrible narrative into somatic symptoms may become the culturally sanctioned "way of knowing" and of processing such stress. Predictably, cultures vary not only in determining whether narratives of extreme stress express themselves by overt psychological disturbance as opposed to somatic symptoms, but also in the patterning of somatic symptoms when they occur.

At the individual level, one also expects variability in the reaction to extreme stress. Because of biologic differences that are genetically determined, or because of varying childhood experiences that create greater or lesser vulnerability to trauma, some individuals may react to severe stress with less psychological disturbance or less somatic symptomatology. That is, within cultures, different biological characteristics or experiences may lead to individual variation in the processing of the terrible narrative. Not all individuals within a given culture, therefore, react to traumatic stress in the same way, and culture influences the pattern by which individuals process their narratives of severe trauma. This variability may depend on the coherence versus incoherence of narrative structure, which links trauma, culture, and somatization.

My colleagues and I have conducted a long-term project that aims to determine how war-related pre-migration experiences, changes in language, and acculturation are related to the presentation of somatoform symptoms in primary care. This study was designed to address gaps in existing knowledge about the links among severe trauma, PTSD, and somatization, and also about cultural differences in the clinical presentation of these problems. We have studied how Central American patients differ from other Latino and non-Latino patients in the expression of somatoform complaints, as well as the association between somatoform symptoms and PTSD among these patients. The research also focuses on the attitudes and behavioral responses of primary care physicians to these patients, and the extent to which barriers to access for health care and mental health services affect the presentation of somatoform symptoms.

In our research (see Holman, Silver, & Waitzkin, 2000), we confirmed cultural differences in the occurrence of somatization, as measured by the structured diagnostic instrument (CIDI). Specifically, among 1,456 subjects interviewed, we found greater rates of somatization among Central American subjects (approximately 30%) than among other Latino (21%) and non-Latino (19%) comparison groups. Although we observed high levels of traumatic stressors in the Central American group (72%), PTSD per se did not differ markedly from that affecting other Latinos and non-Latinos. This observation suggests that culture may mediate the link between severe stress and somatization, even without the development of PTSD, including its full manifestations of flashbacks, dreams, and related psychological phenomena. Our study represents only one of several that will yield new knowledge about mental health disorders among immigrant, refugee, and minority populations who seek primary care services.

The traumas experienced by many refugees, members of minority groups, and nonminority patients have created a new set of conditions and challenges for North American primary care and mental health providers. Much remains to be done in order to understand and to heal the social, cultural, and political dimensions of trauma-related somatoform symptoms.

Needed Changes in the Patient-Doctor Relationship

The changes needed at the levels of the health care system and of the society will not come easily. Such transformations require political action that goes beyond the usual limits of policy proposals. To achieve equitable access to care at reasonable costs, and to achieve improved health outcomes across social classes and races, fundamental changes in the social structures of our society have to occur. In particular, the social structural issues that stand in the way of a just health care system need to be confronted, especially the political and economic power of the private insurance industry; without that confrontation, the United States will retain its distinction as the last economically developed country without a national health program. Similarly, the societal structures that maintain income and racial inequalities must change, if meaningful improvements in health outcomes are to be obtained. These improvements will not occur even with a successful national health program.

In short, an economically developed country ascribing to principles of justice must have a national health program that permits universal access to services. But even more fundamental change in the relationships among social classes and races must occur to improve the pervasive inequalities in health outcomes that members of our society experience. Here, I focus on the level of the primary care encounter, recognizing that what goes on in the encounter, even when aggregated over many encounters, will have less potential impact on health outcomes than changes that are needed at much broader levels in our society. Even so, primary care encounters will continue to occur, both before and after broader social transformations take place. Improvements at the "micro" level of the patient-doctor encounter, and how to get there from here, become a way of concluding this consideration of the quest for solutions.

Dealing with Social Context in Patient-Doctor Encounters

Many practitioners feel reluctant to get involved in helping improve the contextual problems that patients face—no matter how important such problems may be. Before the growth of managed care, doctors commonly experienced such reluctance because they viewed their involvement in patients' contextual difficulties as beyond the medical role, or because they could not find the time to extend their role to the contextual arena. The constraints introduced by managed care have made practitioners' involvement in patients' contextual concerns even more problematic. For instance, the productivity expectations and financial structure of managed care discourage efforts to deal with such problems. Several years ago, members of our research group on patient-doctor communication and I worked out some preliminary criteria to guide practitioners in addressing contextual concerns (Mishler, Clark, Ingelfinger, & Simon, 1989; Waitzkin, 1991).

These criteria try to address the question: To what extent *should* physicians intervene in the social context? The answer to this question depends partly on clarification of the practitioner's role, especially the degree to which intervention in the social context comes to be seen as appropriate and desirable. Practitioners reasonably may respond to this analysis by referring to the time constraints of current practice arrangements, the need to deal with challenging technical problems, and a lack of support facilities and personnel to improve social conditions. How physicians should involve themselves in contextual difficulties, without increasing professional control in areas in which physicians claim no special expertise, therefore takes on a certain complexity.

On the other hand, the presence of social problems in medical encounters warrants more critical attention. Briefly, on the most limited level, physicians should let patients tell their stories with far fewer interruptions, cutoffs, or returns to technical matters. Patients should have the chance to present their narratives in an open-ended way. When patients refer to personal troubles that derive from contextual issues (e.g., overwork and chaotic lives; see Whitley, Kirmayer, & Groleau, 2006), physicians should try not to marginalize these connections by reverting to a technical track. Although such suggestions encourage more "attentive patient care" and more acknowledgment of patients' contextual stories within medical encounters (Mishler et al., 1989; Smith, 1996), some preliminary criteria also may prove helpful for physicians in deciding when and under what circumstances they could initiate, extend, or limit discussions about contextual matters.

First, it is important to recognize that patients differ in their openness and desire for contextual discussion; physicians should take their cues here from the initiative that patients themselves show in raising contextual concerns. When patients do introduce contextual information such as trauma, loss, social isolation, problems accessing care, or financial concerns, supportive listening is only a start. Rather than supportive listening alone, the physician might respond more directly to these patient-initiated concerns by mentioning contextual interventions that could prove fairly easy to arrange: referral to service organizations, home care services, social work support to help with financial issues, information about transportation services, and efforts to coordinate care with the patient's family members and friends.

Second, under other circumstances, physicians should remain sensitive to patients' differing desires and needs. Some patients may prefer no contextual interventions. Physicians' inquiry about contextual concerns requires tactful recognition of patients' autonomy to limit contextual discussion and to refuse such interventions.

In considering the time and costs devoted to contextual discussion and intervention, a point of concern especially to managed care organizations, a third criterion suggests that physicians and patients consider effects of contextual conditions on outcomes of care, such as prognosis, functional capacity, and satisfaction. Contextual concerns such as isolation and related social psychological problems can affect morbidity and mortality. Social isolation and psychological distress, for instance, are associated with higher rates of adverse cardiac events after myocardial infarction, and these effects may be equal or greater in magnitude than previously established cardiac risk factors (Brezinka & Kittel, 1996).

Current productivity standards in managed care are leading to tighter scheduling of shorter appointments, which do not encourage the exploration of contextual concerns (see Real & Street, this volume). When constraints of time and costs require prioritization, existing evidence about the importance of specific contextual problems for health outcomes can help guide physicians and patients in targeting contextual issues for discussion and intervention. Likewise, a reasonable hypothesis for future research is that the marginalization of contextual issues may be inversely related to patient satisfaction, an important outcome of care (Roter & Hall, 1992), and that for many patients more explicit attention to contextual problems would enhance satisfaction. Even from the standpoint of utilization and cost, it can be argued that attention to contextual concerns in many instances can improve functional status, decrease unnecessary utilization, and possibly reduce the costs of care, especially for at-risk people such as the elderly and those affected by poverty. Aiming toward a more supportive and humanistic encounter, one that can address contextual concerns rather than simply marginalizing them, may then emerge as a goal that even some enlightened managed care organizations could support.

As a fourth criterion, practitioners should consider referral to social workers, psychologists, or psychiatrists but also should evaluate whether specific patients would benefit more from dealing with contextual issues exclusively in the primary care setting. In managed care, the primary care practitioner usually initiates such referrals, but administrative reviewers, often through utilization review committees, must approve the referrals for reimbursement. For some patients, experiences with mental health professionals prove unsatisfactory or financially prohibitive. In addition, mental health professionals' role in mediating socially caused distress has received criticism both outside and inside the psychiatric profession (Davis, 1986, 1988; Laing & Esterson, 1970). Even aside from utilization review, because many patients do not feel comfortable seeking help from mental health professionals, primary care practitioners rather than psychiatrists probably will continue to see the majority of patients with emotional problems who present to physicians for care (Depression Guideline Panel, 1993). Although referrals to mental health professionals sometimes may prove necessary or appropriate, a broad mandate encouraging such care for people suffering from contextually based distress is not a solution.

As a fifth criterion, physicians and managed care organizations should try to avoid the "medicalization" of social problems that require long-term reforms in social policy, and medicalization itself requires further critical attention (Waitzkin, Britt, & Williams, 1994; also see Lantz, Lichtenstein, & Pollack, 2007). At the individual level, medicalization can become a subtle process. For instance, there is a fine line between physicians' discussing contextual interventions and assuming professional control over broad arenas of patients' lives. Here it is important that physicians not imply that the solution of contextual difficulties ultimately becomes an individual's responsibility.

Clearly, it would be helpful if patients and physicians could turn to more readily available forms of assistance outside the medical arena to help in the solution of social problems, and current conditions do not evoke optimism about broader changes in medicine's social context. Such changes will require time and financial resources, although not necessarily more than those now consumed in inefficient conversations that marginalize contextual issues. Contextual problems warrant social policies to address unmet needs, and some other countries have gone far beyond the United States in enacting such policies (Waitzkin, 1991; Waitzkin & Britt, 1989). These suggestions are not new. Yet it is evident that meaningful improvements in medical encounters will depend partly on such wider reforms that go beyond the changes inherent in managed care.

Trauma, Somatization, and Narrative

Regarding treatment of somatoform symptoms in primary care settings specifically, an alliance between provider and patient has to recognize the interrelationships among trauma, somatization, culture, and narrative. In this alliance, a principal goal is the patient's feeling of safety. Frequently, refugees and immigrants have lost basic trust in institutions as a result of their previous traumatic experiences. Conditions encountered in exile may impede recovery from premigration trauma. Local violence generated by youth gangs, drug abuse and traffic, physical and sexual abuse, fear of immigration officials (which affects not only undocumented individuals, but also those with temporary visas), police brutality, lack of access to health services, and other forms of ongoing severe stress may reactivate patients' previous trauma and exacerbate physical and emotional symptoms (Asch, 1994; Gonsalves, 1990; Hubbell, Waitzkin, Mishra, Dombrink, & Chavez, 1991). Somatizing patients from diverse cultural backgrounds may respond to different therapeutic interventions, including group treatment and participation by culturally sensitive mental health professionals (Mollica et al., 1990; Morris & Silove, 1992; Waitzkin & Magana, 1997).

Unfortunately, however, the most effective approach to treating somatizing patients remains unclear (for a review of randomized controlled trials of treatment for somatoform disorders, see Kroenke, 2007). Such patients, who usually present to primary care practitioners, often receive extended and expensive diagnostic evaluations, either because the physician does not recognize somatization or because he or she feels the need to exclude organic causes as well. Even when a practitioner diagnoses somatization accurately, treatment options remain limited, partly because patients often resist psychiatric evaluation and therapy.

Still, at least among the high proportion of somatizing patients who have experienced severe trauma, there is little question that bringing to consciousness a narrative of trauma, its relation to somatic symptoms, and the impact of culture at least offers promise as a treatment option to be evaluated. Although this promise is tempered by the consistent observation that ongoing economic, political, and familial issues play an important role in somatization and its treatment, therapeutic approaches that emphasize the construction of coherent narratives of trauma deserve assessment for many patients who suffer from somatoform symptoms.

Work in several fields suggests the possible value of therapeutic strategies that emphasize the formulation of coherent narratives in dealing with severe trauma (Herman, 1992). For instance, psychotherapeutic explorations with survivors of childhood abuse or political trauma such as torture during adulthood suggest the importance of a patient's enunciating a coherent narrative, sometimes referred to as a "testimony," as a critical component of the healing process. Case reports of such testimonies, either in individual therapy or in nonprofessional support groups, indicate the usefulness of narratives that link trauma, culture, and physical symptoms in the treatment of patients who suffer from somatization. Such efforts cohere with findings in psychological research that "putting stress into words" not only alleviates emotional suffering, but also exerts favorable effects on physiological measures of arousal (Pennebaker & Seagal, 1999; Richards, Beal, Seagal, & Pennebaker, 2000).

Several colleagues and I are exploring the efficacy of Paulo Freire's model of consciousness-raising groups, which previously have been used as a technique of empowerment for educational interventions in Latin America (Freire, 1970, 1994, 1998). The techniques resemble the group processes that have provided forums for the "testimonies" of trauma victims (Herman, 1992; Mollica, 1988). Although empowered speech clearly is not equivalent to empowered action, several of these programs that have applied Freire's educational approaches to health care have found that many participants in empowerment groups eventually take greater initiative in dealing with adverse conditions in other arenas, such as housing and employment (Minkler & Wallerstein, 1997). We are trying to study how the processing of narratives occurs in such groups and how the therapeutic (or, as Freire would say, "liberating") process might take place.

Specifically, can such groups provide a culturally sanctioned space in which the terrible narrative finally could be returned to consciousness, expressed explicitly and coherently, and worked through in a supportive social context? Although this question has not yet been answered, intervention studies that evaluate and compare empowerment groups versus other therapeutic options for somatizing patients will clarify the efficacy of approaches encouraging the expression of coherent narratives that link trauma, culture, and somatoform symptoms. This conceptual approach to narratives of trauma and somatization may prove therapeutically more useful than the current tendency to deal with extreme stress in a manner that, though culturally sanctioned, becomes expensive, misleading, and perhaps more painful somatically than need be the case.

Acknowledgment

I gratefully acknowledge the contributions of Rolando Castillo, Javier Escobar, Alison Holman, Holly Magaña, and Roxane Cohen Silver to the work described in this chapter. This chapter is adapted from *At the Front Lines of Medicine: How the Healthcare System Alienates Doctors and Mistreats Patients and What We Can Do about It* (2001, Lanham, MD: Rowan & Littlefield).

Note

1. Sartorius (1992, p. 5) presented the definitions used by the World Health Organization and affiliated organizations: "The definition of the word refugee as '… a person who owing to well-founded fear of being persecuted for reasons of race, religion, nationality, [or] membership in a particular group of political opinion is outside the country of his nationality' served to define the role of the United Nations High Commission for Refugees. It was subsequently amended—for example, by the Organization of African Unity, which added that 'persons fleeing from war, civil disturbance, and violence of any kind' should also be considered refugees. Subsequently, the definition was even further amended to include persons fleeing from extreme economic hardship as well as persons displaced within borders of their own country (provided that they met the other requirement of being in vital danger unless they left their usual abode)."

References

Alejandro, I., Guarnaccia, P. J., Vega, W. A., Gara, M. A., Like, R. C., Escobar, J. I., & Diaz-Martinez, A. M. (2005). The relationship between ataque de nervios and unexplained neurological symptoms: A preliminary analysis. *The Journal of Nervous and Mental Disease, 193,* 32–39.

American Psychiatric Association. (1994). *Diagnostic and statistical manual of mental disorders* (4th ed., pp. 445–469). Washington, DC: American Psychiatric Association.

Asch, S. (1994). Does fear of immigration authorities deter tuberculosis patients form seeking care? *Western Journal of Medicine, 161,* 373–376.

Barsky, A. J., Orav, E. J., & Bates, D. W. (2005). Somatization increases medical utilization and costs independent of psychiatric and medical comorbidity. *Archives of General Psychiatry, 62,* 903–910.

Bhugra, D., & Mastrogianni, A. (2004). Globalisation and mental disorders. Overview with relation to depression. *British Journal of Psychiatry, 184,* 10–20.

Brezinka, V., & Kittel, F. (1996). Psychosocial factors of coronary heart disease in women: A review. *Social Science & Medicine, 42,* 1351–1365.

Castillo, R., Waitzkin, H., Villasenor, Y., & Escobar, J. I. (1995). Mental health disorders and somatoform symptoms among immigrants and refugees who seek primary care services. *Archives of Family Medicine, 4,* 637–646.

Cervantes, C. R., Salgado de Snyder, V. N., & Padilla, A. M. (1989). Post-traumatic stress disorder in immigrants from Central America and Mexico. *Hospital and Community Psychiatry, 40,* 615–619.

Davis, K. (1986). The process of problem (re)formulation in psychotherapy. *Sociology of Health and Illness, 8,* 44–74.

Davis, K. (1988). *Power under the microscope: Toward a grounded theory of gender relations in medical encounters.* Dortecht, Holland: Foris.

DeGruy, F. V., III. (2000). Mental health diagnoses and the costs of primary care. *Journal of Family Practice, 49,* 311–313.

Depression Guideline Panel. (1993). *Depression in primary care* (AHCPR Publication No. 93-0550). Rockville, MD: Agency for Health Care Policy and Research.

Duran, B., Malcoe, L. H., Sanders, M., Waitzkin, H., Skipper, B., & Yager, J. (2004). Child maltreatment prevalence and mental disorders outcomes among American Indian women in primary care. *Child Abuse & Neglect, 28,* 131–145.

Eisenberg, D. M., Kessler, R. C., Foster, C., Norlock, F. E., Calkins, D. R., & Delbanco, T. L. (1993). Unconventional medicine in the United States: Prevalence, costs, and patterns of use. *New England Journal of Medicine, 328,* 246–252.

Eisenberg, M., Davis, R. B., Ettner, S. L., Appel, S., Wilkey, S., Van Rompay, M., et al. (1998). Trends in alternative medicine use in the United States, 1990–1997: Results of a follow-up national survey. *Journal of the American Medical Association, 280,* 1569–1575.

Escalona, R., Achilles, G., Waitzkin. H., & Yager, J. (2004). PTSD and somatization in women treated at a VA primary care clinic. *Psychosomatics, 45,* 291–296.

Escobar, J. I. (1987). Cross-cultural aspects of the somatization trait. *Hospital and Community Psychiatry, 38,* 174–180.

Escobar, J. I., Canino, G., Rubio-Stipec, M., & Bravo, M. (1992). Somatic symptoms after a natural disaster: A prospective study. *American Journal of Psychiatry, 148,* 965–967.

Escobar, J. I., Waitzkin, H., Silver, R. C., Gara, M., & Holman, E. A. (1998). Abridged somatization: A study in primary care. *Psychosomatic Medicine, 60,* 466–472.

Fazel, N., Wheeler, J., & Danesh, J. (2005). Prevalence of serious mental disorder in 7000 refugees resettled in western countries: A systematic review. *Lancet, 294,* 1309–1314.

Flores, G. (2005). The impact of medical interpreter services on the quality of health care: A systematic review. *Medical Care Research & Review, 62,* 255–299.

Freire, P. (1970). *Pedagogy of the oppressed.* New York: Herder & Herder.

Freire, P. (1994). *Pedagogy of hope.* New York: Continuum.

Freire, P. (1998). *Pedagogy of freedom: Ethics, democracy, and civic courage.* Lanham, MD: Rowman & Littlefield.

Gonsalves, C. J. (1990). The psychological effects of political repression on Chilean exiles in the U.S. *American Journal of Orthopsychiatry, 60,* 143–153.

Herman, J. L. (1992). *Trauma and recovery.* New York: Basic Books.

Hoang, G. N., & Erickson, R. V. (1982). Guidelines for providing medical care to Southeast Asian refugees. *Journal of the American Medical Association, 248,* 710–714.

Holman, E. A., Silver, R. C., & Waitzkin, H. (2000). Traumatic life events in primary care patients: A study in an ethnically diverse sample. *Archives of Family Medicine, 9,* 802–810.

Hsieh, E. (2006). Understanding medical interpreters: Reconceptualizing bilingual health communication. *Health Communication, 20,* 177–186.

Hsu, S. I. (1999). Somatisation among Asian refugees and immigrants as a culturally-shaped illness behaviour. *Annals of the Academy of Medicine of Singapore, 28,* 841–845.

Hubbell, F. A., Waitzkin, H., Mishra, S. I., Dombrink, J., & Chavez, L. R. (1991). Access to medical care for documented and undocumented Latinos in a southern California county. *Western Journal of Medicine, 154,* 414–417.

Jackson, J. L., & Kroenke, K. (2008). Prevalence, impact, and prognosis of multisomatoform disorder in primary care: A 5-year follow-up study. *Psychosomatic Medicine, 70,* 430–434.

Kessler, R. C., Berglund, P., Demler, O., Jin, R., Merikangas, K. R., & Walters, E. E. (2005). Lifetime prevalence and age-of-onset distributions of DSM-IV disorders in the National Comorbidity Survey replication. *Archives of General Psychiatry, 62,* 593–602.

Kirmayer, L. J., Groleau, D., Looper, K. J., & Dao, M. D. (2004). Explaining medically unexplained symptoms. *Canadian Journal of Psychiatry, 49,* 663–672.

Kirmayer, L. J., & Sartorius, N. (2007). Cultural models and somatic syndromes. *Psychosomatic Medicine, 69,* 832–840.

Kirmayer, L. J., & Young, A. (1998). Culture and somatization: Clinical, epidemiological, and ethnographic perspectives. Psychosomatic Medicine, 60, *420–430.*

Kleinman, A. (1988). *The illness narratives.* New York: Basic Books.

Kleinman, A., & Becker, A. E. (1998). "Sociosomatics:" The contributions of anthropology to psychosomatic medicine. *Psychosomatic Medicine, 60,* 389–393.

Kroenke, K. (2007). Efficacy of treatment for somatoform disorders: A review of randomized controlled trials. *Psychosomatic Medicine, 69,* 881–888.

Kung, W. W., & Pei-Chun, L. (2008). How symptom manifestations affect help seeking for mental health problems among Chinese Americans. *The Journal of Nervous and Mental Disease, 196,* 46–54.

Laing, R. D., & Esterson, A. (1970). *Sanity, madness and the family.* Baltimore: Penguin.

Lantz, P. M., Lichtenstein, R. L., & Pollack, H. A. (2007). Health policy approaches to population health: The limits of medicalization. *Health Affairs, 26,* 1253–1257.

Lee, R., Rodin, G., Devins, G., & Weiss, M. G. (2001). Illness experience, meaning and help-seeking among Chinese immigrants in Canada with chronic fatigue and weakness. *Anthropology and Medicine, 8,* 89–108.

Lin, E. H. B., Carter, W. B., & Kleinman, A. M. (1985). An exploration of somatization among Asian refugees and immigrants in primary care. *American Journal of Public Health, 75,* 1080–1084.

Minkler, M., & Wallerstein, N. (1997). Improving health through community organizing and community building. In M. Minkler (Ed.), *Community organizing and community building for health* (pp. 30–52). London: Routledge.

Mishler, E. G., Clark, J. A., Ingelfinger, J., & Simon, M. P. (1989). The language of
  attentive patient care: A comparison of two medical interviews. *Journal of General
  Internal Medicine, 4*, 325–335.

Mollica, R. (1988). The trauma story: The psychiatric care of refugee survivors of violence and torture. In F. Ochberg (Ed.), *Post-traumatic therapy and victims of violence*
  (pp. 285–314). New York: Brunner/Mazel.

Mollica, R. F. (2000). Waging a new kind of war: Invisible wounds. *Scientific American,
  282*, 54–57.

Mollica, R. F., Caspi-Yavin, Y., Bollini, P., Truong, T., Tor, S., & Lavelle, J. (1992). The
  Harvard Trauma Questionnaire: Validating a cross-cultural instrument for measur-
  ing torture, trauma, and posttraumatic stress disorder in Indo-Chinese refugees.
  Journal of Nervous and Mental Diseases, 180, 111–116.

Mollica, R. F., Wyshak, G., Lavelle, J., Truong, T., Tor, S., & Yang, T. (1990). Assessing symptom change in Southeast Asian refugee survivors of mass violence and
  torture. *American Journal of Psychiatry, 147*, 83–88.

Moore, L. J., & Boehnlein, J. (1991). Posttraumatic stress disorder, depression, and
  somatic symptoms in U.S. Mien patients. *Journal of Nervous and Mental Diseases,
  179*, 728–733.

Morris, P., & Silove, D. (1992). Cultural influences in psychotherapy with refugee survivors of torture and trauma. *Hospital and Community Psychiatry, 43*, 820–824.

Mull, J. D., & Mull, D. S. (1983). A visit with a curandero. *Western Journal of Medicine,
  139*, 730–736.

Nguyen, D. (1985). Culture shock: A review of Vietnamese culture and its concepts of
  health and disease. *Western Journal of Medicine, 142*, 409–412.

O'Hare, T., & Van Tran, T. (1998). Substance abuse among Southeast Asians in
  the U.S.: Implications for practice and research. *Social Work in Health Care, 26*,
  69–80.

Pennebaker, J. W., & Seagal, J. D. (1999). Forming a story: The health benefits of narrative. *Journal of Clinical Psychology, 10*, 1243–1255.

Richards, J. M., Beal, W. E., Seagal, J. D., & Pennebaker, J. W. (2000). Effects of disclosure of traumatic events on illness behavior among psychiatric prison inmates.
  Journal of Abnormal Psychology, 109, 156–161.

Roter, D. L., & Hall, J. A. (1992). *Doctors talking with patients/Patients talking with doctors*. Westport, CT: Auburn House.

Sarver, J., & Baker, D. W. (2000). Effect of language barriers on follow-up appointments after an emergency department visit. *Journal of General Internal Medicine,
  15*, 256–264.

Sartorius, N. (1992). Refugee mental health: Issues and problems. In H. T. Lo & E.
  Yeh (Eds.), *Critical condition: Refugee mental health* (pp. 5–11). Toronto: Hong Fook
  Mental Health Association.

Shorter, E. (1992). *From paralysis to fatigue: A history of psychosomatic illness in the modern era*. New York: Free Press.

Shorter, E. (1994). *From the mind into the body: The cultural origins of psychosomatic
  symptoms*. New York: Free Press.

Smith, R. C. (1996). *The patient's story*. Boston: Little, Brown.

Smith, R. C., Gardiner, J. C., Lyles, J. S., Sirbu, C., Dwamena, F. C., Hodges, A., et al. (2005). Exploration of the DSM-IV criteria in primary care patients with medically unexplained symptoms. *Psychosomatic Medicine, 67,* 123–129.

Waitzkin, H. (1991). *The politics of medical encounters: How patients and doctors deal with social problems.* New Haven, CT: Yale University Press.

Waitzkin, H., & Britt, T. (1989). Changing the structure of medical discourse: Implications of cross-national comparisons. *Journal of Health and Social Behavior, 30,* 436–449.

Waitzkin, H., Britt, T., & Williams, C. (1994). Narratives of aging and social problems in medical encounters with older persons. *Journal of Health and Social Behavior, 35,* 322–348.

Waitzkin, H., Iriart, C., Buchanan, H. S., Mercado, F., Tregar, J., & Eldredge, J. (2008). The Latin American Social Medicine Database: A resource for epidemiology. *International Journal of Epidemiology, 37,* 724–728.

Waitzkin, H., & Magana, H. (1997). The black box in somatization: Narrative, culture, and unexplained physical symptoms. *Social Science & Medicine, 45,* 811–825.

Whitley, R., Kirmayer, L. J., & Groleau, D. (2006). Public pressure, private protest: Illness narratives of West Indian immigrants in Montreal with medically unexplained symptoms. *Anthropology & Medicine, 13,* 193–205.

Willging, C. E., Waitzkin, H., & Nicdao, E. (2008). Medicaid managed care for mental health services: The survival of safety net institutions in rural settings. *Qualitative Health Research, 18,* 1231–1246.

Chapter 6

Bilingual Health Communication
Medical Interpreters' Construction of a Mediator Role

Elaine Hsieh

Patients with limited-English-proficiency (LEP) often experience inequality in health services and poor health outcomes. Researchers have noted that when language barriers exist in provider-patient communication (i.e., when compared to English-speaking patients), a patient is likely to receive more diagnostic testing (Hampers, Cha, Gutglass, Binns, & Krug, 1999; Waxman & Levitt, 2000); is less likely to receive preventive care (Woloshin, Schwartz, Katz, & Welch, 1997) and follow-up appointments after an emergency department visit (Sarver & Baker, 2000); is less likely to understand health care providers' instructions (Doty, 2003; Gerrish, 2001); and is less satisfied with the quality of care (David & Rhee, 1998). Their findings suggest the urgent need to develop effective interventions to improve the quality of health care services received by patients with LEP, one of which is to provide interpreters in health care settings (Allen, 2000; Jones & Gill, 1998).

Interpreters often are viewed as the standard solution to language barriers between physicians and patients (Department of Health and Human Services, 2001; Flores, 2005; Flores et al., 2002; Woloshin et al., 1997). Interpreters traditionally have been conceptualized as conduits, invisible non-thinking language modems that allow providers and patients who do not share a common language to communicate with each other. *Interpreters-as-conduits* remains the prevalent ideology of translation models and training programs in many different areas. For example, the Cross-Cultural Health Care Program (1999), one of the leading programs in medical interpreter training, views the conduit role as the default role for interpreters. In an analysis of code of ethics documents from more than 20 institutions, Kaufert and Putsch (1997) concluded that many of the codes emphasize a mode of interpretation that calls for an objective and neutral role for medical interpreters. The National Standards of Practice for Interpreters in Health Care recognizes the various responsibilities of interpreters (e.g., advocacy and cultural awareness) but still emphasizes the importance of accuracy and impartiality in interpreters' practice (National Council on Interpreting in Health Care [NCIHC], 2005). Recently, NCIHC has proposed a national code of ethics for interpreters (for a complete discussion on the code of ethics, see NCIHC, 2004), which are based on three core values: beneficence, fidelity, and respect for the importance of culture and cultural differences. In regards to fidelity, NCIHC (2004, p. 13) noted,

> The ethical responsibility of the interpreter, therefore, is to convert messages rendered in one language into another without losing the essence of the meaning that is being conveyed and including all aspects of the message without making judgments as to what is relevant, important, or acceptable. [...] The principle of fidelity requires that interpreters have the ability to detach themselves from the content of information.

The conduit model has been a prominent feature of the transmission models of communication, viewing communication as the transfer of information from a sender to a receiver (for a discussion of Shannon & Weaver's [1963/1949] conduit and noise models, see Dysart-Gale, 2005). The model adopts a monological and linear view of communication, assuming that meanings are created by the speakers (as opposed to co-created by all participants, including the interpreter, involved in the conversation; e.g., Bakhtin, 1981). The model also presupposes linear communication, in which the interactions between the speakers are only possible via the accurate, faithful, and neutral relay of the interpreter.

There are several reasons that a conduit model remains popular. First, interpreters traditionally have been expected to claim an invisible role (i.e., minimizing their presence and influence in the communicative process) so that they can claim authority and credibility for their services (Hsieh, 2002). A conduit model allows interpreters to deny any personal interference with their work. Second, a conduit model appears to be a straightforward way of interpretation and requires minimal training (i.e., an interpreter just needs to relay everything and not make any judgment). When talking about the complexity of interpreters' functions and roles in health care settings, Sara, a participant in our study who is also a practicing interpreter and trainer for medical interpreters, explained that the industry-standard 40-hour training is insufficient to educate the interpreters to be proficient in the variety of roles; however, she concluded, "You had better say, 'Everybody has to be robot.' That way, you don't have to deal with all the other issues. [...] It's easier." Finally, a conduit model suggests that the speakers are the only persons who have control over the process and content of communication. In other words, the speakers (e.g., provider and patient) can confidently assume that the interpreter says *exactly* what they said and that they still have full control over the information exchanged

The ideology of interpreters-as-conduits has been challenged in the past few years. Language and social interaction researchers have argued that human communication exchanges are always dialogical and the meanings and contents of communication are co-constructed by *all* participants of the communicative activity (Georgakopoulou, 2002; Miller, Hengst, Alexander, &

Sperry, 2000). Through both qualitative and quantitative analyses, researchers recently have argued that interpreters are not neutral or impartial participants in medical encounters but actively participate the communicative process (Angelelli, 2002, 2004; Davidson, 2000, 2001; Hale, 1999; Hale & Gibbons, 1999; Metzger, 1999; Rosenberg, 2001). Angelelli (2002, 2004) concluded that interpreters perceive their role as visible regardless of their work settings (e.g., conferences, courts, or hospitals), which also is evident in their role performances in the communicative process (i.e., actively intervening in the interpreter-mediated interactions). Interpreters often need to reconcile between the ideology and the practice of medical interpreting (Hsieh, 2001, 2006a, 2006b). In fact, interpreters may assume a variety of roles (e.g., conduit, co-diagnostician, institutional gatekeeper, patient advocate, and professional) to manage the complexity of bilingual provider-patient interactions (Hsieh, 2004a, 2006a, 2007). These studies successfully challenged the idea of interpreter neutrality and inspired researchers to develop more complex theories of interpreter-mediated activities.

These studies, however, suggest a missing link in researchers' efforts to deconstruct interpreters' claim of neutrality (i.e., a conduit role): If the conduit model remains the dominant ideology in the training programs and code of ethics for medical interpreters (Dysart-Gale, 2005), how do interpreters legitimize their practice? Do they still claim a conduit role? If yes, why and how do they enact the role?

To answer this question, I undertook a study to examine the roles of medical interpreters. Results reported here are part of a larger study, which included ethnographic shadowing of Mandarin Chinese interpreters' daily assignments (i.e., participant observation) and in-depth interviews with interpreters from various cultures. I recruited medical interpreters from two interpreting agencies in the midwestern area in the United States. Both agencies view medical interpreting as their primary task and have contractual relationships with local hospitals. A total of 26 participants from 17 languages (i.e., Arabic, Armenian, Assyrian, Mandarin Chinese, Cantonese, French, German, Hindi, Kurdish, Polish, Russian, Spanish, Turkish, Ukrainian, Urdu, Vietnamese, and Yoruba), of whom 21 were practicing medical interpreters and 5 held management positions in interpreting offices. Interpreters included in this study are all considered *professional* interpreters and work as freelance interpreters in local hospitals. The majority of interpreters ($n = 17$) had participated in a 40-hour training course developed by the Cross Cultural Health Care Program (CCHCP), which has been viewed as an industry-recognized standard for training professional interpreters. Those who had not attended the course either had passed certification programs offered by individual hospitals or had acted as trainers in education programs for medical interpreters.

I shadowed two Mandarin Chinese interpreters for the ethnographic study, following their daily routines, audio-recording the interpreter-mediated medical encounters, and taking fieldnotes to include nonverbal and contextual information. Three months after the beginning of the ethnographic study, I conducted 14 individual and 6 dyadic interviews (each lasted 1 to 1½ hours). All dyadic interviews consisted of two interpreters from different languages (except one that included two Spanish interpreters). In these interviews, I relied on my experience as a medical interpreter and my prior data collected through the participant observation to navigate through the design, preparation, and interview process. Two research assistants and I used grounded theory for the data analysis for both the ethnographic and interview data (Strauss & Corbin, 1998). The focus of the research questions was to explore interpreters' understanding of their roles and to generate rich and diverse views, opinions, and experiences from participants of various cultures. The transcription includes two primary types of notation. The texts are CAPITALIZED when they were the speakers' emphasis and *italicized* when they were my emphasis. Each interpreter is assigned a pseudonym. In the transcript, health care providers are denoted as H, interpreters as I, and patients as P. I also have assigned pseudonyms for all participants so that readers have a better understanding of the interactions and relationships between providers, interpreters, and patients. A total of 11 health care providers, four patients, one patients' family member, and two mandarin Chinese interpreters were included in the participant observation data. All providers' pseudonyms begin with H (e.g., Helen and Henry) and the four patients' pseudonyms begin with P (e.g., Pam and Paula), and the Chinese interpreters are Christie and Claire.

The Construction of an Invisible Role

Conduit was, by far, the role that is identified most explicitly and frequently by the interpreters in this study (i.e., 21 of 26 participants claimed various forms of a conduit role). By examining interpreters' narratives and the metaphors with which they explicitly identified, I will demonstrate that interpreters' conceptualization of the conduit role extends beyond an information or linguistic transferring role. Contrary to an earlier study (Angelelli, 2002), which concluded that interpreters perceived their role as visible across various settings, the interpreters of this study strived to be invisible (i.e., to minimize their presence) in provider-patient interactions. For example, Selena, an interpreter with 32-years experience, stated, "I am sort of in the background, I am the voice, I try to be faceless. That way, I don't interfere with their communication or their rapport between the patient and the provider." Colin described his role, "I try not to exist in a sense. I just sort of let the patient and the provider talk, and I just interpret." Sara explained, "The goal [of medical interpreting] would be to perform such a job that it seems that you were never there."

Interpreters who identify with a conduit role often claimed that all that they do is "just interpret everything" and they are "just interpreters." The constant use of "just" in their narratives reflect their effort to claim a limited role (i.e., they are nothing more than a conduit). Claire explained,

Because when I went through the training, we have to interpret every-thing exactly as what the doctor said, even have to interpret exactly the same tone, and same expression, and the same use of words. So, I just did the same. I would always try to follow what I learned in the class. So, I did the same thing. I just interpreted in Chinese, just equivalent what he said in English.

The pursuit for neutrality challenges interpreters to justify their perfor-mances. Their physical presence in the medical encounters and their func-tions in eliminating language and cultural barriers between providers and patients make it difficult for interpreters to claim that they are truly faceless or nonexistent. Some interpreters claim a *non-thinking* status to justify their inter-preting strategy. In other words, if their performances do not require them to think in the communicative process, they cannot interfere with the process or the content of provider-patient communication. Peter explained, "No matter what my judgment or my opinion, or my feelings [are], in a health care provider setting, I interpreted everything." Roger shared a similar attitude, "You cannot adjust [information] the way you like it or how you think. *You are here to work, not to think.* Remember."

Metaphors for the Conduit Role

In addition to the claims about a non-thinking role, interpreters developed many metaphors that are indicative of a conduit role. For example, interpreters often claimed that they are just the *voice*. The voice metaphor often is associ-ated with the interpreters' desire to establish direct communication between the providers and the patients. Scott explained, "We are like the voice, we are not a person. [...] We become the voice of the professional, but we also become the voice of the patient. We are not a person in terms of being addressed to us directly." Interpreters in this study talked about how they actively incorporate this concept in their practice. For example, Silvia said, "I am only the voice and I keep reminding the doctor and the patient to talk to each other." Sophia said that at the beginning of a medical encounter, she would explain to her clients, "I am just a voice of you. Whatever you said is what I am going to say without adding or removing or anything. I'd rather if you talk directly to [each other]."

Robot (or machine) is another metaphor that interpreters used to describe their roles. The mechanical nature (i.e., non-thinking, non-feeling, and yet highly-skilled characteristics) of a robot corresponds to the values of a con-duit model. A few interpreters talked about their roles as robots or machines. For example, Steve explained, "I mean I'd rather be considered more like a machine. They know that I am there, and then, I am doing my job, but I'd rather not be there as another person controlling the situation at all." Sara even argued, "If you want to keep your job, you want to become, really, a kind of robot in order to keep your job." A mechanical view of interpreting is valued because human beings make mistakes and machines are thought to be more reliable, performing with great consistency. Shirley, a manager of interpreter services, recognized the human nature of interpreters, which may become unreliable as pressure mounts:

> We are human, and we have feelings, it's just like everybody else. However, in that moment, you are the person that the staff is depending on to provide that communication, to convey the same spirit that it is being given. So, the last thing that the team needs is for that *instrument to crumble*.

Alternatively, interpreters used the robot metaphor to describe their struggles to adhere to a conduit role. A robot metaphor often was used to contrast interpreters' emotional reaction in medical encounters. As a result, robot becomes a metaphor that is situated against interpreters' awareness of the challenge (i.e., their human nature) to live up to a conduit role (also see Hsieh, 2006a). Although a robot metaphor often highlights the interpreters' sense of conflict, it, nevertheless, reflects interpreters' understanding of the expected roles that others have placed on them. Rachel talked about such internal conflicts:

> We learned that we don't have to talk to patients. We learned that. We are not allowed, right? I don't like that. I can tell you, 'It's not right.' We are not robots. We have training; I know why we are here. But I say that because it's not true, I am not a robot.

Bridge is another metaphor that often is adopted by interpreters to describe their functions. A bridge, in a sense, is much like a conduit, providing a neutral channel for communication without adding personal interpretation or opinions. Steve explained, "I would just say that I'm there to provide some of the language bridge, to be a conduit." Rachel echoed, "My role is just to be a bridge, a bridge between the doctor and the patient." Although the bridge metaphor seems to be similar to a conduit in the sense that it provides a neutral channel for successful communication, interpreters' comment often reflected their awareness of the educational, socioeconomic, and cultural gaps between providers and patients. Rachel explained,

> [The goal of medical interpreting is] to help other people to bridge the gap, that's pretty much the theme of all the [training] classes. To help other people from our own country who do not speak English, who don't know the system and who don't know the culture, just to help them, guide them along, and help them as much as you can, to get through it.

Interpreters talk about how they adjust speakers' register, interject their own explanations, describe terms that have no linguistic equivalent, check for understanding when necessary, or provide a necessary cultural framework for understanding. It is important to note that although these behaviors do not belong to the conduit role proposed by Cross Cultural Health Care Program (CCHCP, 1999), a major training program for medical interpreters in the United States, interpreters talked about these behaviors *without seeming to be aware that these behaviors require them to become an active participant in the communication*, evaluating the communicative process and interfering as necessary, which in fact makes them more than a conduit. In other words, although interpreters use bridge as a metaphor to describe the conduit role, the metaphor actually encompasses communicative behaviors that do not belong to a conduit role.

It is important to note that the interpreters who used a bridge metaphor still saw themselves as conduits. They also talked about their non-thinking status and neutrality. For example, after identifying his role as a bridge, Peter explained his interpreting strategy, "No matter how I feel, what is my private opinion, I interpreted everything that was said in the room." Colin talked about how interpreters are bridges between two languages, providing cultural frameworks to other conversational partners; however, when one of his patients was asked to leave the clinic because of the lack of funds, Colin decided to not get involved because "It's not my battle. Being an interpreter, that's not our battle." In other words, although interpreters were aware of their functions in bridging the gaps between the provider and the patient in various aspects (e.g., linguistic, cultural, educational, and socioeconomic aspects), they still strived to be and saw themselves as conduits. Nevertheless, the interpreters' use of the bridge metaphor highlighted the fact that their understanding of the "conduit" role has extended beyond the conduit model envisioned in their training programs and the ideology of translation and interpretation.

The Communicative Goals of an Invisible Role

Conduit roles require interpreters to refrain from evaluating the process and the content of communication and interpret all information during the medical encounter. Interpreters talk about conduit roles as a way to accomplish two major communicative goals: (a) transferring complete information, and (b) reinforcing the provider-patient relationship.

Transferring Complete Information

The first goal is consistent with the ideology of conduit as it focuses on the neutral and faithful transfer of information. In Extract 001, the interpreter (Claire) performed a straightforward conduit role, helping the provider (Hillary) to investigate the patient's (Paul) treatment history for his diabetes.

Extract 001

    H: Does he see a diabetic doctor here?
    I: 那你在這裡有沒有見過糖尿的醫生？
    (Have you seen a diabetic doctor here?)
    P: 沒有
    (No)
→ I: No
    P: 以前沒有，是才發現的
    (I didn't before. I just discovered it.)
→ I: I just discovered it. Before, I didn't see a diabetes doctor.
    H: But now he does?
    I: 你現在看過醫生嗎？關於糖尿病的醫生？
    (Now you've seen a doctor? A diabetic doctor?)
    P: 沒有
    (No)
→ I: No
    H: Okay. Who gave you the medication for the diabetes?
→ I: 那你糖尿病的藥是誰給你的？
    (who gave you the medication for the diabetes?)
    P: 是醫生開的
    (A doctor gave me).
→ I: It's from a doctor.

In this interaction, the interpreter followed the speakers' utterances very closely in the highlighted interpretation. A conduit role requires interpreters to interpret not only the verbal messages but also the nonverbal messages. For example, if a speaker demonstrates specific emotions or attitudes, interpreters are expected to re-enact those nonverbal messages. Claire also talked about an incident in which she thought the patient was mistreated and she explained her choice of strategies:

> [The provider was] kind of rude and disrespectful. I just personally think that he is not respectful. [...] So, what can I do? I just interpret exactly in the same tone, in the same expression. *Because when I went through the training, we have to interpret everything exactly as what the doctor said, even have to interpret exactly the same tone, and same expression, and the same use of words.*

In other words, when assuming a conduit role, interpreters transfer *all* information indiscriminately. The interpreter not only includes all verbal information but also emulates *nonverbal information* (e.g., tone of voice and emotion). In Extract 002, during a prenatal examination, the interpreter (Claire) provided verbal interpretation of the provider's (Heather) and the patient's (Pam) nonverbal behaviors:

Extract 002

    P: 就我的牙齦出血。
       (I have bleeding in my gum.)
    I: I have bleeding in my teeth gum.
→ H: Only in her gum but not from below? [pointing at her crotch]
→ I: 下面有沒有流血？陰部有沒有流血？
       (Any bleeding from below? Bleeding from the vagina?)
→ P: [shakes her head]
→ I: Only in the teeth gum. But no vagina bleeding.

Claire explicitly interpreted Heather's nonverbal gesture (line 204), which as used to clarify the meaning of the word "below," as *vagina.* Claire also interpreted Pam's nonverbal gesture (i.e., headshakes, meaning "no") by providing a confirmation to the provider's statement (i.e., "Only in the teeth gum") and an answer to the provider's question (i.e., "But no vagina bleeding"). By replacing nonverbal gestures with verbal messages, Claire ensured the information was relayed with minimal ambiguity. In Extract 003, the ultrasound technician's (Helen) turned the computer screen toward the Patient (Paula) so that she can see the fetus:

Extract 003

    H: Baby's heart. [pointing at the screen]
→ I: 小孩子心臟的位置，她手指的位置。
       (The position of the baby's heart. Where she's pointing)
       [H' clicks the machine a couple of times]
    H: Baby's waist line. [creating a circle on the computer screen.]
→ I: 小孩子的腰圍。他的腰，她現在用白色曲線慢慢圈出來是小孩子的
       腰圍
       (The baby's waist line. His waist. She is using the white line to circle it,
    that's the baby's waistline.)

During this medical encounter, the interpreter (Christie) and Helen were at the different sides of the patient's bed and it was inconvenient for Christie to physically point at the computer screen at Helen's side. However, Christie still tried to transfer complete information. Christie verbalized Helen's nonverbal gesture. In addition, Christie verbalized the information that was provided on the computer screen but not verbalized or gestured by Helen. In Extracts 002 and 003, although the interpreters tried to convey "complete" information, their choice of the communicative channels (i.e., nonverbal vs. verbal) was not the same as the speaker's choice. There were also situations that the interpreter chose the same communicative channel as the speaker. For example,

Extract 004 took place when the patient (Paula) brought her newborn back to the hospital for the first time after the delivery:

Extract 004

>H: Can you say congratulations in China- Chinese. A BEAUTIFUL BABY, SHE MUST BE VERY HAPPY, VERY PROUD, EVERYBODY IN THE BLOCK MUST BE JEALOUS OF HER!! [in a dramatic tone and loud volume]
>
>I: 他說喔，恭喜你有這麼漂亮的小孩子，你們街頭上面的人一定都會對你很羨慕的！！
>(He said, CONGRATULATION FOR SUCH A BEAUTIFUL BABY. People in your neighborhood must be very jealous of you!![in a dramatic tone and loud volume].)
>
>P: Thank you!

Some readers may notice that the literal message of interpreter's (Christie) interpretation is somewhat different from what the provider (Hank) said. Nevertheless, the communicative goal of the provider was to create a congratulatory message with a dramatic flair, which was successfully emulated by the interpreter.

Finally, the complete transfer of information may also include *information that is not directed or relevant to the other speaker* (e.g., conversations between providers). Although a couple of interpreters talked about their indiscriminate treatment of information, the two interpreters I observed did not interpret utterances that were not directed or relevant to the speakers. This may be due to the limited numbers of observed medical encounters ($N = 12$) and interpreters ($N = 2$). Nevertheless, this strategy may be significant for building the provider-patient relationship. For example, at times, a provider may consult with another provider in the presence of the patient (or a family member may speak directly to a patient), and a conduit role would expect an interpreter to interpret that information as well. Interpreters become not only the speakers' voice but also their *ears*. Yetta explained,

> Because everything I hear, when I am there, is like the patient should hear whatever I hear. So, whatever is there, I would say, "This has nothing to do with you, but this is what they are talking about." I would explain to the patient. To make him or her feel comfortable that they are just not there to say something about him. Because that scared a couple of my clients away, so, I would make sure that whatever I hear, [they'd hear too].

A speaker (e.g., a provider or a patient) may not be aware that the messages are not directed or relevant to him or her. Without the knowledge of the information exchanged between other parties, a speaker may grow suspicious about the relationship and interactions between the interpreter and other speakers (e.g., providers or family members). By interpreting all information indiscriminately, an interpreter allows a speaker to become not only a participant in provider-patient interactions but also a competent bystander to other interactions in a medical encounter.

Reinforcing Provider–Patient Relationships

A conduit role creates the illusion of dyadic physician-patient communication, which, in turn, reinforces the provider-patient relationship. In their training, interpreters are taught to strive for an invisible presence in provider-patient interaction by adopting a first-person singular interpreting style (i.e., speaking as if the interpreter were the original speaker) and interpreting indiscriminately. Roat, Putsch, and Lucero argued (1997) that the advantages of first-person interpretation include shortening the communication, avoiding confusion as to who is speaking, and reinforcing the primary relationship between the provider and the patient. In addition, by using first-person singular, the interpreter simplifies the interpreting context by presenting himself or herself as a non-person (cf. Goffman, 1959), creating the *illusion* of dyadic physician-patient communication. For example, in Extract 001, the interpreter stated, "*I* just discovered it. Before, *I* didn't see a diabetes doctor" (line 109), when the patient was actual referent.

At times, ironically, interpreters violate this rule and "interfere" with the content and process of provider-patient communication to reinforce provider-patient relationship. For example, Roger explained, "The only influence on the interaction when it comes to 'say her,' 'tell him,' [...] if she says, 'tell him I feel bad.' I go like, 'I feel bad.'" In Extract 005, the interpreter (Claire) used several different strategies to reinforce the relationship between the provider (Hilda) and the patient (Pam).

Extract 005

    H: Does she have any family history of diabetes?
→ I: 你家庭裡面有沒有成員是有糖尿病的？
      (Do any of your family members have diabetes?)
→ P: 沒有，(No)
    H: Is this her first pregnancy?
→ I: 第一胎？
      (First pregnancy?)
    P: 對
      (Yes)
    I: Yes
    H: Is she on any medication?

→   I: 你有沒有吃什麼藥，現在？
     (Are you taking any medicine now?)
→   P: No

The first-person interpreting style of the provider's comment should be "Does *she* have any family history of diabetes?" After all, this was what the provider exactly said. The interpreter, however, changed the actual comment and interpreted, "Do any of *your* family members have diabetes?", which changed it from second-person to first-person. Whereas the provider's comment implicitly recognized the presence of an interpreter, the interpreter's utterance directed the comment to the patient and thus, created the illusion of direct interaction between the provider and the patient. Although changing pronouns may appear to contradict a conduit style, the communicative goal (i.e., reinforcing the provider-patient relationship) was consistent with the ideology of a conduit role.

In addition, the interpreter did not interpret when the patient communicated directly with the provider. Although a conduit role includes the expectation that interpreters will interpret everything, in this example, the interpreter recognized that the provider was able to understand the patient's comment and did not require any interpretation (i.e., the patient answered in English). By *not* interpreting (or repeating) the patient's comment, the interpreter further minimized her presence in the encounter and reinforced the provider-patient relationship. This strategy suggests that the interpreter actively evaluates the speakers' utterances, deciding whether those comments should be interpreted (i.e., they are not assuming a non-thinking role). Shirley, a trainer in interpreting programs, explained how a silent interpreter allows patients to empower themselves by establishing direct communication with providers:

> [The patients] want to empower themselves, they want to use a little bit of English or whatever language that they do know. [...] The family wants to be able to say as much as they can, who are we to say, "You know what? Your English here is just not good enough!" It's the issue of empowering, and knowing that this person wants to take the initiative, because that goes to a lot more later on that [patient's] diagnosis.

Some interpreters in this study, in fact, believed that a conduit role facilitates patient empowerment by assuming that patients are competent individuals to act on their own behalf. In other words, patient empowerment is accomplished through respecting patients' autonomy (i.e., *not* to intervene on a patient's behalf or assume that the interpreter knows better) and acting as a conduit (i.e., not to provide personal opinions).

Interpreters in this study talked about adopting specific communicative strategies to minimize their presence and reinforce provider-patient relationships. For example, the interpreter (Christie) has assisted a patient (Paula) in several prenatal appointments and was familiar with Paula's concern about her infant having the same genetic disorder as her oldest child. In Extract 006, Paula met a new physician (Heather) for the first time after her delivery:

Extract 006

> P: 我這個兒子這個病，要不要告訴她？
> (My son's disease. Tell her or not?)
> I: Oh, she said that her first son has a disease. If you need to know the name of the disease?
> H: If it's an inherited disease, yeah.
> I: 它那是遺傳性的嗎？
> (Is it inherited?)

This interaction is significant because of Christie's strategies to reinforce the provider-patient relationship. In line 601, Paula's comment was directed to Christie, asking for her opinion about whether disclosing the information was appropriate in this encounter. Christie's interpretation, however, differed from the patient's original question and treated the provider as the targeted audience. Christie also deferred Paula's concern (i.e., the appropriateness of the information) to the provider. Finally, when Heather provided an answer to Christie's question ("If you need to know the name of the disease?" in the form of a *conditional statement* ("If it's an inherited disease, yeah."), Christie interpreted it as *question* (i.e., "Is it inherited?"). By interpreting the provider's statement as a question, Christie projected Paula as the next turn speaker, directing the question to Paula. In Extract 006, from the speakers' perspective, the conversation was logical and orderly. Christie's communicative strategies effectively minimized her presence (i.e., the provider and the patient seemed to be talking directly to each other) while accomplishing the speakers' communicative goals (e.g., checking the appropriateness of information and obtaining details of a child's disease).

A similar example was also present in Extract 004. When the provider (Hank) asked Christie to congratulate the new mom, he first asked Christie, "Can you say congratulations in Chinese." This was not a question to check if Christie was a competent interpreter (because Hank did not pause for Christie to answer); rather, Hank was informing Christie about his communicative goal (i.e., to congratulate the new mom). In her interpretation, Christie eliminated Hank's comment that was directed to her (i.e., "Can you say congratulations in Chinese."). But she kept Hank's dramatic flair in the interpretation and *reformulated* the message to minimize her presence and to focus on Hank's communicative goal. In Extracts 004 and 006, the interpreters modified the message to create the illusion of a dyadic provider-patient interaction.

In addition to the verbal strategies, interpreters may also adopt specific nonverbal behaviors (e.g., positioning in medical encounter and eye contact) to reinforce the provider-patient relationship. In the participant observation data, the two interpreters I observed often positioned themselves in a way that the provider and the patient are closer to each other than to the interpreter. In addition, in all occasions that a provider pulled the curtain to perform a physical exam, the interpreters always stood outside of the curtain and provided interpretation to the speakers' verbal messages (i.e., becoming "the voice"). By managing their physical positioning, the interpreters highlighted the provider and the patient as the primary participants in the medical encounter. Several interpreters in the interviews explained how they use nonverbal behaviors to facilitate the provider-patient relationship:

SHERRY: What happens is when you stand here, the patient is going to look at you and you have to be doing this [looking down at the floor], "I'm the voice, just look at each other." So, if you stand behind the patient, then the patient can't [turn their head backward], and they look at the physician, and then they are looking at each other.

STELLA: Once I step into the examination room, the interpretation begins, I detach myself emotionally from many things that are going on there, and I look at the floor, and I look at the ceiling or something. And I make sure that they talk to each other. [...] I have to detach myself from it and make sure that I don't get involved in it. And I am just the voice. Without my opinion.

Interpreters' narratives of their conduit role suggest that a conduit role actually requires an interpreter to adopt specific communicative strategies that are more than a neutral transfer of information. Interpreters in this study utilize both verbal and nonverbal strategies to reinforce the provider-patient relationship. By manipulating linguistic features, the interpreters create the illusion of a dyadic interaction. By being silent when the primary speakers communicate directly with each other, the interpreter empowers the speakers to establish rapport and trust with each other. By avoiding eye contact or standing behind a speaker, the interpreters not only become less visible but also influence *others'* communicative behaviors, making them to communicate with each other directly (e.g., having eye contact). From this perspective, interpreters' understanding of the conduit role is not a non-thinking, robotic way of interpreting but includes specific strategies to accomplish the communicative goal of reinforcing the provider-patient relationship.

Interpreter Roles in Health Care Settings

It is important to note that interpreters play a variety of roles in health care settings. For example, researchers have observed interpreters acting as institutional gatekeeper (Davidson, 2000), co-diagnostician (Davidson, 2001; Hsieh, 2007), physician assistant (Bolden, 2000; Elderkin-Thompson, Silver, & Waitzkin, 2001), patient advocate (Haffner, 1992), and some variations of these roles (Hsieh, 2004b, 2006a, 2008). Cross Cultural Health Care Program (1999) proposed four roles (i.e., conduit, clarifier, cultural broker, and advocate) of medical interpreters (for a detailed review of roles, see Roat et al., 1997). CCHCP explained, "the 'appropriate' role for the interpreter is the least invasive role that will assure effective communication and care" (Roat et al., 1997, p. 18). In other words, all roles are legitimate and different situations may call for different roles. It is then interesting to find that the conduit role remains the most predominant role in the code of ethics for medical interpreters (Kaufert & Putsch, 1997; for a detailed discussion of the code of ethics, see Dysart-Gale, 2005) and the most explicitly and frequently claimed role by the interpreters of this study. The objective of this chapter is to examine how interpreters understand and enact the conduit role.

Interpreters as Active Participants

The current study supports earlier studies in finding that interpreters are actively involved in the process and content of provider and patient interactions. Past studies have used interpreters' non-conduit behaviors (e.g., acting as patient advocate or screening for illness-related information) as examples of their active involvement in provider-patient interactions (e.g., Davidson, 2000, 2002; Roy, 2000). In contrast, this study demonstrated that even when interpreters believed that they were assuming the neutral, faithful, and impartial role of a conduit, they still were active participants in the medical encounters. From this perspective, it is important not to simply categorize all deviations from the source texts as interpreters' errors because some of them may be motivated by specific communicative goals (e.g., reinforcing provider-patient relationship).

Interpreters in this study claimed the conduit role by utilizing metaphors (e.g., voices of others, robot, and bridge) that minimize their role in influencing the content and process of provider-patient interactions. However, an analysis of the strategies they employed to enact the role, it was evident that they were calculated and purposeful performances for specific goals. The conduit role enacted by the interpreters in this study is not the conduit proposed or prescribed in the code of ethics and the trainings for interpreters (i.e., a role that does not interfere with the process or content of communication). This is, in fact, an unexpected finding. The current study challenges the legitimacy of using this term to describe interpreters' performances for this role. Because interpreters' communicative strategies for this role have extended beyond a conduit model, it is necessary for researchers to use a new model to describe the role performances that reflects the communicative goals of (a) transferring complete information and (b) reinforcing provider-patient relationship. In other words, although interpreters in this study demonstrated their desire to accomplish the communicative *goals* of a conduit role, these goals were not accomplished through a conduit *role*.

Interpreters' performance of the two communicative goals emerged in this study reflects an institutional view of the values and norms of provider-patient interaction. Interpreters' communicative strategies reinforce the institutional objective to create the illusion of a dyadic interaction, promoting direct interactions between the provider and the patient (Roat et al., 1997; Hsieh, 2001) and empowering them to control the content and process of interactions. This institutional objective is embedded in interpreter training as well as the health care system's focus on the provider-patient relationship. In other words, the interpreters enact an invisible role that is motivated to enforce specific institutional objectives. For example, interpreters talked about verbal and nonverbal strategies used to empower their clients and reinforce the provider-patient relationship. They provide interpretation for both verbal and nonverbal information. They metacommunicate to encourage providers and patients to direct comments to each other and to look at each other. They stand behind a patient and look at the floor to avoid eye contact, both of which encourage primary speakers to interact directly with each other. Finally, interpreters even actively change the verbal messages to create direct conversations between the provider and patient. Despite the changes in translated utterances, interpreters utilizing these strategies should be considered to be assuming a conduit role because the changes were made for the purpose of reinforcing the provider-patient relationship. Researchers have noted that providers' verbal and nonverbal behaviors may influence patients' disclosure patterns (Duggan & Parrott, 2000; Robinson, 1998), treatment choices (Roter & Hall, 1992), and perception of providers' attention (Ruusuvuori, 2001). By forcing providers and patients to modify their verbal and nonverbal behaviors and creating the illusion of a dyadic interaction, interpreters may effectively influence speakers' communicative behaviors, perceptions about quality of care, and health outcomes.

Interpreters' manipulation of (or influence over) other speakers' communicative behaviors is a topic that rarely has been examined in past literature. Most studies have focused on interpreters' communicative interpreting strategies, examining whether their interpretation was problematic (e.g., Elderkin-Thompson et al., 2001) or how their interpretation has influenced the contexts or dynamics of the interpreter-mediated interaction (Roy, 2000). No studies, however, discussed how interpreters adopt specific strategies to *influence* other speakers' behaviors. The interpreters in this study have explicitly talked about their intention and strategies to change others speakers' behavior as a way to manage interpreter-mediated interaction. Influencing other speakers' communicative behaviors is not consistent with the interpreting style of a conduit model. Nevertheless, the interpreters still see themselves as conduits because these strategies focus on maximizing the speakers' role in the communicative process.

If a model that is the traditional model for training of interpreters fails to describe the practice of professional interpreters, we should no longer attribute the deviations from the conduit role as interpreters' mistakes or incompetence. Rather, we need to recognize the complex responsibilities and functions of interpreters and consider if the conduit model is realistic or even acceptable. In essence, the fundamental problem of putting emphasis on the conduit model forces researchers as well as interpreters to oversimplify their roles and the complexity of interpreting as a communicative activity.

From this perspective, it is important to reconsider the definition of interpreters' neutrality. In the conduit model, interpreters are taught to achieve neutrality by remaining passive, allowing the speakers to do the talking, thinking, negotiating, and even arguing. This approach aims to minimize an interpreter's presence in and influence over provider-patient interactions. Interpreters' neutrality is enacted through their impartiality (e.g., "I interpret everything."), invisibility (e.g., "I try to be faceless." or "I am the voice."), and the lack of personal opinions or judgment (e.g., "I don't think."). The conduit model assumes that an interpreter does not have any communicative goals or personal agenda. The interpreters in this study, however, suggested that they *do* have specific communicative goals (i.e., transferring complete information and reinforcing provider-patient relationship), which may motivate them to not only deviate from the speakers' original utterances but also to influence other speakers' communicative behaviors. For these interpreters, their neutrality is not maintained though the lack of (personal) agenda; rather, it is enacted through maximizing the speakers' access to all information, ensuring the speakers' control of the information exchanged, and reinforcing the primary relationship. All these strategies reflect the institutional views of provider-patient communication and interpreter-mediated interactions. In other words, although the interpreters remain neutral to the speakers during the communicative process, their strategies are not "neutral" in the sense that they carry specific agenda to accomplish an institutional view of interpreter-mediated medical encounters that is appropriate and effective.

Moving Beyond a Conduit Model: Interpreters as Bilingual Mediators

By recognizing interpreters as active participants, researchers have opportunities to move beyond a conduit model and explore the complexity of interpreting as a communicative activity coordinated between multiple parties. I am not suggesting that medical interpreters no longer need to pursue accuracy, neutrality, or faithfulness to the source text and other traditional criteria that have been valued in a conduit model. However, I believe that by conceptualizing interpreters as mediators (as opposed to conduits), researchers and interpreters can have a more solid and comprehensive foundation to further the theoretical development and practical guidelines for interpreter-mediated interactions.

Rather than claiming neutrality through passivity, I propose to use the *mediator* model to reconceptualize interpreters' role performances that aim to achieve neutrality, faithfulness, and impartiality. The mediator model adopts the values (i.e., impartiality and faithfulness) embodied in a conduit model and extends its theoretical basis to phenomena that cannot be explained by a conduit model (Payne, Kohler, Cangemi, & Fugua, 2000). The conceptualization of the roles of mediator emerged from the field of conflict resolution (McCorkle, 2005). Folberg and Taylor (1984) argued that mediators allow the participating parties to be self-empowered by taking the responsibility for the decision-making process. Mediators accomplish neutrality and impartiality through active and careful management of verbal and nonverbal strategies to manage the dynamics of participants as well as the content and process of interactions (Cobb & Rifkin, 1991; Jacobs, 2002; Payne et al., 2000). Although researchers still debate about the appropriate enactment of neutrality and impartiality for mediators, the mediator model highlights the human agents in the communicative process and situates the mediators as the skilled expert in facilitating the multi-party communication in which individuals may share competing or conflicting goals (McCorkle, 2005). Jacobs and Aakhus (2002, p. 200) concluded that a competent dispute mediator should have: "(1) the ability to choose which model to apply to any particular session and to any particular moment in the session and (2) the skills with which a mediator implements any particular model." A competent interpreter should also follow the same standards and practices of mediators.

Unlike dispute mediators, however, medical interpreters do not presume that the participating parties have conflicting goals. Nevertheless, it is not uncommon for providers and patients to have competing or conflicting objectives due to cultural differences and treatment preferences (Brashers, Goldsmith, & Hsieh, 2002). The challenge faced by interpreters is not resolving conflict for parties that are often at odds with each other, but rather they are being vigilant in identifying potential or hidden differences and needs of participating parties, which often emerge in the dynamic process of provider-patient interaction and are inferred rather than explicitly communicated (Tracy, 2004). As mediators, interpreters focus on facilitating the providers' and patients' common and collaborative goals of ensuring the quality and delivery of care. Once they identify the competing or conflicting goals of the participating parties, however, they need to actively manage the interaction through communicative strategies to ensure appropriate and effective communication.

The mediator model in medical interpreting has several key characteristics. First, it recognizes the values (e.g., faithfulness, neutrality, and accuracy) that are inherent in a conduit model (McCorkle, 2005). Second, it centers on the speakers' equal voice and presence in an interpreter-mediated activity (i.e., a focus on the human agent, as opposed to the text, in the communicative process). A mediator is an active but neutral participant (Jacobs, 2002). Although they actively intervene in the communicative process, their primary objective is to allow the speakers to be equally represented in the communicative process. Third, it provides an interpreter leverage to intervene in the communicative process (i.e., as an active but neutral co-participant in the provider-patient interaction; Payne et al., 2000). A mediator does not take sides but serves only to facilitate a conversation between the speakers. Although interpreters may adopt specific communicative strategies to influence the communicative process, their strategies are acceptable and appropriate provided that they do not side with the speakers and the speakers have equal access to and control over the information exchanged. Finally, it assumes that interpreters are skilled professionals who can make online and fair judgment to manage the communicative process (Jacobs & Aakhus, 2002). With the mediator model, interpreters find legitimate grounds to exercise their expertise as linguistic, cultural, and communicative experts. They are expected to shift between various role performances and adopt different strategies to ensure the appropriateness and effectiveness of provider-patient interactions.

A mediator model is consistent with the values and communicative goals of a conduit model, but also provides practical solutions to dilemmas faced by interpreters who wish to be neutral facilitators in medical encounters. For example, a conduit model does not expect an interpreter to interfere with the communicative process. An interpreter speaks after a speaker presented a comment; however, in everyday life, overlapping talk is not uncommon (e.g., arguments) and interpreters may feel frustrated because they are unable to listen to multiple individuals and interpret different comments at the same time. Nevertheless, a strict adherence to a conduit model does not provide them leeway to intervene the problematic situation. On the other hand, a mediator model allows an interpreter to intervene the communicative process so that the provider and the patient can effectively and equally voice their opinions. In these situations, a mediator model expects an interpreter to interrupt the interaction, providing suggestions of an effective process (e.g., an interpreter may say, "Please let me interpret the doctor's comment first and then I will tell the doctor about your concerns."). In a mediator model, interpreters' primary concern is to intervene the communicative process in a way that ensures the speakers' equal access to and control over information.

Another predicament faced by a conduit model is the conversations that take place in front of but do not include the primary speakers. For example, an additional participant in provider-patient interaction (e.g., a nurse or a family member) may challenge the assumptions of dyadic provider-patient communication (e.g., all conversations are between the provider and the patient and center on the patient's illness; Hsieh, 2006a). In these situations, the spoken utterances may not be directed to the primary speakers (i.e., the provider or the patient) who the interpreter serves or be relevant to the medical encounter. In addition, because an interpreter's service is not needed for these conversations to take place, the speakers usually talk to each other at a faster pace and do not leave time for the interpreter to interpret. These conversations, at times, may include private information (e.g., two providers discussing another patient's diagnosis or family members talking about issues unrelated to the illness) that the speakers may not want others to know. A conduit model requires an interpreter to relay everything, regardless the relevance of the information. An interpreter may feel awkward or unethical to interpret verbatim when he or she believes that it is privileged information (Hsieh, 2006a); nevertheless, a conduit model expects an interpreter to relay all information without making any personal judgment about the appropriateness or effectiveness of the information.

A mediator model, in contrast, allows an interpreter to actively evaluate the emergent interactions and take interventions to ensure that the communicative process is fair and unbiased. Interpreters do not need to try to squeeze in their interpretation when their services are not relevant or needed in the interaction. When an interpreter believes that the conversation took place is not relevant to the provider-patient interaction (i.e., the interaction is still fair and unbiased), he or she can just inform the speakers that the conversation is unrelated to the medical encounter, provide a brief summary of the context (e.g., "The doctors are talking about another patient."), and allow privileged information to remain private. These behaviors do not violate the faithfulness, impartiality, or neutrality the public expects from an interpreter; at the same time, they still ensure that both speakers are not marginalized and their voices and rights are protected in the communicative process. Whereas in a conduit model, transferring complete information means interpreting without evaluating whether the information is relevant to the speakers, in a mediator model, transferring complete information means that an interpreter make judgments about the best way to relay information so that the both speakers' control over the provider-patient interaction is secured and equitable.

Finally, a mediator model does not presume that other speakers are familiar with the communicative process of interpreter-mediated activities. For example, most speakers are layperson who may not be aware of or have problems to understand the code of ethics or the specific communicative styles that interpreters are required to follow. As a result, unlike interpreters who are trained to adopt specific frames (e.g., interpreters as nonpersons), a layperson may not know that they should address another speaker directly and should not interact with the interpreter. A strict adherence to a conduit model, however, requires an interpreter to provide a verbatim relay of a provider's third-person comment (e.g., "Ask him if it hurts;" a communicative norm in multiple-party interactions), which would simply confuse the patient (i.e., because in this case "him" is the patient; Hsieh, 2006a). A mediator model allows an interpreter to actively evaluate the speakers' communicative goals and to modify their strategies accordingly. In other words, in a mediator model, an interpreter can modify their verbal and nonverbal messages without feeling conflicted about violating their expected role.

In summary, whereas a conduit model focuses on the equivalence between the source and target texts, a mediator model emphasizes the interpreters' responsibility to maintain an equitable process of communication between the speakers. In a mediator model, interpreters are viewed as expert communicators who are capable of making effective judgment and active interventions to accomplish specific goals: (a) both speakers have equal access and control over information exchanged, (b) their roles and interpretations are neutral and faithful, and (c) the relationship between primary speakers is the focus of the interpreter-mediated interaction. A mediator model presents specific limits for interpreters' communicative strategies in the sense that it expects interpreters to be neutral and faithful throughout the communicative process. Interpreters' intervention or modification of information is acceptable only when these behaviors reinforces provider-patient relationships and ensures the equal voices and presentation of both speakers. A mediator model does not allow an interpreter to advocate for a speaker, to suppress a speaker's problematic behavior, or to interpret information selectively. In short, a mediator model does not give an interpreter unlimited freedom in intervening in provider-patient interactions; rather, it provides specific role expectations and communicative goals for interpreters to conduct bilingual provider-patient interactions that maximize the speakers' roles in the communicative process.

A mediator model is superior to the conduit model in prescribing and regulating interpreters' performances. A conduit model allows interpreters to claim authority and credibility for the services they provide by renouncing the active roles of interpreters in the communicative process; in contrast, a mediator model does so by recognizing interpreters' expertise. Whereas a conduit model treats deviation from the source texts as errors or exceptions, a mediator model provide researchers to examine the effectiveness and appropriateness of those deviations. In doing so, the research and health care community can explore the necessary trainings and guidelines that are critical for interpreters to accomplish the various role performances in health care settings. In addition, rather than demanding the blind trust from other speakers, a mediator model encourages the participants to be vigilant about the interpreters' communicative strategies, questioning and challenging the interpreters' performances as they see fit.

Conclusion

As trained experts, interpreters adopt and move between various roles to facilitate provider-patient interactions (Bolden, 2000; Davidson, 2001; Hsieh, 2004a). I want to emphasize that this chapter does not argue that bilingual mediator should be the only role that an interpreter can play; in fact, by being versatile in various roles (or role models), interpreters may best ensure the appropriateness and effectiveness of provider-patient interactions. The main objective of this chapter is to propose a new model (i.e., the mediator model) to replace the conduit model, a default role of medical interpreters. My goal is not to drastically modify the conduit model, but rather to provide a different way to conceptualize a specific role that often is placed on medical interpreters. As researchers have noticed the problems of a conduit model, the discrepancies of interpreters' practice and ideology, and the values of interpreters' active involvement in the communicative process, it is important to develop a model that not only explains interpreters' practices but also provides theoretical basis to guide their code of ethics, training programs, and everyday practice.

A mediator model views interpreters as neutral but active participants in provider-patient interactions. It allows interpreters to intervene in the communicative process, but also requires them to assume specific communicative goals (e.g., reinforcing provider-patient relationships and maximizing the speakers' role), which already are embedded in interpreters' training programs. Whereas a conduit model envisions a type of neutrality (i.e., an exact duplication of information and interactive contexts) that is impractical (if not impossible; see Hsieh, 2001), a mediator model challenges an interpreter to maintain a neutral position (or at least appearance) in the communicative process. Interpreters' ability to effectively, appropriately, and smoothly accomplish the communicative goals of a mediator role and to maintain a neutral position will significantly influence the quality of provider-patient communication and relationship.

Finally, researchers need to investigate the complexity of medical interpreters' practices and its corresponding consequences. In recent studies, researchers have explored possible factors for interpreters' non-conduit behaviors. Interpreters' non-conduit behaviors may reflect their effort to improve a patient's health literacy (Angelelli, 2004), to protect institutional resources (e.g., providers' time; Davidson, 2002), to reduce the cultural gap between the provider and the patient (Angelelli, 2004), to reconcile provider-patient conflicts (Hsieh, 2006a), and to ensure the quality of provider-patient interactions (Dysart-Gale, 2005, Metzger, 1999). As interpreters become active participants, however, they inevitably infringe on others' control over the medical encounter (Hsieh, 2006a, 2006b). Health care providers have gone through rigorous education and certification to validate their ability to solicit, screen, and evaluate medical-related information; in contrast, interpreters generally have minimum training in those skills. In fact, Flores and colleagues (2003) found that 63% of interpreting errors had potential clinical consequences. As researchers notice interpreters' active involvement in the communicative process, it is important to examine interpreters' ethics (e.g., Davidson, 2001) and explore the impacts of their communicative strategies (Hsieh, 2006a). In other words, although the recent findings of bilingual health communication highlight the importance of interpreters' role in provider-patient interactions, they also highlight the significance of developing ethical boundaries for interpreters to function effectively without compromising providers' authority and patients' autonomy.

References

Allen, J. E. (2000, November 6). Worlds and words apart: Inadequate interpreter services for non-English-speaking patients has medical experts and civil rights advocates concerned. *Los Angeles Times*, p. S1.

Angelelli, C. V. (2002). *Deconstructing the invisible interpreter: A critical study of the interpersonal role of the interpreter in a cross-cultural linguistic communicative event.* Doctoral dissertation, Stanford University, Stanford, CA. (ProQuest Digital Dissertation, AAT 3026766)

Angelelli, C. V. (2004). *Medical interpreting and cross-cultural communication.* Cambridge, England: Cambridge University Press.

Bakhtin, M. M. (1981). *The dialogic imagination: Four essays by M. M. Bakhtin* (M. Holquist & C. Emerson, Trans.). Austin: University of Texas Press.

Bolden, G. B. (2000). Toward understanding practices of medical interpreting: Interpreters' involvement in history taking. *Discourse Studies, 2,* 387–419.

Brashers, D. E., Goldsmith, D. J., & Hsieh, E. (2002). Information seeking and avoiding in health contexts. *Human Communication Research, 28,* 258–271.

Cobb, S., & Rifkin, J. (1991). Practice and paradox: Deconstructing neutrality in mediation. *Law and Social Inquiry, 16,* 35–62.

Cross Cultural Health Care Program. (1999). *Bridging the gap interpreter handbook* (Rev. ed.). Seattle, WA: Author.

David, R. A., & Rhee, M. (1998). The impact of language as a barrier to effective health care in an underserved urban Hispanic community. *Mount Sinai Journal of Medicine, 65,* 393–397.

Davidson, B. (2000). The interpreter as institutional gatekeeper: The social-linguistic role of interpreters in Spanish-English medical discourse. *Journal of Sociolinguistics, 4,* 379–405.

Davidson, B. (2001). Questions in cross-linguistic medical encounters: The role of the hospital interpreter. *Anthropological Quarterly, 74,* 170–178.

Davidson, B. (2002). A model for the construction of conversational common ground in interpreted discourse. *Journal of Pragmatics, 34,* 1273–1300.

Department of Health and Human Services. (2001, January 30). *Limited English Proficiency (LEP).* Washington, DC: Author. Retrieved November 7, 2005, from http://www.hhs.gov/ocr/lep/

Doty, M. M. (2003). *Hispanic patients' double burden: Lack of health insurance and limited English.* The Commonwealth Fund. Retrieved August 22, 2005, from http://www.cmwf.org/usr_doc/doty_hispanicdoubleburden_592.pdf

Duggan, A. P., & Parrott, R. L. (2000). Research note: Physicians' nonverbal rapport building and patients' talk about the subjective component of illness. *Human Communication Research, 27,* 299–311.

Dysart-Gale, D. (2005). Communication models, professionalization, and the work of medical interpreters. *Health Communication, 17,* 91–103.

Elderkin-Thompson, V., Silver, R. C., & Waitzkin, H. (2001). When nurses double as interpreters: A study of Spanish-speaking patients in a US primary care setting. *Social Science & Medicine, 52,* 1343–1358.

Flores, G. (2005). The impact of medical interpreter services on the quality of health care: a systematic review. *Medical Care Research & Review, 62,* 255–299.

Flores, G., Fuentes-Afflick, E., Barbot, O., Carter-Pokras, O., Claudio, L., Lara, M., et al. (2002). The health of Latino children: Urgent priorities, unanswered questions, and a research agenda. *Journal of American Medical Association, 288,* 82–90.

Flores, G., Laws, M. B., Mayo, S. J., Zuckerman, B., Abreu, M., Medina, L., et al. (2003). Errors in medical interpretation and their potential clinical consequences in pediatric encounters. *Pediatrics, 111,* 6–14.

Folberg, J., & Taylor, A. (1984). *Mediation: A comprehensive guide to resolving conflicts without litigation.* San Francisco: Jossey-Bass.

Georgakopoulou, A. (2002). Narrative and identity management: Discourse and social identities in a tale of tomorrow. *Research on Language and Social Interaction, 35,* 427–451.

Gerrish, K. (2001). The nature and effect of communication difficulties arising from interactions between district nurses and South Asian patients and their carers. *Journal of Advanced Nursing, 33,* 566–574.

Goffman, E. (1959). *The presentation of self in everyday life.* Garden City, NY: Doubleday.

Haffner, L. (1992). Translation is not enough: Interpreting in a medical setting. *Western Journal of Medicine, 157,* 255–259.

Hale, S. (1999). Interpreters' treatment of discourse markers in courtroom questions. *Forensic Linguistics, 6,* 57–82.

Hale, S., & Gibbons, J. (1999). Varying realities: Patterned changes in the interpreter's representation of courtroom and external realities. *Applied Linguistics, 20,* 203–220.

Hampers, L. C., Cha, S., Gutglass, D. J., Binns, H. J., & Krug, S. E. (1999). Language barriers and resource utilization in a pediatric emergency department. *Pediatrics, 103,* 1253–1256.

Hsieh, E. (2001, November). *To be or not to be: Discrepancies between the ideology and the practice of interpreters.* Paper presented at the annual meeting of National Communication Association, Atlanta, GA.

Hsieh, E. (2002). Necessary changes in translation ideology. 翻譯學研究集刊 *Fan I Hsueh Yen Chiu Chi K'an* [Studies of Translation and Interpretation], *7,* 399–435.

Hsieh, E. (2004a). *Bilingual health communication and medical interpreters: Managing role performances and communicative goals.* Doctoral dissertation, University of Illinois at Urbana-Champaign. (ProQuest Digital Dissertation, AAT 3153318)

Hsieh, E. (2004b, November). *"I am not a robot!": Interpreters' Roles and Communicative Goals in Health Care Settings.* Paper presented at the annual meeting of National Communication Association, Chicago.

Hsieh, E. (2006a). Conflicts in how interpreters manage their roles in provider-patient interactions. *Social Science & Medicine, 62,* 721–730.

Hsieh, E. (2006b). Understanding medical interpreters: Reconceptualizing bilingual health communication. *Health Communication, 20,* 177–186.

Hsieh, E. (2007). Medical interpreters as co-diagnosticians: Overlapping roles and services between providers and interpreters. *Social Science & Medicine, 64,* 924–937.

Hsieh, E. (2008). "I am not a robot!" Interpreters' views of their roles in health care settings. *Qualitative Health Research, 18,* 1367–1383.

Jacobs, S. (2002). Maintaining neutrality in dispute mediation: Managing disagreement while managing not to disagree. *Journal of Pragmatics, 34,* 1403–1426.

Jacobs, S., & Aakhus, M. (2002). What mediators do with words: Implementing three models of rational discussion in dispute mediation. *Conflict Resolution Quarterly,* *20,* 177–203.

Jones, D., & Gill, P. (1998). Breaking down language barriers. The NHS needs to provide accessible interpreting services for all. *British Medical Journal, 316,* 1476.

Kaufert, J. M., & Putsch, R. W. (1997). Communication through interpreters in health-care: Ethical dilemmas arising from differences in class, culture, language, and power. *The Journal of Clinical Ethics, 8,* 71–87.

McCorkle, S. (2005). The murky world of mediation ethics: Neutrality, impartiality, and conflict of interest in state codes of conduct. *Conflict Resolution Quarterly, 23,* 165–183.

Metzger, M. (1999). *Sign language interpreting: Deconstructing the myth of neutrality.* Washington, DC: Gallaudet University Press.

Miller, P. J., Hengst, J., Alexander, K., & Sperry, L. L. (2000). Versions of personal storytelling/versions of experience: Genres as tools for creating alternate realities. In K. S. Rosengren & C. N. Johnson (Eds.), *Imagining the impossible: Magical, scientific, and religious thinking in children* (pp. 212–246). New York: Cambridge University Press.

National Council on Interpreting in Health Care. (2004). A National Code of Ethics for Interpreters in Health Care. Retrieved March 28, 2007, from http://www.ncihc. org/NCIHC_PDF/NationalCodeofEthicsforInterpretersinHealthCare.pdf

National Council on Interpreting in Health Care. (2005). National Standards of Practices. Retrieved March 28, 2007, from http://www.ncihc.org/NCIHC_PDF/ National_Standards_of_Practice_for_Interpreters_in_Health_Care.pdf

Payne, K., Kohler, P., Cangemi, J. P., & Fugua, H., Jr. (2000). Communication and strategies in the mediation of disputes. *Journal of Collective Negotiation, 29,* 29–47.

Roat, C. E., Putsch, R., & Lucero, C. (1997). *Bridging the gap over phone: A basic training for telephone interpreters serving medical settings.* Seattle, WA: Cross Cultural Health Care Program.

Robinson, J. D. (1998). Getting down to business: Talk, gaze and body orientation during openings of doctor-patient consultations. *Human Communication Research, 25,* 97–123.

Rosenberg, B. A. (2001). *Describing the nature of interpreter-mediated doctor-patient communication: A quantitative discourse analysis of community interpreting.* Doctoral dissertation, University of Texas at Austin. (ProQuest Digital Dissertations, AAT 3008433)

Roter, D. L., & Hall, J. A. (1992). *Doctors talking with patients/patients talking with doctors: Improving communication in medical visits.* Westport, CT: Auburn.

Roy, C. B. (2000). *Interpreting as a discourse process.* New York: Oxford University Press.

Ruusuvuori, J. (2001). Looking means listening: Coordinating displays of engagement in doctor-patient interaction. *Social Science & Medicine, 52,* 1093–1108.

Sarver, J., & Baker, D. W. (2000). Effect of language barriers on follow-up appointments after an emergency department visit. *Journal of General Internal Medicine, 15,* 256–264.

Shannon, C., & Weaver, W. (1963). *The mathematical theory of communication.* Urbana: University of Illinois Press. (Original work published 1949)

Strauss, A., & Corbin, J. (1998). *Basics of qualitative research: Techniques and procedures for developing grounded theory* (2nd ed.). Thousand Oaks, CA: Sage.

Tracy, K. (2004). *Everyday talk: Building and reflecting identities.* New York: Guilford.

Waxman, M. A., & Levitt, M. A. (2000). Are diagnostic testing and admission rates higher in non-English-speaking versus English-speaking patients in the emergency department? *Annals of Emergency Medicine, 36,* 456–461.

Woloshin, S., Schwartz, L. M., Katz, S. J., & Welch, H. G. (1997). Is language a barrier to the use of preventive services? *Journal of General Internal Medicine, 12,* 472–477.

Chapter 7

Negotiating the Legitimacy of Medical Problems
A Multiphase Concern for Patients and Physicians

John Heritage

In this chapter, I explore a theme that often emerges in the context of patient problem presentation, but that also surfaces elsewhere in the medical visit. This is the theme of legitimacy: Specifically, the idea that the patient's visit to seek medical care should be properly motivated by an appropriate medical problem. From the physician's perspective, this theme is summed up in a rather hard-nosed fashion by the New Zealand primary care physician who observed that "In order to have the privilege of talking to your doctor, you must fulfil the essential precondition of being sick. Then you may go to him and ask him if he will perform his professional services upon you" (Byrne & Long, 1976, p. 20). At the societal level, this theme is enshrined in everyday language that contains numerous terms for patients who inappropriately seek medical care: hypochondriac, malingerer, crock, and so on, and the pathological disposition to do so (as manifested in Munchausen's Syndrome) is itself treated as a medical condition. And it is also present in contemporary popular culture. A recent cartoon in the *New Yorker* magazine depicts a nurse entering a crowded waiting room and saying, "We're running a little behind, so I'd like each of you to ask yourself 'Am I really that sick, or would I just be wasting the doctor's valuable time.'" (*New Yorker*, May 14, 2001). And this concern helps to explain the peculiar conflict we sometimes experience when we go to the doctor: we want to be told that we are well, but we also would like to have had 'good reasons' for wrongly believing that we were not. As another *New Yorker* cartoon, depicting the delivery of a diagnosis, caricatures the concern: "You're not ill yet, Mr. Blendell, but you've got potential" (*New Yorker*, September 11, 1998).

These common sense normative orientations have been systematized by social scientists. In his classic formulation of the "sick role," Parsons (1951, pp. 436–439) observed that persons entering the sick role are entitled to some exemption from normal social tasks but that, correspondingly, they have the obligation to view being sick as undesirable and to resist any temptation to take advantage of the "secondary gains" of the sick role in the form of economic, social, and emotional support. It is this latter set of obligations, of course, that inform the morally loaded terminology and orientations sketched above.

By the very act of making the appointment and walking into the physician's office, patients commit themselves to two interrelated premises. They assert (a) the existence of a concern or problem that they lack the knowledge, skill, or other forms of expertise to manage on their own, and (b) project the concern or problem as one that is properly handled through the exercise of medical expertise. Given this commitment, a significant part of the patient's project during the visit can concern the justification of the visit itself. In providing for their decision to seek medical assistance, patients may find themselves designing their descriptions of events, experiences and circumstances so as to communicate "good reasons" that will justify them being in the physician's office.

Thus, from the outset of the medical visit, patients can face a *doctorability issue*. For patients, a doctorable problem is one that is "worthy of medical attention, worthy of evaluation as a potentially significant medical condition, and worthy of advice and, where necessary, medical treatment" (Heritage & Robinson, 2006, p. 58). Establishing that they have a doctorable problem is a method of justifying the decision to visit a physician. It is a means for patients to show that they are reasonable people, which in this context means showing that they have a problem or a concern for which seeking medical assistance is a reasonable solution. The presentation of a complaint determined to be nondoctorable can deprive the patient of authoritative medical support for their claim to financial and other benefits from entering the "sick role" (Freidson, 1970; Parsons, 1951, 1975), and engender a vulnerability to the judgment that they were misguided in seeking medical assistance, are over-concerned about their own or their children's health, or in illegitimate search of "secondary gains" from the sick role itself. Patients' concerns with doctorability thus center on showing that they are reasonable people, with "good reasons" to present themselves at the doctor's office. Providing for that reasonableness effectively converges with providing for the doctorability of the concern that they present.

Although patients may vary in the extent to which they feel obligated to legitimate a medical visit, and, of course, many conditions—for example, accidental injuries—scarcely require elaborate justification, patients who present with the normal run of primary care complaints frequently manifest a concern with the legitimation of the visit. In the remainder of this chapter, I will illustrate the emergence of this issue in the context of (a) problem presentation, (b) (verbal) history taking and physical examination, and (c) the diagnosis and counseling phase of the medical visit. My objective is to show that the problem of legitimacy is indeed a multiphase concern.

Problem Presentation

Let me illustrate this claim with a case in which the patient's concern with the doctorability of her problem is unmistakable. This patient has previously been treated for a small basal cell carcinoma on the back of her neck, and she has recently discovered a suspicious raised spot (or "mole" (line 7)) at, or close to, to the place where she was previously treated. If this discovery represents a recurrence of the earlier condition, the patient's situation may be quite dangerous:

```
(1) [Heritage and Robinson, 2006]
 1  Pat:    (I'm here on fal[se pre- pretenses.)<I think.
 2  Doc:                   ['hh
 3  Doc:    [<Yes.
 4  Pat:    [ehh! hih heh heh heh!
 5          ((Five lines omitted))
 6  Pat:    I asked my husband yesterday 'cause I could feel: (0.8) (cause)
 7           I: could feel this li'l mo:le coming. An:d: uh (0.5) (he) (.) I:
 8          hh thought I better letchya know-<uh well I asked my husband 'f
 9          it was in the same place you took off thuh (0.5)  °thee (mm)
10          thee:°( [                   )
11  Doc:             [That's why you've come in be[cause of the mo:le.
12  Pat:                                          [that's why I ca:me, but=
13  Doc:    =H[ow long 'as it been-]
14  Pat:      [t h i s  m o r ning-] I: I didn' I hadn't looked yesterday
15          he said it was in the same place but 'hh but I: can feel it
16          nah- it's down here an' the other one was up here so I don't
17          think it's: th'same one at a:ll.
18  Doc:    Since when.
19          (0.8)
20  Pat     Y(h)ea(h)h I(h) just felt it yesterday 'n
21  Doc:    Does it hurt?
22  Pat:    No?
23          (.)
24  Pat:    No it's just a li:ttle ti:ny thing bu:t=I (.) figured I
25          sh(h)ou(h)ld l(h)et y(h)ou kn(h)ow .hhh i(h)f i(h)t was (on)
26          the same pla:ce, b't
27  Doc:    So when you push [on it it doesn't hur[t.
28  Pat:                     [(Right.)            [No it's
29  Pat:    just a little- li:ttle tiny skin: [(tag) really.
30  Doc:                                      [I: (.) see=
31  Doc:    =Yeah it's different than whatchu had be[fore.
32  Pat:                                            [Uh huh.
33  Doc:    Your scar is up here,
34  Pat:    Yeah that'[s what I figured (an-)
35  Doc:             [An'
36  Doc:    An' this is down below.
37  Pat:    hh When he s- When he told me it was in the same place I
38          thought Uh: Oh: I better ca:ll a(h)nd te(h)ll yo(h)u .hhh
39  Doc:    Ri:ght.
40          (.)
41  Doc:    That's- I'm <ve:ry gla:d that you uh> did that.
```

A number of aspects of this patient's problem presentation exhibit a concern with the doctorability of her complaint:

1. In the headline of the narrative (line 1), she explicitly expresses some doubts that her complaint is doctorable and that her visit is justified. At most, the patient presents her problem as a possible problem.

2. She constructs her reason for the visit as a *narrative* and projects that narrative with an abstract or headline at line 1. Narrative is a device that can permit speakers to retain relatively strong control over the content and trajectory of their talk (Sacks, 1974). It provides the narrator with control over the content of their complaint and context in which it will be heard, and for this reason is often used in preference to submitting to questioning when persons are obliged to justify a need for service (Whalen & Zimmerman, 1990; Zimmerman 1992).

3. At lines 6, 8, 15, and 37, the patient invokes her husband, a third party, to bolster the validity of her decision to come to the physician with her problem, in effect co-implicating him in the decision to make the visit. At the same time, she disaffiliates (lines 15–17) from the judgment that she reports him as having made about as to the positioning of the "mole" that is worrying her.

4. When the physician starts to question her at line 11/13, she responds to him briefly in overlap, and then continues on with her narrative, refusing to concede to the interruption to the account-in-progress. It is unusual for a patient to compete in overlap with a physician, and to resist responding to a course of questioning that a physician initiates during the problem presentation (Beckman & Frankel, 1984). In this case, the patient competes with the physician specifically to express her doubts about the doctorability of her condition.

5. When the patient, at line 25, reports making her decision to come in for the visit, she inflects her talk at exactly that place with "breathy" laugh particles. Speakers have the capacity to do this very precisely (Jefferson, 1985), and the injection of laugh particles into talk is often associated with the reporting of "misdeeds" of some kind (Jefferson, Sacks, & Schegloff, 1987), especially in medical consultations (Haakana, 2001).

Up to this point in the patient's account, we have considered the issue of doctorability as a prospective one that can dominate the problem presentation phase of the consultation. Although this issue is particularly apparent during problem presentation, it can also resurface at later moments during the consultation. This is also shown in this datum. The patient's preoccupation with doctorability continues after the physician's evaluation at line 31, "Yeah it's different than whatchu had before." In particular:

6. The patient, who has positioned herself as skeptical about the nature of the problem prior to the physician's "no problem" evaluation, exhibits agreement with that evaluation (line 34).

7. Then, in redescribing the basis of her decision to come in for the consultation, the patient reinvokes her husband's judgment, and again infiltrates her report of the decision to make the appointment with laugh particles (lines 37–38).

8. The patient's redescription of the rationale for her decision has the effect of inviting the physician to offer reassurance as to the legitimacy of her decision to seek medical assistance, and he does so at line 41, by saying "That's- I'm <ve:ry gla:d that you uh> did that.".

Although, in this case, the patient's preoccupation with justifying the visit is clearly and vividly present, the same concerns emerge in more routine problem presentations. For example, routine upper respiratory ailments are often presented as being accompanied by symptoms that offer special justification for the medical visit:

(2) [Cold]
```
 1  Doc:          What can I do for you,
 2  Pat:          It's just- I wouldn' normally come with a cold,=but I
 3                'ad this: co::ld. (0.4) fer about.hh >m's been< on
 4                (Fri:day).=I keep coughin' up green all the time?
```

(3) [Flu - Expanded]
```
 1  Doc:          What's been goin' o:n?
 2  Pat:          I just got (0.4) chest cold a:nd it's been uh
 3                goin' on for a week- I don't seem to be able to
 4                [shake it-
 5  Doc:          [O:kay
 6  Pat:   →      And uh what caused me to call is uh 'bout fourth
 7         →      or fifth day in a row in thuh mornin- [I was
 8  Doc:                                                 [Mm hm
 9  Pat:   →      tryin' to get the engine started-
10  Doc:          Mm hm
11  Pat:   →      Coughin' up a buncha green stuff.
12  Doc:          Oka:y.
13  Pat:          So,
14  Doc:          Oka:y .hh uh now have you had much in thuh way
15                of fevers or chills with this?
```

In both these cases, the patients refer to "green" stuff (purulent rhinorrhea) as a special symptom: the symptom implicitly justifies the visit because patients treat it as an index of bacterial infection for which an antimicrobial prescription is appropriate (Mainous, Zoorob, Oler, & Haynes, 1997; Stivers, 2002; Stivers, Mangione-Smith, Elliott, McDonald, & Heritage, 2003).

In other cases, the presentation of minor and potentially self-limiting symptoms is justified by past medical history:

(4) [Strep Throat]
```
 1  Doc:      .hh U:m: (2.0) what's been goin' o:n.
 2  Pat:      Ah just achiness sore throat, an' .h I jus' thought
 3      →     rather than wait, um (0.2) I just have seen up a
 4      →     predisposition t' pick up strep throat durin' the school
 5            year.=I teach kindergarten.=
 6  Doc:      =Oh you do.=
```

```
 7  Pat:        =So but thuh ↑school year hasn't [↑started yet,
 8  Doc:                                        [eh heh heh heh heh heh
 9              heh ((laughs)) [.hhh
10  Pat:                      [I jus' thought rather than wait, °I want
11              to stop in and check.°
```

Or by reference to the advice of third parties, as in (1) above and (5) below, especially if the third parties have some kind of "medical" connection (6):

```
(5) [Sore Throat]
 1  Doc:          So you're having a bad sore throat huh.
 2  Pat:     →    Yes:: um (.) a- a girl friend of mine kinda made me
 3          →    paranoid about it. =She said u:m (.) uh it could be
 4          →    strep throat but I've never had it before
 5               [so I have no idea what that is but um (.) I was just=
 6  Doc:          [Uh huh
 7  Pat:          =explaining to her that my throat's been hurtin' up.
```

```
(6) [Asthma-like Symptoms]
 1  Doc:          You went camping and now have some difficulty breathing,
 2               since the camping or something else?
 3  Pat:     →    Yeah actually a friend of mine is a pharmaceutical sales rep,
 4          →    and she noticed the way I've been talking?
 5  Doc:          Okay.
 6  Pat:          I've been like (.) (breathing in) and she thought maybe I was
 7               having some kinds of symp[toms.
 8  Doc:                                  [Okay.
```

In cases in which patients believe that their symptoms indicate a recurrence of a problem, they may risk self diagnosis as a short-cut to legitimacy:

```
(7) [UTI]
 1  Doc:     →    How do you do.<
 2               (0.9)
 3  Pat:          I got a 'U' 'T' 'I',
 4               (0.2)
 5  Pat:          I think,
 6  Doc:          Uhh huh ((laugh)) £Okay look. that makes
 7               my job easy,£ y(h)ou've a(h)lr(h)ead(h)y
 8               d(h)i(h)ag[n(h)osed (h)it.
 9  Pat:                    [I know.
10  Doc:          hhh £Okay.£ .hh £have a seat over here.£
```

More complex still are narrative problem presentations that are predominantly occupied with displays of "troubles resistance" (Halkowski, 2006; Heritage & Robinson, 2006; Jefferson, 1988) in which patients are concerned to show that they attempted to manage their medical problem by watchful waiting or self-medication, and/or to document that the problem is outside their previous experience. In (8) below, the patient's struggle to explain his medical problem illustrates both of these elements:

(8) [Ringworm]
```
 1  Doc:   Yeah=I was lookin' through your chart before I
 2          came in looks [like you've been a pretty]
 3  Pat:                 [      <Oh yeah>      ]
 4  Doc:   healthy g□u:y.□
 5  Pat:   (I've)- (.) pretty healthy, as far as I'm aware
 6          of. ( [          ) ]
 7  Doc:          [□Goo:d.□] Good [for you:.]
 8  Pat:                         [Uh:    ]
 9  Doc:   What happened.
10          (.)
11  Pat:   Oh I got_ (.) what I thought_ (.) in Ju:ne (.)
12          uh was an insect bite.=in thuh back of my neck
13          here.
14  Doc:   Okay,
15  Pat:   An' I (0.2) you know became aware of it 'cause
16          it was itching an'=I (.) scratched that,
17          (0.2)
18  Pat:   An' it persisted fer a bit so I tried calamine
19          lotion,=
20  Doc:   =Okay,
21          (0.2)
22  Pat:   An' that didn't seem to make it go away
23          completely, an' it=s:tayed with me,=w'll its
24          still with me. Thuh long and thuh short of it.
25  Doc:   [Okay.      ]
26  Pat:   [Cut to thuh] chase is its- its still with
27          me, (0.3) but (its) got a welt associated
28          °with it.°
29  Doc:   Okay,
30          (0.5)
31  Pat:   Its got a welt that's (.) no:w increased in
32          size to about that big=it was very (.) small
33          [like a di:me] initially you know, an' now
34  Doc:   [Okay,      ]
35  Pat:   its (0.3) like a (.) bigger than a half do:llar
36          (I bet [it's like-)] [(        )-]
37  Doc:          [   So you] [said it's] no: longer
38          itchy. Is [that correct,]
39  Pat:             [O c c a:      ]sionally.
```

Here, the patient depicts an initial noticing of the problem about 10 weeks prior to this visit (line 11), depicts his becoming aware of it as the product of an entirely normal experience (Halkowski, 2006), and offers a routine and benign self-diagnosis as his first interpretation (Jefferson, 2004) of its cause (lines 11–12). Subsequently, he describes the persistence of the symptoms and his unavailing efforts at self-medication (lines 18–19, 22–24) and, bringing the time-line of the narrative into the here-and-now of the visit, he depicts his current symptoms as increasing in extent (lines 31–33, 35–36), and prominence (a "welt"—line 31). In all of these ways, the patient portrays himself as someone

(a) who would not ordinarily come to the doctor's office for no reason, and (b) who is suffering from escalating and unexplained symptoms. It may be added that the presentation of difficulties in interpreting symptoms opens up a second line of justification for medical visits—counseling for benign but unknown conditions. Thus, actual treatment is not required for the visit to be legitimated.

An overwhelming majority of problem presentations are built towards, and conclude with, the description of current symptoms (Robinson & Heritage, 2005). There is ample evidence that the presentation of current symptoms is designed to be the proximal point at which medical investigation begins and thus the point of transition into (usually verbal) history taking. If developing their concern as a doctorable problem is a primary task for many patients during the reason for the visit phase of the consultation, that task becomes somewhat less pressing after the doctor asks the first history-taking question. At that point, the patient's concern becomes "medicalized" by being reconstructed within a course of questioning that embodies a medical frame of reference. With the first-history taking question, the patient ceases to build the case for their concern alone and becomes a party to the co-construction of their concern as a medical problem. Thus, the first history-taking question provisionally validates the patient's belief that the concern is worthy of medical attention. The reason for the visit phase is occupied with a progression towards that bargain, at which point patients can surrender their control of the encounter in exchange for the medical questioning that prospectively underwrites the doctorability of their problems.

Although the validation of the medical visit as legitimate is ordinarily implied by a first history-taking question, it is important to underscore that this validation is provisional only. New information may emerge in the history that undermines the legitimacy of the concern, and the concern may be perceivably or actually delegitimated by diagnoses and counseling which do not match the patient's level of expressed concern. It is to these themes that we now turn.

History Taking and Physical Examination

Although history taking is ordinarily occupied with the co-constructive elaboration of patient symptoms into medical signs, the provisional validation of the patient's problem as legitimate can nonetheless remain problematic. As many have documented, history taking that is driven by differential diagnostic goals tends to be constructed using yes/no questions. The construction of these questions unavoidably involves setting agendas, and will also embody communicated presuppositions and expectations about the patient's circumstances and concerns (Boyd & Heritage, 2006; Mishler, 1984). Thus, as Cassell (1985, p. 4) observed, "'taking a history' is unavoidably and actually an *exchange* of information."

This is particularly apparent when we consider that the design of yes/no questions, as social survey methodologists know only too well, must perforce incorporate indications of the likelihood or desirability of responses (Boyd & Heritage, 2006; Heritage, 2002; Stivers & Heritage, 2001). For example, though some of the questions in the following example from a comprehensive history invite "yes" responses (lines 1 and 9) and some "no" (line 5), all of them are designed for, anticipate, and convey an expectation in favor of "optimized" or "no problem" responses:

(9) [History Taking]
```
 1  Doc:   → Are your bowel movements normal?
 2             (4.0)   ((patient nods))
 3  Pat:      °(Yeah.)°
 4             (7.0)
 5  Doc:   → Tlk Any ulcers?
 6             (0.5)   ((patient shakes head))
 7  Pat:      (Mh) no,
 8             (2.5)
 8  Doc:   → Tl You have your gall bladder?
 9             (2.0)
10  Pat:      I think so. uh huh=hh
```

Acute care histories are not exempt from this process. In the following pediatric case, the mother has presented her child's symptoms in terms of diarrhea and vomiting:

(10) [History Taking]
```
 1  Doc:    So it's (.) four da:ys? isn't i[t?
 2  Mom:                                   [yeah.
 3           (0.7)
 4  Doc:    mtch.='hhh o:ka:y
 5           (.)
 6  Doc:  → A::nd (.) no blood with the diarrhea.
 7  Mom:    No.
 8  Doc:    (Just water[ ).
 9  Mom:               [(                    ).
10           (1.0)
11  Doc:    How many times a da:y?
```

The physician's question at line 1 confirms the total period that the child has been experiencing symptoms, but her subsequent question at line 6—"A::nd (.) no blood with the diarrhea." (and its "reversed" follow-up "Just water" at line 8)—convey that this is an unlikely (and more serious) symptom. In Cassell's formulation (1985), information has been "exchanged" here.

A more explicit case is the following:

(11) [Diarrhea and Vomiting]
```
 1  Doc:  → 'hh What's she bringing up?<any[thing exciti°n-
 2  Mom:                                  [(like just)
```

```
 3  Mom:      [Just fluid rea[lly,
 4  Doc:      [ʰhh         [hhh  Just fluid.
 5  Mom:      [Nothing now. I don[ʾ- obviously I don't know what it was=
 6  Doc:      [Nuh-              [ʰhh
 7  Mom:      =earlier on,  I wasn't her[e, you know,=
 8  Doc:                               [ʰhhʾhh
 9  Doc:   →  =Right, but the: th I mean- n:othing nasty no blood er
10          →  anything ʾhh and the diarrhea: you say is quite (0.9)
11  Mom:      Very strong, yea[h.
12  Doc:                      [Smelly.=What color is it.<is a hih![ʰhh
13  Mom:                                                          [A (.) a
14             white yuhh (0.4) yellowy
```

Here, the physician's question references the potential for the child to be vomiting something "exciting," but does so within the scope of the negative polar-
ity term "anything" which invites a negative response. His follow-up question
(lines 9 and 10) strongly indexes the seriousness of "blood" as a medical sign
while conveying his expectation that this is not the case.

Although these serious medical signs are addressed in optimized questions
that invite negative responses, questions addressed to core elements of the presenting concern embody what Stivers (2007) termed the principle of "problem
attentiveness:" They are built so as to invite the confirmation of expectable
medical signs. It is in this context that concerns with justifying the need for
medical attention can re-surface.

In the following case, a child is presenting with an upper respiratory condition. The physician's "problem attentive" question at line 1 is responded to
defensively by the mother:

```
(12)  [History Taking]
 1  Doc:   1→  Has he been coughing uh lot?
 2             (0.2)
 3  Mom:   2→  .hh Not uh lot.=h[h
 4  Doc:                        [Mkay:?,
 5  Mom:   3→  But it- it <sound:s:> deep.
 6             (1.0)
 7  Mom:   4→  An' with everything we heard on tee v(h)ee=hhhh
 8             £we got sca:re.£
 9  Doc:      Kay. (An fer i-) It sounds deep?
10             (.)
11  Mom:      Mm hm.
12  Doc:      Like uh barky cough?
```

Here, rather than responding to the question with a straight "no" (Raymond,
2003), the mother gives a qualified negative response and then offers an additional characterization of the cough that goes beyond the terms of the question (line 5). Subsequently, she proceeds to elaborate on her concern as based
on a television news report (which had described a case of meningitis in the
area).

Paul Drew (2006) described this activity as "defensive detailing." Here, the mother has called the physician outside normal surgery hours, again in connection with a likely upper respiratory condition:

```
(13) [History Taking]
 1  Doc:   →  Any problems with 'er breathing,=
 2  Doc:      =°(m[m,) n[o? no?
 3  Mom:   →       [No:, [no she's alright she's 'er eyes are very red.
 4         →  <'Er eyes are extremely bloodshot,
 5  Doc:      Mm hm,
 6  Mom:   →  U:m: a::nd she's su- sayin' ow! all the ti:me, ehm
 7            sort'u holdin' 'er stomach an' 'er head is very
 8            hot (an') 'er 'hhh like a back an' (uh) (uh) chest
 9            (an' uh)('hh[h)
10  Doc:                [Ri:gh[t,
11  Mom:   →                 [An' then she's (sit) dozy now,
```

Here, the mother responds in the negative to a "problem attentive" question, but then proceeds to describe a range of additional and unasked-for symptoms, including the state of the child's eyes, the child's communication of stomach pain, fever, and so on. Notwithstanding the truth of these descriptions, their "defensive" presentation in the aftermath of the mother's no-problem response to the question about the child's breathing appears designed to convey the symptomatic foundations of her concerns, and hence to bolster the legitimacy of her decision to make the call.

Similar issues can surface in the physical examination. In the following case, the child is presenting with pain in the left ear which the mother has characterized as an "infection"—a formulation that implicitly lobbies for antibiotic medication (Stivers, 2002; Stivers et al., 2003):

```
(14) [Physical Examination]
 1  Doc:      Which ear's hurting or are both of them hurting.
 2            (0.2)
 3  Pat:      Thuh left one,
 4  Doc:   →  °Okay.° This one looks perfect, .hh
 5  Mo?:      (U[h:.???)
 6  Doc:   →     [An:d thuh right one, also loo:ks, (0.2) even more
 7         →  perfect.
 8  Pa?:      (        )
 9  Doc:      Does it hurt when I move your ears like that?
10            (0.5)
11  Pat:      No:.
12  Doc:      No?,
13  Doc:      hh Do they hurt right now?
14            (2.0)
15  Pat:   →  Not right now but they were hurting this morning.
16  Doc:      They were hurting this morning?
17            (0.2)
18  Doc:      M[ka:y,
```

19 Mom: →   [(You've had uh-) sore throat pain?
20 Mom: (°Yes°)
21 Doc: → Let's check your throat.

During the child's ear examination, at lines 4 and 6–7, the physician engages in online commentary (Heritage & Stivers, 1999; Mangione-Smith, Stivers, Elliott, McDonald, & Heritage, 2003) that projects a negative finding on the child's presenting concern. At line 9, the physician resumes the verbal history in pursuit of ear symptoms, designing his questions to facilitate affirmative answers. The child's negative responses are delayed (note the silences at lines 10 and 14) and hearably reluctant, and her final response (line 15) is a defensive justification for the visit (and possibly for being away on a school day). At this point, the mother interjects with a further symptom that could be pursued, and the physician takes it up at line 21. Here, online commentary projecting a "no problem" diagnostic outcome that is in flat contradiction with the child's reported symptoms elicits responses from both the child and the mother that function to defend the legitimacy of the visit.

Diagnosis and Counseling

The diagnostic phase of the medical visit is arguably the phase in which the physician's authority as an expert on disease and its treatment is paramount (Byrne & Long, 1976; Heath, 1992; Heritage, 2005; Peräkylä, 1998, 2002, 2006; Stivers 2005a, 2005b, 2006); however even here a "no problem" evaluation can engender patient or parent resistance. For example, in (15) the physician's announcement of a viral diagnosis and recommendation for over the counter medication (lines 1–5) is followed by the father's defense of the decision to visit the clinic—a defense that invokes the child's mother (who is not present) as a key decision maker (lines 8–12):

(15) [Diagnosis/Counseling]
  1 Doc: → As you know they're viral infections, so there's
  2   → no point in any a- any ant- antibiotics.
  3   (0.5)
  4 Doc: → Simply control thuh cou:gh with .hh whatever
  5   → your favorite cough medicine is,
  6   (1.8)
  7 Doc: #hmg hmg#=h[h
  8 Dad: →   [That's what I figured. (0.5) it
  9   → was her mo:m who called. I said you got (tuh be
 10 Dad: → k(h)idd(h)ing)he's probably- .hh heard about:
 11   → couple hundred cases already=there's not much
 12   → he's gonna be able to do: so_

In the following case, the patient resists the physician's diagnosis on the grounds that the presenting symptoms only emerge at night (lines 6–11, 14–15):

(16) [Diagnosis/Counseling: Heath, 1992]
```
 1  Doc:        Well yer ches:t is:: (.) absolutely cle:ar: today::,
 2              (1.0)
 3  Doc:        which is helpful: (0.4) and your pulse is: (0.7)
 4               only eighty .thhhh (.) which is er:: (1.2) not so bad.
 5              (1.2)
 6  Pat:    →   (Right it's::) there:: night time (uh) (.) it's:: 'ts
 7          →   not clear there, I've got er::: (        ) (1.4) (       )
 8          →   (0.3) I've more or less gone to bed when it starts: on us:?
 9              (2.5)
10  Pat:    →   I wake all the way through the night without getting
11          →   any sleep (un open))
12              (0.5)
13  Doc:        Mm
14  Pat:    →   (I don't know what's fetchin it up) during the nights (.) but
15          →   it comes in at the nights.
```

And in (17), which is translated from Finnish, a diagnosis that minimizes the patient's problem is resisted with an alternative diagnostic suggestion (lines 9–11), which the physician takes up (lines 12–15):

(17) [Diagnosis/Counseling: Perakyla, 1998]
```
 1  Doc:        As [tapping on the vertebrae didn't cause any pain
 2              and there aren't (yet) any actual reflection symptoms
 3              in your legs it corresponds with a muscle h (.hhhh)
 4              complication so hhh it's [only whether hhh (0,4) you
 5                                       [((Dr lands on her chair.))
 6              have been exposed to a draught or has it otherwise=
 7  Pat:        =Right,
 8  Doc:        .Hh got irrita[ted,
 9  Pat:    →                 [It couldn't be from somewhere inside then
10          →   as it is a burning feeling there so it couldn't be
11          →   in the kidneys or somewhere (that p[ain,)
12  Doc:                                           [Have you
13              had any tr- (0.2) trouble with urinating.=
14              =a pa- need to urinate more frequently or
15              any pains when you urinate,
```

And in (18), the physician's (line 2) attempt to reassure a mother that her child's gastric symptoms are relatively non-serious ("Doesn't look like it's too significant,") attracts vigorous resistance:

(18) [Diagnosis/Counseling]
```
 1  Doc:        So it looks like she has an acute gastroenteritis:,
 2  Doc:        Doesn't look like it's too sig[nificant,
 3  Gir:                                      [(              )
 4  Mom:    →   °Okay: th-° .hh th- I was con[cerned cause uh-
 5  Doc:                                     [ (And expect 'er-).
 6  Mom:    →   Usually: if- she:- when she=if she vo:mits: she-
 7          →   (0.8) it- it doesn't last as long or as o:ften.
 8              (.)
```

```
 9  Mom:   → La[st night (was  -)
10  Doc:         [('ts-) jus- jus' uh few throw ups an' that's
11                  thee end of it. #Yeah [thee-#
12  Mom:   →                  [Yea:h_ Like I
13         → sa[y she was probably at least=h_
14  Doc:         [(It) was uh little u-
15  Mom:   → It was at least ten [ti:mes.
16  Doc:                       [(s- s-)
17  Mom:   → [more like: ten to twe:lve (yeah.)
18  Doc:   → [Sh #uh:#=yeah. well she had very significant=uh:
19         → (5.5) Significant  throw-up, but i:t=uh:
20  Mom:     [(Yeah [                    .)
21  Doc:   → [.hh  [there wasn't uh whole lot of bile in it so
22         → she's not obstru- I don't (wanta th=[say)
23  Mom:                                          [No.
24  Doc:   → .h[ likely be ob[structed □it_#
25  Mom:       [No.        [No it was just once that [I saw [that.
26  Doc:                                              [.mlh [Or: uh°.
27            (2.8)
28  Mom:     °But=uh:=h° (0.5)
29  Doc:   → Okay: every- An' everything checks out fi:ne,
```

Here, the mother invokes the unusual extent and frequency of her child's vomiting episodes (lines 4–7), together with the extreme nature of her child's symptoms the previous night (lines 12–13, 15–17) to rebut the physician's suggestion
and, in the process, to defend against the imputation that she has brought her
child to the physician's office for something that is not "too significant." In
turn, the physician defends his comment by reference to a much more serious
condition: gastro-intestinal obstruction (lines 18–24).

Finally, in the following case, the female patient has presented with a small
cyst-like growth on the back of her shoulder. The physician announces that
the growth is a "fatty tumor" (lines 1, 3), and reassures her that the growth is
benign (lines 9–10, 12–17), whereupon the patient invokes a third party as a
determining factor in her decision to make the appointment (lines 13–14, 16,
18):

```
(19) [Diagnosis/Counseling]
 1  Doc:   This is uh fatty tumor.
 2  Pat:   .hh Is that what it is?
 3  Doc:   (Right.) Uh little fatty tumor.
 4
 5         ...(7 lines omitted)
 6  Doc:   Nothing tuh worry about.
 7  Pat:   °Okay.°
 8  Doc:   Okay?
 9  Doc:   .hh They: .hh- (1.5) al:most never never (.) turn into
10         into cancer,
11  Pat:   °Mm hm,°
12  Doc:   And (0.2) they don't interfere with anything except if
13         they're so big #tha:t# (.) you can't lean on it or >ya know<
```

```
15                  if they're big. Mechanical[ly they cause uh problem.
16  Pat:                                [Oh okay.
17  Doc:     .hh But (in some sense) it's really nothing to worry about.
18        →  <It feels just like fat. An' that's what it [is.
19  Pat:    →                                            [Yeah:
20        →  th=somebody told me it might be that bu[t (they seh-)
21  Doc:                                            [>(a fatty tumor)<
22  Pat:    →  (they said tuh go) (0.5)
23  Doc:       (Yeah [w  )
24  Pat:    →        [(ya know/have it) check(ed).
25  Doc:     Right. That's what this is.
26  Pat:    →  .h I guess my concern was=('t)=since I had skin cancer
27        →  befo:re,
28  Doc:     Uh [huh,
29  Pat:    →     [they say you're at higher risk for getting: but it's in
30        →  uh strange place tuh be_=
31  Doc:     =Yeah >this is- .hh ya know< it feels like=h uh fatty tumor.
32  Pat:     Okay.
```

Subsequently, the patient reveals her underlying concern (lines 26–27, 29–30)—having previously had skin cancer, she was entertaining a cancer diagnosis as a possibility. Given that the physician has explicitly ruled out this possibility early in the diagnosis at lines 9–10, this later reinvocation of a cancer diagnosis, while attracting a further round of reassurance (data not shown), also serves to bolster the legitimacy of the visit as a whole as one in which getting the lump "checked" (line 24) is the sensible and appropriate thing to do.

Conclusion

This chapter has offered a range of examples in which a concern with the legitimacy of visiting the physician's office is more or less apparent at the surface of the medical conversation. This concern is most transparently visible during the problem presentation phase of the visit. Here, the presentation of symptoms is almost unavoidably intricated with justifying the appropriateness of the search for medical care. However, as subsequent examples have demonstrated, a concern with legitimacy can and does surface at later stages of the medical encounter. This concern emerges most prominently when lines of questioning, comments during the physical examination, and reassuring "no problem" diagnoses and counseling renew the patient's sense that the physician may not be treating the decision to visit the surgery as fully justified. At such moments, patients can find themselves engaging in descriptions and observations whose import is transparently defensive.

The observation that symptomatology and morality are intimately intertwined is not a surprising one. For many years social psychologists have recognized that a description of a state of affairs is simultaneously a presentation of self. Since Jefferson's (1980, 1984a, 1984b, 1988; Jefferson & Lee, 1992) work on troubles telling, we have known that the presentation of any personal problem is circumscribed by very tight forms of normative regulation. And, in the special normative context of medicine in which the presentation of problems is fully justified, the operation of this principle of social life is particularly interesting. However the fact that physician and patient alike are first and foremost members of our ordinary society and bound by the quotidian norms of everyday life means that facts and morals can never be entirely separated in the medical encounter, and that the evaluation of these facts in the course of differential diagnosis cannot be fully separated from the moral evaluation of the patient. This unavoidable intertwining of medical expertise with normative and moral considerations injects a significant source of complication into the practice of medicine.

References

Beckman, H., & Frankel, R. (1984). The effect of physician behavior on the collection of data. *Annals of Internal Medicine, 101*, 692–696.

Boyd, E., & Heritage, J. (2006). Taking the history: Questioning during comprehensive history taking. In J. Heritage & D. Maynard (Eds.), *Communication in medical care: Interactions between primary care physicians and patients* (pp. 151–184). Cambridge, England: Cambridge University Press.

Byrne, P. S., & Long, B. E. L. (1976). *Doctors talking to patients: A study of the verbal behaviours of doctors in the consultation.* London: Her Majesty's Stationary Office.

Cassell, E. (1985). *Talking with patients, Vol. 2: Clinical technique.* Cambridge, MA: MIT Press.

Drew, P. (2006). Mis-alignments in 'after-hours' calls to a British GP's practice: A study in telephone medicine. In J. Heritage & D. Maynard (Eds.), *Communication in medical care: Interactions between primary care physicians and patients* (pp. 416–444). Cambridge, England: Cambridge University Press.

Freidson, E. (1970). *Profession of medicine: A study of the sociology of applied knowledge.* Chicago: University of Chicago Press.

Haakana, M. (2001). Laughter as a patient's resource: Dealing with delicate aspects of medical interaction. *Text, 21*, 187–219.

Halkowski, T. (2006). Realizing the illness: patients' narratives of symptom discovery. In J. Heritage & D. Maynard (Eds.), *Communication in medical care: Interactions between primary care physicians and patients* (pp. 86–114). Cambridge, England: Cambridge University Press.

Heath, C. (1992). The delivery and reception of diagnosis and assessment in the general practice consultation. In P. Drew & J. Heritage (Eds.), *Talk at work: Social interaction in institutional settings* (pp. 235–267). Cambridge, England: Cambridge University Press.

Heritage, J. (2002). Ad hoc inquiries: Two preferences in the design of 'routine' questions in an open context. In D. Maynard, H. Houtkoop-Steenstra, N. K. Schaeffer, & H. van der Zouwen (Eds.), *Standardization and tacit knowledge: Interaction and practice in the survey interview* (pp. 313–333). New York: Wiley Interscience.

Heritage, J. (2005). Revisiting authority in physician-patient interaction. In D. Kovarsky & J. Duchan (Eds.), *Diagnosis as cultural practice* (pp. 83–102). New York: Mouton De Gruyter.

Heritage, J., & Robinson, J. (2006). Accounting for the visit: Patients' reasons for seeking medical care. In J. Heritage & D. Maynard (Eds.), *Communication in medical care: Interactions between primary care physicians and patients* (pp. 48–85). Cambridge, England: Cambridge University Press.

Heritage, J., & Stivers, T. (1999). Online commentary in acute medical visits: A method of shaping patient expectations. *Social Science & Medicine, 49,* 1501–1517.

Jefferson, G. (1980). On "trouble-premonitory" response to inquiry. *Sociological Inquiry, 50,* 153–185.

Jefferson, G. (1984a). On stepwise transition from talk about a trouble to inappropriately next-positioned matters. In J. M. Atkinson & J. Heritage (Eds.), *Structures of social action* (pp. 191–221). Cambridge, England: Cambridge University Press.

Jefferson, G. (1984b). On the organization of laughter in talk about troubles. In J. M. Atkinson & J. Heritage (Eds.), *Structures of social action* (pp. 346–369). Cambridge, England: Cambridge University Press.

Jefferson, G. (1985). An exercise in the transcription and analysis of laughter. In T. A. Dijk (Ed.), *Handbook of discourse analysis* (Vol. 3, pp. 25–34). New York: Academic Press.

Jefferson, G. (1988). On the sequential organization of troubles-talk in ordinary conversation. *Social Problems, 35,* 418–441.

Jefferson, G. (2004). "At first I thought": A normalizing device for extraordinary events. In G. Lerner (Ed.), *Conversation analysis: Studies from the first generation* (pp. 131–167). Amsterdam: John Benjamins.

Jefferson, G., & Lee, J. (1992). The rejection of advice: Managing the problematic convergence of a 'troubles-telling' and a 'service encounter'. In P. Drew & J. Heritage (Eds.), *Talk at work: Social interaction in institutional settings* (pp. 521–548). Cambridge, England Cambridge University Press.

Jefferson, G., Sacks, H., & Schegloff, E. A. (1987). Notes on laughter in the pursuit of intimacy. In G. Button & J. R. E. Lee (Eds.), *Talk and social organisation* (pp. 152–205). Clevedon, England: Multilingual Matters.

Mainous, A. G., Zoorob, R. J., Oler, M. J., & Haynes, D. M. (1997). Patient knowledge of upper respiratory infections: Implications for antibiotic expectations and unnecessary utilization. *The Journal of Family Practice, 45,* 75–83.

Mangione-Smith, R., Stivers, T., Elliott, M., McDonald, L., & Heritage, J. (2003). Online commentary during the physical examination: A communication tool for avoiding inappropriate prescribing? *Social Science & Medicine, 56,* 313–320.

Mishler, E. (1984). *The discourse of medicine: Dialectics of medical interviews.* Norwood NJ: Ablex.

Parsons, T. (1951). *The social system.* New York: Free Press.

Parsons, T. (1975). The sick role and the role of the physician reconsidered. *Milbank Memorial Fund Quarterly, 53,* 257–278.

Peräkylä, A. (1998). Authority and accountability: The delivery of diagnosis in primary health care. *Social Psychology Quarterly, 61,* 301–320.

Peräkylä, A. (2002). Agency and authority: Extended responses to diagnostic statements in primary care encounters. *Research on Language and Social Interaction, 35,* 219–247.

Peräkylä, A. (2006). Communicating and responding to diagnosis. In J. Heritage & D. Maynard (Eds.), *Communication in medical care: Interactions between primary care physicians and patients* (pp. 214–247). Cambridge, England: Cambridge University Press.

Raymond, G. (2003). Grammar and social organization: Yes/No interrogatives and the structure of responding. *American Sociological Review, 68*, 939–967.

Robinson, J., & Heritage, J. (2005). The structure of patients' presenting concerns: The completion relevance of current symptoms. *Social Science & Medicine, 61*, 481–493.

Sacks, H. (1974). An analysis of the course of a joke's telling in conversation. In R. Bauman & J. Sherzer (Eds.), *Explorations in the ethnography of speaking* (pp. 337–353). Cambridge, England: Cambridge University Press.

Stivers, T. (2002). Presenting the problem in pediatric encounters: "Symptoms only" versus "candidate diagnosis" presentations. *Health Communication, 14*, 299–338.

Stivers, T. (2005a). Non-antibiotic treatment recommendations: Delivery formats and implications for parent resistance. *Social Science & Medicine, 60*, 949–964.

Stivers, T. (2005b). Parent resistance to physicians' treatment recommendations: One resource for initiating a negotiation of the treatment decision. *Health Communication, 18*, 41–74.

Stivers, T. (2006). Treatment decisions: Negotiations between doctors and patients in acute care encounters. In J. Heritage & D. Maynard (Eds.), *Communication in medical care: Interactions between primary care physicians and patients* (pp. 279–312). Cambridge, England: Cambridge University Press.

Stivers, T. (2007). *Prescribing under pressure: Parent-physician conversations and antibiotics.* New York: Oxford University Press.

Stivers, T., & Heritage, J. (2001). Breaking the sequential mold: Answering "more than the question" during medical history taking. *Text, 21*, 151–185.

Stivers, T., Mangione-Smith, R., Elliott, M. N., McDonald, L., & Heritage, J. (2003). Why do physicians think parents expect antibiotics? What parents report vs. what physicians perceive. *The Journal of Family Practice, 52*, 140–148.

Whalen, M., & Zimmerman, D. (1990). Describing trouble: Practical epistemology in citizen calls to the police. *Language in Society, 19*, 465–492.

Zimmerman, D. (1992). The interactional organization of calls for emergency assistance. In P. Drew & J. Heritage (Eds.), *Talk at work: Social interaction in institutional settings* (pp. 418–469). Cambridge, England: Cambridge University Press.

Chapter 8

Keeping the Balance and Monitoring the Self-System

Towards a More Comprehensive Model of Medication Management in Psychiatry

Bruce L. Lambert, Naomi A. Levy, and Jerome Winer

> If his (Dr. Cabot's) patients wanted to talk diagnosis, he talked drugs. If they wanted to talk symptoms, he talked drugs. Stress? Drugs. Suffering? Drugs. Family problems? Drugs. Job? Drugs. (Basch, as cited in Shem, 1997, p. 299)

> Your little "talk therapy" is now a minor sub-specialty. A hundred twenty an hour tops. Chump change... Managed care and insurance won't pay for talk. They pay for drugs. (Cabot, as cited in Shem, 1997, p. 301)

> I was prepared to expose myself, but they didn't want to listen, only medicate. Take this and shut up, they said. (Johansson & Eklund, 2003, p. 343)

> I don't think very highly of psychiatrists ... I tolerate them because I have to take this medicine ... They've got a drug for everything ... they like to tinker with the body through these drugs rather than have people express what they're feeling. (Karp, 1996b, p. 85)

> There remains plenty of room for human misery after the drugs have been most skillfully applied. (Ostow, as cited in Goldhamer, 1983, p. 176)

> When medications take the place of relationships, not only do patients suffer the side effects of aggressive medication, but they lose the healing power of the relationship. (Luhrmann, as cited in Gabbard & Kay, 2001, pp. 1961–1962)

Beginning with the discovery of rauwolfia (i.e., reserpine) in 1931 and chlorpromzine in 1952, and accelerating during the 1960s, drug therapy has become an increasingly central part of psychiatric care (Cruz & Pincus, 2002; H. I. Kaplan & Sadock, 1998; Tasman, Riba, & Silk, 2000). In the last 10 years, however, several forces have converged to create a situation in which drug therapy is the dominant and, at times, the only type of treatment some chronically mentally ill patients receive (Kandel, 1998). The recent rise to prominence of drug therapy and brief medication management are part of a larger set of changes currently affecting the U.S. health care delivery system. The effects of these changes on cost and quality are poorly understood (Durham, 1998). However, there is reason to suspect that key patient, professional, and societal goals may not be achieved by drug therapy and brief medication management alone. For many patients, the quality of psychiatric care depends on the quality of drug therapy and medication management. It is, therefore, important to carefully consider some of the factors that may improve the quality of this type of care.

The purpose of this chapter is to contribute to the development of a model of psychiatric medication management that better reflects the needs, beliefs and preferences of both psychiatrists and people living with mental illness. We begin by reviewing the recent increase in psychiatric medication use during the last decade. Next, we review negative indicators that highlight challenges in the current practice of drug therapy and medication management within psychiatry, and we attempt to identify problems with existing models of medication management. We then sketch the outlines of a new perspective that is emerging around a more comprehensive model of medication management and review theories from several different intellectual traditions that converge on the idea that medication management must focus on the meanings of medication and medication effects, especially the manner in which these meanings affect a patient's ability to sustain a preferred identity and maintain a cohesive sense of self. The final section represents our initial effort to turn the conceptual model into a set of concrete suggestions for improving the practice of medication management. This section consists primarily of recommendations about how to communicate in medication management interviews.

This chapter is directed at several audiences. Our arguments are developed primarily in the context of psychiatry, but we believe they have much broader relevance. Practicing psychiatrists at all levels of training (i.e., residents and attendings) will be interested in the analysis of negative quality indicators in psychiatry, as well as in the specific ideas for improving the quality of medication management interviews with psychiatric patients. Non-physician therapists who provide treatment in conjunction with psychiatrists will be interested in the sections on the meanings of medication as they relate to identity and biography. Health communication researchers will be interested in symbolic interactionist accounts of health and illness and their implications for provider-patient interaction, especially in the context of medication management. Finally, health professionals involved in medication counseling, including pharmacists, nurses, and physicians from outside psychiatry, will be interested in the meaning and identity-centered analysis of medication adherence.

The Growth of Drug Therapy and Medication Management

This section reviews the evidence of recent growth in the use of drug therapy and brief medication management for psychiatric outpatients. With respect to the receipt of drug therapy generally, the National Ambulatory Medical Care Survey (NAMCS) indicates that the percentage of psychiatric outpatients receiving one or more medications has increased from 46% in 1985 to 71% in 1996 to 73% in 1997 (Olfson, 1992; Woodwell, 1997). In 1997, only cardiologists and family physicians prescribed drug therapy to a higher percentage of their patients (Woodwell, 1999). Drugs commonly used for mental illness accounted for roughly 11% of all drugs mentioned in outpatient visits during 1997 (Woodwell, 1999). Four of the 20 most frequently prescribed drugs in outpatient practice were for the treatment of depression and/or anxiety (Prozac®, Xanax®, Zoloft®, and Paxil®). These drugs alone accounted for 3% of all office-based prescriptions (Woodwell, 1999). By 2002, antidepressants were the second most frequently mentioned class of drugs in U.S. outpatient medical visits, trailing only non-steroidal anti-inflammatory drugs (e.g., ibuprofen; Woodwell & Cherry, 2004).

Medication management visits (defined as any visit of 20 minutes or less during which a medication was prescribed) increased from 6.7% of all visits in 1985 to 40.4% of visits in 1997 (Olfson, 1992; Woodwell, 1999). Olfson's recent analysis of trends in office-based psychiatric practice showed that, from 1985 to 1995, office visits "became shorter, less often included psychotherapy, and more often included a medication prescription" (Olfson, Marcus, & Pincus, 1999, p. 451). For the most common type of psychiatric visit, one related to depression, the use of drug therapy has increased dramatically in the last 10–15 years, and this increase has been more pronounced among psychiatrists than among other office-based physicians (Mechanic, McAlpine, & Rosenthal, 2001; Olfson et al., 1998; Pincus et al., 1998). The proportion of psychiatric outpatients receiving an antidepressant more than doubled in the period between 1985 and 1994, from 23% to nearly 49% (Olfson et al., 1998). More recent data confirm this trend. Between 1987 and 1997, the number of patients receiving outpatient treatment for depression increased, the proportion of treated patients receiving antidepressant medications doubled to 74.5%, and the proportion of patients receiving psychotherapy declined from 71% to 60% (Olfson, Marcus, Druss, Elinson, et al., 2002). During the same period, medication use by psychotherapy patients increased significantly, from 14.4% to 48.6% for antidepressants, from 5.3% to 14.5% for mood stabilizers, and from 1.9% to 6.4% for stimulants (Olfson, Marcus, Druss, & Pincus, 2002). These same patients also were increasingly likely to be receiving psychotherapy from physicians as opposed to psychologists or other non-physician mental health professionals.

Outcomes of Drug Therapy and Brief Medication Management: Negative Indicators

In spite of the successes of psychopharmacology, documented elsewhere (Schatzberg & Nemeroff, 1998), there is ample room to improve the quality and effectiveness of medication management in psychiatry (Gabbard & Kay, 2001; Lamberg, 2000; Medawar & Hardon, 2004; Tasman et al., 2000). Evidence takes the form of negative quality indicators, most notably in regard to poor adherence to medication regimens, poor rates of appointment keeping, and significant rates of patient and professional dissatisfaction. Clearly, not all problems in psychiatry are due to poor medication management, but the following section illustrates that there is room for quality improvement in this core area of psychiatric practice.

Medication Adherence

Poor adherence (i.e., noncompliance) with medical regimens is commonplace across all medical specialties (DiMatteo, Giordani, Lepper, & Croghan, 2002; Kravitz et al., 1993). It is not unique to drug therapy nor to psychiatry. What's more, low rates of adherence to drug therapy regimens are not solely the responsibility of health professionals, nor do they always reflect poor outcomes (e.g., some patients discontinue therapy because they feel better, though they may relapse later) (Demyttenaere, 1998; Demyttenaere et al., 2001). Nevertheless, in an optimal system of care, patients and providers should be able to agree on a therapy that patients can stick to (Chewning & Sleath, 1996; DiMatteo, Reiter, & Gambone, 1994). Even if they are not a perfect indicator of the quality of medication management, low adherence rates often represent evidence of the failure of treatment to achieve its desired effects. According to one review, "acceptance or rejection of prescribed pharmacological regimens is often the single most important determinant of these treatments' effectiveness" (Fenton, Blyler, & Heinssen, 1997, p. 637).

In psychiatry, adherence to drug therapy regimens is notoriously poor, regardless of the underlying illness. In a study of depressed patients, roughly half stopped taking the medication after 12 weeks (Maddox, Levi, & Thompson, 1994). Another study showed more than two thirds of patients had stopped drug therapy after 90 days (Demyttenaere, 1998). It should be noted that one common reason for stopping was that the patient felt better. Overall, Demyttenaere estimated 2–3 month adherence to antidepressant drug therapy at 25%–50% (Demyttenaere, 1998; Demyttenaere et al., 1998). Other reviews of noncompliance in depression report similar rates (Demyttenaere et al., 2001; E. M. Kaplan, 1997; Lin et al., 1995; Lingam & Scott, 2002; Pampallona, Bollini, Tibaldi, Kupelnick, & Munizza, 2002; Souery & Mendlewicz, 1998). The situation is no better among patients with schizophrenia, for whom median rates of noncompliance across a large number of studies range from 25% to

55% (Bebbington, 1995; Fenton et al., 1997; Olfson, Hansell, & Boyer, 1997; J. L. Young, Zonana, & Shepler, 1986; Zygmunt, Olfson, Boyer, & Mechanic, 2002). In a recent landmark study of the newest drugs for schizophrenia, 74% of patients had discontinued drug therapy within 18 months of initiating (Lieberman et al., 2005). Short- and long-term noncompliance rates of 50% have also been observed among people with bipolar disorder (i.e., manic depression; Hilty, Brady, & Hales, 1999; Johnson & McFarland, 1996; Keck et al., 1996; Lingam & Scott, 2002).

Thus, it is clear that poor adherence to prescribed drug therapy is a significant problem in the three most serious psychiatric illnesses. As a consequence of poor adherence, patients often suffer unnecessarily, relapse faster, and are rehospitalized sooner and more often than would be the case if adherence were improved (Fenton et al., 1997; Hilty et al., 1999; Kelly, Scott, & Mamon, 1990; Lingam & Scott, 2002; Olfson et al., 1997; Valenstein et al., 2002).

Appointment Keeping

Another (imperfect) indicator of quality and satisfaction is the extent to which patients keep scheduled appointments. Our assumption is that if patients feel safe, respected, cared for, and listened to, they will be more likely to keep scheduled appointments than if they are dissatisfied, alienated, or estranged from their doctor. Missed appointments are a problem across all medical specialties, but the problem seems especially acute in psychiatry, in which the rate of missed appointments may be twice as high as in other specialties (Killaspy, Banerjee, King, & Lloyd, 2000). Of course, dissatisfaction is not the only reason for missing an appointment. Demographics, diagnosis, chaotic lives, rapid recovery, homelessness, drug addiction, and lack of transportation also play a role. Nevertheless, missed appointments can be viewed as a negative quality indicator because an association has been found between appointment keeping and subsequent outcomes. For example, patients who miss appointments tend to be sicker and more likely to be readmitted to the hospital than those who do not miss appointments (Grunebaum et al., 1996; Killaspy et al., 2000; Matas, Staley, & Griffin, 1992; Nelson, Maruish, & Axler, 2000; Sparr, Moffitt, & Ward, 1993). Overall rates of missed appointments range from 10%–55% (Dotter & Labbate, 1998; Grunebaum et al., 1996; Matas et al., 1992; Pang, Lum, Ungvari, Wong, & Leung, 1996). Half of the patients referred by primary care providers failed to keep their psychiatric clinic appointment in another study (Grunebaum et al., 1996). The problem is not unique to the United States. In a 2-month study of outpatients in Hong Kong, 15.4% of all follow-up appointments were missed (Pang et al., 1996). In a 2- and one-half-year Canadian study, 17.8% of appointments were missed (Matas et al., 1992). Rates of missed appointments tend to be higher for medication checks than for psychotherapy, intake, or other types of appointments (Sparr et al., 1993).

Dissatisfaction

Patient   Although levels of patient satisfaction are generally quite high in psychiatry (as they are in most specialties), dissatisfaction tends to focus on treatment planning and medication management issues (Howard, El-Mallakh, Kay Rayens, & Clark, 2003). For example, substantial minorities of mental health patients at Kentucky hospitals reported not receiving medication education (13.8%) or not being told what side effects to watch out for (17.4%). Fourteen percent said they were not asked what they thought would help to make them feel better, and 17% did not feel free to complain (Howard et al., 2003). Qualitative studies of satisfaction also reveal strong feelings about the quality of medication management: "I hardly know what treatment I get; which medication I get or why I get it" (Johansson & Eklund, 2003, p. 344). Quantitative results reinforce these perceptions. For example, 27% of respondents to a British survey of mental health patients reported never having a discussion about their medications with their doctor; 46% received no written drug information, and 62% were not offered any choice of medications (Demyttenaere, 2003).

Practitioner   There is widespread concern and discussion about job dissatisfaction among physicians (Zuger, 2004). During the 1990s, this concern was especially acute in psychiatry as the number of residents choosing psychiatry as a specialty steadily declined. This trend has reversed since 2000. Recent surveys suggest that most psychiatrists are satisfied with their jobs; however, older, typically less biomedically-oriented psychiatrists are significantly more dissatisfied than their younger colleagues, presumably as a result of the increased emphasis on drug therapy (Sturm, 2001). Across medical specialties, satisfaction has declined only slightly in recent years (Landon, Reschovsky, & Blumenthal 2003). When dissatisfaction is expressed, it often is attributed to time pressures, perceived lack of autonomy, the decreased significance of the narrative history, and the dominance of drug therapy over psychotherapy (Andreasen, 2001).

Understanding the Negative Quality Indicators

No single fact can explain why, in such large numbers, patients miss appointments, report dissatisfaction, and do not follow their drug therapy regimens. There are undoubtedly many system-, provider-, and patient-level factors at work. In this chapter, we focus on the quality of medication management because it has become such an integral part of modern psychiatric treatment and because it poses such an interesting challenge for health communication research. So why, one might ask, is psychiatric medication management achieving less than optimal results? Many explanations have been offered:

not enough time to spend on medication issues; not enough collaboration between patients and providers; not enough collaboration between different types of providers; too much emphasis on biological reductionism; not enough training in psychotherapy or the art of medication management; and not enough focus on the meaning of medications and illness experience (Charmaz, 2000; Chewning & Sleath, 1996; Conrad, 1994; Demyttenaere, 1998; Gabbard & Kay, 2001; Holzinger, Loffler, Muller, Priebe, & Angermeyer, 2002; Karp, 1996c; Lambert et al., 1997; Medawar & Hardon, 2004; Tasman et al., 2000). In addition to these system and provider factors, some of the negative quality indicators are also due to patient factors such as poverty, substance abuse, homelessness, and to the severity of the underlying illnesses. Among all these explanations, we find the arguments about self, identity, and the meaning of medication to be the most compelling: They cut across the other explanations, they seem central to the lived experience of illness, they are rooted in deep traditions in both psychiatry and sociology, and they appear to offer new and constructive suggestions about how to move out of the present situation. Specifically, we believe that to improve medication management, providers will first have to deepen their understanding of the relationship between the meaning of medication, the patient's identity, and the dynamics of the underlying chronic illness. Of course, a deepened understanding alone will not be sufficient unless it is accompanied by new and different ways of communicating with patients about their medications, identities, and biographical narratives.

The Trajectory Model of Chronic Illness: Conceptual Foundation for Better Medication Management

Although recovery is not unheard of, all of the major psychiatric illnesses (e.g., depression, schizophrenia, bipolar disorder) are regarded as chronic and incurable. A great deal has been written in the last 20 years about chronic illness from a social scientific viewpoint, most of which has focused on nonpsychiatric illness and injury (Charmaz, 2000; Corbin & Strauss, 1988b; Roth & Conrad, 1987). The models of chronic illness that have been developed are consistent with the traditional commitments of psychiatry: patient-centeredness, biopsychosocial framework, focus on the meaning of medications and of illness, the importance of the doctor-patient relationship and on the centrality of the narrative history (Andreasen, 2001). We believe psychiatrists would benefit by integrating these contemporary models of chronic illness into their practices. By internalizing a detailed conceptual model of the lived experience of chronic illness, practitioners might better be able to anticipate problems and conflicts, to read between the lines of patients' questions and complaints, to understand patients' goals and motivations, and to understand where suffering comes from and how it might more effectively be alleviated.

The Trajectory Model of Chronic Illness and the BBC Chain

Inspired in many respects by Goffman's analysis of identity, stigma, and chronic illness (Goffman, 1961, 1963), the trajectory model was developed by Juliet Corbin (a nurse) and Anselm Strauss (a sociologist) and further refined by sociologist Kathy Charmaz and others (Charmaz, 1987a, 1987b, 1991, 1999, 2000; Corbin & Strauss, 1987, 1988b; Strauss & Corbin, 1988b). The full complexity of the model cannot be summarized here. Instead, we focus on one main idea: the BBC chain. According to the trajectory model, one enjoys a subjective sense of health and well-being only when the three elements of the BBC chain—body, biographical time, and conceptions of self—are in balance, interactively stabilizing and reinforcing one another (Corbin & Strauss, 1987, 1988a; Lambert et al., 1997).

The Body   The body is the physical, material self; skin and bones, organs, cells, molecules, and DNA. Most importantly for the model, the body is the means through which performances in the world can be enacted (Goffman, 1959). Body failure—in the form of paralysis, tremors, limps, memory loss, incontinence, fatigue, constipation, shortness of breath, impotence, weakness, pain, blindness, deafness, slurred speech, scars, sores, deformities, and so on—is the prototypical concern of biomedically-oriented physicians. But in the trajectory model, body failure takes on significance only when it impacts identity-relevant performances (Corbin & Strauss, 1987, 1988a; Lambert et al., 1997). An identity-relevant performance is one that is essential to the maintenance of a given identity. A gardener needs to be able to dig in the dirt; a musician needs to be able to play her instrument; a grandfather needs to be able to play with his grandchildren; a baseball player needs to be able to run, jump, throw, catch, and hit.

Biography   Biography (or biographical time as Corbin and Strauss, 1987 refer to it) refers to the more-or-less explicit narrative that gives meaning, coherence, purpose, and direction to a person's life (McAdams, 1993). In the trajectory model, chronic illness is understood primarily as biographical disruption (Bury, 1982; Corbin & Strauss, 1987; Frank, 2000; Williams, 2000). At its worst, body failure can prevent chronically ill people from engaging in performances that are crucial to the maintenance of their identities and thereby keep them from realizing the plans, hopes, dreams, and aspirations that are expressed in their biographies. According to the trajectory model, one of the three types of work that chronically ill patients must do (in addition to illness work and household work) is biographical work (Boeije, Duijnstee, Grypdonck, & Pool, 2002; Corbin & Strauss, 1987; Ville, 2005). Biographical work refers to all of the effort spent preserving, restoring or recasting one's self-image and identity as well as the work done to rewrite the story of one's life and to mourn for hopes, dreams, and identities rendered unachievable by body failures.

Conceptions of Self   Conceptions of self refer to all of the constructs that are typically described as self-image and identity (Ashmore & Jussim, 1997; James, 1961; McCall & Simmons, 1978). These may include role identities (father, teacher, brother, friend), social identities (American, Republican/Democrat, baseball fan), or spiritual identities (Christian, Muslim, Jew, child of God). Conceptions of self also include information about both actual or real selves as well as ideal selves. In the wake of a chronic illness, the discrepancy between real and ideal selves often is exacerbated by body failure and failed performances, and this discrepancy may bring about feelings of sadness, depression, guilt, shame, and anxiety (Corbin & Strauss, 1987, 1988a; Higgins, 1987; James, 1961). The primary form of suffering in chronic illness, according to Charmaz, is the progressive loss of self that results from mounting body failures, repeated failed performances, and subsequent social isolation (Charmaz, 1987a).

When these three component structures—body, biography, and conceptions of self—form a coherent alignment, reinforcing and interactively stabilizing one another, one enjoys a subjective sense of well-being (Albrecht & Devlieger, 1999; Lambert et al., 1997). When the BBC chain is destabilized by changes in body, self, or biography, then one has the subjective feeling of being unwell or ill.

The BBC chain has many desirable qualities as a model of health, not the least of which is that it is a biopsychosocial model (Engel, 1977; Gabbard & Kay, 2001). It does not succumb to the temptation of either biological reductionism or "mere" social constructionism (Pickering, 1990). By placing the body in the BBC chain, the model is thoroughly materialist, admitting a central role for biology. At the same time, by including biography and conceptions of self, the model captures most of what seems important about anthropological and sociological theories of health and illness (Charmaz, 2000; Kleinman & Seeman, 2000). By defining health in terms of stable alignment and balance between these component structures, it gives equal weight to each and draws attention to the processes by which a stable alignment among the components is disrupted, restored, and maintained.

The BBC Chain and Patient Motivation

Seeing health and illness in terms of stability or instability in the BBC chain leads to new insight into patient motivation. Patients are motivated, above all, to maintain or restore stability among the elements of the BBC chain. What were once puzzling patient behaviors begin to make sense in this context. Why do some types of body failure, even very serious body failures, sometimes appear not to bother patients at all? When they are offered medications to deal with these body failures, they do not seem motivated to take the medication. On the other hand, why do seemingly insignificant body failures or medication side effects sometimes cause patients to stop taking medications, even when the medication has other obvious benefits that, from a biomedical perspective, far outweigh the side effects? To put it more concretely, why do many patients forget to take their blood pressure medication but not their erectile dysfunction or acne or weight loss medication?

The answer is obvious when seen from the point of view of the BBC chain. A person only feels healthy when the three elements of the BBC chain are in a stable, mutually reinforcing alignment, when the body enables a person to do the performances that are consistent with one's self-concept and that allow one to realize the life narrative that is spelled out in one's biography. Body failures only matter if they destabilize this alignment by impacting on identity-relevant performances. When body failures impede identity-relevant performances, patients are strongly motivated to repair the body failure. When body failures fail to impact on identity-relevant performances, then patients are less motivated to do anything about them, especially if the recommended treatment for the body failure causes new body failures that may have identity-relevant consequences. These observations also lead to a very simple (perhaps overly simplistic) theory of adherence to regimens: If a recommended regimen helps a patient maintain or regain stability in the BBC chain, then the patient will stick with the regimen; if the regimen destabilizes or fails to impact the BBC chain, then it will likely be abandoned.

The biomedical model and the trajectory model attribute significance to body failure in starkly different ways (Lambert et al., 2000). In the biomedical model, a body failure is significant if it is objectively measurable, if it impacts on a fundamental physiologic process, and if it can be linked, however remotely, to increased risk of future morbidity or mortality. The goal for biomedically-oriented physicians is to restore all measurable physiological parameters to their normal ranges. In psychiatry, in which physiological measures are rare, rating scales and symptom checklists take their place. In the trajectory model, in which the focus is on maintaining the integrity of the BBC chain, body failure is significant if and only if it disrupts the alignment of the BBC chain—if it has identity consequences. The goal for patients is to preserve or restore the integrity of the BBC chain, regardless of the biomedical consequences. We want to argue that the trajectory model, through its emphasis on the stability of the BBC chain, does a better job than the biomedical model of capturing the lived experience of illness.

The Meaning of Medications

Along with the trajectory model's focus on body–self–biography, another major insight from social scientific work on chronic illness concerns the meaning of medications (Adams, Pill, & Jones, 1997; Conrad, 1994; Gabbard & Kay, 2001; Karp, 1996b; Mintz, 2000, 2002; Montagne, 1996; Pound et al., 2005; Rogers et al., 1998; Trostle, Hauser, & Susser, 1983). Again, the contrast between biomedical and social scientific (i.e., symbolic interactionist) conceptions of medications is instructive. From a biomedical perspective, medications are certainly meaningful. They have brand (Prozac®) and generic names (fluoxetine), strengths (e.g., 20 mg), dosage forms (e.g., tablet, capsule), routes of administration (e.g., oral, intramuscular), indications (e.g., antidepressant, antipsychotic), pharmacologic categories (e.g., benzodiazepines, selective serotonin reuptake inhibitors), chemical structures, mechanisms of action, side effects, contraindications, and so on. The biomedical model explains medication effects in terms of mechanical actions at the molecular, cellular, or organ-system level. The efficacy of a medication may be assessed with respect to its ability to affect objectively measurable physiological parameters (e.g., blood pressure, blood glucose, respiration rate, temperature) in predictable ways. In psychiatry, in which such measures are not available, efficacy may be measured by changes in rating scales or symptom checklists.

Along side the biomedical meanings, medications may have many additional meanings to patients living with chronic illnesses. Drugs may symbolize, among other things, dependence or independence, malevolence or benevolence, toxin or tonic, normality or stigma, sickness or health, fuel, food, status, affection, or escape (Adams et al., 1997; Conrad, 1994; Gabbard & Kay, 2001; Helman, 1981; Karp, 1996c; Montagne, 1988, 1996; Nichter & Vuckovic, 1994; Rogers et al., 1998; Trostle et al., 1983; Vuckovic, 1999; Vuckovic & Nichter, 1997). A medication itself may have potent symbolic meanings, as in the case of *Prozac®* or *Viagra®* (Mintz, 2000) or AZT or opiates or birth control pills. The meanings may be idiosyncratic or widely shared in popular culture. Apart from the meaning of any specific medication, the very fact of "being on" any medication, especially lifetime regimens, can have powerful significance for patients, often in relation to themes of autonomy, dependence, illness causation and control. What is important about all of this is that medications can destabilize the BBC chain not only by their physiologic effects (e.g., when they cause fatigue, nausea, hair loss, weight gain, or sexual dysfunction), but also by virtue of their symbolic effects.

Medication and the Self-system   To understand people's medication-use behavior, psychiatrists and other prescribers must understand not just the physiologic mechanism of action and its effects on biological systems, but also the *symbolic* mechanism of action of the drug and its effects on the *self-system*. Failure to understand medication effects on the self-system is analogous to failure to understand the effects of medications on the liver. A medication might "cure" depression while causing liver failure. Doctors rarely fail to consider the potential effects of a drug on a nontargeted organ system, but they often fail to consider the effects of medication on the self-system. This is because doctors are well trained in physiology and in *pharmacodynamics* (the way drugs have their physiological effects), but they are relatively poorly trained in *psychodynamics* (i.e., the way the meaning of medications effects the self-system via its effects on cognitions, interactions and performances; see Gabbard & Kay, 2001; Mintz, 2005).

Medications are the linchpin that connects the space of molecules (i.e., biomedicine) to the space of meanings (i.e., the trajectory model, the sociology and anthropology of health and illness). Medications have biochemical potency and they have symbolic potency. They have a biochemical mechanism of action and a symbolic mechanism of action, a biochemical route of administration and a symbolic route of administration. The have effects in the space of molecules and in the space of meanings. Medication management is the most common form of treatment in modern psychiatry (and in the rest of medicine as well); therefore, clinicians must be trained to manage the biochemical and the symbolic (i.e., meaningful) effects of medication.

The Meaning of Asthma Medication   To begin, a non-psychiatric example helps to make the point about the connection between medication-taking and illness self-definition. Adams and colleagues (1997) interviewed people with asthma in Great Britain. Asthma is a common chronic condition worldwide. It can be effectively controlled with a combination of medications for prophylaxis (the "preventer" medications) and symptom control (the "reliever" medication). Unfortunately, asthma mortality rates are still quite high. Much of this mortality is what experts call unnecessary or excess mortality, so called because the deaths could be avoided if only patients received appropriate primary care and followed the prescribed drug regimens. One underlying purpose of Adams' study was to understand how and why people made decisions about whether or not to take their asthma medications.

Based on their interview responses, patients were placed into three groups: denier/distancers, accepters, and pragmatists (Adams et al., 1997). The deniers denied that the label "asthmatic" applied to them. In spite of this denial, they acknowledged frequent coughing and difficulty breathing, and they reported heavy use of the "reliever" medications. Deniers did not take the preventer medication, because it was only for people with "proper asthma," which they did not acknowledge having. Deniers viewed "true asthmatics" as being crippled, infirm, and unable to engage in most ordinary work and leisure activities. Deniers perceived the asthmatic's identity in plainly negative terms, and they were not willing to accept a diagnostic label or an illness identity that would lead to such a negative redefinition of self. Rejecting preventer medications was the primary way these patients could dramatize their rejection of the asthma identity. The decision to take a medication is a transformative event for self and identity (Karp, 1996c). When the identity transformation is seen to be negative—to involve a loss of self—then the decision is made not to take the medication.

Accepters, on the other hand, saw asthma as more of an annoyance, something to be managed and lived with, not something to be dreaded or avoided (Adams et al., 1997). As a consequence, the accepters readily took both their preventer and their reliever medications. In fact, for the accepters, the medication was seen as enabling them to avoid stigma, illness, and infirmity, by helping them prevent hospitalizations as well as public episodes of breathing trouble and outright asthma attacks. Accepters were able to integrate asthma into their existing identities without significant loss of self. Pragmatists fell somewhere in between the deniers and accepters, for the most part taking their medication as directed but not embracing or integrating their asthma identities as fully as the accepters. Of course, what this analysis does not tell us is how we transform deniers into accepters so that they can enjoy the benefits of drug therapy without the attendant loss of self. Nor does it tell us which of the deniers might be engaging in reasoned and sensible nonadherence, based on their own cost-benefit analyses. What is does show is that the decision to take medication is often grounded in the acceptance or rejection of an illness identity implied by the drug regimen.

Medications Destabilize the BBC Chain via Physical Effects and via Meaning

There are several pathways by which medications can destabilize the BBC chain. The first and most obvious is when the medication, by virtue of its biological mechanism of action, brings about changes in bodily functioning. The classic example concerns side effects or unintended effects of drugs. With psychiatric drugs, common side effects include weight gain, dizziness, drowsiness, sexual dysfunction, urinary problems, increased cholesterol, increased blood sugar, tremors, and mental clouding. If any of these side effects intersects with an identity-relevant performance, then the BBC chain will be destabilized. The extent of the destabilization will depend on the severity and persistence of the side effect and on the salience of the affected performance. This type of medication problem is the one that psychiatrists are probably most comfortable addressing. A great deal of present-day medication management consists of searching for the drug (or combination of drugs) that maximizes intended effects while minimizing unintended effects (Sin & Gamble, 2003). One opportunity for improvement here is in discerning which side effects are most likely to be disruptive of a given patient's BBC chain. To do this requires good understanding of the patient's identity and biography so that one can identify the crucial identity-relevant performances that need to be shielded from side effects. In the absence of side effects, the mere need to be on (even an effective and easily tolerated) medication can still be disruptive to identity and biography. Thus, providers should consider offering nondrug therapies to the patients who are most troubled by the need to start a long term drug regimen. Once a regimen is started, providers must be attentive to and respectful of patients' identity concerns, and must not minimize patient concerns about side effects or be judgmental about the cost-benefit formulas patients use to weigh their own decisions.

The BBC Chain in Psychiatric Illness

The trajectory model was developed primarily in the context of chronic physical illness (e.g., migraine headaches, back pain, paraplegia, congestive heart failure, stroke, rheumatoid arthritis, diabetes, asthma, Parkinson's disease, cancer, multiple sclerosis, heart attack, myasthenia gravis, ulcer, hypertension, lupus, emphysema, renal failure, incontinence, chronic fatigue syndrome) (Charmaz, 1991; Corbin & Strauss, 1988b). One might ask, then, whether there are differences between chronic mental and chronic physical illnesses that would prevent application of the trajectory model to chronic mental illnesses without significant revisions or elaborations. The main difference would appear to be that mental illnesses, especially those with psychotic symptoms, impair cognition in ways that most (but not all) physical illnesses do not. The crucial question is whether or not these cognitive impairments stop people with chronic mental illnesses from doing the biographical work that is central to the maintenance of the BBC chain.

Part of the process of maintaining a stable alignment between body, biography, and self-image is being able to interpret one's own performances in relation to one's biography and identity and to revise and reconstruct biographical narratives in light of ongoing body failures (Charmaz, 2000; Corbin & Strauss, 1987; Lambert et al., 1997). Observation and evaluation are processes fundamental to the development and maintenance of the self-system (McCall & Simmons, 1978). We observe our own performances, and we evaluate our own performances both with respect to our ideals of performance and with respect to their consistency with our biography and identity (Corbin & Strauss, 1987, 1988a; Higgins, 1987). In addition, to develop, sustain, and revise one's own biography or self-narrative, one also requires the capacity for temporal integration of information, for minimal self-reference, for storing and recalling autobiographical memories, for personal agency, and for reflective metacognition (Gallagher, 2003; Lysaker, Carcione, et al., 2005). One potentially important difference between chronic physical conditions and chronic psychiatric problems is that in many psychiatric conditions, the *self-system itself is impaired* (Lysaker & Lysaker, 2002; Sass & Parnas, 2003). That is to say, when a chronic condition brings about primarily physical limitations, the cognitive ability to do interpretation, evaluation and narrative construction is left mostly intact. There are obvious exceptions to this generalization (e.g., Alzheimer's disease, stroke, head injury, brain tumor, etc.).

In contrast, in some chronic psychiatric conditions (schizophrenia in particular), the cognitive skills needed to do the interpretations, evaluations, and narratives may themselves be impaired (Franck et al., 2001; Kapur, 2003;

Lysaker, Wickett, & Davis, 2005; Lysaker, Wickett, Wilke, et al., 2003; Sass & Parnas, 2003). The most obvious examples involve delusions and hallucinations, in which a person's observations may not jibe with reality. But even patients without active delusions or hallucinations may have impaired or distorted evaluations of their own performances as well as limitations in memory, perception, attention, judgment, decision making, and the ability to construct coherent self-narratives (Hofer et al., 2005; Kurtz, 2005; Lysaker & Lysaker, 2002; Lysaker, Wickett, & Davis, 2005; Lysaker, Wickett, Wilke, et al., 2003).

Because it was developed primarily to explain chronic physical illness, the trajectory model has not had much to say about how to deal with cognitive impairments that may distort or disable the narrative and interpretive mechanisms that allow for the maintenance of a cohesive sense of self. If the trajectory model is going to be applied successfully to psychiatric medication management, this is an important area for future research. Several questions need to be answered (Lysaker, Wickett, & Davis, 2005; Lysaker, Wickett, Campbell, et al., 2003): What cognitive functions (e.g., attention, memory, perception) are essential for the accomplishment of biographical work? In which chronic mental illnesses and under what circumstances are these cognitive functions impaired? To what extent do impairments in cognitive functioning impede biographical work? What interventions are available to improve cognitive functioning and thereby improve one's ability to engage in biographical work? At what level of severity do the cognitive impairments begin to impede biographical work? What are the consequences of pursuing biographical work with patients who are cognitively impaired?

Although not minimizing the cognitive impairments that may accompany chronic psychiatric illness (notably schizophrenia), there is reason to believe that these impairments may not always be severe enough to preclude biographical work. For example, the majority of seriously mentally ill people in America are not institutionalized, and large numbers of seriously mentally ill people live independently. Furthermore, when given standard tests of neurocognitive function, noninstitutionalized (i.e., community-dwelling) patients with schizophrenia performed only slightly worse than population norms, and their overall mean scores were not in the range normally defined as "impaired" (Ganguli et al., 1998). The level of cognitive functioning appears to be stable over time (Kurtz, 2005). Supportive employment intervention and vocational rehabilitation can be successful even among seriously mentally ill people (Cook, Leff, et al., 2005; Cook, Lehman, et al., 2005). Lysaker and colleagues have demonstrated improvements in narrative structure among schizophrenic patients after psychotherapy and vocational rehabilitation (Lysaker, Davis, Hunter, Nees, & Wickett, 2005; Lysaker, Lancaster, & Lysaker, 2003; Lysaker, Wickett, Campbell, et al., 2003). From the point of view of professionals and people suffering from mental illnesses, there is an increasing recognition that fostering the ability to reconstruct a coherent narrative of one's own life is a key step in recovery and a central goal of treatment (Corin, 1998; Davidson & Strauss, 1992; Holma & Aaltonen, 1997, 1998; S. L. Young & Ensing, 1999).

It also should be noted that chronic mental illness, like chronic physical illness, is episodic, not constant. It may be true that, in the midst of an acute depressive episode, a manic phase or bipolar disorder, or psychotic break in schizophrenia, that a person may be too sick to do biographical work. But this is really no different than in physical illness, in which biographical work can only be done during relatively stable phases of the illness, and in which exacerbations, acute episodes, and physical setbacks temporarily derail biographical work. What's more, the cognitive impairments that limit the capacity for biographical work are most common in psychotic illnesses such as schizophrenia, but patients with schizophrenia comprise only 6%–7% of patients with mental illness in America (U. S. Department of Health and Human Services, 1999). The remaining 93%–94% have other mood or anxiety disorders that are unlikely impair cognition severely or persistently enough to prevent people from engaging in biographical work.

In summary, the cognitive impairments that accompany serious mental illness present a theoretical and practical challenge for the trajectory model. Such impairments are not unheard of in chronic physical illnesses, for which the trajectory model has most often been applied, but they are likely to be both more common and more severe among people with chronic mental illnesses. Still, even among these patients, whose insight, memory, perception, attention, language skills, and capacity for self-narrative may at times be impaired, we believe there remains significant capacity to do biographical work, especially as it relates to the meaning of medication in relation to illness identity. In the end we conclude that, with a few exceptions, patients with chronic mental illnesses can do biographical work, and there is no reason to believe that the trajectory model cannot be used to understand their experience. In spite of the linguistic distinction between mental and physical illnesses (with all of its Cartesian dualistic implications), what both have in common, and what the trajectory model excels at explaining, are the challenges and consequences of *chronicity* itself—that is, how does one cope with and adapt to a serious, identity-threatening, life-limiting, unending illness? The following two sections illustrate what this process looks like in the context of patients taking medication for depression and psychosis.

The Meaning of Antidepressant Medication   Perhaps the best illustration of the relationship between medication, identity and illness in psychiatry comes from David Karp's interview study of 50 people with depression (Karp, 1996c). Many of Karp's interview subjects described a distinctive sequence of identity transformations—what he termed their depression career (Karp, 1996a). Depression careers began with inchoate feelings of sadness, emptiness, or despair. In the early stages, these feelings were not labeled as depression, nor were they seen as pathological, just normal sadness. Inchoate feelings were followed by a phase during which people sensed that something was really wrong, that the bad feelings they were having went beyond ordinary sadness. Next came a crisis, often a "breakdown" and subsequent hospitalization, and finally a period during which they attempted to come to grips with a new identity as a depressed person.

One important characteristic of the depression career concerns attributions of causality. As the participants in Karp's study moved through their careers, there was a general progression from external to internal attributions of cause. In the early stages, feelings of sadness were often attributed to the external environment (e.g., work, family, or intimate relationships). As time passed, crises mounted, illness became undeniable, and as medical definitions were gradually accepted, the feelings were blamed instead on a pathological self (Karp, 1996a). What is interesting for our purposes is the role medication experiences play in these identity transformations. According to Karp (1996c),

> a patient's willingness to begin a drug regimen and stick with it involves an extensive interpretive process that includes consideration of such issues as the connection between drug use and illness self-definitions, the meanings of drug side effects, attitudes toward physicians, evaluations of professional expertise, and ambiguity about the causes of one's problems. (p. 81)

Most of Karp's informants were initially reluctant to take medication. Some of this reluctance had to do with fear of side effects or a general unwillingness to use medication, but for the most part the reluctance stemmed from the realization that agreeing to take antidepressant medication would lead to negative changes in identity and illness self-definition (Karp, 1996b). For many people, the decision to take antidepressant medication signals an acceptance of the biomedical definition of depression. Accepting a biomedical definition may cause substantial dissonance for people who had defined their troubles as rooted in external social, economic, or family circumstances. Biomedicine defines depression as a chronic, incurable disease. Accepting this definition requires coming to terms with lifelong consequences that may be difficult to integrate into one's pre-illness identity and biography. The biomedical definition of depression also raises difficult challenges vis-à-vis autonomy. On the one hand, the biomedical conception of depression as a "chemical imbalance" or serotonin deficiency frees a person from responsibility for their condition. On the other hand, it puts them in the grip of a biomedical determinism that leaves little opportunity for patients to minimize or escape the consequences of depression by their own persistence, creativity, or hard work. Ironically, the more effective the medicine is, the more difficult it is to deny the biomedical definition—because if the condition was not biological, then the medication would not work so well.

The lesson to draw from Karp's interviews is that medication decisions are never separate from identity struggles. If health professionals insist on thinking about medications only in terms of their biomedical meanings, they will continue to be puzzled by patients' apparently irrational "noncompliance." If they think instead about the meaning of medications in relation to the BBC chain, then patients' decisions about medications may begin to appear rational, sensible, and predictable.

The Meaning of Antipsychotic Medication   Rogers' interviews with patients on antipsychotic medication produced similar insights (Rogers et al., 1998). Patients with schizophrenia often saw neuroleptic medication as a means of controlling symptoms that were either personally or socially undesirable. In this example, the lay and professional meanings of the medication overlap. Patients weighed the benefits of symptom control against the cost of side effects. Reinforcing what we said earlier about identity-relevant side effects being most significant, patients were not bothered by the side effects themselves but by "the way in which physical and psychological side effects acted to inhibit everyday social interaction" (Rogers et al., 1998, p. 1317). What is important is that side effects were most likely to take on negative meanings when they interfered with identity-relevant performances.

Summary   Karp's study of the meaning of antidepressant medication (Karp, 1996c), Rogers' study of the meaning of neuroleptic (i.e., antipsychotic) medication (Rogers et al., 1998), and Adams' study of asthma sufferers (Adams et al., 1997) illustrate the many meanings medications may have and the various ways in which these meanings enter into patients' decision-making process. The key is for health professionals to appreciate that decisions about whether to take medication, as well as the experience of being on medication, are deeply embedded in the ongoing process of identity transformation—the biographical work—that occupies so much of the time and energy of people with chronic illnesses. To the extent that medications bring about positive transformations in identity—for example, by helping to maintain or restore identity-relevant performances—they will be embraced. But when medications bring about negative identity transformations, either directly, by causing identity-damaging side effects, or indirectly, by virtue of what it means to "be on" a given medication, then they will be resented, avoided, and eventually abandoned. If there is one take-home message from this chapter, that is it.

Comprehensive Medication Management: From Theory to Practice

Thus far we have offered a review of negative quality indicators related to medication management in psychiatry and the theoretical outlines of an approach that might improve the situation. In this final section, we offer some suggestions about how to put our theoretical ideas about chronic illness and the meaning of medication into practice. This is not primarily a "how to" chapter, but we would be remiss in not offering at least some ideas about how to address these issues during typically brief (i.e., 15–30 minute) medication management visits. For more thorough and detailed practical guidance about how to do medication management in psychiatry, the interested reader should follow up on the excellent work that has been done in this area recently (Chewning & Sleath, 1996; Cruz & Pincus, 2002; Gabbard & Kay, 2001; Mintz, 2002, 2005; Tasman et al., 2000; Weiden & Rao, 2005). The paragraphs below focus on several key issues: Which patients are most likely to benefit from discussion of medication, identity, and illness? How can clinicians resolve conflicts over treatment goals and methods while still respecting patients' autonomy over medication decision making? What are some of the key issues to be handled in initial and follow-up medication management appointments?

Which Patients Might Benefit?

Not all patients will benefit equally from a consideration of the meaning of medications in clinical practice. For example, some patients have "purely biological" problems that the medicine alleviates. For them the medication has either benign or beneficent meanings which don't need to be discussed. Indeed, by engaging in this type of discussion clinicians may be perceived by patients as playing devil's advocate or second guessing the decision to take medications. In contrast, there are some patients who have a problem that is treated well by the medication, but for whom the side effects create problems in the space of meanings and identity (e.g., impotence, a humiliating tremor, hair loss, and so on). Here the task is to deal with the identity-damaging, personal meanings so that the patient can enjoy the biomedical benefits.

The decision to try and deal at length with the meaning of medications may also depend on the severity of a patient's illness. At one extreme on this continuum, severely psychotic patients may be too sick to tolerate long appointments, or their speech or thoughts may be too disorganized for discussion to be worthwhile. Active drug addicts (i.e., those not in recovery) may be uninterested in this sort of self-examination and may simply want to get medications. In the middle of the continuum are large numbers of patients who are sick enough to want and need longer appointments and well enough to tolerate and benefit from them. This middle group is likely to benefit most from detailed discussion of the meaning of medications. Finally, at the other end of the severity spectrum, there are very high functioning patients who have good social support and just want to refill their medications. Although these patients are capable of discussing the meanings of medication, their high functioning suggests that they have already successfully integrated the drug regimens into their identities and biographies and therefore may benefit less than others. These are generalizations, of course, but they illustrate the types of patient- and disease-specific factors that may impact the usefulness of the approach we have been advocating.

Anticipate Resistance and Disagreement

It is often a mistake to assume that the patient likes, trusts, or values the relationship with the clinician. Patients often are brought to a psychiatrist's office under duress—a family member is insisting that he/she get care, an employer is requiring an evaluation or documentation to support disability, or treatment may be court-ordered. It is reasonable to expect some level of conflict, whether it be internal on the patient's part, interpersonal between patient and other parties including the clinician, or intrapsychic around the issue of medications and identity. In addition, in some cases, combativeness, resistance, and a tendency toward interpersonal conflict may be symptoms of a patient's underlying illness (Mintz, 2002).

As a result, medication management needs to be approached as a negotiation. Attempts to exert undue influence over patients, by using fear appeals, appeals to expert knowledge, or threats of abandonment ("either follow my advice or find another doctor"), will ultimately backfire since patients can exercise absolute autonomy over medication use once they leave the hospital or clinic. A more productive approach may be to acknowledge and accept patients' autonomy from the outset, and to view one's role as that of an advisor, not as one who dictates proper medication use behavior (Butler, Rollnick, & Stott, 1996; Chewning & Sleath, 1996; Cruz & Pincus, 2002). In spite of the likelihood that patients and clinicians will define problems and goals differently, it is often possible to find common ground between clinicians' biomedical goals and patients' quality of life goals (Lambert et al., 2000). The purpose of medication management should be to seek this common ground and expand it whenever possible.

The Initial Visit

During a medication management evaluation, which can range between 30 and 60 minutes, there is a significant amount of information to be obtained. This includes current information regarding symptoms, precipitating events, substance abuse, current medications and any medical conditions, relationships and work, mental and cognitive status (e.g., suicidal or homicidal ideation, as well as psychotic symptoms). It also may include past psychiatric history, past medications and other treatment modalities, family history of mental or medical illness, past trauma, childhood history, and so on. This is a daunting amount of information to be obtained and doesn't even include problem solving with a patient and establishing a mutually acceptable plan of care. The trend toward briefer (i.e., 30 minute) evaluations is disturbing not only because important information may be missed due to lack of time, but the pace of such initial contact may convey to the patient that being rushed will be the rule rather than the exception, an expectation that can affect future interactions; that is, not wanting to initiate discussion about more personal or intimate details because of limited time. Given this limited time frame, it is important to set up a situation wherein the meanings of medication can become knowable. This means listening without judgment and without interruption as much as possible.

By the end of an initial interaction, a clinician will want answers to several questions. Some of these questions can be asked directly: What brings you into treatment? Why now? Why here? Later in the interview, one can ask: How do you feel about being here? What do you want to achieve? How do you feel about me being the person talking to you? Patients will differ in their willingness to respond to these questions. A patient who comes of her own accord and identifies her symptoms as being alien and unwanted may be open to answering these questions directly. A patient who is ambivalent about treatment or who has come to treatment under duress may not be as forthcoming. In this case, a clinician has to listen with the "third ear" (Reik, 1948). This is a process of active listening in that one observes the verbal and nonverbal behavior of the patient and anyone accompanying her. It means being aware of what is being said, what is not being said, and any inconsistencies in the process or content of the interaction.

Clinicians must then generate and test inferences based on these observations. For example, a patient sits silently with her arms crossed while her spouse reports on her symptoms. When asked about the accuracy of these reports, the patient replies, "I don't see it the same way." One might infer that the patient is in denial about her symptoms. When this is offered to the patient in the form of, "it sounds like you don't believe that you have a problem," she might respond with, "I don't." Yet in the context, it may be that the real issue is that her symptoms have become an interpersonal issue between her and her spouse. Admitting that she is symptomatic means admitting that her spouse is right and she is wrong, which, in the context of their relationship, may be difficult to do. Inferences need to be tested out with patients. If an inference is incorrect, the clinician can correct a misinterpretation that could have adversely affected the patient-doctor relationship. If the inference is correct, the patient will feel heard and understood by the clinician, and this can impact the patient-doctor relationship positively. One inference that often needs to be tested is that the patient will have a positive response to symptom relief. This may not always be true. Illnesses serve multiple social functions for patients. Often, a cure based on medication is threatening and unwelcome because it threatens the secondary gains of the sick role—that is, the extra sympathy and attention, as well as the temporary exemption from normal obligations (Mintz, 2002; Wolinsky, 1980).

Building the Therapeutic Alliance During Subsequent Visits

Psychiatric residents must learn and master the skills that are needed to create a positive relationship wherein a patient will be forthcoming about the
raw material that underlies the meaning of medication. These skills include
active listening, minimizing interruptions, testing inferences and recalibrating
any assumptions based on the patient's behavior, and involving the patient in
decision making (Chewning & Sleath, 1996; Cruz & Pincus, 2002; Tasman et
al., 2000). It's vital to establish an authentic nonjudgmental, person-to-person
contact in the midst of the authoritarian relationship between doctor and
patient (Berger, 1993). After a therapeutic alliance is established, the patient
may open up.

In the absence of a therapeutic alliance, patients are unlikely to disclose the
meanings of medication, because those meanings can be highly personal, private, intimate, and threatening to self. One way to welcome these disclosures
is to normalize "noncompliance" by reminding patients that self-regulation of
drug therapy is the rule not the exception (Conrad, 1994). Part of this involves
providers learning how to be passive and receptive. Providers must realize that
despite their privileged professional position, the patient needs to be in control
of the treatment process. Patients must have autonomy with respect to their
medications. As outpatient practitioners, residents may have difficulty transi-
tioning from managing patients on an inpatient unit during which they are
writing orders and managing 24-hour control of the patient. The reality is that
patients are capable of making numerous types of decisions for themselves, and
except in the cases of threat of harm to self or others, they are also capable
of making decisions about their treatment. In this context, clinicians—both
in and out of training—are merely consultants (Chewning & Sleath, 1996).
The key to promoting a therapeutic alliance is to convey that you, the health
professional, understand that the patient is doing the best she can to get better
and that you can provide additional strategies to augment whatever steps she
has already taken to get better.

In this context, patients' behavior can be best understood as improvisation
directed at maximizing quality of life as they define it. This means that patients
will often not take medication recommendations literally. They will gather
information from multiple sources about how to alleviate their own suffering,
and then they will go home and implement the parts of those recommendations
that make the most sense to them, modifying them as needed. This pattern of
behavior too often is construed as noncompliance, but is actually self-regulation
of medication therapy (Conrad, 1994). It's critical to be nonjudgmental about
this process. The clinician needs to see this as a normal expression of autonomy
on the part of the patient—it may not be a personal rejection of the doctor or
the diagnosis, but rather a means to maintain some control over what can be a
frightening, destabilizing, and unpredictable life experience.

Most young clinicians will readily accept that the meaning of medication is important, but they know no techniques to get at those meanings. The following questions may be a useful starting point: What does your medication mean to you? How does your medication fit into your life? How does it make you feel about yourself to be on medication? What does the medication symbolize? What does it represent? Does the medication help you be the person you want to be or does it keep you from being the person you want to be? Do you think you have been given the right medication? What side effects have you had? Often the patient will not be able to answer these questions, nor is it always appropriate to ask them directly. Nevertheless, these questions should remain in the clinician's consideration as s/he tries to understand the patient's unique situation.

From a client-centered perspective, medication management is about facilitating achievement of patient's goals (Chewning & Sleath, 1996). It's not about symptom control (i.e., doctor's goals) unless symptoms are getting in the way of patient's goals. Not dealing with the meaning of medications may lead to loss of the patient, but dealing with the meaning is not always therapeutic. Dealing with the meaning of medication may be a necessary but not a sufficient step. There may be meanings of the medication that are not relevant to the patient's underlying discrepancy between real and ideal selves (Higgins, 1987). Because our perspective sees this discrepancy as the main source of suffering, the meaning of medications should only be dealt with when it affects identity/discrepancy issues.

Implications for Structural Change and Patient Empowerment

We have focused primarily on the implications of the trajectory model for practicing clinicians and how they conduct medication management interviews, but the trajectory model has larger implications as well for both structural change in the health care system and for patient empowerment. Many of the structural changes implied by the trajectory model are summarized by Strauss and Corbin in their book *Shaping a New Healthcare System* (1988a). There they identify five main themes for reform efforts: (a) health care should focus on quality of life in addition to biomedical outcomes; (b) home should be recognized as the central site of care; (c) resources should be more evenly distributed between home care and hospital care; (d) access to nonmedical supportive services (e.g., financial, marital, legal, sexual, etc.) should be greatly expanded; and (e) services should be tailored to fit the stage and phase of the illness (Strauss & Corbin, 1988a, p. 49). One additional structural reform suggested by our analysis is the need to reimburse physicians and pharmacists for the time it takes to talk about the meaning of medication and its relationship to illness and identity. In discussing the policy implications of their client-centered model of medication decision making, Chewning and Sleath (1996, pp. 395–396) make several more recommendations: (a) to evaluate reimbursement policies with respect to their ability to encourage patient involvement in medication decision making; (b) to use regulation, especially in large federally funded programs like Medicare and Medicaid, to require a certain minimum amount of "medication counseling;" (c) to pass and enforce laws like HIPAA (the Health Insurance Portability and Accountability Act of 1996) to protect the privacy of patients' medical information, including their preferences (U. S. Department of Health and Human Services, 2005); and (d) to reform health professions education so that newly trained doctors, nurses, and pharmacists both understand the importance of patient involvement in decision making and accept their roles as consultants in (as opposed to dictators of) drug therapy.

In regard to patient empowerment, we endorse Chewning and Sleath's (1996) notion of client-centered medication decision making. In this model, patients and health professionals collaborate to identify treatment goals, choose regimen options, monitory symptoms and evaluate regimens, and refine or change regimens when needed (Chewning & Sleath, 1996, p. 390). The role of the health professional is more like that of a consultant, making sure that the patient understands the alternatives, and the consequences associated with each alternative. Patients empowered in this manner would have many responsibilities, including the duty to communicate their preferences, to be honest about their self-care practices, to monitor and communicate the outcomes of care, and to share insights and concerns about regimens (Chewning & Sleath, 1996, p. 394). Of course, not all patients will be willing or able to take on these responsibilities, so one goal for research is to determine how to identify these patients and how to care for them once they are identified.

Limitations

The analysis presented here has several limitations. One is that we have focused quite narrowly on medication management. There is more to mental health care than medication management. One important additional component is the rehabilitative mission, which we have only addressed in passing. Rehabilitation involves, among other things, collaborating with patients to develop treatment plans that are meaningful to them, helping patients become more self-sufficient, and facilitating the development of a wider range of pleasurable and productive activities.

With regard to the meaning of medications, we have focused almost exclusively on what the medications mean to patients. But medications also have meaning for the physicians, nurses, pharmacists, family members, friends, coworkers, and the public at large. At any moment these other meanings may impinge on the patient's experience of illness, affecting the decision to start or stop or change the therapy in ways that we have not discussed (Mintz, 2005; Montagne, 1988, 1996; Tasman et al., 2000).

Much of our presentation has been theoretical. As such, practicing health professionals and communication professionals looking for more concrete examples and suggestions are likely to be frustrated by the paucity of clinical cases presented here. For those readers we can recommend several more didactic presentations that come from a similar point of view (Beitman, Blinder, Thase, & Safer, 2003; Mintz, 2002, 2005; Tasman et al., 2000).

We have focused on psychiatric medication management because of the relatively recent trend toward increasing medication use and decreasing use of talk therapy in psychiatry, but we believe essentially all of the arguments we have offered apply beyond mental health to all other medical specialties (Pound et al., 2005). Nearly all of the work on the trajectory model and the meaning of medications has been done outside the domain of mental health. Still it bears repeating that understanding the meaning of medication in relation to a sick person's identity and biography will be essential to successful drug therapy in any setting.

Summary and Conclusion

Brief medication management is increasingly the most common form of treatment that patients with psychiatric illnesses receive. This is a historically significant trend, one that illustrates psychiatry's transition from a marginalized medical specialty that offered talk as its primary form of treatment to one that is thoroughly committed to the biological basis of mental illnesses. Evidence of noncompliance, missed appointments, and poor patient and provider satisfaction suggests that there is room for improvement in the way medications are managed. Social scientists, working outside psychiatry and focusing primarily on physical impairments, have developed detailed theoretical models of the lived experience of chronic illness. These models define health as a balance between body, self, and biography, and they portray chronically ill patients as primarily motivated to reverse or minimize the loss of self that results from body failures.

The main point of this chapter is that the quality of psychiatric medication management might be improved if it were based more closely on this social scientific analysis of chronic illness experience. From this perspective, medication management is not merely about symptom control. It is about assisting patients in restoring the balance between body, self, and biography. Medication therapy is one among many strategies that patients will try in their attempts to restore this balance. If clinicians want to understand what appears on the surface to be harmful, ignorant, or uncooperative medication use behavior, they will need to understand each patient's identity struggles, the impact of the illness on each patient's biography, and the meaning of the medication and its side effects in relation to all of these issues. Then, with the modesty that comes from acknowledging patient's ultimate autonomy over decision making, they will need to negotiate treatment goals and drug therapy regimens that patients can live with. None of this can be done quickly or easily. It may not work with all types of patients, and it cannot be done at all without first establishing a therapeutic alliance based on mutual trust and respect. But if medication management is reframed in the ways suggested above, it may be possible to improve the overall quality of medication management in psychiatry and thereby reverse many of the negative quality indicators reviewed above.

Acknowledgment

This preparation of this chapter was supported in part by a grant from the Program for Mental Health Services Research on Women and Gender, Research Infrastructure Support Program, Department of Psychiatry, University of Illinois at Chicago (NIMH Grant #R24 MH54212-02, Dr. Joseph Flaherty, PI). We are grateful for the comments of Gregory Dalack, David Karp, Michael Montagne, Mark Olfson, Don Rucker, and Betsy Sleath.

References

Adams, S., Pill, R., & Jones, A. (1997). Medication, chronic illness and identity: The perspectives of people with asthma. *Social Science & Medicine, 45*, 189–201.

Albrecht, G. L., & Devlieger, P. J. (1999). The disability paradox: High quality of life against all odds. *Social Science & Medicine, 48*, 977–988.

Andreasen, N. (2001). Diversity in psychiatry: Or, why did we become psychiatrists? *American Journal of Psychiatry, 158*, 673–675.

Ashmore, R. D., & Jussim, L. (Eds.). (1997). *Self and identity: Fundamental issues.* New York: Oxford University Press.

Bebbington, P. E. (1995). The content and context of noncompliance. *International Clinical Psychopharmacology, 9*(Suppl. 5), 41–50.

Beitman, B. D., Blinder, B. J., Thase, M. E., & Safer, D. L. (2003). *Integrating psychotherapy and pharmacotherapy: Dissolving the mind-brain barrier.* New York: W. W. Norton.

Berger, B. (1993). Building an effective therapeutic alliance: Competence, trustworthiness, and caring. *American Journal of Hospital Pharmacy, 50*, 2399–2403.

Boeije, H. R., Duijnstee, M. S. H., Grypdonck, M. H. F., & Pool, A. (2002). Encountering the downward phase: Biographical work in people with multiple sclerosis living at home. *Social Science & Medicine, 55*, 881–893.

Bury, M. (1982). Chronic illness as biographical disruption. *Sociology of Health and Illness, 4*, 167–182.

Butler, C., Rollnick, S., & Stott, N. (1996). The practitioner, the patient and resistance to change. *Canadian Medical Association Journal, 154*, 1357–1362.

Charmaz, K. (1987a). Loss of self: A fundamental form of suffering in the chronically ill. *Sociology of Health and Illness, 5*, 168–195.

Charmaz, K. (1987b). Struggling for a self: Identity levels of the chronically ill. In J. Roth & P. Conrad (Eds.), *Research in the sociology of health care: Vol. 6. The experience and management of chronic illness* (pp. 283–321). Greenwich, CT: JAI.

Charmaz, K. (1991). *Good days, bad days: The self in chronic illness and time.* New Brunswick, NJ: Rutgers University Press.

Charmaz, K. (1999). From the "sick role" to stories of self. In R. J. Contrada & R. D.

Ashmore (Eds.), *Self, social identity, and physical health* (pp. 209–239). New York: Oxford University Press.

Charmaz, K. (2000). Experiencing chronic illness. In G. L. Albrecht, R. Fitzpatrick, & S. C. Scrimshaw (Eds.), *Handbook of social studies in health & medicine* (pp. 277–292). Thousand Oaks, CA: Sage.

Chewning, B., & Sleath, B. (1996). Medication decision-making and management: A client-centered model. *Social Science & Medicine, 42,* 389–398.

Conrad, P. (1994). The meaning of medications: Another look at compliance. In P. Conrad & R. Kern (Eds.), *The sociology of health and illness: Critical perspectives* (pp. 149–161). New York: St. Martin's.

Cook, J. A., Leff, H. S., Blyler, C. R., Gold, P. B., Goldberg, R. W., Mueser, K. T., et al. (2005). Results of a multisite randomized trial of supported employment interventions for individuals with severe mental illness. *Archives of General Psychiatry, 62,* 505–512.

Cook, J. A., Lehman, A. F., Drake, R., McFarlane, W. R., Gold, P. B., Leff, H. S., et al. (2005). Integration of psychiatric and vocational services: A multisite randomized, controlled trial of supported employment. *American Journal of Psychiatry, 162,* 1948–1956.

Corbin, J. M., & Strauss, A. L. (1987). Accompaniments of chronic illness: Changes in body, self, biography, and biographical time. In J. A. Roth & P. Conrad (Eds.), *Research in the sociology of health care* (Vol. 6, pp. 249–281): Greenwich, CT: JAI.

Corbin, J. M., & Strauss, A. L. (1988a). Experiencing body failure and a disrupted self image. In J. Corbin & A. L. Strauss (Eds.), *Unending work and care: Managing chronic illness at home* (pp. 49–67). San Francisco: Jossey-Bass.

Corbin, J. M., & Strauss, A. L. (1988b). *Unending work and care: Managing chronic illness at home.* San Francisco: Jossey-Bass.

Corin, E. (1998). The thickness of being: Intentional worlds, strategies of identity, and experience among schizophrenics. *Psychiatry, 61,* 133–146.

Cruz, M., & Pincus, H. A. (2002). Research on the influence that communication in psychiatric encounters has on treatment. *Psychiatric Services, 53,* 1253–1265.

Davidson, L., & Strauss, J. S. (1992). Sense of self in recovery from severe mental illness. *British Journal of Medical Psychology, 65,* 131–145.

Demyttenaere, K. (1998). Noncompliance with antidepressants: Who's to blame? *International Clinical Psychopharmacology, 13*(Suppl. 2), S19–S25.

Demyttenaere, K. (2003). Risk factors and predictors of compliance in depression. *European Neuropsychopharmacology, 13*(Suppl. 3), S69–S75.

Demyttenaere, K., Mesters, P., Boulanger, B., Dewe, W., Delsemme, M.-H., Gregoire, J., et al. (2001). Adherence to treatment regimen in depressed patients treated with amitriptyline or fluoxetine. *Journal of Affective Disorders, 65,* 243–252.

Demyttenaere, K., Van Ganse, E., Gregoire, J., Gaens, E., Mesters, P., & Belgian Compliance Study Group. (1998). Compliance in depressed patients treated with fluoxetine or amitriptyline. *International Clinical Psychopharmacology, 13,* 11–17.

DiMatteo, M. R., Giordani, P. J., Lepper, H. S., & Croghan, T. W. (2002). Patient adherence and medical treatment outcomes: A meta-analysis. *Medical Care, 40,* 794–811.

DiMatteo, M. R., Reiter, R. C., & Gambone, J. C. (1994). Enhancing medication adherence through communication and informed collaborative choice. *Health Communication, 6,* 253–266.

Dotter, J. F., & Labbate, L. A. (1998). Missed and canceled appointments at a military psychiatry clinic. *Military Medicine, 163,* 58–60.

Durham, M. L. (1998). Mental health and managed care. *Annual Review of Public Health, 19,* 493–505.

Engel, G. (1977). The need for a new medical model. *Science, 196,* 129–136.

Fenton, W. S., Blyler, C. R., & Heinssen, R. K. (1997). Determinants of medication compliance in schizophrenia: Empirical and clinical findings. *Schizophrenia Bulletin, 23,* 637–651.

Franck, N., Farrer, C., Georgieff, N., Marie-Cardine, M., Dalery, J., d'Amato, T., et al. (2001). Defective recognition of one's own actions in patients with schizophrenia. *American Journal of Psychiatry, 158,* 454–459.

Frank, A. W. (2000). Illness and autobiographical work: Dialogue as narrative destabilization. *Qualitative Sociology, 23,* 135–155.

Gabbard, G. O., & Kay, J. (2001). The fate of integrated treatment: Whatever happened to the biopsychosocial psychiatrist? *American Journal of Psychiatry, 158,* 1956–1963.

Gallagher, S. (2003). Self-narrative in schizophrenia. In T. Kircher & A. David (Eds.), *The self in neuroscience and psychiatry* (pp. 336–357). New York: Cambridge University Press.

Ganguli, R., Brar, J. S., Vemulapalli, H., Jafar, H., Ahuja, R., Sharma, S., et al. (1998). Mini-mental state examination (mmse) performance of partially remitted community-dwelling patients with schizophrenia. *Schizophrenia Research, 33,* 45–52.

Goffman, E. (1959). Performances. In E. Goffman (Ed.), *The presentation of self in everyday life* (pp. 17–76). New York: Anchor Doubleday.

Goffman, E. (1961). *Asylums: Essays on the social situation of mental patients.* New York: Doubleday.

Goffman, E. (1963). *Stigma: Notes on the management of spoiled identity.* New York: Simon and Schuster.

Goldhamer, P. M. (1983). Psychotherapy and pharmacotherapy: The challenge of integration. *Canadian Journal of Psychiatry, 28,* 173–177.

Grunebaum, M., Luber, P., Callahan, M., Leon, A. C., Olfson, M., & Portera, L. (1996). Predictors of missed appointments for psychiatric consultations in a primary care clinic. *Psychiatric Services, 47,* 848–852.

Helman, C. G. (1981). 'Tonic', 'fuel' and 'food': Social and symbolic aspects of the long-term use of psychotropic drugs. *Social Science & Medicine, 15B,* 521–533.

Higgins, E. T. (1987). Self-discrepancy: A theory relating self and affect. *Psychological Review, 94,* 319–340.

Hilty, D. M., Brady, K. T., & Hales, R. E. (1999). A review of bipolar disorder among adults. *Psychiatric Services, 50,* 201–213.

Hofer, A., Baumgartner, S., Bodner, T., Edlinger, M., Hummer, M., Kemmler, G., et al. (2005). Patient outcomes in schizophrenia ii: The impact of cognition. *European Psychiatry, 20,* 395–402.

Holma, J., & Aaltonen, J. (1997). The sense of agency and the search for a narrative in acute psychosis. *Contemporary Family Therapy: An International Journal, 19,* 463–477.

Holma, J., & Aaltonen, J. (1998). Narrative understanding in acute psychosis. *Contemporary Family Therapy: An International Journal, 20,* 253–263.

Holzinger, A., Loffler, W., Muller, P., Priebe, S., & Angermeyer, M. C. (2002). Subjective illness theory and antipsychotic medication compliance by patients with schizophrenia. *Journal of Nervous and Mental Disease, 19*, 597–603.

Howard, P. B., El-Mallakh, P., Kay Rayens, M., & Clark, J. J. (2003). Consumer perspectives on quality of inpatient mental health services. *Archives of Psychiatric Nursing, 17*, 205–217.

James, W. (1961). *Psychology.* Notre Dame, IN: University of Notre Dame Press.

Johansson, H., & Eklund, M. (2003). Patients' opinion on what constitutes good psychiatric care. *Scandinavian Journal of Caring Sciences, 17*, 339–346.

Johnson, R. E., & McFarland, B. H. (1996). Lithium use and discontinuation in a health maintenance organization. *American Journal of Psychiatry, 153*, 993–1000.

Kandel, E. R. (1998). A new intellectual framework for psychiatry. *American Journal of Psychiatry, 155*, 457–469.

Kaplan, E. M. (1997). Antidepressant noncompliance as a factor in the discontinuation syndrome. *Journal of Clinical Psychiatry, 58*(Suppl. 7), 31–36.

Kaplan, H. I., & Sadock, B. J. (1998). *Synopsis of psychiatry (behavioral sciences/clinical psychiatry).* Baltimore, MD: Williams and Wilkins.

Kapur, S. (2003). Psychosis as a state of aberrant salience: A framework linking biology, phenomenology, and pharmacology in schizophrenia. *American Journal of Psychiatry, 160*, 13–23.

Karp, D. (1996a). Illness and identity. In *Speaking of sadness* (pp. 51–77). Oxford, England: Oxford University Press.

Karp, D. (1996b). The meanings of medication. In *Speaking of sadness* (pp. 78–103). Oxford, England: Oxford University Press.

Karp, D. (1996c). *Speaking of sadness.* Oxford, England: Oxford University Press.

Keck, P. E., Jr., McElroy, S. L., Strakowski, S. M., Stanton, S. P., Kizer, D. L., Balistreri, T. M., et al. (1996). Factors associated with pharmacologic noncompliance in patients with mania. *Journal of Clinical Psychiatry, 57*, 292–297.

Kelly, G. R., Scott, J. E., & Mamon, J. (1990). Medication compliance and health education among outpatients with chronic mental disorders. *Medical Care, 28*, 1181–1197.

Killaspy, H., Banerjee, S., King, M., & Lloyd, M. (2000). Prospective controlled study of psychiatric out-patient non-attendance. Characteristics and outcome. *British Journal of Psychiatry, 176*, 160–165.

Kleinman, A., & Seeman, D. (2000). Personal experience of illness. In G. L. Albrecht, R. Fitzpatrick, & S. C. Scrimshaw (Eds.), *Handbook of social studies in health & medicine* (pp. 230–242). Thousand Oaks, CA: Sage.

Kravitz, R. L., Hays, R. D., Sherbourne, C. D., DiMatteo, M. R., Rogers, W. H., Ordway, L., et al. (1993). Recall of recommendations and adherence to advice among patients with chronic medical conditions. *Archives of Internal Medicine, 153*, 1869–1878.

Kurtz, M. M. (2005). Neurocognitive impairment across the lifespan in schizophrenia: An update. *Schizophrenia Research, 74*, 15–26.

Lamberg, L. (2000). Patient-physician relationship critical even during brief "medication checks". *Journal of the American Medical Association, 284*, 29–31.

Lambert, B. L., Butin, D. N., Moran, D., Zhao, S. Z., Carr, B. C., Chen, C., et al. (2000). Arthritis care: Comparison of physicians' and patients' views. *Seminars in Arthritis and Rheumatism, 30*, 100–110.

Lambert, B. L., Street, R. L., Cegala, D. J., Smith, D. H., Kurtz, S., & Schofield, T. (1997). Provider-patient communication, patient-centered care, and the mangle of practice. *Health Communication, 9*, 27–43.

Landon, B. E., Reschovsky, J., & Blumenthal, D. (2003). Changes in career satisfaction among primary care and specialist physicians, 1997–2001. *Journal of the American Medical Association, 289*, 442–449.

Lieberman, J. A., Stroup, T. S., McEvoy, J. P., Swartz, M. S., Rosenheck, R. A., Perkins, D. O., et al. (2005). Effectiveness of antipsychotic drugs in patients with chronic schizophrenia. *New England Journal of Medicine, 353*, 1209–1223.

Lin, E. H. B., Von Korff, M., Katon, W., Bush, T., Simon, G. E., Walker, E., et al. (1995). The role of the primary care physician in patients' adherence to antidepressant therapy. *Medical Care, 33*, 67–74.

Lingam, R., & Scott, J. (2002). Treatment non-adherence in affective disorders. *Acta Psychiatrica Scandinavica, 105*, 164–172.

Luhrmann, T. M. (2000). *Of two minds: The growing disorder in American psychiatry.* New York: Vintage.

Lysaker, P. H., Carcione, A., Dimaggio, G., Johannesen, J. K., Nicolo, G., Procacci, M., et al. (2005). Metacognition amidst narratives of self and illness in schizophrenia: Associations with neurocognition, symptoms, insight and quality of life. *Acta Psychiatrica Scandinavica, 112*, 64–71.

Lysaker, P. H., Davis, L. W., Hunter, N. L., Nees, M. A., & Wickett, A. (2005). Personal narratives in schizophrenia: Increases in coherence following five months of vocational rehabilitation. *Psychiatric Rehabilitation Journal, 29*, 66–68.

Lysaker, P. H., Lancaster, R. S., & Lysaker, J. T. (2003). Narrative transformation as an outcome in the psychotherapy of schizophrenia. *Psychology & Psychotherapy, 76*, 285–299.

Lysaker, P. H., & Lysaker, J. T. (2002). Narrative structure in psychosis: Schizophrenia and disruptions of the dialogical self. *Theory & Psychology, 12*, 207–220.

Lysaker, P. H., Wickett, A. M., Campbell, K., & Buck, K. D. (2003). Movement towards coherence in the psychotherapy of schizophrenia: A method for assessing narrative transformation. *Journal of Nervous and Mental Disease, 191*, 538–541.

Lysaker, P. H., Wickett, A., & Davis, L. W. (2005). Narrative qualities in schizophrenia: Associations with impairments in neurocognition and negative symptoms. *Journal of Nervous and Mental Disease, 193*, 244–249.

Lysaker, P. H., Wickett, A. M., Wilke, N., & Lysaker, J. (2003). Narrative incoherence in schizophrenia: The absent agent-protagonist and the collapse of internal dialogue. *American Journal of Psychotherapy, 57*, 153–166.

Maddox, J. C., Levi, M., & Thompson, C. (1994). The compliance with antidepressants in general practice. *Journal of Psychopharmacology, 8*(Suppl. 1), 48–53.

Matas, M., Staley, D., & Griffin, W. (1992). A profile of the noncompliant patient: A thirty-month review of outpatient psychiatry referrals. *General Hospital Psychiatry, 14*, 124–130.

McAdams, D. P. (1993). *The stories we live by.* New York: Guilford.

McCall, G. J., & Simmons, J. L. (1978). *Identities and interactions: An examination of associations in everyday life.* New York: Free Press.

Mechanic, D., McAlpine, D. D., & Rosenthal, M. (2001). Are patients' office visits with physicians getting shorter? *New England Journal of Medicine, 344*, 198–204.

Medawar, C., & Hardon, A. (2004). *Medicines out of control? Antidepressants and the conspiracy of good will*. Amsterdam: Askant.

Mintz, D. L. (2000). Unusual case report: Nonpharmacologic effects of sildenafil. *Psychiatric Services, 51*, 674–675.

Mintz, D. L. (2002). Meaning and medication in the care of treatment-resistant patients. *American Journal of Psychotherapy, 56*, 322–337.

Mintz, D. L. (2005). Teaching the prescriber's role: The psychology of psychopharmacology. *Academic Psychiatry, 29*, 187–194.

Montagne, M. (1988). The metaphorical nature of drugs and drug taking. *Social Science & Medicine, 26*, 417–424.

Montagne, M. (1996). The pharmakon phenomenon. In P. Davis (Ed.), *Contested ground: Public purpose and private interest in the regulation of prescription drugs* (pp. 11–25). New York: Oxford.

Nelson, E. A., Maruish, M. E., & Axler, J. L. (2000). Effects of discharge planning and compliance with outpatient appointments on readmission rates. *Psychiatric Services, 51*, 885–889.

Nichter, M., & Vuckovic, N. (1994). Agenda for an anthropology of pharmaceutical practice. *Social Science & Medicine, 39*, 1509–1525.

Olfson, M. (1992). Psychiatric outpatient practice: Patterns and policies. *American Journal of Psychiatry, 149*, 1492–1498.

Olfson, M., Hansell, S., & Boyer, C. (1997). Medication noncompliance. In D. Mechanic (Ed.), *New directions for mental health services* (pp. 39–49). San Francisco: Josey-Bass.

Olfson, M., Marcus, S. C., Druss, B., Elinson, L., Tanielian, T., & Pincus, H. A. (2002). National trends in the outpatient treatment of depression. *Journal of the American Medical Association, 287*, 203–209.

Olfson, M., Marcus, S. C., Druss, B., & Pincus, H. A. (2002). National trends in the use of outpatient psychiatry. *American Journal of Psychiatry, 159*, 1914–1920.

Olfson, M., Marcus, S. C., & Pincus, H. A. (1999). Trends in office-based psychiatric practice. *American Journal of Psychiatry, 156*, 451–457.

Olfson, M., Marcus, S. C., Pincus, H. A., Zito, J. M., Thompson, J. W., & Zarin, D. A. (1998). Antidepressant prescribing practices of outpatient psychiatrists. *Archives of General Psychiatry, 55*, 310–316.

Ostow, M. (1966). The complementary roles of psychoanalysis and drug therapy. In P. Soloman (Ed.), *Psychiatric drugs* (pp. 91–111). New York: Grune and Stratton.

Pampallona, S., Bollini, P., Tibaldi, G., Kupelnick, B., & Munizza, C. (2002). Patient adherence in the treatment of depression. *The British Journal of Psychiatry, 180*, 104–109.

Pang, A. H., Lum, F. C., Ungvari, G. S., Wong, C. K., & Leung, Y. S. (1996). A prospective outcome study of patients missing regular psychiatric outpatient appointments. *Social Psychiatry and Psychiatric Epidemiology, 31*, 299–302.

Pickering, A. (1990). Knowledge, practice, and mere construction. *Social Studies of Science, 20*, 682–729.

Pincus, H. A., Tanielian, T. L., Marcus, S. C., Olfson, M., Zarin, D. A., Thomson, J., et al. (1998). Prescribing trends in psychotropic medications: Primary care, psychiatry, and other medical specialties. *Journal of the American Medical Association, 279*, 526–531.

Pound, P., Britten, N., Morgan, M., Yardley, L., Pope, C., Daker-White, G., et al. (2005). Resisting medicines: A synthesis of qualitative studies of medicine taking. *Social Science & Medicine, 61*, 133–155.

Reik, T. (1948). *Listening with the third ear: The inner experience of a psychoanalyst.* New York: Farrar Straus.

Rogers, A., Day, J. C., Williams, B., Randall, F., Wood, P., Healy, D., et al. (1998). The meaning and management of neuroleptic medication: A study of patients with a diagnosis of schizophrenia. *Social Science & Medicine, 47*, 1313–1323.

Roth, J. A., & Conrad, P. (Eds.). (1987). *The experience and management of chronic illness* (Vol. 6). Greenwich, CT: JAI.

Sass, L. A., & Parnas, J. (2003). Schizophrenia, consciousness, and the self. *Schizophrenia Bulletin, 29*, 427–444.

Schatzberg, A. F., & Nemeroff, C. B. (Eds.). (1998). *The American Psychiatric Press textbook of psychopharmacology.* Washington, DC: American Psychiatric Press.

Shem, S. (1997). *Mount misery.* New York: Fawcett Columbine.

Sin, J., & Gamble, C. (2003). Managing side effects to the optimum: Valuing a client's experience. *Journal of Psychiatric and Mental Health Nursing, 10*, 147–153.

Souery, D., & Mendlewicz, J. (1998). Compliance and therapeutic issues in resistant depression. *International Clinical Psychopharmacology, 13*(Suppl. 2), S13–S18.

Sparr, L. F., Moffitt, M. C., & Ward, M. F. (1993). Missed psychiatric appointments: Who returns and who stays away. *American Journal of Psychiatry, 150*, 801–805.

Strauss, A., & Corbin, J. M. (1988a). *Shaping a new health care system.* San Francisco: Jossey-Bass.

Strauss, A., & Corbin, J. M. (1988b). Understanding what it means to be chronically ill. In *Shaping a new health care system* (pp. 46–58). San Francisco: Jossey-Bass.

Sturm, R. (2001). Datapoints: Are psychiatrists more dissatisfied with their careers than other physicians? *Psychiatric Services, 52*, 581.

Tasman, A., Riba, M. B., & Silk, K. R. (Eds.). (2000). *The doctor-patient relationship in pharmacotherapy.* New York: Guilford.

Trostle, J. A., Hauser, W. A., & Susser, I. S. (1983). The logic of noncompliance: Management of epilepsy from the patient's point of view. *Culture, Medicine and Psychiatry, 7*, 35–56.

U.S. Department of Health and Human Services (1999). *Mental health: A report of the surgeon general.* Retrieved May 21, 2002, from http://www.surgeongeneral.gov/library/mentalhealth/home.html

U.S. Department of Health and Human Services. (2005, July 19). *Office for civil rights - HIPAA. Medical privacy - National standards to protect the privacy of personal health information.* Retrieved January 4, 2006, from http://www.hhs.gov/ocr/hipaa/

Valenstein, M., Copeland, L. A., Blow, F. C., McCarthy, J. F., Zeber, J. E., Gillon, L., et al. (2002). Pharmacy data identify poorly adherent patients with schizophrenia at increased risk for admission. *Medical Care, 40*, 630–639.

Ville, I. (2005). Biographical work and returning to employment following a spinal cord injury. *Sociology of Health and Illness, 27*, 324–350.

Vuckovic, N. (1999). Fast relief: Buying time with medications. *Medical Anthropology Quarterly, 13*, 51–68.

Vuckovic, N., & Nichter, M. (1997). Changing patterns of pharmaceutical practice in the United States. *Social Science & Medicine, 44*, 1285–1302.

Weiden, P. J., & Rao, N. (2005). Teaching medication compliance to psychiatric residents: Placing an orphan topic into a training curriculum. *Academic Psychiatry, 29,* 203–210.

Williams, S. J. (2000). Chronic illness as biographical disruption or biographical disruption as chronic illness? Reflections on a core concept. *Sociology of Health and Illness, 22,* 40–67.

Wolinsky, F. (1980). The sick-role concept. In F. Wolinsky (Ed.), *The sociology of health* (pp. 99–121). Boston: Little, Brown & Co.

Woodwell, D. A. (1997). National ambulatory medical care survey: 1996 summary. US National Center for Health Statistics. *Advance Data from Vital and Health Statistics, 305,* 1–28.

Woodwell, D. A. (1999). National ambulatory medical care survey: 1997 summary. US National Center for Health Statistics. *Advance Data from Vital and Health Statistics, 305,* 1–28.

Woodwell, D. A., & Cherry, D. K. (2004). National ambulatory medical care survey: 2002 summary. *Advance Data from Vital and Health Statistics.* Retrieved October 1, 2004, from http://www.cdc.gov/nchs/data/ad/ad346.pdf

Young, J. L., Zonana, H. V., & Shepler, L. (1986). Medication noncompliance in schizophrenia: Codification and update. *Bulletin of the American Academy of Psychiatry and Law, 14,* 105–122.

Young, S. L., & Ensing, D. S. (1999). Exploring recovery from the perspective of people with psychiatric disabilities. *Psychiatric Rehabilitation Journal, 22,* 219–231.

Zuger, A. (2004). Dissatisfaction with medical practice. *New England Journal of Medicine, 350,* 69–75.

Zygmunt, A., Olfson, M., Boyer, C. A., & Mechanic, D. (2002). Interventions to improve medication adherence in schizophrenia. *American Journal of Psychiatry, 159,* 1653–1664.

Chapter 9

The HIV Social Identity Model

Lance S. Rintamaki

Advances in antiretroviral treatments have dramatically increased the life spans of those infected with the Human Immunodeficiency Virus (HIV), such that clinicians now treat it as a chronic condition rather than terminal disease (e.g., Burgoyne, Rourke, Behrens, & Salit, 2004). Clinical and social scientific emphasis subsequently has expanded beyond the study of purely bio-medical concerns to now encompass the complete gamut of issues inherent to the HIV experience. Guided by the biopsychosocial model of health (Engel, 1977, 1980), researchers are now striving to better understand factors that may influence the psychological and social well-being of people living with HIV (PLWHIV).

One issue of considerable importance to the quality of life of PLWHIV is the stigma that accompanies infection. Stigma is a socially constructed phenomenon that creates boundaries between the stigmatized and the non-stigmatized, as well as places the stigmatized into an undesirable out-group (Devine, Plant, & Harrison, 1999; Goffman, 1963). Stigmatized people are "pejoratively regarded by the broader society and are devalued, shunned, and otherwise lessened in their life chances and in their access to the human-izing benefit of free and unfettered social intercourse" (Alonzo & Reynolds, 1995, p. 304). The social stigma surrounding HIV subsequently relegates those infected to a new and outcast social group that further compromises their already impaired well-being. Studies show that large proportions of the U.S. public misunderstand HIV and its routes of transmission, express fear and disgust towards those infected with the virus, and support public policies that would deprive PLWHIV of their civil rights (e.g., Herek, Capitanio, & Widaman, 2002). Many PLWHIV report being stigmatized and, as a result, experience anxiety, depression, and a disruption in their positive social inter-actions with others (for a review, see Rintamaki & Weaver, 2008). Discrimina-tion resulting from stigma has led to loss of employment, housing, and health care for PLWHIV (Gostin & Webber, 1997, 1998; Levin, Krantz, Driscoll, & Fleischman, 1995; Rintamaki, Scott, Kosenko, & Jensen, 2007). The social stigma surrounding HIV infection clearly can pervade the lives of PLWHIV and affect them in many deleterious ways; however, stigma may also serve as the catalyst for the development of a new social identity.

HIV and Social Identity

Upon HIV diagnosis, there is a shift in a person's social group membership from the healthy, normal group to an illness community that is broadly stigmatized by the larger society. Due to this shift in social group membership, along with the salience of this shift both to those with HIV and the general public, social identity theory and self-categorization theory together help describe the HIV experience. In particular, these theories (a) provide insight into social and psychological phenomena that likely affect PLWHIV and (b) direct research towards these issues.

Tajfel and Turner (Tajfel, 1978, 1982; Tajfel & Turner, 1979, 1986) have argued that much of the self-concept is derived from social group memberships. In essence, people incorporate the values, norms, and behaviors of the groups to which they see themselves belonging. People also place considerable importance on these group memberships, as they help define who they are, particularly when they compare themselves to others (e.g., Asch, 1951; Turner, Wetherell, & Hogg, 1989; Wegner & Bargh, 1998). Building on these ideas, Turner and his colleagues (e.g., Turner, Oakes, Haslam, & McGarty, 1994) have developed self-categorization theory, asserting that people constantly are identifying not only to which social groups they belong, but also to which social groups others belong. As a result, a person's self-concept is dependent on social context and shifts toward the collective self in intergroup contexts and toward the individual self in intragroup contexts (Turner, 1999; Turner, Hogg, Oakes, Reicher, & Wetherell, 1987). In other words, people see themselves as unique individuals when compared to other members of their group, but as members of their group when they interact with people who belong to groups other than their own. Understanding the social identity experience of PLWHIV ultimately is crucial to understanding how they manage the stigma surrounding the virus and their social interactions with others.

The utility of social identity theory and self-categorization theory for understanding HIV stigma and its implications derives from the comparative aspects of the categorization process. According to Tajfel and Turner (1986), social identities are fundamentally relational and comparative. They defined the individual as similar to or different from (or better or worse than) members of other groups. It is this shift and its resulting implications that are of special importance for the stigmatized. Social identity research reveals how people from stigmatized groups are mindful in the presence of others, are worried about how their performances may be interpreted by those around them, and are alert to any behaviors from others that might signal negative feelings about the stigmatized.

In general, members of stigmatized social groups are concerned with others' attitudes and are sensitive to any clues that may signal others' feelings or beliefs about them (e.g., Devine, Evett, & Vasquez-Suson, 1996; Frable, Blackstone, & Scherbaum, 1990). Members of stigmatized groups also may be aware that, despite verbal assurances to the contrary, others may nonetheless possess prejudices against them (e.g., Major & Crocker, 1993). Because others may even actively work to conceal their prejudicial attitudes (e.g., Carver, Glass, & Katz, 1978), stigmatized people may be particularly alert for the more subtle and indirect clues that belie others' genuine attitudes (Devine et al., 1996; Frable et al., 1990; Goffman, 1963). PLWHIV report a heightened sense of guardedness around others (Bennett, 1990) and are likely to be sensitive to the behaviors of other people that signal prejudicial attitudes about HIV (e.g., Chapman, 2002; Rintamaki et al., 2007).

The mindful state that stigmatized people maintain has consequences for how other's behaviors are assessed and evaluated by PLWHIV. Kleck and Strenta (1980) demonstrated that individuals with physically deviant characteristics may attribute other's reactions to their stigma, even when stigma had no bearing on the other person's behavior. Other studies have shown that stigmatized individuals are more likely to attribute negative outcomes to prejudice when this attribution is plausible rather than implausible (e.g., Crocker, Major, & Steele, 1998). Accordingly, it is likely that PLWHIV experience attribution ambiguity during social interaction, which causes uncertainty in interpreting other people's behavior. If the interaction is positive or negative, PLWHIV may be uncertain if the other's behavior is a response to their HIV status, the other's personality traits, or the specific circumstances surrounding the interaction. Knowing that others are aware of one's HIV status may make one even more likely to interpret other's behavior as reactionary to the stigma or stereotypes associated with HIV (see Kleck & Strenta, 1980).

Understanding of social comparison at the group level is one of the primary contributions social identity theory makes to the study of intergroup behavior (Tajfel & Turner, 1986). When people who are socially disadvantaged (such as PLWHIV) compare themselves to people who are not, they process their comparisons at the collective level rather than the personal level (e.g., Vanneman & Pettigrew, 2001). In other words, they tend to focus on how their entire group fairs in comparison to other groups. Social comparisons at this level are particularly likely when one's social group membership is made salient (Brewer & Weber, 1994; Major, 1994). Given the derogation and social exclusion they experience, this process seems almost inevitable for PLWHIV. This will likely work against people with HIV if they see themselves as disadvantaged in comparison to people without HIV, as upward comparisons can threaten self-esteem (for a review, see Crocker et al., 1998).

Developmental Literature

Social identity theory contributes much to our understanding of how people with HIV manage the social stigma surrounding the virus. It helps explain the categorization and exclusion processes that degrade PLWHIV and provides insight into how PLWHIV might perform in the presence of others; however, social identity theory is not without limits that leave unanswered a number of questions about the HIV experience. Social identity theory tends to discuss group membership in static terms, such as ingroup/outgroup and low-identifier/high-identifier; yet it is reasonable to assume that people can transition from one category to another during different points in time. In contrast, research in counseling and developmental psychology identifies how people integrate social identities into their self-concepts and how they demonstrate developmental change across these social identities (i.e., becoming stronger or more affiliated with their social group membership). These models describe how people go from low identifiers to high identifiers and explain the relationship between identity development and stigmatized social group membership.

Research within these traditions identifies stigma as an important catalyst to social identity development for members of stigmatized and disenfranchised social groups. The identity models from these traditions also describe social identity experiences in ways that help account for how and why people respond to different types of identity threats. To date, these research traditions have focused on the social identity and developmental processes of racial and ethnic identity (e.g., Atkinson, Morten, & Sue, 1989; Cross, 1991), gay and bisexual identity (e.g., Cass, 1979, 1984), age identity (e.g., R. E. Goldsmith & Heiens, 1992; Logan, Ward, & Spitze, 1992), gender identity (e.g., Ashmore, 1990; Gurin & Townsend, 1986), and (dis)ability identities (e.g., Charmaz, 1995; Low, 1996). Although the groups focused on in the various theories may be different in several respects, they all are stigmatized and/or disenfranchised subgroups of the larger population.

The researchers in this tradition have conceptualized identity development in surprisingly uniform ways, primarily as a set of stages across linear trajectories that mark developmental advancement in the formation of a social identity. Although researchers differ in the number of stages they use to organize and describe social identity formation (e.g., three, four, five, or six stages), comparison across these models reveals numerous parallels in the stages researchers conventionally have proposed as fundamental to these different social identities. Each begins with a negative self-concept, progresses to dissonance between self-appreciating and self-depreciating attitudes, continues through an empowered and confrontational stage, and finally develops into a synergistic and highly socially conscious stage. Although researchers in this tradition describe multiple stages across their respective models, they are quick to suggest that advancement across all stages may not transpire among all individuals and that some will never fully progress to the final developmental stages. To that end, they also often suggest catalysts may exist for both developmental advancement, as well as identity foreclosure (the halting of developmental advancement) in each model.

There is much to be gained from this literature that can help us understand the experiences of PLWHIV; however, care must be taken in adopting concepts from this earlier body of research and applying them to the context of HIV. This need for care is due, in part, to aspects of the HIV experience that may be unique and, therefore, shape the lives of PLWHIV in ways that are unlike those of the groups previously studied. As such, it is important not to superimpose the HIV experience over those of previous models, but rather, to let the experiences described by PLWHIV reveal both how they might be different, as well as similar, to the experiences of members of other stigmatized groups.

Previous research on developmental aspects of social identity also is vulnerable to several criticisms that can be avoided in future research. First and foremost is the rigid, linear nature of the stage models within the developmental and counseling psychology traditions. Linearity predicts specific start and stop points across the development of any given social identity, as well as a singular trajectory between these two points. As such, members of the social groups described by each model are expected to start at a specific developmental stage and systematically progress into more advanced developmental stages. Although each model proposes that advancement to the highest developmental stages is not guaranteed for every individual, these models assume that all people in a given social group will begin the process of social identity development in exactly the same way and proceed to encounter the exact same set of identity experiences. This excludes the possibility that people may enter the identity development process at a number of different developmental conditions; however, the diversity found within any given social group necessarily calls this assumption into question. This criticism is especially valid in the context of HIV, in which diversity (including that of age, race, sex, sexual orientation, and economic status) is considered the hallmark of the HIV community. As such, future theories and research on social identity development must be able to account for the possibility that social identity processes may not all commence and converge in a similar fashion across all members of a given social group.

A second concern pertaining to previous identity models follows a similar logic: People should not be expected (as is assumed in linear models) to only move in a singular direction through these developmental processes. Previous models of social identity development posit that the process is uni-directional and that people cannot regress in their development; however, this assumption seems inappropriate, especially in the context of stigmatized groups. Gays and lesbians, for instance, may begin to embrace their sexual identity but regress back into shame and malcontent if their initial attempts at coming out are met with hostility or reproach. Future models on social identity processes, therefore, must be sensitive to nonlinear progression throughout identity development.

A third concern pertains to the mutually exclusive nature of the stages used in previous social identity models. When combinations of variables are being used to describe members of a social group at each stage of a model, only one such combination is described for each stage; however, the limited set of stages described in each of these models is assumed capable of describing every single person within a particular model's social group. In other words, each of these models assumes that at a single point in time, any one person belonging to a group described by a model should clearly fall into one particular stage described by that model. This assumption also violates expectations for diversity found across the human experience. Future identity models, therefore, must be able to account for the dynamic (and potentially limitless) experiential and developmental variations found naturally occurring throughout any given population.

A fourth concern pertaining to earlier social identity development models involves the variables described within each of these models. In particular, many models move beyond concepts of identity to include a variety of behavioral variables. For instance, some models of identity development include such things as political involvement (e.g., Cross, 1991) or the incorporation of peers into an individual's social network (e.g., Cass, 1984). These interactions may be both important to, and descriptive of, social identity development, but it is questionable whether or not they are, themselves, variables of identity. It may be more appropriate to consider how these variables might impact the development of a person's social identity, or how a person's social identity may affect these variables, rather than referring to a set of behaviors as identity.

A fifth concern regarding earlier identity models pertains to what it is they claim to describe. Models addressing sexual identity, racial identity, age identity, (dis)ability identity, and gender identity all claim to describe social identity development. This muddies the definition of social identity, which is simply the sum of aspects that constitute of a person's sense of self that are derived from a group membership. This connotes issues of becoming aware of belonging to a group and possessing a sense of group membership. This may be appropriate for issues of sexual identity, age identity, and (dis)ability identity, as these are often identities people discover over time; however, the same does not always apply to matters of race or gender identity, which are social identities into which people are born and often are aware of from an early age. What many of these models are doing, in fact, actually describes changes in the level of importance people place on their given group memberships to their sense of self. Researchers in social psychology have reinforced this notion (e.g., Branscombe, Ellemers, Spears, & Doosje, 1999; Turner & Oakes, 1997). As a result, future research on social identity and identity development should better distinguish between social identity and level of identification.

Despite the limitations of earlier research and conceptualizations of social identity development in stigmatized groups, this research has greatly advanced the understanding of the identity processes many people experience. Given that PLWHIV are relegated into a stigmatized social group, it is likely that they also experience developmental identity processes. Lewis (1999) presented evidence of this in the status passages of HIV-positive gay males. PLWHIV experience identity loss and transition when they are diagnosed as HIV-positive. Given the parallels between the social experiences of people with HIV and those of the aforementioned stigmatized groups, it is both relevant and timely to construct a system for describing HIV social identity. Such a system will not only be useful in explaining how PLWHIV manage the social stigma surrounding the virus, but will likely shed light on how they manage the communicative dynamics of numerous other social experiences, as well.

Two Studies of Coping with HIV Stigma

Two studies were conducted to explore the social identity and stigma management experiences of PLWHIV. The first study included 33 PLWHIV who participated in focus group interviews regarding how they managed the effects of HIV on their lives. The second study built upon the findings of the first, utilizing one-on-one qualitative interviews with 72 PLWHIV to further understand how they cope with the virus. Together, these studies utilized a broad set of questions pertaining to the HIV experience, combining the benefits of synergy provided during focus groups and the in-depth probing acquired during one-on-one interviews.

As part of a larger study on the HIV experience, Study 1 included 33 participants in eight focus groups who discussed how HIV had affected their lives and how they managed the uncertainty in their lives. Recruitment for the study was conducted at an AIDS Clinical Trials Unit (ACTU) at a large midwestern university. Clients at this center were contacted by a member of the ACTU based on their previous willingness to participate in similar research. Participation in the first stage of the study consisted of joining one of six focus group interviews that each lasted approximately 120 minutes. Four years later, attempts were made to contact all of the original 33 participants in these focus groups to invite them to participate in a second set of focus groups. Nine of the original 33 returned for the two reunion focus groups (several members of the original groups were deceased and others had moved out of the area), the purpose of which was to explore how the lives of the participants had changed over the previous four years. Participants were given $40 remuneration for each focus group in which they participated (up to $80).

Of the 33 participants in the original six focus groups, 29 were men. Twenty-eight participants identified as White, 4 as African American, and 1 as Latino. Additionally, 29 of the participants identified as gay or bisexual, and 4 identified as heterosexual. Participants ranged in age from 22 to 59 years old (mean of 37.1 years old). Participants had been diagnosed with HIV from less than 1 year to 12 years, with 21 of the participants having been diagnosed with AIDS (an advanced stage of HIV infection at which point opportunistic infections and malignancies are increasingly likely).

Of the 9 participants who returned for the two reunion focus groups, 7 were men and 2 were women. Six participants identified as White, 2 as African American, and 1 as Latino. Additionally, 7 participants identified as gay or bisexual and 2 identified as heterosexual. The ages of participants ranged from 30 to 65 years old (mean of 44.1 years old). Participants had been diagnosed with HIV for 6 to 16 years, with 3 of the participants having been diagnosed with AIDS.

Once the focus groups were scheduled, three members of the research team met the participants at a designated location in the ACTU and conducted the focus groups there. The interview schedule entailed two major areas: demographics and life experiences. The interviewer began by eliciting demographic information using a short demographic questionnaire. The interviewer then asked participants questions regarding their experiences with the study's focal issues. To elicit accounts of the life experiences of people with HIV, participants were asked a series of open-ended questions pertaining to how HIV had affected their lives, what being HIV positive meant to them, and what important changes had occurred in their lives since diagnosis. Probe and follow-up questions were included, when appropriate, to clarify issues and validate the interviewer's interpretations of responses.

Study 2 sought to answer research questions similar to those in Study 1; however, this second study involved examining the life history narratives of 72 PLWHIV through the use of one-on-one, semi-structured interviews. Data were collected at an AIDS Clinical Trials Unit at a large midwestern university and two AIDS service organizations in one small city and one large city in the central United States. Participation in the study consisted of single interviews that lasted between 60 and 120 minutes. Interviews were conducted on location at the respective care facilities, the facilities of the primary investigator's institution, or the participants' homes. Participants were provided $40 remuneration for their involvement in the study.

A total of 81 participants volunteered for this study. This included 69 men and 12 women, of whom 48 identified as White, 27 as African American, 4 as Latino, and 2 as Asian. Sixty-five of the participants identified as gay, lesbian, or bisexual, and 16 identified as heterosexual. The ages of participants ranged from 24 to 65 years old (mean of 40.1 years old). Participants' time since diagnosis ranged from 1 to 19 years, with 36 of the participants having been diagnosed with AIDS.

Qualitative interviews were used in this study to explore the experiences of PLWHIV. The interview schedule included two major areas: demographics and life experiences. The interviewer began by eliciting demographic information (divorced from subsequent transcripts) and then asked about the participants' experiences, beginning from diagnosis ranging to the present. To elicit accounts of the life experiences of PLWHIV, participants were asked a series of open-ended questions that included (a) how the participants' lives were affected by HIV, (b) how social support was used in managing the issues surrounding HIV, (c) how stigma and embarrassment caused by issues surrounding HIV were managed, and (d) how participants managed their sense of control regarding the virus and its effects on their lives. Probe and follow-up questions were included, when appropriate, to clarify issues and validate the interviewer's interpretations of responses.

The interviews were scheduled after the participants contacted the research team. Once scheduled, a member of the research team met each participant at a designated location (either the ACTU, the AIDS service organization facilities, the research team's educational institution, or the participants' homes) and conducted the interview there. Each interview was audio recorded and later transcribed by members of the research team. Equipment problems prevented nine interviews from being transcribed (which left 72 to be analyzed). Care was taken during the transcription process to obscure overtly identifying information (such as names) revealed during the interviews to protect participant anonymity. After transcription was completed, the audio-tapes have been kept in a secure place and the transcripts made accessible only to research team members.

In both Study 1 and Study 2, a coding team consisting of the author and three undergraduate students analyzed the transcripts using latent content analysis and constant comparative techniques (Strauss & Corbin, 1990), looking at how people's experiences changed over time, what attributes of various processes were perceived by the coders to constitute social identity, what factors served as catalysts for movement throughout these processes, and what aspects of the participants' lives (such as their social interaction with others) were affected by these processes. The research team independently coded the transcripts to identify general categories before reconvening to discuss and compare general findings. After a compilation of the findings was agreed upon by the research team, the author then re-examined the transcripts to assess the fit of the research team's analysis. The author then corresponded with the three undergraduate coders who worked on the two studies to discuss the overall findings. As a result, consensus was reached among the coders on the HIV social identity process dimensions, their antecedents, and implications these processes have for communication.

Results

A social identity involves the aspects of a person's sense of self derived from a social group membership. Understanding how PLWHIV relate to their HIV status as a social identity provides insight into how they interact with others, both HIV-positive and HIV-negative alike. Doing so requires the identification of processes that affect affiliation with this identity and how these processes relate to social interaction and other variables, such as overall health. In the two studies, the coding team identified four process dimensions as important to how people relate to the HIV social identity. These involve aspects of how people place value on their HIV social group membership and the salience of this identity. Value of the social group membership consists of three identity processes: (a) managing negative meaning, (b) managing positive meaning, and (c) orienting to stigma. Salience consists of how mindful people are of their HIV-positive status.

The HIV social identity process dimensions identified in these studies appear to have significant implications for social interaction. In particular, participants described how their interactions with others were affected by the value and salience they placed on the HIV social identity. Conversely, participants described how social interaction with others had considerable effects on movement across the four process dimensions. The relationships between the process dimensions and social interaction (along with other behavioral outcomes, such as self-care) found within this study are described below.

Managing Negative Meaning

Managing negative meaning refers to how PLWHIV manage the negative affect generated by various HIV-related experiences and the weight they place on these negative experiences. Weight, in this context, refers to how important or powerful a person perceives an event or the affect it produces. People may place more weight on certain negative events than on others (e.g., not all forms of HIV stigma may have the same impact on people). Additionally, weight is not constant and can change over time. People may experience negative events soon after diagnosis upon which they place a great deal of weight; however, over time people may adjust or learn to minimize these negative events and place less weight on the negative meaning they ascribe to them. The more weight people place on negative meaning derived from the HIV experience, the less they will value HIV as a social identity. HIV-related outcomes and various social interactions that heighten negative meaning construction are described below, followed by descriptions of ways in which negative meaning construction can affect behavioral outcomes, such as social interaction and self-care.

Antecedents   People's success in managing negative meaning across the HIV experience appears related to numerous variables, many of which involve social interaction. To begin, people's general health plays an important role in affecting negative meaning, with multiple HIV-related health problems increasing the likelihood of negative meaning construction. Medications used to treat HIV have the potential to both heighten and diminish negative meaning across people's experiences with HIV (also see Lambert, Levy, & Winer, this volume). On one hand, when treatments are effective at combating the virus, negative meaning is diminished; however, when medications fail or produce serious side effects, negative meaning is increased.

Disruption of life goals also can increase negative meaning, as does the loss of friends who die from HIV-related causes. Regardless of how they die, the loss of peers can be acutely felt by people struggling to help their friends pass on. Tyrone recounted the following story when describing the personal costs of comforting a friend dying from the disease:

Two nights before he died, he was really sick. Basically the support I gave him wasn't in words or anything like that. He was really scared and it was like he knew he was dying. He kept on screaming, "Get them away from me, get them away from me!" So I would get out of my bed and go sit on the bed with him. While he was screaming during his last two days, I was in the bed with him just letting him know, "I'm here with you. They aren't going to get you while I'm here with you." That was really the only kind of support I knew how to give him at that point. I couldn't die for him, but if I could have I probably would have. He was a really good person.

People also can face discrimination from others, as might the people they care about. For instance, Marcella described concern for her family and explained that her loved ones "will be discriminated against if [it's discovered by others that] someone in the family has it [HIV]." Subsequent feelings of loneliness or alienation also serve to increase the negative meaning people ascribe to the HIV experience. Christian explained that after his diagnosis, "I have not made many friends since that happened … I'm alone a lot more now." Dealing with incompetent or fearful care providers serves to increase negative meaning in the HIV experience, whereas dealing with competent care providers who show respect for their clients can reduce it. Tommy noted,

That whole "care team" concept they have is marvelous. You got a doctor, got a nurse practitioner, you have a diet nurse, a prescription nurse, and then you have a research nurse. I tell you all them put together I probably wouldn't need my family. There is so much support that has kept me happy and feeling good.

Information meant to help people manage HIV also has the potential to alleviate negative meaning and inspire hope in PLWHIV, but can sometimes be overwhelming, which results in heightened negative meaning. Martin noted,

Some of these people who are being diagnosed right now—it's overwhelming, and I don't blame them for just running away from it and saying, "I can't handle all that information." You know, how, what drugs am I not supposed to take with these drugs, and all the complications of taking drugs is—if I were diagnosed right now, I'd be overwhelmed too.

Personality and outlook on the illness experience appear important in moderating how intensely people feel negative outcomes of the HIV experience, with such outlooks often being shaped by people's spiritual affiliations. A strong sense of faith or connection to a divine presence appears to lessen the negative meaning people place on living with HIV. As Charlie explained, "a lot of people wonder how I went through all of that and I tell them God helped me and that's what it is." Finally, social support appears to play an important role in mitigating negative meaning, with support from friends, family, and peers all having the potential to reduce the negative meaning people may ascribe to the HIV experience; however, when the social support provided involves bad information or comes from domineering sources, negative meaning may be heightened for the recipient. Receiving support from domineering peers may not be uncommon, as Steven noted, "unfortunately, what I have often times found is people saying 'well, this is what I do and therefore this is the way it should be done.'" Receiving both beneficial and ineffective social support from others is not restricted to the experiences of PLWHIV and has been well documented among people dealing with various difficult events (e.g., Herbert & Dunkel-Schetter, 1992).

Outcomes   How people manage negative meaning in the HIV experience also appears to have important implications for various behavioral outcomes, including self-care, support provision, and networking. People who are high in negative meaning may be more likely to report suicidal ideation and refuse treatment in order to hasten their own deaths. Thomas explained,

> I just decided not to take the treatments, but I couldn't tell you why. It could be a lot of reasons. It could be because I don't want to live with this disease as long as maybe the medications will help me to live. I think that's torture.

People also may have difficulty providing support to others living with HIV. LaTisha described numerous struggles in her life as a result of her HIV status, stating, "I wouldn't say anything. I'd just be quiet." People also may try to avoid others living with the virus in order to avoid thinking about the negative ramifications of HIV. Arnold stated, "I don't want to be in a room with a bunch of people who are HIV-positive. I don't want to hear other people's pain and suffering. I think it would just bring me down farther." On the other hand, people may seek out peers in their search for successful ways of mitigating negative meaning in the HIV experience. Clark explained,

> The main reason I went [to a support group] was to socialize and get to know people again, because I felt kind of out of the loop and not knowing what was going on. I was feeling kind of lonely and depressed. So that was my main reason for going … it has helped me to laugh a little bit more.

Managing Positive Meaning

Managing positive meaning refers to the events people experience as a result of living with HIV that generate positive affect and the weight people place on them. The more weight people place on positive meaning derived from the

HIV experience, the more they will value the HIV social identity. Participants throughout the data described maintaining positive and negative meaning in combinations, suggesting that positive meaning and negative meaning are conceptually distinct constructs and not simply opposing ends of the same continuum. For instance, participants described experiencing high levels of both negative and positive meaning simultaneously, low levels of both simultaneously, high in one but not the other, or combinations of moderate levels of the two meaning types.

The construction of positive meaning is a well-documented strategy for coping (either reactively or proactively) with the negative affect that can result from difficult experiences (e.g., Taylor & Armor, 1996; Taylor & Brown, 1994). In the case of HIV, health outcomes and various social interactions that heighten positive meaning construction are described below. This is followed by a description of the ways in which positive meaning construction can affect behavioral outcomes, particularly social interaction, as described by participants in the two studies.

Antecedents   People's ability to manage positive meaning throughout the HIV experience appears to be affected by numerous variables. After diagnosis, the families of some PLWHIV come together to provide their loved one with support, which several participants reported as an important positive outcome of the HIV experience. Luther stated,

> In a way, it brought me and my internal family, the next of kin, so to speak, very close. If I had to do it all over again, I wouldn't have changed a thing because today my mother and father and I have a wonderful relationship. I can talk to them about anything—even the gayness, which I could never talk to them about before because they are very strict, very religious people.

Others reported becoming friends with many new people who they otherwise would not likely have met, which also was seen as a positive outcome of living with HIV. Phil explained,

> There certainly is a bond there that is different from other friends. We have some commonality as far as talking about lab work and medications. I have made friends with people that I would never have made friends with because of the disease. I think once you get past that commonality of HIV you find other things you have in common.

For some, HIV serves as a catalyst for positive behavioral changes, shifts in perspective, and increased sensitivity to others, all of which were seen by participants as positive outcomes of the HIV experience. For some, this leads to reorganizing their lives, such as Harold, who stated,

I took more control of putting things in order, getting things more focused, working hard on my personal needs; putting me first instead of everything I was doing. I think I got straighter or it made me more conscious of what needed to be taken care of and put my priorities in the right perspective.

Tyrone credited HIV for his still being alive:

I believe it [being diagnosed with HIV] probably saved my life. I believe if I had not had it, this might sound stupid, but I believe if I'd never had got AIDS, I'd probably be dead a long time ago. I used to be real wild and stuff… It changed me and it changed me for the best. I wouldn't have had time because I was a busy trooper out there in the streets. I would not have had time to sit and think about what I was doing. I probably wouldn't be here. I'd be dead by now from a bullet or something else.

Some people reported either a newfound sense of spirituality after their diagnosis or a strengthening of their pre-existing faith, both of which were identified as positive outcomes of the HIV experience. As David explained, "it's [living with HIV] brought me a lot closer to God. It strengthened the faith system that I already had in place [and] it forced me to call upon that system." As a result of these positive outcomes of the HIV experience, some participants described engaging in educational outreach or HIV supportive services, which in turn lead to even more positive meaning from the HIV experience. Maria explained how her activism and educational outreach affected her:

It feels good. I have a hard time being objective or quantified but it's just one of those things that feels worthwhile. It emotionally feels good and when that happens I generally feel good. It is something that I value and will want to continue. It's like eating. It's a multi-faceted thing. It's an opportunity to intellectually educate; emotionally it is one other way I can be less secretive; spiritually I feel more connected with those around me. It works.

Outcomes   Positive meaning construction across the HIV experience also has implications for how people interact with others. In particular, people who construct positive meaning across HIV experiences described wanting to seek out and provide support to those who are newly diagnosed in order to help them do the same. For example, Florence stated,

I want to be somebody's backbone because somebody was mine … I was down and out. For real, I'm telling you, I was a female Freddy Krueger. I was [gurgling sound effect]. Now that people have reached out and showed me what it was and I just asked for wisdom and tried to regain as much as I can. If they [other people with HIV] feel like they want to fall they can fall on my hand and it'll be just like a pillow, a comfort. That's the way I want it.

At the same time, some people who construct positive meaning do not want to be around those who are high in negative meaning, instead preferring to interact only with others who have minimized negative meaning or constructed positive meaning in their experiences living with HIV. Robert explained about his experience with a support group: "There were some people who were there to wallow, and I wasn't there to wallow. I was there to try and cope. So it just seemed like a very negative type of group, so I got out of it." For those people intent on managing the negatives of HIV, being around people who cannot or are not yet able to do so is a frustrating and undesirable experience. Wanting to affiliate with those dealing with similar circumstances and those who share similar attitudes is not uncommon, particularly in the context of illness (e.g., Kulik & Mahler, 1997), nor is desire to affiliate with others who share attitudes similar to oneself (e.g., Schachter, 1959); however, in the context of HIV, this helps explain how and why people may network with peers, as well as provide insight on who might best provide support to newly diagnosed individuals.

Orienting to Stigma

Orienting to stigma refers to how people cognitively come to either accept or reject the social stigma that surrounds HIV. The more people internalize and accept HIV social stigma, the less likely they will value HIV as a social identity. Conversely, the more they reject HIV stigma, the more capable they may be of constructing positive meaning from the HIV experience, which can lead to increased value placed on the HIV social identity. Rejecting HIV stigma also may lead people to embrace the HIV social identity and place more value on it. HIV-related outcomes and various social interactions that reinforce internalized stigma or lead people to reject stigma are described below, followed by descriptions of ways in which orienting to stigma may affect behavioral outcomes, such as self-care and social interaction.

Antecedents   How people orient to stigma is affected by several variables, including people's experiences with stigma, their involvement with activist organizations, and the social support they receive from others. Encountering stigmatizing behaviors from others can reinforce internalization and acceptance of stigma in PLWHIV, but in some, stigmatizing behaviors from others appear to have the opposite effect, serving instead as motivation to reject HIV stigma. Martin puts it in the following way, "we [PLWHIV] don't take shit from nobody now, 'cause we don't have time to take shit." In addition, involvement in HIV activist organizations can help people reject stigma due to interactions with like-minded peers. Neil explained,

It's important to have some place and people that you can go to. Even if nothing else to vent your anger at the world for how they're treating you and to realize that there are legal ways that you can do things if you feel like you are discriminated against. That there are people there that, maybe you don't even know them, but they care and are going to help.

Interaction with peers is an important antecedent to how people orient to social stigma, as supportive peers can help people manage emotions after they encounter stigmatizing behaviors and lead people to move from internalization to rejection of HIV stigma. Conversely, interaction with peers who fit negative stereotypes may reinforce internalized stigma among some PLWHIV.

Outcomes   How people orient to HIV stigma also has important implications for how they may manage their own health care and interact with others. People who internalize HIV stigma or are fearful of being victimized by it may avoid seeking testing or treatment for fear of others finding out they are HIV positive. Such was the case for Don, who explained,

> I was pretty sure throughout the 80s that I had HIV but I didn't get tested because people were advocating putting people with AIDS in concentration camps and stamping them with some sort of tattoo and all this kind of stuff.

People also may develop patterns of irregular treatment adherence if they choose not to take medications in the presence of others (such as at work or among family members). For instance, Ben recalled a time before disclosing his diagnosis to his parents when he planned to visit them. He was forced to either leave his medication at home or deal with unnerving questions that he was unprepared to discuss:

> There was this one drug that came on the market and I was on it and it was twelve hour, twice a day, but it had to be refrigerated and it's like "uh, no! I'm going to Florida in a few weeks to visit my parents. They don't know anything about this. I'll be damned if I'm going to put this shit in their refrigerator!"

In addition to self-care, how people orient to stigma also impacts the ways in which they interact with others. Those who internalize HIV stigma may be reluctant to self-disclose their status to others. In contrast, those who reject HIV stigma may disclose their status as a form of activism or educational outreach, such as Maria, who did a great deal of public speaking on issues surrounding HIV:

One of the reasons I like to be vocal is from the education standpoint. First of all, you got to teach people there are a lot of us out there. Lot more than they may realize. It's encouraging to me when I see them go, "Oh, you mean you can live with this" or "You've got it? You don't look like you got HIV." "Well what does a person with HIV look like?" They can't tell me. "Well I want to teach you a little bit and I'm not a good teacher." There's certain places where it's okay to get on your soapbox. When I have talked to the people who didn't know, because I don't fit the typical, I'm big and round, and a woman and older and I didn't do IV drugs. I don't fit any of the common profiles. They say, "Well you're the first person I've ever known with HIV," and I say, "No, I'm the first person who ever talked about it."

Similarly, people who reject stigma also appeared more prone to join HIV activist organizations than those who internalize HIV stigma, as well as more likely to engage in advocacy and educational outreach programs. Hugh, someone who also openly rejected HIV stigma throughout his interview, stated,

I think the dramatic change has been the realization that I wanted to change my life. And when I saw my health getting better I saw that as an opportunity to focus my life on—I know this sounds pretentious—but on affecting social change in the world, as opposed to affecting parties.

How people orient to stigma also relates to the strategies they employ when responding to stigmatizing behaviors from others. People who internalize HIV stigma may do little in response to encountered HIV stigma and seek to avoid people who might stigmatize them. Burt, who demonstrated shame at being HIV-positive in his interview, described how he silently listens to derogatory comments from his own son about PLWHIV:

I guess there's one thing that bothers me when my son talks about, he doesn't know, he'll say "he has AIDS" and say something derogatory and it's like, "I need to say something" but I can't tell him. That bothers me.

In contrast, people who reject HIV stigma appear more prone to confront their stigmatizers in either educational or aggressive ways, or a combination thereof. Participants expressed a variety of scenarios in which this played out, as evidenced by Norton:

I guess the main thing is that I'm probably not as tolerant as I used to be … I know I probably should be more tolerant, but people who are prejudiced, or whatever … in the past I would just, "Oh, this is the way people are." Now it just makes me mad and I get confrontational. Not yelling or anything like that, but I address it.

Lastly, how people orient to stigma appears to affect their social networking. Those who internalize HIV stigma may withdraw from their social ties through a form of self-imposed isolation. This was evident in the comments of participants such as Karen, who commented, "The biggest thing has probably been the self imposed isolation I've put on myself. [I] kind of have that attitude [that I'm] damaged merchandise." They also may work hard to avoid interacting with other PLWHIV. For some, this has to do with losing control over who might learn of their HIV status. Mike described his struggle with this issue and how it affected his desire to interact with his peers:

> The confidentiality part is what kept me away. I was like, "Now, will this be really confidential if I go to this [HIV support] group?" and finally I was like, "You should probably go." I went that first time and they never mentioned anything about confidentiality. So I left the group that night and I was like, "Okay, we'll try this one more time," and I went back the next week and they did mention the confidentiality and everything that happens in this group should be considered confidential. But the first week that I went they did not mention that and that almost totally scared me away.

It is important to note that how people orient to stigma may be predictive of particular behaviors (such as how people will respond to stigmatizing encounters), but people also may act in ways that seem inconsistent with the general cognitive way in which they internalize or reject HIV stigma. For instance, someone may cognitively reject stigma, but choose not to confront the stigmatizing behaviors of others (such as the case of people who are conflict avoidant); therefore, it is important to use the labels of acceptance and rejection of HIV stigma as references to cognitive states and not descriptions of behavior.

Managing Salience

Salience describes how aware and mindful people are of their HIV social group membership. The value people place on the HIV experience is important to how they relate to HIV as a social identity and helps explain whether they see this identity as favorable or undesirable. Those who ascribe positive value to the HIV experience, and its subsequent social identity, may be more likely to highly identify with HIV, whereas those who see both the HIV experience and social identity as undesirable may more likely disassociate from HIV. Salience serves as a moderator of identification among these different levels of association. Among the people who place a negative value on the HIV experience and disassociate from this social identity, those for whom HIV has low salience, are considered to have the lowest level of identification. Those who place a negative value on the HIV experience and disassociate from this social identity, but for whom HIV has a high salience (such as one who is overwhelmed by

HIV-health problems), are also considered low identified, but more identified than those who deny their status. Among the people who place a positive value on the HIV experience and subsequent social identity, those for whom HIV is salient (such as those volunteering to do HIV educational outreach) will be the most highly identified with the HIV social identity. Those who place a positive value on the HIV experience and social identity, but for whom HIV is not salient, will be highly identified, but not so much as those for whom HIV is salient. HIV-related outcomes and various social interactions that affect salience are described below, followed by descriptions of ways in which salience affects behavioral outcomes among PLWHIV, such as self-care and social interaction.

Antecedents   How people manage salience is affected by a number of variables, three of which include the negative outcomes of HIV in their lives, people's involvement in activism, and their encounters with social stigma. When people are confronted with HIV-related problems, such as poor health or a constant regimen of medications, salience may be high. Such is the case for Martin, who explained,

> I went on medication a year ago and that really, I mean, I have to take it at every meal, and I'm constantly being reminded about it. It's like every time I take the medicine I feel like the virus has complete control over my life. Because I can't eat without taking the medicine, and then it ruins my meal because it leaves a bad taste in my mouth.

Similarly, dealing with stigmatizing behaviors from others may also increase the salience of HIV in people's lives. As Christian explained, his experiences during the early days after his diagnosis, the fear of stigma and the negative reactions he encountered from others made HIV highly salient for him: "During that time I didn't want to be out in public because I felt shunned. It was all I could think about, was I had this virus." At the same time, when people engage in HIV-related programs, such as educational outreach or activist organizations, the salience of HIV in their lives is likely to remain high.

Outcomes   Salience also has implications for a number of behavioral outcomes, including how people manage their own health care. After diagnosis, some people work hard to deny their diagnosis and to block out any thoughts pertaining to it. In one instance, Daniel recounted how he was reminded he had HIV after going in for a second HIV test again several years later:

> I was diagnosed in '89 and that was in New York. I put that out of my mind. Denied it, blocked it, until I got retested when I came back to school. Even when I first got re-tested, I had forgotten that I was HIV since '89. You know, the denial, the mental blocks, and so forth.

This means of coping with negative affect has been identified in various research traditions (e.g., Cloitre, 1998; Dombeck, Siegle, & Ingram, 1996). People who force low salience in this way may avoid interactions with care providers until their immune systems are severely compromised. Norton explained how several of his friends chose not to consider the possibility that they could be infected and put off testing until it was too late for treatments to be effective in managing their health:

> [Some of my] friends got a diagnosis in January and were dead in June. And a couple cases I know for a fact that those persons that got their diagnosis in January they knew for sure they were HIV-positive, they were positive a year before but they were in such denial that they didn't go and have it checked. And my feeling on that is, they knew it. And had they done something a year or two years prior they would probably still be around today. But that was the "I don't want to know" kinda thing.

Similarly, people who do seek treatment but force low salience may become irregular in their treatment adherence. Such was the case with Florence, who explained,

> I didn't want to hear it [about her HIV diagnosis]. I would just go [to health care appointments] because sometimes it was a way to get out and get air. I'd get a bus ticket, get on the bus and go. They'd say such and such and then they'd tell you "Well, you need to take such and such." So, I'd go to the pharmacist, get the medicine. Then turn around and come back home. And then the next appointment, "well, Florence?" "What? Oh. No, well, I forgot." That's because I wasn't in control. I was living in denial.

In either case, this form of low salience has dangerous implications for people's self-care.

Salience also has a number of implications for the ways in which people are likely to interact with others. In particular, people who are trying to lower the salience of HIV in their lives may actively avoid other people with HIV. This is true both for people who are newly diagnosed as well as for people who previously have been highly involved in HIV-related activities (such as former activists, volunteers at HIV-service organizations, or members of educational outreach programs). Numerous participants for whom HIV was primarily a negative experience described their own efforts to diminish the salience of HIV in their lives. For instance, Justin commented,

> To go into a support group and that's [HIV] the focus of the whole meeting, it would make me feel miserable. It's constantly reminding me that I have this. I know I have this and I don't need to be reminded every Thursday night from 7 to 8 o'clock.

For someone like Bill, a person who lost several friends to HIV, backing away from others infected with the virus and distancing himself from his own HIV status was his means of coping with grief and loss:

> I withdrew because it was too much. I haven't been to a support group probably in two years. I'll pick up the books or things on my own, but I just had to back away from it. I think information is what you're going to need to get you through this, and choices, but I couldn't do it any longer. I've buried all the friends I want to bury, and I've stopped putting, associating myself with those people I was burying … It was just too much.

Similarly, those who accept that HIV is a part of their lives but resist the idea of allowing their entire life to revolve around HIV may try to avoid people for whom HIV has high salience. Greg stated,

> When I'm in that phase of not wanting HIV to be the focus of my life I don't spend a lot of time around my HIV positive friends. For many of them that is their focus and that tends to be the main topic of our conversation. I don't always want it to be the topic of our conversation. I don't mean to imply that I'm in denial or anything, but there is more to life than my disease and someone else's disease. It is part of what we go through and it has a big effect on our lives and yet it is not the whole person.

Discussion

The four social identity process dimensions acknowledged in these studies describe how people orient to living with HIV, including how people place value on their HIV social group membership and the salience of this identity. The value component consists of three identity processes: (a) managing negative meaning, (b) managing positive meaning, and (c) orienting to stigma. Salience involves people's awareness of their HIV-positive status. When considered together, the four identity dimensions constitute a theoretical HIV social identity model (HIV SIM) that can be used to both understand the behaviors of PLWHIV and affect their capacity to manage the HIV experience.

Rather than claiming that people experience these identity processes in a uniform way after diagnosis, it is better to understand HIV social identity development as consisting of infinite combinations of meaning, orientation to stigma, and salience. Utilization of these independent dimensions as components of a theoretical social identity model for PLWHIV is an important advancement over the earlier stage models used to describe social identity development. One criticism of stage models is their linear nature, which predicts specific start and stop points across a social identity, as well as a singular trajectory between these two points. Earlier stage models assume that all people in a given social group will begin the process of social identity development in exactly the same way and proceed to encounter the exact same set of experiences, which excludes the possibility that people may enter the identity development process at a number of different stages. Considering the four HIV social identity process dimensions separately allows for the possibility that people may enter the social identity development process in an infinite number of combinations across the four dimensions. The flexibility of the HIV SIM allows it to account for the diversity found within the human experience. Also, the HIV SIM does not suggest that people must follow a singular trajectory across the four dimensions. As such, the HIV social identity process dimensions account for the variability found in the ways that social identity development both commences and converges after people are diagnosed with HIV.

In addition to accounting for the variability found across people's social identity experiences after HIV diagnosis, the HIV SIM also is an improvement over earlier stage models in that it does not suggest a linear trajectory across identity development. Previous models of social identity development suggest that it is a forward-moving process in which people do not regress; however, this theory allows for the possibility that people may move in one direction across these dimensions at one point in the HIV experience, only to move in the opposite direction across these dimensions at later points in time. For instance, people may find ways to minimize negative meaning soon after their diagnosis, only to later deal with difficult HIV-related health problems that cause the negative meaning they ascribe to the HIV experience to increase. Therefore, the HIV SIM is sensitive to nonlinear progression across identity development.

The flexibility of the HIV SIM also addresses a third concern of previous stage models, which is the mutually exclusive nature of the stages these models used in describing social identity development. The possible combinations of identity variables that can describe people's social identity development is limited when a small number of mutually exclusive stages are used, as is the case with earlier stage models. Additionally, it seems unlikely that the limited set of stages described in earlier models is capable of describing every single person within a particular model's social group. As the HIV SIM provides a broad set of possible combinations of the four process dimensions, it is better able to account for the experiential and developmental variation found naturally occurring throughout the HIV community.

A fourth concern regarding earlier social identity development models involves the inclusion of behavioral variables used to describe social identity development. For instance, earlier social identity development models included such things as social networking as part of social identity, when it is more appropriate to think of social networking as both an antecedent and an outcome of social identity development. The HIV SIM includes only variables that describe how people relate to their identity as a person living with HIV, but does consider how these variables relate to behavioral outcomes, such as social networking and social support.

Lastly, earlier researchers claimed to describe identity development among members of various social groups; however, it is clear that these earlier models actually describe common changes in the value and importance people place on their social group memberships. Social identity refers to the aspects of a person's sense of self that are derived from a group membership, whereas earlier models, in essence, describe changes in people's level of identification with their various social identities. In the HIV SIM, people are considered to possess an HIV social identity upon their diagnosis. When people discover they are HIV-positive, they shift from belonging to the larger, HIV-negative social group to the HIV-positive social group. The HIV SIM tracks how people change in the way they place value on this new social group membership and the salience of this group membership in their lives. Each of the four process dimensions can be used to describe any person living with HIV. When considered together, they give an overall impression of the importance of the HIV social identity for a person living with HIV. Those who reject stigma and place more weight on the positive outcomes of living with HIV than on the negative outcomes of living with HIV tend to be more highly identified with their HIV social identity than will those who internalize HIV stigma and place more weight on the negative outcomes of living with HIV than they do on the positive outcomes of living with HIV. In the social identity literature, the importance a person places upon any given social identity most often is referred to as level of identification with a social identity. Therefore, the HIV SIM can be used not only to identify where a person is across each of the individual process dimensions, but, when considered together, these dimensions can help explain people's level of identification with their HIV social identity. In simplest terms, people may range from either low to high identification; therefore, by stating that the HIV SIM tracks level of identification with a person's HIV social identity across his or her experiences living with HIV, this theory is more precise in what it claims to describe than are earlier social identity development models.

In addition to advancing the literature on social identity development, this model and its process dimensions suggest what factors might affect people's movement across the four process dimensions, such as social support and encounters with stigma. This is important both for the assessment and provision of needs across the HIV experience and may serve to aid in the care of people living with the virus. This model additionally identifies how people's movement across these dimensions might influence their behavior, including how they are likely to develop or disband their social networks, seek and provide support, and interact with others, including their health care providers. As such, this theoretical model of HIV social identity is not only conceptually useful when considering the experiences of PLWHIV, but when used as an assessment tool by care providers it also has the potential to improve the quality of life for people dealing with the various physical and social ramifications of HIV infection.

Despite the ways in which the HIV SIM improves upon previous stage models of social identity, care must be taken not to discard the utility inherent to these forerunners of the process dimension approach. Stage models have been used in higher education and counseling psychology since their inception, primarily as tools by which educators and practitioners can assess and provide for the needs of their students and clientele who belonged to groups for which these models were designed. Although lacking in precision, these models may be accounting for general trends across identity development, which means common combinations or trajectories may be found across the four HIV process dimensions. Should future research identify such trends within the HIV SIM, these findings would bridge the precision of a process dimension approach with the utility of a stage model approach in identifying common combinations of identity variables educators and clinicians might encounter with the HIV population.

As a next step in this line of inquiry, future research is required to develop instruments that will enable the quantitative identification of people's location across these dimensions if useful interventions meant to help people using this model are to be constructed. Future research will also need to explore these process dimensions across different social groups (such as race and sex). Although these studies included participants from numerous social groups, several groups had few representatives (such as women). This may be important if common differences exist in the experiences of PLWHIV who possess different demographic attributes (e.g., the HIV experiences of Black, gay men may tend to differ in important ways from those of straight, White women).

Future research also may consider the applicability of these process dimensions outside of the HIV context. All forms of illness may be stigmatized in some way (Vash, 1981), and both meaning management and salience may be common processes for people across illness communities. As such, although the social identity theory described in this project has utility for the HIV experience, it may also be applicable to numerous illness contexts.

Findings from this study highlight the need to further explore meaning making and social support in HIV. The management of both positive and negative meaning is a social identity process dimension described in this study. These areas include how people process through the HIV experience and focus either on negative elements or on finding positive aspects of their experience. As suggested in this study, people who are high in negative meaning and low in positive meaning are at risk for suicidal ideation and irregular treatment adherence. Interventions using communication and social support may be useful in affecting people's management of meaning and help them attain psychologically healthy configurations of the meaning dimensions. Research in communicating social support (e.g., Burleson & Goldsmith, 1998; D. J. Goldsmith, 2004) suggests that the most effective social support messages focus, in part, on helping people put their experiences into perspective. This, in turn, can lead people to find or focus on positive aspects of their current circumstances.

Helping people manage negative meaning in the HIV experience and bolster positive meaning construction could be achieved through communication interventions using social support. Training those who work with people newly diagnosed with HIV in how to best craft social support messages that help people find positive meaning in the HIV experience could be a powerful contribution of communication scholarship to the care of PLWHIV.

Findings of this study also show how PLWHIV are particularly sensitive to behaviors that might signal that other people will stigmatize them; however, it is unclear as to what behaviors might signal that a person will become an enemy or ally. Future research that identifies these behaviors may help to prevent well-meaning friends, family, and care-providers from unintentionally sending antagonistic signals. Similarly, this research may also identify what behaviors people can perform in order to disarm stigma anxiety in PLWHIV.

Conclusion

How people relate to HIV as a social identity involves a set of four process dimensions that have important implications for communication and other behavioral outcomes. How PLWHIV manage meaning, orient to stigma, and determine salience throughout the HIV experience can affect how they perform a variety of behaviors; however, communication and other variables also affect people's movement across these four process dimensions. For these reasons, understanding how people relate to HIV as a social identity is both of theoretical and practical importance, as it furthers understanding of why PLWHIV may perform certain behaviors, provides insight on psychosocial needs important to people's well-being, and suggests ways through which to best help people manage the HIV experience.

Acknowledgment

This study was supported by a grant from the National Institutes of Health (National Institute of Mental Health, NR04376, and National Institute of Allergies and Infectious Diseases, AI25924). The author wishes to thank Dale Brashers for his considerable guidance and mentorship throughout the development of this manuscript.

References

Alonzo, A. A., & Reynolds, N. R. (1995). Stigma, HIV and AIDS: An exploration and elaboration of a stigma trajectory. *Social Science & Medicine, 41*, 303–315.

Asch, S. E. (1951). Effects of group pressure upon the modification and distortion of judgments. In H. E. Guetzkow (Ed.), *Groups, leadership and men: Research in human relations* (pp. 177–190). Pittsburgh, PA: Carnegie Press.

Ashmore, R. (1990). Sex, gender, and the individual. In L. Pervin (Ed.) *Handbook of personality: Theory and research* (pp. 486–526). New York: Guilford.

Atkinson, D. R., Morten, G., & Sue, D. W. (Eds.). (1989). *Counseling American minorities: A cross-cultural perspective* (3rd ed.). Dubuque, IA: William C. Brown.

Bennett, M. J. (1990). Stigmatization: Experiences of persons with acquired immune deficiency syndrome. *Issues in Mental Health Nursing, 11,* 141–154.

Branscombe, N. R., Ellemers, N., Spears, R., & Doosje, B. (1999). The context and content of social identity threat. In N. Ellemers, R. Spears, & B. Doosje (Eds.), *Social identity: Context, commitment, content* (pp. 35–58). Oxford, UK: Blackwell.

Brewer, M. B., & Weber, J. G. (1994). Self-evaluation effects of interpersonal versus intergroup social comparison. *Journal of Personality & Social Psychology, 66,* 268–275.

Burgoyne, R. W., Rourke, S. B., Behrens, D. M., & Salit, I. E. (2004). Long-term quality-of-life outcomes among adults living with HIV in the HAART era: The interplay of changes in clinical factors and symptom profile. *AIDS and Behavior, 8,* 151–163.

Burleson, B. R., & Goldsmith, D. J. (1998). How the comforting process works: Alleviating emotional distress through conversationally induced reappraisals. In P. A. Andersen & L. K. Guerrero (Eds.), *Handbook of communication and emotion: Research, theory, applications, and contexts.* (pp. 245–280). Thousand Oaks, CA: Sage.

Carver, C. S., Glass, D. C., & Katz, I. (1978). Favorable evaluations of Blacks and the handicapped: Positive prejudice, unconscious denial, or social desirability? *Journal of Applied Social Psychology, 8,* 97–106.

Cass, V. C., (1979). Homosexual identity formation: A theoretical model. *Journal of Homosexuality, 4,* 219–235.

Cass, V. C. (1984). Homosexual identity formation: Testing a theoretical model. *Journal of Sex Research, 20,* 143–167.

Chapman, E. (2002). Patient impact of negative representations of HIV. *AIDS Patient Care & STDs, 16,* 173–177.

Charmaz, K. (1995). The body, identity, and self: Adapting to impairment. *Sociological Quarterly, 36,* 657–680.

Cloitre, M. (1998). Intentional forgetting and clinical disorders. In J. M. Golding & C. M. MacLeod (Eds.), *Intentional forgetting: Interdisciplinary approaches* (pp. 395–412). Mahwah, NJ: Erlbaum.

Crocker, J., Major, B., & Steele, C. (1998). Social stigma. In D. T. Gilbert & S. T. Fiske (Eds.), *The handbook of social psychology* (4th ed., Vol. 2, pp. 504–553). New York: McGraw-Hill.

Cross, W. E. (1991). *Shades of black: Diversity in African-American identity.* Philadelphia: Temple University Press.

Devine, P. G., Evett, S. R., & Vasquez-Suson, K. A. (1996). Exploring the interpersonal dynamics of intergroup contact. In R. M. Sorrentino & E. T. Higgins (Eds.), *Handbook of motivation and cognition: The interpersonal context* (Vol. 3, pp. 423–464). New York: Guilford.

Devine, P. G., Plant, E. A., & Harrison, K. (1999). The problem of "us" versus "them" and AIDS stigma. *American Behavioral Scientist, 42,* 1212–1228.

Dombeck, M. J, Siegle, G. J., & Ingram, R. E. (1996). Cognitive interference and coping strategies in vulnerability to negative affect. In I. G. Sarason, G. R. Pierce, & B. R. Sarason (Eds.), *Cognitive interference: Theories, methods, and findings* (pp. 299–323). Mahwah, NJ: Erlbaum.

Engel, G. L. (1977). The need for a new medical model: A challenge for biomedicine. *Science, 196*, 129–136.

Engel, G. L. (1980). The clinical application of the biopsychosocial model. *American Journal of Psychiatry, 137*, 535–544.

Frable, D. E., Blackstone, T., & Scherbaum, C. (1990). Marginal and mindful: Deviants in social interactions. *Journal of Personality & Social Psychology, 59*, 140–149.

Goffman, E. (1963). *Stigma: Notes on the management of spoiled identity.* Englewood Cliffs, NJ: Prentice-Hall.

Goldsmith, D. J. (2004). *Communicating social support.* New York: Cambridge University Press.

Goldsmith, R. E., & Heiens, R. A. (1992). Subjective age: A test of five hypotheses. *Gerontologist, 32*, 312–317.

Gostin, L. O., & Webber, D. W. (1997). The AIDS Litigation Project: HIV/AIDS in the courts in the 1990s, Part 1. *AIDS & Public Policy Journal, 12*, 105–121.

Gostin, L. O., & Webber, D. W. (1998). The AIDS Litigation Project: HIV/AIDS in the courts in the 1990s, Part 2. *AIDS & Public Policy Journal, 13*, 3–19.

Gurin, P., & Townsend, A. (1986). Properties of gender identity and their implications for gender consciousness. *British Journal of Social Psychology, 25*, 139–148.

Herbert, T. B., & Dunkel-Schetter, C. (1992). Negative social reactions to victims: An overview of responses and their determinants. In L Montada, F. Sigrun-Heide, & M. J. Lerner (Eds.), *Life crises and experiences of loss in adulthood* (pp. 497–518). Mahwah, NJ: Erlbaum.

Herek, G. M., Capitanio, J. P., & Widaman, K. F. (2002). HIV-related stigma and knowledge in the United States: Prevalence and trends, 1991–1999. *American Journal of Public Health, 92*, 371–377.

Kleck, R. E., & Strenta, A. (1980). Perceptions of the impact of negatively valued physical characteristics on social interaction. *Journal of Personality & Social Psychology, 39*, 861–873.

Kulik, J. A., & Mahler, H. I. (1997). Social comparison, affiliation, and coping with acute medical threats. In B. P Buunk & F. X. Gibbons (Eds.), *Health, coping, and well-being: Perspectives from social comparison theory* (pp. 227–261). Mahwah, NJ: Erlbaum.

Levin, B. W., Krantz, D. H., Driscoll, J. M., & Fleischman, A. R. (1995). The treatment of non-HIV-related conditions in newborns at risk for HIV: A survey of neonatologists. *American Journal of Public Health, 85*, 1507–1513.

Lewis, J. (1999). Status passages: The experience of HIV-positive gay men. *Journal of Homosexuality, 37*, 87–115.

Logan, J. R., Ward, R., & Spitze, G. (1992). As old as you feel: Age identity in middle and later life. *Social Forces, 71*, 451–467.

Low, J. (1996). Negotiating identites, negotiating environments: An interpretation of the experiences of students with disabilites. *Disability & Society, 11*, 235–248.

Major, B. (1994). From social inequality to personal entitlement: The role of social comparisons, legitimacy appraisals, and group membership. In M. O. Zanna (Ed.), *Advances in experimental social psychology* (pp. 293–348). San Diego, CA: Academic Press.

Major, B., & Crocker, J. (1993). Social stigma: The consequences of attributional ambiguity. In D. M. Mackie & D. L. Hamilton (Eds.), *Affect, cognition, and stereotyping:*

Interactive processes in group perception (pp. 345–370). San Diego, CA: Academic Press.

Rintamaki, L. S., & Weaver, F. M. (2008). The social and personal dynamics of HIV stigma. In T. Edgar, S. M. Noar, & V. S. Freimuth (Eds.), *Communication perspectives on HIV/AIDS for the 21st century* (pp. 67–99). Mahwah, NJ: Erlbaum.

Rintamaki, L. S., Scott, A. M., Kosenko, K., & Jensen, R. (2007). Male patient perceptions of HIV stigma in healthcare contexts. *AIDS Patient Care and STDs, 21,* 956–969.

Schachter, S. (1959). *The psychology of affiliation.* Stanford, CA: Stanford University Press.

Strauss, L., & Corbin, J. (1990). *Basics of qualitative research: Grounded theory procedures and techniques.* Thousand Oaks, CA: Sage.

Tajfel, H. (1978). *Differentiation between social groups: Studies in the social psychology of intergroup relations.* New York: Academic Press.

Tajfel, H. (1982). Social psychology of intergroup relations. *Annual Review of Psychology, 33,* 1–39.

Tajfel, H., & Turner, J. C. (1979). An integrative theory of intergroup conflict. In W. Austin & S. Worchel (Eds.), *The social psychology of intergroup relations* (pp. 33–48). Pacific Grove, CA: Brooks/Cole.

Tajfel, H., & Turner, J. C. (1986). The social identity theory of intergroup relations. In W. Austin & S. Worchel (Eds.), *Psychology of intergroup relations* (pp. 7–24). Chicago: Nelson-Hall.

Taylor, S. E., & Armor, D. A. (1996). Positive illusions and coping with adversity. *Journal of Personality, 64,* 873–898.

Taylor, S. E., & Brown, J. D. (1994). Positive illusions and well-being revisited: Separating fact from fiction. *Psychological Bulletin, 116,* 21–27.

Turner, J. C. (1999). The social identity perspective. In N. Ellemers, R. Spears, & B. Doosje (Eds.), *Social identity* (pp. 11–35). Oxford, UK: Blackwell.

Turner, J. C., & Oakes, P. J. (1997). The socially structured mind. In C. McGarty & S. A. Haslam (Eds.), *The message of social psychology: Perspectives on mind in society* (pp. 355–373). Oxford, UK: Blackwell.

Turner, J. C., Hogg, M., Oakes, P., Reicher, S., & Wetherell, M. (1987). *Rediscovering the social group: A self-categorization theory.* Oxford, UK: Basil Blackwell.

Turner, J. C., Oakes, P. J., Haslam, S. A., & McGarty, C. (1994). Self and collective: Cognition and social context. *Personality & Social Psychology Bulletin, 20,* 454–463.

Turner, J. C., Wetherell, M. S., & Hogg, M. A. (1989). Referent informational influence and group polarization. *British Journal of Social Psychology, 28,* 135–147.

Vanneman, R. D., & Pettigrew, T. F. (2001). Race and relative deprivation in the urban United Stated. In M. A. Hogg & D. Abrams (Eds.), *Intergroup relations: Essential readings. Key readings in social psychology* (pp. 316–336). Philadelphia: Psychology Press.

Vash, C. L. (1981). *The psychology of disability.* New York: Springer.

Wegner, D. M., & Bargh, J. A. (1998). Control and automaticity in social life. In D. T. Gilbert & S. T. Fiske (Eds.), *The handbook of social psychology* (4th ed., Vol. 2, pp. 446–496). New York: McGraw-Hill.

Chapter 10

Stories and Silences

Disclosures and Self in Chronic Illness

Kathy Charmaz

Stories and silences simultaneously frame and constitute meanings among people who experience disrupted lives and, subsequently, inform the content of much qualitative inquiry. The narrative turn in the social sciences has buttressed this inquiry through renewed attention to research participants' stories and researchers' renditions and interpretations of them (Brody, 1987; Bury, 1982, 2001; Charmaz, 1999a, 1999b; Frank, 1995, 1998, 2001; Hyden, 1997; Kleinman, 1988; Maines, 1993; Richardson, 1990; Riessman, 1993; Robinson, 1990). Considerable scrutiny has been given to how researchers represent their subjects' stories and bring the reader into the written narrative (see, e.g., Clough, 1992; Denzin, 1997, 2000; Fine, Weis, Weseen, & Wong, 2000; Lincoln, 1997; Tedlock, 2000). But do stories encompass all experiences? How do we account for silences?

The narrative turn has significantly broadened how we report research. Polkinghorne (1997) advocated narrative as an alternative to traditional research reports because it retains temporality and links events to a common purpose. He noted that we researchers select events to tell the story, yet, by bringing events together, we impose a higher level of order on them than actually occurred. Tierney (1997) further observed, "events and stories do not always unfold sequentially" (p. 30). Scholars such as Polkinghorne and Tierney have advanced our awareness of both the place and logistics of storytelling in research; however, the notion of story, per se, itself largely remains unquestioned (but see Frank, 1997) in research.

Serious chronic illness presents an intriguing case for social scientists to study disclosures within subjective stories—and their absence. Imposing a narrative frame on research participants' experience may mask rather than illuminate its meanings, particularly those of suffering. From a participant's perspective, the raw experience of suffering may fit neither narrative logic nor the comprehensible content of a story. Some participants can only articulate a story about suffering long after experiencing it. Further, when stories are research data, the participant's and researcher's meanings of the story may differ and whose story it becomes may change. Lines blur between stories that we adopt from our research texts and the stories of distressed people. Whether or not *their* stories and *our* stories reflect or retell their experienced realities raises other questions. Nonetheless, lay persons and scholars alike valorize stories and storytellers.

Not all experiences are storied, nor are all experiences stored for ready recall. Silences have meaning, too. In this case, silences often reflect meanings about having a chronic illness and feelings about disclosing it. Silence signifies an absence—of words and/or perceivable emotions. Sources of this absence include a lack of awareness, inability or unwillingness to express thoughts and feelings, attempts to control information, and, at times, tacit messages. Absent sounds sometimes reflect active signals—of meanings, boundaries, and rules.[1] As such, these silences are the other side of spoken language.

To date, studies of chronically ill adults have emphasized how they make sense of their lives through stories (see, e.g., Karp, 1996; Maines, 1991). By understanding both stories and silences—and what lies between them—as well as when, why, and how they emerge, social scientists may gain a nuanced, processural analysis of how their research participants and, they, themselves, construct meanings about self and subjective existence. Studying the stories and silences of chronically ill people permits us to see how crucial features of their existence emerge. I propose that participants' fundamental, though often liminal, concerns underlie their illness stories and intentional silences, and result in tensions between them. These concerns include the place of suffering (see for example, Charmaz, 1999b; Frank, 1991, 2001; Jackson, 1992; Karp, 1996; Kotarba, 1980, 1983), the potential of disconnection and isolation (Goffman, 1963; Jones et al., 1984; Schneider & Conrad, 1980, 1983), the relativity of moral status—that is, the extent of virtue or vice attributed to a person's standing (Charmaz, 1999b, 2000), and the threat of loss of a way of life and the self embedded in it (Frank, 1991, 2000; Murphy, 1987; Sandstrom, 1990).

Throughout this chapter, I juxtapose stories and silences for clarity and contrast; however, my analysis also pertains to everything between them— unspoken signals, impassive responses, implied messages, emotive sounds, fragmented statements and false starts. My focus on stories picks up threads in earlier works and weaves them together with new ideas (Charmaz, 1991, 1995, 1999a, 1999b; Mitchell & Charmaz, 1996).[2] This analysis begins to correct an over-reliance on research participants' stories in qualitative inquiry in general and, specifically, within the growing literature about experiencing illness. What participants do not say may be as telling as what they do say.

This exploration of stories and silences illuminates four issues that affect inquiry. First, silences are often pregnant with subjective meaning (see also Poland & Pederson, 1998). Yet, those meanings may not be shared by everyone involved. Even if people with illnesses do not give their silences meaning, their family and friends may. In turn, we social scientists may confer new meanings on layered patterns such as a participant's unacknowledged silence, other actors' response to this silence and stories of it, and subsequent actions and events. Studying stories and silences offers new possibilities for understanding processes through which research participants construct meanings of their experience. Otherwise we might focus solely on the products of meaning construction: their stories. Then our research story interprets participants' stories rather than offering an interpretive view of their experiences. Moreover, studying meanings from the vantage points of both stories and silences—and what occurs in between—reduces the narrative hazard of imposing stories on our subjects.

Second, my approach begins to balance the rational order of experience that stories foster with the chaos, uncertainty, and emotion that typify disrupted lives. Interviews, which inform my discussion below, elicit rational accounts that explain events and justify actions (Scott & Lyman, 1968).[3] Third, ill people attempt to make sense of an often unpredictable, now disorderly, and sometimes overwhelming and indescribable body. Addressing their stories and silences also brings bodily experiences into analytic purview. This approach also acknowledges the realities of those who see their experience as beyond words, those who have lost their ability to speak, those who remain silent, and those who have been silenced. Fourth, studying research participants' stories and silences has implications for our social scientific stories and how we form and frame them.

Stories

Stories define actions and events, articulate their meanings, and give them coherence and direction: stories make sense of experience. People create stories through reflecting upon their experience, drawing upon or reinterpreting extant narratives, and attending to their audiences. Stories, thus, are fundamentally social in form and content. Storytellers select and connect events from the flow of experience and recast them within an overall theme. The experiences that participants select and how they recast them and create connections between them all draw upon collective understandings of narrative form, purpose, order, and movement as well as of specific content.

A story contains a form, plot, sequence, and ending that shape its framework. When we study stories, certain analytic questions arise: What is the story about? What does the storyteller select to be told? What emerges during the story? What is the storyteller's purpose? How and when might that purpose change?

An illness story makes a reality claim; it contains rhetorical elements of purpose, problem solving, persuasion, and passion. Any story has characters, action, a plot, mood, scenes, as well as a point of view (Mitchell & Charmaz, 1996). Like other storytellers, an ill person's point of view shapes how he or she portrays characters, plot, and action in the story. Hence, an illness story does not replicate experienced or observed reality(ies). Rather, stories are renderings of realities.

Which stories people tell and how they tell them turns on permutations of meaning, context, and audience (Charmaz 1991, 1994, 1999a). Thus, for example, people may not make distinctions between "appropriate" and "inappropriate" audiences when they are shocked by their diagnoses but seek to know what they portend. They tell and retell the same story to anyone who will listen. Months later, these individuals may have established meanings of their illness and subsequently make discerning assessments about whom to tell their stories.

Stories take different forms and serve varied purposes (Bury, 2001; Charmaz, 1999a; Riessman, 1993); hence, stories of the same event may differ depending on when and to whom they are told. Stories themselves do not replicate experience. Thus, all storytellers— including social scientists—select content, enact stories, and interpret their meanings (also see Mattingly, 1998). In typical narrative form, storytellers present an obstacle, form a plot around it, and resolve the problems it causes. Subsequently, the obstacle may produce surprises, redirect attention, introduce tensions, and quicken the pace of the story. The obstacle causes dilemmas, conflict—drama. Through the story, mundane characters and actions become memorable.

As Mattingly (1998) argued, stories are socially enacted and they unfold through mutual enactment; however, narrative disjunctures may pierce the appearance of shared meanings at every turn. Different actors may begin at different narrative starting points. A woman who defined herself as an ill person with intermittent serious disabilities took a contrasting narrative starting point than her husband. He defined her as in good health, although periodically afflicted with illness. Various actors may bring different facts, sensibilities, and stakes to the enactment of the story—a story, for they may construct different stories. Even if they contribute to the same story, what may constitute a narrative plot for one actor may represent evanescent fragments of experience for another. One woman defined her impairment as all encompassing, although its significance remained masked even to her college-age sons. Her attractiveness combined with the invisible nature of her disability led them to ignore her daily struggles. She said, "They only think I'm sick when I can't get out of bed."

The gap between expectations and experiences may shock one actor but present little dramatic twist for another. The story in the making for one participant may be but a chapter; for the other it is the entire narrative. Short stories evoke different images of self than found in multiple chapters, layered upon each other. Subsequently, narrative form shifts, content changes, and meanings vary. After participants grant a story narrative truth, retellings of it may give rise to new versions and narrative emphases. One 35 year-old-man struggled with multiple complications of kidney failure that immersed him in illness. During an interview, he described a recent visit from a friend:

> I realized I wasn't talking about anything *but* my medical problems. In one way it was OK because that's what was going on anyway and so it is reasonable to share that with your friends and on the other side, like for lately

that's all they've been hearing and for me it sounds like all I've been saying. Then it's time to stop and ask, "what is going on?" It seemed like that [illness] was pretty much dominating my life. (Charmaz, 1991, p. 101)

This man's realization caused him to try to broaden his horizons. He could not halt the onslaught of complications that kept him almost housebound; however, he made further attempts to stay in touch with old friends and to bring them back into his life.

It may help to draw connections between the framework and content of the story. A framework for a story often emerges during an interview. This frame reflects an individual's understandings of his or her situation and efforts to shape views—of situation, self, and other actors.[4] Hence, the experiential content of an illness story affects how people frame it. Understandings and efforts are not necessarily coterminous. Ill people magnify, mirror, or minimize their understandings depending upon their current intentions and past assessments of both their experience of illness and their earlier disclosures.

Assessments of relative gains and losses figure here. These assessments are contingent upon the person's current experience and view of it. When in the midst of crisis, for example, someone who wants help is unlikely to hide illness. In ordinary interactions, ill people magnify illness when they believe doing so promises gains without losses. For example, a woman exaggerated her disability to receive a coveted parking spot near the pool where she attended water exercise classes. However, she reversed her stance toward her illness and disability when it came to telling friends of her diagnosis of multiple sclerosis. She said that she kept it quiet because she hated sick people herself, and expected that her friends would also. Sharp contrasts are evident in both the contexts for this woman's disclosures and their consequences. In the former scenario, her investment in magnifying disability was conditional, relatively invisible, and limited. Thus, she had no difficulty reconciling her divergent stances toward disclosure. From her view, the first could benefit her; the second could cause her suffering and loss of moral status.

Stories about one's life may connect inner and outer worlds and thus serve to locate self in time, place, and circumstance (see Plummer, 2001). Not only do these stories integrate past, present, and future, they also create coherence between disparate images of self (Charmaz, 1999a; McAdams, 1997). Forming a story, telling it, and retelling it—to self and others—enable people who have sustained losses to adapt to them.

What may begin as stories of sickness become stories of self when people recount events again and again (Charmaz, 1999a). The original story may recount inexplicable events, harrowing experiences, and shocking discoveries. It may help the storyteller make sense of illness and cope with stigma and difference (Charmaz. 1999b); however, the story may shift and change over time. What began as a story of loss, may become quite another. Men sometimes used stories to make invidious comparisons with others and to show their valor and victory over death (Charmaz, 1994). "You only had a double by-pass? I had a quadruple by-pass and almost died on the operating table." People may use the story to bolster their claims to recovery and to regaining the self before illness rather than the self experienced during crisis and uncertainty. One can claim greater moral status and can distance the illness from self when suffering recedes into the past.

Frequently, however, stories of illness become stories of redemption, transformation, and transcendence of self. The self in the story grows in purpose, meaning, and depth. Then tales of loss are transformed into stories of a reconstructed self. Musa Mayer (1997, p. 354) talked with a woman who had metastatic breast cancer. This woman said:

> I feel that getting cancer was one of the luckiest things that has happened to me. It taught me to love myself for what is inside. It taught me to respect myself and others for who they are and not what they look like. Cancer has taught me to love life and to live and love each day to the fullest.

Silences

The word "silence" denotes stillness, soundlessness. Yet, the stillness of silence arises from varied sources that emerge in particular social contexts. What are the sources of silence? In the case of people with chronic illness, silences often reflect meanings about suffering and feelings about disclosing it. They remain silent rather than being devalued and losing moral status. Silences result from intent—ranging from a strategic message to polite restraint to active withholding. Rapidly unfolding events and awkward situations may prolong silence, although a person may now wish to talk. Silences also result from unintended lapses and misunderstandings. The juxtaposition of meaning and awareness comes into play here and silences vary accordingly. Certainly silences derive from what people do not know, understand, forget, or fail to take into account. Hence, these silences reflect a lack of meaning and lack of awareness.

Other silences occur when people grope for words to say something on the edge of awareness that had been unclear and unstated (Devault, 1990). A glimmer of awareness spawns the search for meaning. Then, too, some silences result from people's awareness of and actions toward their situations. Awareness is complete and meanings emerge through interactions. Thus, depending on the audience, a person may use the timing, placement, length, and context of his or her silence to impart certain messages.

Silences may be imposed: some people are silenced.[5] Once silence has been imposed, the person may choose it rather than risk demeaning judgments. For example, one woman had sequential mastectomies for breast cancer. The chemotherapy and radiation treatments made her deathly ill. Despite her extreme weight loss, baldness, and lack of energy, friends and family trivialized her illness. She said, "For my father and his wife this was kind of like get over it,

Martha, it was like I had a toothache or an earache or something, it was like just get over it. I mean they were not supportive at all." Such experiences relegate people with serious illnesses to silence. Similarly, the devalued moral status that arises from sustained suffering without medical legitimation enforces silence.

Nonetheless, silences are elusive because they result from the unknown as well as the unstated. Silences occur when events and bodily sensations overwhelm the person. Events move too quickly—chaotically—to anchor in words. In addition, words make experience real and stories confirm and congeal its meaning. Remaining silent may be a form of resistance, an attempt to disallow events and refusal to accept the meanings portended in them. A woman who had long struggled with fibromyalgia was diagnosed with breast cancer, but did not tell anyone:

> Actually I have to tell you something, when I first found a lump in May, I didn't tell a soul. Now you must know that I'm the kind of person if it's on my lung it's on my tongue, everybody knows everything about me, especially I'm very close to my family, my sisters and my mother, and you know, subconsciously I so didn't want to deal with it that I didn't tell a soul for almost six months.

Silences may be broken by sounds, not stories. Raw emotions of shock, fear, anger, or sorrow may fill psychic and social space. Later, however, people tell coherent stories about these events although their troubled feelings may lurk just beneath the surface. Annika Lillrank (2002) found that her research participants' interview transcriptions recorded rational accounts of crises that belied their unsettled emotions evident in the actual interviews.

Although people experience some telling moments while alone, silences occur within a social context of language and meaning. Then, too, silences, like stories, mirror patterns of interaction before and during illness. People who seldom expressed their inner thoughts before illness or lacked the ability to articulate them may be relegated to silence. Beliefs about appropriate masculine behavior precluded some men from telling their stories or acknowledging self-deprecating stories. One 62-year-old man who experienced a harrowing bypass surgery told the tale with glee; however, he mentioned that he never even told his doctor of mistakenly taking too much heart medication "because I felt so dumb." Then, too, ill people's proclivity toward silence may intensify when they view others as more knowing, even about self. To the extent that doctors, spouses, and sometimes siblings or parents claimed superior knowledge and ill people accept it, they remain silent. A woman had long blamed herself about her crumbling marriage and difficulties in coping with her life. Her doctor had decreed that her symptoms of nausea and vomiting were psychosomatic in origin and her husband had denounced her as using ploys to keep the marriage together. Until she ended up in the local emergency room and saw another physician who diagnosed a rare condition, she tried to hide her symptoms and suffering.

What lessons do silences teach about an emerging self? Olesen and Whittaker (1968) constructed a foundation for understanding silent acts and speechless moments. They show that student nurses develop a professional self through mundane routines, reluctant moments, and comparisons with peers. Meanings emerge that gain clarity and collective power but remain understood and, often, unspoken. Mundane moments also shape a changed self in illness. Yet, this self is framed in experiences more fleeting and diffuse than in professional socialization, but no less real. Sustained symptoms, immediate medical crises, and lasting stigma undermine an established self-conception. Intermittent bodily sensations, implicit negative messages, and liminal identity questions may erode taken for granted images of self as well.

Like stories, although more subtly, silences frame individuals' past and present and inform their future. As researchers, we must acknowledge when we reframe these silences in our narratives but participants did not. Studying silences means finding gaps in stories, observations, or sequential interviews. It also means witnessing them, observing their social and emotional context, seeing participants' body language, and looking for implicit meanings. Moreover, it means making participants' meanings and metaphors the starting point of analysis rather than forcing our narrative frames on them. Hence, we may take Tierney's (1997) concern with narrative temporality and meaning one step further: Silences, false starts, and fragmented thoughts form and mark experience and thus become part of subjective temporality, as well as lucid stories. Individuals may, of course, cite these markers later in revised or new stories. In addition, Poland and Pederson (1998) observed that silence in interviews does not always mean a passive withholding of speech or denote a devalued status. When and why people tell stories or remain silent not only reflects their immediate concerns, but also their historical, social, cultural, and interactional contexts. What sparks stories in one context may invoke silence in another.

Relationships between Stories, Silences, and Suffering

Stories of and silences about sickness hold promise for exploring narrative meaning, temporal duration and sequence, and reconstruction of self after loss. Studying these stories and silences opens a window on frequently suppressed views (also see Mishler, 1984). In a similar way as stories, silences take different forms and serve varied purposes for individuals and their audiences. Furthermore, how, when, and where silences are defined can become part of other stories. Both stories and silences may reflect meanings of suffering.

Still, much lies between silences and stories. Mere speech differs from stories—a story has form, purpose, order, and movement. In contrast, words may express raw, inchoate feelings, spontaneous responses to immediate concerns, or halting efforts to understand (Charmaz, 1991, 1999a) but not be cast into a story or even a clear statement. Then, too, other statements consist of announcements, personal musings, pressing questions, or unconnected thoughts, but not stories.

Shifting forms and many versions of stories and silences may then reflect a storyteller's multiple selves rather than a single self presented to the world.[6] Hence, these people's stories and silences serve varied purposes that reflect their shifting, strained, or now complicated identities, rather than fueling debates about whether narrative meaning is a search for coherence or a source of creating drama (see Garro & Mattingly, 2000; Mattingly, 1998). While experiencing turmoil, once anchored identities become mobile and so do the selves imbedded in those identities. Thus, these individuals' stories and silences may resemble "mobile subjectivities" (Ferguson, 1993) that stand on shifting grounds—palpable, provisional, and unreliable. Our task is to portray participants' lives in all their complexity—from silent moments to storied claims—while revealing their empirical and theoretical significance.

The stories and silences of chronically ill people remain part of the same process: reconstructing life after disruption and loss (Becker, 1997; Charmaz, 1991, 1995, 1999a, 1999b). Ill people experience tensions between storytelling and remaining silent when they believe that they have a story to tell and have attributed some meaning to it.[7] To tell the story, a story, or not to tell? Certain situations call for a story that accounts for behavior. A rhetoric of self is requested. This rhetoric provides an expressive set of claims to convince an audience, including oneself, of a particular view of self. People then have to decide whether to tell their stories as they view them or to provide some plausible account that justifies or excuses their behavior (Scott & Lyman, 1968).

Initial questions about telling arise in the context of a person's life; subsequently, other questions immediately follow. What to tell? When to tell? How much to tell? What slant should be taken in the telling? Who should be told? "Shoulds" and "oughts" quickly enter into consideration (Charmaz, 1991). And so do imagined views of self that might emerge in the contemplated telling. People may choose silence to resist dominant views although others may interpret this silence as resignation, depending on the context and expressed behavior.

Stories and silences are emergent but seldom wholly idiosyncratic; they emerge within social contexts and, thus, are historically, socially, and culturally specific. Any consideration of stories or silences must take these contexts into account (Charmaz, 1999a). Poland and Pederson (1998), for example, observed that some Eastern cultures value silence, rather than seeing it as problematic, as North Americans do. More specifically, Basso (1970) showed how ethnographic description can reveal how people enact cultural norms about silence. He found that silences in Western Apache culture occurred in uncertain situations and among participants with ambiguous statuses.

Stories serve purposes; silences are often deliberate. Like stories, silences can be laden with meaning, be directed toward particular audiences, and, subsequently, affect the kind and quality of interaction an ill person shares with others. Olesen and Whittaker (1966) discovered that organizational strains and interactional errors spawn silences. Both stories and silences may constitute performances enacted within a scene and for a particular audience (Goffman, 1959). People act and impart meaning through expression and symbol without talking. For example, a middle-aged woman with cancer had taken pride in appearing younger than her years. When she abruptly stopped dyeing her hair and using make-up as her condition worsened, her daughters believed that she had abandoned concerns about appearance, accepted her suffering, and became resigned to dying. Physical appearance may also impart silent cues without an ill person's intent. An ashen face, frightened eyes, or frail body says much about illness—despite a lack of statements or stories (Charmaz, 1991). Similarly, expressions, gestures, and tone can say much about suffering and loss of moral status. The drama of silence depends upon how the audience views the overall context, specific events, and the ill person. Certain meanings of illness may not be lost upon an audience, although nothing is said. For example, a recurrence of cancer after a woman has had breast cancer often foretells impending death.

A lack of knowledge about one's diagnosis and prognosis fosters silence, which may be sustained by a lack of foreboding symptoms. Suffering, devalued moral status, and disconnection remain unreal. These people have little story to tell—now. Their symptoms, when experienced, remain mundane and seemingly manageable. Events and interactions that might arouse their suspicions of something amiss also have other plausible explanations. The story starts for them when events, symptoms, and sensations no longer can be explained—they learn about their fates through their bodies. Their story builds bit by bit upon unstated mundane actions and silent realizations as well as drama and dialogue (Olesen & Whittaker, 1968).

Most people with chronic illnesses partition their experience to some extent. They keep illness and suffering out of the view of particular people and off the stage of certain significant scenes. They monitor their bodies and pace themselves. They learn strategies to manage their bodies and their lives after experiencing loss or disconnection, particularly after they suffer the sting of diminished moral status (Charmaz, 1999b). They subsequently invoke silence as a strategy to manage difficult people or situations; however, they may also partition their experience without realizing it. In certain relationships and settings, expectations of continuity of self and self-presentation outweigh illness and suffering; hence, partitioning experience becomes a habit. They allow themselves to be sick and acknowledge suffering only in private places and close relationships. Otherwise they try to remain silent about illness and suffering. For example, a single mother had to keep her job. She propped herself up to maintain appearances during the work day but collapsed each evening and accepted the care of her oldest daughter. This woman viewed her silence as a taken-for-granted prerequisite for keeping her job; she assumed no other choice. She said, "I can't talk about it at work…. Nobody wants to hear about my sickness and pain. Besides, the administration is looking for places where they can make cuts. I can't make it easy for them." This woman held deeper meanings about keeping her job; it sustained her moral status as a functioning adult despite her supervisor's questions about her work performance. Keeping the job symbolized fulfilling her duties as her daughters' only parent. It also symbolized her last tie to the world of adults. Four years of illness and increased responsibilities at work had narrowed her life.

Silence becomes a deliberate strategy when ill people reflect upon possible actions. Ill people intentionally remain silent when they believe that (a) other people cannot comprehend their situations, (b) their views would hurt a significant person, (c) voicing them would prove too costly, and/or (d) no one wants to hear the story. In effect, such individuals are silenced, even if their assessments are wrong. For example, Ron's advanced multiple sclerosis had left him a bedridden young adult with total paralysis in 10 years. As his body failed, his world narrowed, and his autonomy shrank. His main contacts dwindled to the male caregiver in whose home he lived and a young church volunteer. After being stuck in a nursing home for months against his will, he appreciated living in a "real" home and savored his volunteer's visits. However, his inability to do any bodily self-care, much less anything else, left him feeling useless. He wanted to die. But he could not voice his feelings. Talk of wanting to die or to commit suicide had kept him in a nursing home for months before, and anyone without money who required so much physical care was hard to place in the community. His caregiver told me that Ron knew he was pledged to report any death or suicide talk. For Ron, that meant being sent back into a nursing home, a fate he saw as worse than death. He also knew that such talk would hurt his mother and his volunteer. Thus, he chose not to burden them with his feelings.

If people narrate their way into being, this young man was silenced out of being. Low moral status and earlier disconnection foster silence. Part of the drama of Ron's story rests on his youth. Being silenced may be most evident among institutionalized elders who have no one to hear their stories, much less to value them. Being silenced occurs throughout the experience of illness, albeit in less dramatic and visible forms. Ill people experience being silenced in partial, perhaps edited, or circumscribed ways. Like Ron, voicing their concerns is too costly. For example, one man's corporate manager and coworkers had willingly made scheduling and workload accommodations for him after his initial episode of illness. As time went on, he discovered that coworkers treated his special needs with increasing resistance. He felt silenced. His eyes filled with tears when he told of the growing distance between himself and his co-workers.

Like ordinary adults, ill people use silence to withhold information, control encounters, hide feelings, or even to provide cryptic cues. Intentional silence, for example, can be used as a form of resistance. A frail elderly woman felt that she had lost all choices as her middle-aged son took charge of relocating her to new housing. For a time, she quietly challenged the plans; however, after four months, she found that could not manage living alone in her apartment but resisted entering the assistive care facility that he had chosen for her. Through an angry silence with a steely gaze and scornful disregard of queries about her well-being, this woman revealed how she felt about losing her autonomy.

Resistance played out in unstated acts proclaims a right to moral status; however, other people attempt to break silences. Meanings of suffering shaped the content of the stories they wanted to tell. Perhaps most commonly in my study, women struggled for the right to speak and to make their suffering known. These women attempted to gain moral status through acknowledgment of their suffering. Men often struggled to protect having their preferences honored; they attempted to preserve moral status despite suffering.[8] Both men and women risked disconnection through their actions.

Tumultuous experience can spawn silence. When suffering feels inchoate, incomprehensible—overpowering—events may shoot by before being grasped. Here, suffering lies beyond words—what can one say? Physical suffering may usurp speech. No words fit; one cannot speak, much less construct a story of suffering. The experience feels strange, alien, apart from life ... then silence.

Individuals tacitly may choose silence rather than frame meanings of suffering with words. To form a story of suffering enlarges its meaning (Charmaz, 1991). Someone may form the story of his or her suffering but find it too painful to tell. As a result, concrete tensions arise between an ill person's desire to share an experience and willingness to suffer the pain of retelling of it. Words and stories make suffering real and objectify it. What people may have defined as fleeting and unreal now becomes fixed and real. A story locks experience in time and catches it in social space and meaning. Thus, by giving voice to suffering, people make it theirs. Not everyone wishes to do that. Some people refuse to take a problematic situation and identify themselves with and by it. These people saw themselves as struggling against illness as they struggled to maintain their sense of identity. The risk of further suffering and loss is too great, as is the tacit risk of permitting illness to take over self-concepts. Telling one's story of suffering risks becoming caught in strong feelings; it also risks intensifying earlier feelings. Some ill people realized that telling might undermine their current views: "I didn't want to talk about it because then everyone would think it was worse than it is and then I might believe it." Several people equated talking about their suffering with making their fears a self-fulfilling prophecy: "If I said that I was worried about the kidney failing, then that might make it happen."

Stories, Silences, and Self

How people experience reality may contrast sharply with whether and how they talk about it. What they say may diverge from what they know and do (Deutscher, Pestello, & Pestello, 1993). Some stories may conceal other silences and mask silent realizations about self. Moreover, stories assist storytellers in forming a rhetoric of self for presentation to others and for preservation of self (Charmaz, 1994).

A Rhetoric of Self

A rhetoric of self claims certain attributes, values, and beliefs about past and/ or present self as defining it (also see Riessman, 1990). Silences shape a rhetoric of self as well as storied claims. This rhetoric makes truth claims, posits a specific logic, and aims to sway views, but may leave out other aspects of self and experiences—through knowing or unwitting silence. Serious illness raises questions about self and identity. People who once could take their personal and social identities as givens now may need to reclaim or revise them. The identity claims embedded in illness stories form one basis for a rhetoric of self. Claims of continuity with the past form another. Identity claims often require remaining silent about events, actions, and concerns that undermine the asserted rhetoric.

Thus, silence can form the backdrop against which a rhetoric of self is constructed—and judged. Alcoholism accelerated one man's illness. Although he told his brothers that he had stopped drinking, he had not. In an unmailed, seldom shared, letter he wrote of his shame and guilt about his drinking. In this silent space, he acknowledged being on a downward spiral—his body was failing organ by organ, system by system. He had lost jobs, contacts, and friends along the way. At the same time, however, his silent disclosure contradicted the social persona he claimed. This man masked his silent awareness through stories of his invincibility under duress, of contests and collaborations with doctors, and of victories in handling the health care maze. Tales of outsmarting his doctors underscored the persuasiveness of his view of reality. The discrepancy between this man's silent disclosure and the self presented in his stories suggests that what is most significant may remain unstated. Here silence consisted of an absence of telling while speaking something else. As the discrepancy grew between silent realities and social stories, the self reflected in this man's stories became more heroic. They were replete with claims of remaining undefeated by illness and of maintaining personal competence despite declining health.

Thus, people use silence about crucial facts of their current existence to keep them secret, or at least politely unspoken, as they invoke vivid past images of self. The man above created a rhetoric of self in which the past informed his present identity claims. By aligning himself in the present with the commanding man he had been in the past, he attempted to raise his now-diminished moral status, to limit further disconnection, and to reduce identity questions—from others and, likely, from self. Hence, ill people can use stories to retrieve and restore the past and the self within it although this rhetorical self may little resemble the self given in their present circumstances. Simultaneously, however, ill people may invoke these stories to distance themselves from negative images in the present. In addition, treating the rhetorical self as real fosters reclaiming the sense of control that they now attribute to this past. Of course, this sense of control in the past is relative. During the specific past, ill people may not have particularly perceived themselves as having control of events or their lives. In fact, they may have been struggling with major areas such as managing family upheavals, keeping a difficult job, or handling financial problems. When compared to the present, however, the past now looks as if it had been controllable. This response intensifies when people look back at the past without the felt emotions of the past.

Stories may celebrate resolution—not only of problematic identities and moral statuses but also resolution of lifelong questions—that previously had been relegated to silence. The rhetoric of self takes new form that contrasts with the self in the past. A new sense of self may put to rest nagging identity questions from the past. When celebrating this reconstructed self, ill people tell stories tied to the present and subsequently, also, to their new images of self. Here, a person may gain moral status and reduce suffering by relinquishing identity standards of the past. The person's rhetoric of self subsequently reflects these shifts.

In the following story, Nancy Swenson, who had many symptoms from carcinoid tumors, learned to relinquish the silent although pervasive standard of womanhood to which she once had subscribed. She gave up activities but gained new criteria for a valued identity. Nancy said,

> My mom's illness [advanced Alzheimer's disease] taught me the patience I haven't had before and this illness has taught me a whole lot more, and the hardest part I still have to deal with is not being superwoman. But it's taught me a lot and I have found that you can say "no" to people and it's okay, and you cannot, don't have to be doing everything, and that's okay, too....It's taught me that you don't have to do everything letter perfect and you don't have to take it all on yourself, you can delegate and you can put some things aside and if the house isn't perfect, that's fine and a little dust doesn't kill anybody.

A rhetoric of self may then go beyond a mere account. Rather, it can reflect new realities and realizations. Nancy's story articulates lessons about herself and about managing a life with illness and reveals that she saw her illness as the teacher. Silent, unshared events reveal stark lessons when these events mark turning points. One night Nancy retreated to the couch after completing her mother's care because she could not crawl upstairs to her room. She realized that her body was changing. Other events occurred in conversation as she adopted her counselor's viewpoint, resisted her adult children's demands, and countered her friends' attempts to silence her claims of being sick. Nancy's story above was built on these events although her narrative only hinted of them.

Obviously, the present informs interpretations of the past (Mead, 1934) for both storytellers and their audiences, although some participants may remain unaware of *how* this occurs. Thus, a story may change radically over months and years as a person changes his or her slant and tone toward earlier events and experiences of suffering during them. In the first story, the man suffered from his loss of moral status and sense of failure as well as from his physical symptoms; he retreated from the present into a more honorable past and claimed a rhetoric of self based on it. In the second story, Nancy claimed her suffering as part of her story and part of herself. Her rhetoric of self drew upon current realities and past silences. To adopt Frank's (1998) terms, Nancy was rising *in* her suffering rather than rising *above* it. Her rhetoric of self now included lessons learned from suffering.

Stories of Sickness and Stories of Self

Stories form a repository for storing events in meaning and memory; they provide ways of looking at the past. When accepted, or even when continually reiterated, stories can become reified, and therefore, treated as a "true" account of events rather than one rendering among many possible versions. Stories of sickness recount events and imbue them with meaning. These stories may be told for a variety of purposes: to inform others, to remind them of special needs or invisible disabilities, to elicit sympathy, to establish rapport or intimacy, to persuade others to act, or to entertain with dramatic flair (Charmaz, 1991). Stories of sickness may describe a self in the past without necessarily embedding the self in the present in it. Often present identity claims lie more in the stance of the storyteller *toward* the story than given within the tale itself. Thus, the self of the storyteller is not necessarily embedded in the content of the story.

Stories of sickness are of a different order than stories of self. Stories of suffering are *of* the self—they touch and transform the self (Charmaz, 1994, 1999b). These stories do not merely reference reality; they create reality. As such, the person lives within and through the story. Like Frank (2001), I view suffering as the crucial issue here. One can have pain without suffering and suffering without pain; both hold different implications for stories and for self. Suffering is immediate, consuming, and profoundly disrupting. As such, suffering connotes an awareness of loss and consciousness of how distressing experiences may affect present and future self.

When a story becomes tied to self, images of self and indications of moral status within it become defining. A revised self emerges as these new views supersede past, likely entrenched, images. The transformation of stories of sickness into stories of self allows and sometimes enforces new images of self (Charmaz, 1999b).

A series of events reconstructed Nancy's story above and reshaped her defining images of self. She gained pride from giving her mother good care and from professionals' recognition of it, and even gained her doctor's grudging respect. She learned to interpret her physical sensations and to trust her assessments of them, despite lack of medical confirmation. Friends and family let her know that they could not tolerate hearing about her pain, fatigue, and fears. Nancy had always been the strong one. They discounted her descriptions of symptoms and ignored her worries about flare-ups. As they trivialized her suffering, they relegated her to silence. That worked for some years. When I first met Nancy, she asked herself over and over about her illness, "Is it all in my head?" Yet, as she dealt with debilitating symptoms for years, she gained confidence in herself for handling her life and her duress with illness, finances, grown children, and her mother's care. She later broke the silence with a counselor who also had an esoteric chronic illness. In Nancy's case, the story became one of personal gains that transcended physical losses:

> I had so little self-worth, and now I see things [differently]....When I started evaluating all of—everything I always felt before was my fault, no matter what, was my fault. And I understand now that it wasn't my fault. And I don't know, I just started feeling better about myself, and when that started happening, then I started thinking—you know, every once in a while, these instances [of feeling guilty] would come up, and I guess it would be like taking something out of the freezer, I mean it defrosts and when you put it back—it's not—you don't have as much.

Nancy wove fragments of experience into a coherent story through reflecting on the past while she gained new images of self in the present. The form, plot, sequence, and ending of a story moves the listener toward a sense of completion; however, for many people with illness, actual experience may not reflect any of these characteristics—chronic illness does not end, nor do the stories it spawns.

Stories of self reveal beliefs about essential attributes of self—both lost and gained through illness. These stories often mark a transformation of self that emerges through suffering and subsequent struggling to maintain one's moral status. Suffering from illness means more than immediate physical pain. Pain can be relegated to the body; suffering is embedded in self and existence. Frank's (2001) experience of excruciating pain from tendinitis in his shoulder provides important clues to differentiate pain and suffering. The significance of his pain from tendinitis dwindled when contrasted with his suffering while waiting to know whether the nodes on his lungs and diaphragm meant a recurrence of cancer:

> Fortunately, I did not forget everything I had learned during the previous years. One thing I remembered was to ask myself, in a meditative way, what I was suffering from at that immediate moment. The answers were all memories and anticipations, because at that moment I did not feel sick. (Frank, 2001, p. 353)

Thus, people suffer when they step back into a frightening past and leap forward into dark futures feared in that past (Charmaz, 1991). These steps and leaps challenge the person's sense of control and belief that he or she had already conquered or resolved past fears through will, grit, and action.

Stories change as time elapses, and the immediacy of suffering wanes or new experiences cast a different perspective on it. A new medication or surgical procedure may offer a reprieve from a much worse fate (see Brashers et al., 1999). Subsequently, a story of suffering may later become a story *about* sickness and, therefore, permits disavowal of being marked by it. The changed story provides fertile ground for revising identity claims, informing audiences, regaining superior moral status, and dominating interactions. For example, people can use their stories of pain to show how tough and resilient they are. A story about earlier suffering can also testify to a life of pain and sorrow—to be dredged up and displayed as an identity announcement when useful (Charmaz, 1991). Of course, storytellers must be careful about choosing audiences because they may deny, trivialize, or ridicule suffering; hence, storytellers risk losing the impact of the story and negating their present identity claims based upon their earlier suffering.

Where does the story fit? Stories are embedded in contexts—not only do they arise in certain situations and in particular lives, but also they often occur within relationships and the course of an illness. What kind of story can be constructed and which story can be told arise within these contexts. For example, men and women frequently found that the story they could tell early in their illness became unacceptable as illness continued. Often friends, occasionally spouses, resisted hearing the story as time passed and troubles grew. These ill people became silenced. Before his illness, Mike Reilly had constructed a rhetoric of self that reflected his competitiveness and financial success. His business had failed a few months before his heart attack but contract disputes and marital upheavals lasted long after:

> We'd gotten into tremendous legal problems and I had legal problems that, just what you don't need after having a heart attack—that financially just put a great burden on the family.... I didn't have any disability insurance, so we lived mainly off our savings; we had to borrow some money from my

brother.... things like that. Quite expensive, quite stressful....That actually put a greater strain on our marriage then, than we had prior to my heart attack [when the business actually failed].

Mike lost his court case, sunk further into debt, abandoned his regimen, and plunged into depression. He stopped eating with the family, fixed himself sandwiches, and retreated to his bedroom by 6:00 p.m. Mike said his wife refused to listen to either his business woes or his struggles with health. From his view, "It was so tight economically that it was probably why we stayed together." Silences underscored his losses of moral status and emotional connection.

Stories and Audiences

Stories and silences are relative to particular social worlds and discourses with their own standards of acceptability and adequacy. Whether a rhetoric of self gains acceptance depends upon its audience. Silence may not only be acceptable, but demanded, as Ron's story exemplifies. Other people may demand silence if illness contradicts their taken for granted image of whom the person should be, as Mike's story indicates. Demands for silence intensify when others view a person's illness stories as self-indulgent. Thus, statements like these silence ill people: "Just tough it out." "You *used* to be fun." "You're using it as an excuse." Yet, people live in multiple worlds with different discourses: some call for stories and others demand silences. Transposing stories and silences from one frame of discourse to another becomes a problematic venture fraught with misunderstandings and, at times, consequential judgments.

For an audience to take a rhetoric of self as real, the story on which it rests must be credible. Storytellers try to make their stories credible by positioning them in relation to past events and future possibilities. Their audiences also position the story but may not invoke the same events and situations. In the case above, quite conceivably, the wife resisted accepting the situations on which her husband's story was predicated. Earlier definitions about the ill person's age, gender, and racial identities as well as social location in interactional hierarchies may figure here. Contested definitions and images arise about who the person is and should be. Mike was too young and tough to become suddenly "old" and frail with a life-threatening illness. Subsequently, his story did not sustain the credibility of his earlier rhetoric of self to his most significant audiences—himself and his wife.

Credibility relies on context. An incredible story becomes credible when others see the storyteller as a reliable observer of his or her own experience. In Mike's case, the series of misfortunes abruptly reduced his credibility and then his life-threatening illness caused it to plummet further. Credibility increases when ill individuals have a history of being reliable witnesses and when other participants independently define pivotal events in similar ways as the ill person does. If, however, a story continues a saga of trouble or the person has long been defined as troubled or troublesome, credibility rapidly diminishes and with it, the person descends into forced silence. The uncle who drank, smoked, and ate too much and the mother who made poor marital choices, not once, but several times may already have decreased credibility. Thus, they must frame their stories and select the content with care to be heard at all.

Expressing raw feelings, sharing emotions about suffering, and telling stories about it poses risks. Other people may revoke any earlier encouragement they gave the ill person to talk. (Often their family members, for that matter, receive a similar response.) Subsequently, ill people and their families measure, avoid, or hide medical updates (Charmaz, 1991; Schneider & Conrad, 1980). General statements replace earlier detailed medical reports, if mentioned at all. Chronically ill and disabled people often become masters at reading cues about how much to tell and when to tell it. They size up the other person, begin gingerly, test the response, and decide whether to proceed. The greater the risks they define in telling, the more circumspect they become about remaining silent.

How someone measures the audience affects his or her telling. So does experience *in* telling. Secrets and silences may reflect lifelong patterns or, conversely, self-disclosures may have long been readily imparted. Several men and women had earlier been involved in group therapy or Twelve–Step programs. They believed that having learned skills of self-disclosure helped them to handle illness. Moreover, they felt that they had gained tools that allowed them to create a perspective on their lives. Dave, a professional actor and storyteller, had attended Overeaters Anonymous meetings and had been an AA member for years. My research assistant asked him, "What do you value about yourself right now?"

DAVE: I don't know. Most value. Hmm. I suppose integrity. That's important to me.
JOAN: What do you mean by integrity?
DAVE: How I treat others, how I treat myself. Am I fair; am I honest?
JOAN: Is that any different than it was before?
DAVE: No. That's still pretty much how I live.
JOAN: Uh huh. It's sort of been a lifelong thing?
DAVE: Whenever I've not done that, I've always paid for it myself. For years when I was in business I often did things that were not in my best interest. They were supposedly in the best interest of the company, and that was not integrity. And I can look back at any one of those and see that I've paid a very damaging price for it….Because you continue to remember them and remember the horror, not the approval by the [corporate] Board because you made the company another five hundred thousand bucks, or whatever it is. You remember the horror of what you did and who you abused doing it.

This excerpt indicates how a conversation during an interview may spark new reflections and, thus, elicit stories of self that go beyond stories of illness. As the excerpt suggests, a participant's trust in the interviewer permits a flow of ideas to emerge. The person reaffirms self and moral status through forming the story and articulating the moral message within it.[9] The presence of a responsive interviewer further affirms the view of self in the story.

I have emphasized the moral aspect of ill people's stories and their quest to maintain or regain moral status through them. Stories and silences may be put to other uses. Not all stories reflect moral virtue or heroic struggles with suffering. Some people turn their illness stories into cover stories that hide long-standing troubles in their lives (see Cole & Lejune, 1972). Other people use stories of illness or telling silences about it to challenge the moral concerns of other people for some personal edge or interactional advantage. For example, one woman confronted her parents and siblings about their silence about her illness to force them to address what being a family meant to them.

An aggressive "sad tale" (Goffman, 1961) can be used strategically to evoke sympathy, guilt, and help from a receptive audience. This strategy may succeed with a spouse, parents, adult children—who then heed the ill person's wishes or demands. Adopting this strategy, however, risks driving people away, particularly when anger and resentment forms the tone of the story. These storytellers try to set the terms of ensuing interactions. Their tone implies, not just "why me?" but "why do you have what I need?"—be it health, wealth, or help. One middle-aged woman's sad tales had convinced her elderly mother to give her money. After her mother died, this woman invoked a similar strategy with friends with the added twist of ensuring that each knew what other friends had already contributed. This woman lost credibility among several friends who interpreted her sad tale as a manipulative whine. The potential comparative value of her story faltered because most of these friends had not yet experienced either serious illness or financial ruin. They could not comprehend her situation. A sad tale has more impact when an audience compares themselves with the storyteller and empathizes with her plight. Similarly, remaining silent about crises—for a time—may produce maximum concern when others are shocked by the schism between the storyteller's fate and their own and, subsequently, believe that they should be involved.

Stories, Silences, and Social Science

As social scientists, we start with research participants' stories but we tell them in another way. Which stories *we* tell, how we tell them, and how our audiences, including research participants, receive them all differ from the stories we heard. Sometimes we relate facts, often we provide fragments of stories, and, frequently, provide analytic stories. Now such stories are challenged from within the interpretive social sciences.

Thirty years ago, positivists criticized qualitative research in general, as impressionistic, unsystematic, and subjectivist, and in particular, remained skeptical about studies that drew upon subjects' stories. The development and renewed legitimacy of qualitative research has generated numerous studies in health and illness that rely on subject's stories, frequently through interview accounts (see, e.g., Bury, 1988, Charmaz, 1991, 1994, 1995; Corbin & Strauss, 1988; Herzlich & Pierret, 1987; Mathieson & Stam, 1995; Radley, 1988; Radley & Billig, 1996; Radley & Green, 1987; Robinson, 1988, 1990; Sandstrom, 1990; Schneider & Conrad, 1983; Speedling, 1982; Strauss et al., 1984). Yet, the narrative turn has elicited challenges from within as to how researchers obtain these stories and what they do with them.

Current challenges to researchers' stories include the nature of our relationship with those we study, our representation of them and their stories, and the ethics of observing and reporting. Dorothy Smith (1999) asserted that the scientific quest for explanation leads to reproducing ruling relationships because researchers' interests, questions, and interpretations dominate both interactions with study participants and subsequent texts about them. In Smith's view, these ruling relations separate and objectify our participants' experience from its situated local context and within the thinking, feeling *embodied* individual. Smith sought to reveal ruling relations and to preserve the presence of thinking, acting, feeling, individuals who live in their bodies, which she proposed should be the starting point of analysis.

Qualitative researchers typically try to enhance the presence of the thinking, acting, feeling person in the research. We may unwittingly silence certain stories, although some research participants may insist upon airing theirs. Research participants occasionally may silence us, too. When my assistant asked Dave, her interviewee above, one question, he countered: "That's a bad question," and simply refused to answer it. The tone of the interview supported his response. He saw himself as the expert and viewed her as the novice.

Generalizations about what stands as a qualitative research story and what it means often fail to take into account its contextual frame and emergent, negotiated character. Our methods intend to elicit reflections, rather than reactions; our writing is evocative, rather than conclusive. Study participants, like us, hold diverse meanings and live in multiple realities. Thus, like paintings, our portrayals of them and their worlds reflect certain, although not all, images of their lives.

Do we reproduce ruling relations? Might we misrepresent research participants' stories? Possibly. The setting, research objectives, and social context matter. Like health care professionals, we may don authoritative postures. If participants also view our presence as invasive and their participation as involuntary, then likely, both we and they will adopt a frame of ruling relations, however tacitly that occurs. Yet, if we develop a more egalitarian relationship and establish trust, we may open a place for reflection in which participants' stories take form, and their experience is honored and validated. If so, then they are unlikely to see our presence in their lives as intrusive or voyeuristic—the ethical concerns that poststructuralists and university Human Subjects Committees raise. The context of the research and conditions of participation shape whether ruling relations are enacted or unconstrained reflections are elicited. For example, a call for research volunteers in a newsletter sets a different context and different research conditions than when employers order workers to cooperate with the researcher. The first is individual and voluntary; the second occurs in a crucial organizational context and is coercive.

Whether a social scientist's analytic story offers a more significant interpretation of a participant's story depends on its purpose. If the purpose is, for example, to break silence about an experience whether it be surviving the Holocaust, cancer, or dying with AIDS, then the participant's story provides direct, compelling testimony to help others speak. If the purpose is to discover and report *patterns* of thoughts, feelings, and actions, then the social scientist's collective story may form the more persuasive account.

New understandings and significant interpretations can arise through the researcher's analytic rendering of participants' stories. A story often differs when told from another viewpoint (Maines, 2001). That's true. However, the researcher must try to understand and piece together the participant's story with care and detail. Not all research participants tell their stories with clarity and skill. Adept researchers assemble the story and illuminate the meanings they glean from their participants. They may also place a story into a larger context that distills rather than dilutes its meaning.

Fragmentation of a participant's story derives from compiling many stories and adopting pieces of them to tell an analytic story. Analytic writing, particularly grounded theory analysis, does fragment the story but also contains safeguards against transposing the researcher's agenda on to participants' stories or merely importing juicy details from them (Charmaz, 2006, 2007). Inductive methods such as grounded theory move the analysis forward from the start, by beginning with the data. Systematic qualitative coding keeps the analysis and the researcher close to the data. Analytic categories require weighing and evidence. Snippets and stories embedded in the analysis must earn their way into the narrative.

When analytic guidelines are followed systematically, the researcher cannot easily create post hoc analyses. Moreover, the researcher may crystallize meanings through editing participants' verbatim texts, revealing the interactive construction of their stories, offering description of what remained unsaid, and showing its significance. This approach fosters seeing images through participants' eyes, finding hidden poetry in their voices, and sensing the texture of their lives. In this sense, rather than fragmenting the participant's story, we can enhance its presentation. This approach means adapting traditional ways of analyzing qualitative data and adopting new modes of writing about it. With them, we can aid storytellers to break the silences that surround their situations while we present patterns of thought, feeling, and action that had previously remained implicit. My perspective resonates with Meyerhoff's (1992) notion of a "third voice," one that condenses verbatim texts, invisibly embeds empirical knowledge in participants' tales, demonstrates their dialogic and cultural contexts, and provides a seamless bond between experience and ethnographic analysis (Kaminsky, 1992). Such approaches allow us to illuminate certain aspects of empirical reality with clarity and beauty, although we never cover it all (Marcus, 1994); however, knowing that we cannot view, much less render, the full reality before us should not preclude our efforts to see and interpret experience within it.

Most contemporary critiques of qualitative methods are based on assertions rather than inquiry. Methodological angst has long been a part of qualitative research. It may particularly afflict those of us who study disrupted lives and those who enjoy relatively privileged lifestyles knowing full well that their respondents do not. Does that mean we need to relinquish either our methods or the disciplinary perspectives that shape our view? Not necessarily. It does mean that we need to be reflexive about them. Harding's (1991) concept of strong reflexivity is instructive here. Consistent with Harding, we can envision our research participants gazing back at us and the research process from their standpoints. Then we stand behind them and look back at the social and cultural specificity of our project and its location with other projects—*while we look forward to shape the next step in the process.*

Subsequently, we must assess our concrete decisions. I, too, am sensitive about possible voyeurism. How much should we enter our research participants' lives? When should we enter them? Sometimes there is no question. When one woman invited me to her wedding in Yosemite National Park, I went gladly. I would have also accepted a man's invitation to his graduation party had it not conflicted with a conference thousands of miles away. For him, living long enough to finish his graduate program was a crowning achievement. I later attended his memorial service without hesitation. Whether or not to attend a memorial service for a 37-year-old woman posed greater dilemmas. I had long known about her parents' acrimonious divorce years before, her sisters' reluctance to help her, one sister's agreement, then refusal to donate bone marrow, and her former boyfriend's desertion. Might not I intrude upon private scenes and raw emotions? Yes. I went to the ceremony, however, because I knew that she would have wanted me to come, but I lingered only for a little while afterward.

After each service, the man's best friend and the woman's father thanked me profusely for coming. Neither had met me before, but each knew that a sociologist had conducted numerous interviews with the deceased. The woman's father seemed to appreciate having someone there who knew her well, but was not part of the family drama. Her death had been imminent; the man's had not. Unlike so many times before, he simply did not survive this last crisis. Before leaving the gathering after the service, I introduced myself to the woman who was his best friend and caregiver. Her sadness about him dying alone had flooded the tribute she gave him. We arranged to meet to talk about what happened to help her put it into perspective.

I recently came across the obituary of a respondent who I had interviewed at length over a 7-year period. I hadn't seen her for several years. Hers, too, was a story of a splintered family, problematic siblings, and abandonment by friends. Her life story was, in so many ways, a chronicle of sorrow and suffering. I could have gone to the services and now think I probably should have. I believe she would have liked me to be there, however, I lacked the sense of certainty that had shaped my earlier decisions. I reflected about her concerns. During the first two interviews, she had questioned whether I was being paid to do this work (I wasn't) and hinted that the book could make a great deal of money. Several years after the book was published, her concerns seemed to diminish. She was surprised and, perhaps, relieved to learn that I still owed the publisher a return on the modest advance they had given me. This woman spoke from a position of poverty and struggle; her ability to remain financially and physically independent had been hard-won. The question of possible voyeurism arose again, and I chose not to attend. I mention this story as an example of how our allegiance to social scientific ethics, however uncertain and ambivalent, can take precedence over human relationships and caring. And that may be the greater ethical error.

Conclusion

I conclude by offering a few remarks about our social scientific stories. The contemporary call for reflexivity includes the injunction to remain alert to possibilities of imposing our disciplinary views on our participants' stories. I agree—to the extent that we might do so unwittingly. We must pay attention to research participants' language—spoken *and* unspoken. The data we need to analyze consists of more than spoken words on printed pages; they must go beyond expressed stories. How we couch our story should reflect, but not necessarily reproduce, our participants' stories. Williams (1993) pointed out that social scientists cannot reduce interview respondents' expressive terms to instrumental terms such as adaptation, adjustment, and coping that contain moral judgments. For him, such terms are unrelated to the context of the person's moral life. Williams's point is well-taken; we need to end with concepts that preserve this context and the person's moral life within it. Adopting Meyerhoff's (1992) "third voice" offers one methodological route to this end.

Can we also adapt disciplinary concepts to move us in this direction? What cues can we glean from the analysis above? Disciplinary concepts that do not import hidden moral judgments may serve as points of departure. By asking about research participants' worlds and actions, for example, we can learn from their perspectives. Such concepts can help us begin to converse with our participants and, subsequently, through analyzing these conversations we enter a discussion with our colleagues and ourselves. This way, we can translate, not transpose these disciplinary concepts into research practice and use them to inform our research stance to open dialogue rather than to shut it down. An aware interviewer knows that tacit agreements develop between researcher and participant about what to tell and how much to tell.

An interview story is both process and product. How a research participant views the interviewer influences the kind of story told and how the storyteller tells it. A receptive listener elicits stories, as occurred within the interview excerpt above. The interviewer tacitly, if not explicitly, validates not only that the described experience is real and true, but also the self who lived and described it. Thus, depending on the situation, an interview may help the person either to recapture the past for a moment and the meanings of self within that past.

A research interview opens possibilities for storytellers to give voice to previously silenced suffering. We can offer our research participants a safe place to reveal their silences and tell their stories when we open ourselves to the fullness of their experience. That means that we must avail ourselves to look at sorrow, suffering, and uncertainty and neither flinch nor turn away. We must also allow the story to unfold in bits and pieces as well as in coherent narratives. Storytellers, like social scientists, may need time to contemplate experience and interactional space to develop their interpretations. Thus, the story that we hear on first meeting may not be a reflective and complete rendition. Moreover, we too may evoke a rhetoric of self that silences the realities of suffering.

The voice of suffering and the void of silence alert us to the perils of imposing narratives on oft fragmented, elusive stories participants struggle to tell. If, as Mattingly (1998) argued, "narrative derives its power by transforming and distorting life as lived" (p. 25), then we must ask which narrative and whose story? A rare social scientific narrative may transform reality, but ordinary research reports can interpret life as lived. Rather than forcing a story on participants' inchoate experience and distorting it, we can piece events into an analytic story and claim it as *our* narrative. Hence, we minimize the narrative paradox of producing stories that profess to depict experience but instead distort it.

Social scientific stories are not just there, waiting to be selected like dessert in a cafeteria. Our story is not simply given in the speech of interviewees; it is not merely derived from the institutional discourse of medicine. More likely, participants' stories hint, rather than proclaim, and foreshadow, rather than foretell, our social scientific story. To grasp this larger story, *we* may need to remain silent. Otherwise, we may not be able to discern or understand our research participants' silences—and stories. We must look as well as listen and, thus, discover glimmers of the unknown. In doing so, researchers enter the experience and sense or share the actor's meanings of it. This means being in that liminal place where the unexpected occurs, where stories lose coherence, and speech neither captures nor conveys meaning. The research story may emerge through our sustained listening, watching—*and* studying what we hear and see—and what we do not. As we struggle to understand, our symbolic reach extends to envision something authentic that reflects experience and illuminates anew. Meaning is at once emergent, slippery, and changing. And so it is with the research story that we tell.

Acknowledgments

This chapter was adapted from "Stories and Silence: Disclosures and Self in Chronic Illness" originally published in *Qualitative Inquiry*, Sage (2002, vol. 8, pp. 302–328). I am much indebted to Dale Brashers, Norman K. Denzin, Arthur W. Frank, Daena Goldsmith, Stuart Henderson, Lyn H. Lofland, Virginia Olesen, James W. Pennebaker, and Christopher Schmitt who offered constructive critiques at various stages of the development of my ideas. I was also fortunate to be able to bring reditions of this chapter in its earliest and most developed forms to the Sonoma State University Faculty Writing Program seminars. I thank the following members for their stimulating comments: Judith Abbott, Julia Allen, Karin Enstam, Dorothy Fridel, Diana Grant, Carole Heath, Kim Hester-Williams, Scott Miller, Elaine McHugh, Catherine Nelson, Tom Rosin, Richard Senghas, Meri Storino, and Greta Vollmer.

Notes

1. I am indebted to Julia Allen for defining silence as absence (personal communication, November 10, 2000) and to Richard Senghas for emphasizing that silence may represent an active signal. Also see Olesen and Whittaker (1966) for silences that mark violations of role distance.
2. I draw upon 140 interviews of chronically ill working and middle-class White adults in the United States to clarify the following discussion of stories and silences and to ground the analytic points in concrete experience (see Charmaz 1991, 1995, 1999a, 1999b).
3. See Pennebaker and Keough (1999) for the ill effects of silence on health and an innovative way of encouraging storied accounts.
4. As Jarvinen (2001) observed, the interviewer may play an active role in defining this situation, subject, and the salience of other actors' views. Holloway and Jefferson (1997) further point out that whether the respondent trusts the interviewer and subsequently recounts stories depends upon (a) the topic, (b) anxiety-laden events concerning it, (c) expectations about the interview, (d) interpretations of the interviewer's status characteristics, and (e) the emergent relationship.
5. See Poland and Pederson (1998) for an excellent discussion of being silenced. They emphasize how women are silenced; however, chronic illness may present possibilities for studying how men are simultaneously silenced and choose to remain silent.
6. I am indebted to Virginia Olesen for making this point explicit (personal communication, June 21, 2001).

7. For analyses of problematic meanings, see Bury, 1988; Locker, 1983; Radley, 1988.
8. This finding indicates a possible gender difference that merits further investigation through quantitative research that could also specify the extent to which variation occurs according to age, class, race, marital status, and social support categories as well as the type, length, and severity of illness and disability.
9. Note that this man's moral message is couched in monetary metaphors. I thank Greta Vollmer for making this point explicit. For works that address use of metaphors in illness see Bury, 1982; Radley and Billig, 1996; Radley and Green, 1987; Williams, 1984, 1993.

References

Basso, K. H. (1970). To give up on words: Silence in Western Apache culture. *Southwestern Journal of Anthropology, 26*, 213–230.

Becker, G. (1997). *Disrupted lives: How people create meaning in a chaotic world.* Berkeley: University of California Press.

Brashers, D. E., Neidig, J. L., Cardillo, L. W., Dobbs, L. K., Russell, J. A., & Haas, S. M. (1999). "In an important way, I did die": Uncertainty and revival in persons living with HIV or AIDS. *AIDS Care, 11*, 201–219.

Brody, H. (1987). *Stories of sickness.* New Haven, CT: Yale University Press.

Bury, M. R. (1982). Chronic illness as disruption. *Sociology of Health & Illness, 4*, 167–182.

Bury, M. R. (1988). Meanings at risk: The experience of arthritis. In R. Anderson & M. Bury (Eds.), *Living with chronic illness* (pp. 89–116). London: Unwin Hyman.

Bury, M. R. (2001). Illness narratives: Fact or fiction? *Sociology of Health & Illness, 23*, 253–285.

Charmaz, K. (1991). *Good days, bad days: The self in chronic illness and time.* New Brunswick, NJ: Rutgers University Press.

Charmaz, K. (1994). Discoveries of self in illness. In M. L. Dietz, R. Prus, & W. Shaffir (Eds.), *Doing everyday life: Ethnography as human lived experience* (pp. 226–242). Mississauga, Ontario: Copp Clark, Longman.

Charmaz, K. (1995). The body, identity, and self: Adapting to impairment. *The Sociological Quarterly, 36*, 657–680.

Charmaz, K. (1999a). From the sick role to stories of the self: Understanding the self in illness. In R. D. Ashmore & R. A. Contrada (Eds.), *Self and identity, Vol. 2: Interdisciplinary explorations in physical health* (pp. 209–239). New York: Oxford University Press.

Charmaz, K. (1999b). Stories of suffering: Subjects' tales and research narratives. *Qualitative Health Research, 9*, 369–382

Charmaz, K. (2000). Grounded theory: Objectivist and constructivist methods. In N. K. Denzin & Y. S. Lincoln (Eds.), *Handbook of qualitative research* (2nd ed., pp. 509–535). Thousand Oaks, CA: Sage.

Charmaz, K. (2006). *Constructing grounded theory: A practical guide through qualitative analysis.* Thousand Oaks, CA: Sage.

Charmaz, K. (2007). Constructionism and the grounded theory method. In J. A. Holstein & J. F. Gubrium (Eds.), *Handbook of constructionist research* (pp. 397–412). New York: Guilford.

Clough, P. (1992). The ends of ethnography. Thousand Oaks, CA: Sage.

Cole, S., & Lejune, R. (1972). Illness as failure. *American Sociological Review, 37,* 347–356.

Corbin, J. M., & Strauss, A. (1988). *Unending work and care: Managing chronic illness at home.* San Francisco: Jossey-Bass.

Denzin, N. K. (1997). *Interpretive ethnography: Ethnographic practices for the 21st century.* Thousand Oaks, CA: Sage.

Denzin, N. K. (2000). The practices and politics of interpretation. In N. Denzin & Y. Lincoln (Eds.), *Handbook of qualitative research* (pp. 897–922). Thousand Oaks, CA: Sage.

Deutscher, I., Pestello, F. P., & Pestello, H. F. G. (1993). *Sentiments and acts* (2nd ed.). New York: Aldine de Gruyter.

Devault, M. (1990). Talking and listening from women's standpoint: Feminist strategies for interviewing and analysis. *Social Problems, 37,* 96–116.

Ferguson, K. E. (1993). *The man question: Visioning subjectivity in feminist theory.* Berkeley: University of California Press.

Fine, M., Weis, L., Weseen, S., & Wong, L. (2000). For whom? Qualitative research, representations, and social responsibilities. In N. Denzin & Y. Lincoln (Eds.), *Handbook of qualitative research* (pp. 107–132). Thousand Oaks, CA: Sage.

Frank, A. W. (1991). *At the will of the body: Reflections on illness.* Boston: Houghlin-Mifflin.

Frank, A. W. (1995). *The wounded storyteller: Body, illness and ethics.* Chicago: University of Chicago Press.

Frank, A. W. (1997). Enacting illness stories: When, what, and why. In H. L. Nelson (Ed.), *Stories and their limits: Narrative approaches to bioethics* (pp. 31–49). New York: Routledge.

Frank, A. W. (1998). Stories of illness as care of the self: A Foucaldian dialogue. *Health: An Interdisciplinary Journal for the Social Study of Health, Illness, and Medicine, 2,* 329–348.

Frank, A. W. (2000). Illness and the interactionist vocation. *Symbolic Intereaction, 23,* 321–333.

Frank, A. W. (2001). Can we research suffering? *Qualitative Health Research, 11,* 353–362.

Garro, L. C., & Mattingly, C. (2000). Narrative turns. In C. Mattingly & L. C. Garro (Eds.), *Narrative and the cultural construction of illness and healing* (pp. 259–269). Berkeley: University of California Press.

Goffman, E. (1959). *The presentation of self in everyday life.* Garden City, NY: Doubleday.

Goffman, E. (1961). *Asylums.* New York: Doubleday.

Goffman, E. (1963). *Stigma: Notes on the management of spoiled identity.* Englewood Cliffs, NJ: Prentice-Hall.

Harding, S. (1991). *Whose science? Whose lives?: Thinking from women's lives.* Ithaca, NY: Cornell University Press.

Herzlich, C., & Pierret, J. (1987). *Illness and self in society.* Baltimore: Johns Hopkins University Press.

Holloway, W., & Jefferson, T. (1997). Eliciting narrative through the in-depth interview. *Qualitative Inquiry, 3,* 53–70.

Hyden, L. (1997). Illness and narrative. *Sociology of Health &Illness, 19,* 48–69.

Jackson, J. E. (1992). "After a while no one believes you:" Real and unreal pain. In M. D. Good, P. E. Brodwin, B. J. Good, & A. Kleinman (Eds.), *Pain as human experience: An anthropological perspective* (pp. 138–168). Berkeley: University of California Press.

Jarvinen, M. (2001). Accounting for trouble. *Symbolic Interaction, 24,* 263–284.

Jones, E. E., Farina, A., Hastrof, A., Markus, H., Miller, D. T., & Scott, R. A. (1984). *Social stigma: The psychology of marked relationships.* New York: W.H. Freeman.

Kaminsky, M. (1992). Introduction. In B. Meyerhoff (with D. Metzger, J. Ruby, & V. Tufte), *Remembered lives: The work of ritual, storytelling, and growing older* (pp. 1–98). Ann Arbor: University of Michigan Press.

Karp, D. A. (1996). *Speaking of sadness: Depression, disconnection and the meanings of illness.* New York: Oxford University Press.

Kleinman, A. (1988). *The illness narratives.* New York: Basic Books.

Kotarba, J. A. (1980). Discovering amorphous social experience: The case of chronic pain. In W. B. Shaffir, R. A. Stebbins, & A. Turowetz (Eds.), *Fieldwork experience: Qualitative approaches to social research* (pp. 57–67). New York: St. Martin's.

Kotarba, J. A. (1983). *Chronic pain: Its social dimensions.* Beverly Hills, CA: Sage.

Lillrank, A. (2002). The tension between overt talk and covert emotions in illness narratives: Transition from clinician to researcher. *Culture, Medicine and Psychiatry, 26,* 111–127.

Lincoln, Y. S. (1997). Self, subject, audience, text: Living at the edge, writing in the margins. In W. G. Tierney & Y. S. Lincoln (Eds.), *Representation on the text: Reframing the narrative voice* (pp. 37–56). Albany: State University of New York Press.

Locker, D. (1983). *Disability and disadvantage: The consequences of chronic illness.* London: Tavistock.

Maines, D. R. (1991). The storied nature of health and diabetic self-help groups. In G. Albrecht & J. Levy (Eds.), *Advances in medical sociology: Vol. 5* (pp. 35–45). Greenwich, CT: JAI.

Maines, D. R. (1993). Narrative's moment and sociology's phenomena: Toward a narrative sociology. *The Sociological Quarterly, 34,* 17–38.

Maines, D. R. (2001). Writing the self vs. writing the other: Comparing autobiographical and life history data. *Symbolic Interaction, 24,* 105–11.

Marcus, G. E. (1994). What comes (just) after "Post"? The case of ethnography. In N. K. Denzin & Y. S. Lincoln (Eds.), *Handbook of qualitative research* (pp. 563–574). Thousand Oaks, CA: Sage.

Mathieson, C. M., & Stam, H. J. (1995). Renegotiating identity: Cancer narratives. *Sociology of Health & Illness, 17,* 283–306.

Mattingly, C. (1998). *Healing dramas and clinical plots: The narrative structure of experience.* Cambridge, UK: Cambridge University Press.

McAdams, D. P. (1997). The case for unity in the (post)modern self: A modest proposal. In R. D. Ashmore & L. Jussim (Eds.), *Self and identity: Fundamental issues* (pp. 46–78). New York: Oxford University Press.

Mayer, M. (1997). *Holding tight, letting go: Living with metastatic breast cancer.* Sebastopol, CA: O'Reilly.

Mead, G. H. (1934). *Mind, self and society.* Chicago: University of Chicago Press.

Meyerhoff, B. (with Metzger, D., Ruby, J., & Tufte, V.) (1992). *Remembered lives: The work of ritual, storytelling, and growing older.* Ann Arbor: University of Michigan Press.

Mitchell, R. G., & Charmaz, K. (1996). Telling tales, writing stories: Postmodern visions and realist images in ethnographic writing. *Journal of Contemporary Ethnography, 25,* 144–166.

Mishler, E. G. (1984). *Discourse of medicine.* Norwood, NJ: Ablex.

Murphy, R. F. (1987). *The body silent.* New York: Henry Holt.

Olesen, V. L., & Whittaker, E. W. (1966). Adjudication of student awareness in professional socialization: The language of laughter and silences. *The Sociological Quarterly, 7,* 381–96.

Olesen, V. L., & Whittaker, E. W. (1968). *The silent dialogue.* San Francisco: Jossey-Bass.

Pennebaker, J. W., & Keough, K. A. (1999). Self and identity in adaptation to stress and emotion. In R. Ashmore & R. Contrada (Eds.), *Self and identity: Vol. 2. Interdisciplinary explorations in physical health* (pp. 101–124). New York: Oxford University Press.

Plummer, K. (2001). The call of life stories in ethnographic research. In P. Atkinson, A. Coffey, S. Delamont, J. Lofland, & L. H. Lofland (Eds.), *Handbook of ethnography* (pp. 395–406). London: Sage.

Poland, B., & Pederson, A. (1998). Reading between the lines: Interpreting silences in qualitative research. *Qualitative Inquiry, 4,* 293–312.

Polkinghorne, D. E. (1997). Reporting qualitative research as practice. In W. G. Tierney & Y. S. Lincoln (Eds.), *Representation on the text: Reframing the narrative voice* (pp. 3–21). Albany: State University of New York Press.

Radley, A. (1988). *Prospects of heart surgery: Psychological adjustment to coronary bypass grafting.* New York: Springer-Verlag.

Radley, A., & Billig, M. (1996). Accounts of health and illness: Dilemmas and representations. *Sociology of Health & Illness, 18,* 220–240.

Radley, A., & Green. R. (1987). Illness as adjustment: A methodology and conceptual framework. *Sociology of Health & Illness, 9,* 179–207.

Richardson, L. (1990). Narrative and sociology. *Journal of Contemporary Ethnography, 19,* 116–135.

Riessman, C. (1990). Strategic uses of narrative in the presentation of self and illness: A research note. *Social Science & Medicine, 30,* 1195–1200.

Riessman, C. (1993). *Narrative analysis.* Thousand Oaks, CA: Sage.

Robinson, I. (1988). *Multiple sclerosis.* London: Tavistock.

Robinson, I. (1990). Personal narratives, social careers and medical courses: Analysing life trajectories in autobiographies of people with multiple sclerosis. *Social Science & Medicine, 30,* 1173–1186.

Sandstrom, K. L. (1990). Confronting deadly disease: The drama of identity construction among gay men with AIDS. *Journal of Contemporary Ethnography, 19,* 271–294.

Schneider, J. W., & Conrad, P. (1980). In the closet with illness: Epilepsy, stigma potential, and information control. *Social Problems, 28,* 32–44.

Schneider, J. W., & Conrad, P. (1983). *Having epilepsy.* Philadelphia: Temple University Press.

Scott, M., & Lyman, S. (1968). Accounts. *American Sociological Review, 33,* 46–62.

Smith, D. E. (1999). *Writing the social: Critique, theory and investigations.* Toronto: University of Toronto Press.

Speedling, E. J. (1982). *Heart attack: The family response at home and in the hospital.* New York: Tavistock.

Strauss, A. L., Corbin, J., Fagerhaugh, S., Glaser, B. G., Maines, D., Suczek, B., et al. (1984). *Chronic illness and the quality of life* (2nd. ed.). St. Louis, MO: Mosby.

Tedlock, B. (2000). Ethnography and ethnographic representation. In N. Denzin & Y. Lincoln (Eds.), *Handbook of qualitative research* (pp. 455–486). Thousand Oaks, CA: Sage.

Tierney, W. G. (1997). Lost in translation: Time and voice in qualitative research. In W. G. Tierney & Y. S. Lincoln (Eds.), *Representation on the text: Reframing the narrative voice* (pp. 23–36). Albany: State University of New York Press.

Williams, G. (1984). The genesis of chronic illness: Narrative reconstruction. *Sociology of Health & Illness, 6,* 175–200.

Williams, G. (1993). Chronic illness and the pursuit of virtue in everyday life. In A. Radley (Ed.), *Worlds of illness* (pp. 92–107). New York: Routledge.

Chapter 11

Understanding the Helper

The Role of Codependency in Health Care and Health Care Outcomes

Ashley Duggan, Beth A. Le Poire,
Margaret E. Prescott, and Carolyn S. Baham

The family system recently has been the focus of research regarding factors promoting substance abuse (e.g., Amey & Albrecht, 1998), eating disorders (e.g., Humphrey, 1989; Stern et al., 1989; Waller, Slade, & Calam, 1990), domestic violence (e.g., Infante, Chandler, & Rudd, 1989; Pence & Paymar, 1993), and depression (e.g., Beach & O'Leary, 1993). Recent research extends the role of the family member and focuses on the role of family members' communication strategies in modifying negative health behaviors. Family members who seek to curtail negative health behaviors also may be caught in cycles of ineffective control attempts, perhaps because successfully controlling the negative health behavior may be inconsistent with relational goals. Inconsistent Nurturing as Control (INC) theory provides a way to interpret the relational processes and asserts that relational partners (spouses/cohabitators) and parents in relationships with individuals who engage in negative health behaviors unintentionally and subtly encourage the negative health behavior through their well-intentioned efforts to discourage it (Le Poire, 1992, 1995; Le Poire & Cope, 1999; Le Poire, Erlandson, & Hallett, 1998; Le Poire, Hallett, & Erlandson, 2000).

The current chapter integrates literature on codependency, an individual's sacrificing his or her own personal and/or psychological needs for the sake of continued participation in a relationship (e.g., O'Gorman, 1993), with INC theory in order to examine the communication process in four contexts: (a) substance abusive individuals and their partners, (b) mothers and eating disordered daughters, (c) physically abused women and their violent partners, and (d) depressed individuals and their partners. This work explores these helping relationships in an attempt to understand the role of communication in assisting to change behavioral patterns related to physical and mental health. Implications for altering a partner's "at-risk" behaviors also are explored with the assertion that family members potentially can help curtail negative health behaviors and enhance their own mental health by enacting persuasive strategies that have been shown to be more effective.

Codependency in Helping Behaviors

An essential characteristic of codependent individuals is that they invest their self-esteem, identity, and self-worth in the ability to control and influence behavior and feelings in others even when they are faced with adverse consequences (Cowan, Bommersbach, & Curtis, 1995; Springer, Britt, & Schlenker, 1998). The codependent individual might subvert his or her own needs to cater to the relational partner and is likely to remain in, and even perpetuate, a painful relationship and to use denial, rationalization, and projection to reframe negative relational implications (Cermak, 1991). Codependency has been associated with partners of alcoholic and drug-abusing individuals in the clinical field for the last two decades, but neither definitions of codependency nor empirical evidence for codependency clearly differentiate whether codependency is an individual-level trait or a relational process (Gomberg, 1989). Controversy is grounded in distinctions between codependency as a dyadic tool, a psychological assessment, and a disease entity (Morgan, 1991). Some clinicians who refer to codependency imply that a consistent pattern of traits and behaviors is recognizable across individuals (Cermak, 1986). In counseling, codependency is identified as a syndrome of internalized traits, self-perceptions, and relational styles associated with an individual's having been reared in a dysfunctional home (Wright & Wright, 1999).

The National Council on Codependence developed a consensus definition that described codependency as reliance on people and things outside the self that neglect and diminish one's own identity and suggested that the false self that emerges is often expressed through compulsive habits, addictions, and other disorders that further increase alienation for the true identity and foster a sense of shame (Whitfield, 1989). Codependency may be observed in denial or delusion (distorted thinking), emotional repression (distorted feelings), and compulsions (distorted behavior) (Wegscheider-Cruse & Cruse, 1990). Similarly, the core symptom of codependency has been described in research as other focus/self neglect, comprised of a combination of control and boundary issues that manifests as a compulsion to help or control events or people through manipulation or advice-giving (Hughes-Hammer, Martsolf, & Zeller, 1998). Associated symptoms include unhappiness as a result of growing up in a troubled family, low self-worth, repression of negative feelings by using a positive front, and preoccupation with imagined health difficulties (Hughes-Hammer et al., 1998). Examining codependency across four contexts provides insight into the role of the helper in health care and outcomes.

Inconsistent Nurturing as Control Theory

Inconsistent nurturing as control theory (INC) explains the unique position that nurturer-controllers (commonly known as codependents) find themselves in as they attempt to maintain a relationship with their partner while they simultaneously attempt to alter their partners' behavioral compulsions (see Le Poire, 1992, 1995, for a review). Referencing Watzlawick, Beavin, and Jackson's (1967) delineation of relational paradoxes, Le Poire (1995) argued that several paradoxical injunctions exist in relationships that include individuals who engage in negative health behaviors that interfere with everyday functioning (e.g., substance abuse, eating disorders, aggression, and depression), and that these paradoxes, ultimately, impact expressions of control by the functional partner or family member (i.e., the individual in the relationship with no problem that interferes with everyday functioning). The most deleterious effects of these paradoxes result from the contradictory nature of the functional family member's nurturing and subsequently controlling behavior. These two competing goals of nurturing and controlling frequently result in mixed messages and failed persuasive strategies. For instance, relational partners and parents desire maintenance of the relationship with the individual who engages in negative health behaviors, but relational partners and parents also attempt to extinguish the undesirable behavior (e.g., Duggan & Le Poire, 2006; Le Poire et al., 2000; Prescott & Le Poire, 2002). Further, it may be that one of the reasons the substance abusive person maintains the relationship with the functional family member is because the relational partner's or parent's nurturing behavior is highly rewarding during times of "crisis" (Le Poire, 1995). The resulting conclusion is that if relational partners or parents actually control the undesirable, negative health behavior, they also lose their ability to utilize their nurturing resource base in response to that undesirable behavior. Thus, relational partners and parents may ultimately be driven by the fear that extinguishing the undesirable behavior will decrease the individual's dependency on the partner or parent. Given this insight, it is not surprising that the control attempts of relational partners and parents may not always be effective at diminishing the undesirable, negative health behavior.

INC theory argues, in learning theory terms, that the relational partners and parents' nurturing behavior may actually *reinforce* the negative health behavior, and thus increase the likelihood that the behavior will happen again (Le Poire, 1995). More problematically, relational partners and parents may *intermittently* reinforce behaviors they actually want to extinguish. More specifically, if relational partners and parents nurture the substance-dependent, eating disordered, violent, or depressed individual when they are in crisis, this caretaking may ultimately reinforce the negative health behavior. When relational partners and parents become resentful, however, as is likely to happen (Asher, 1992; C. M. Steiner, 1974; Wiseman, 1991), they may fail to nurture the individuals, and thus fail to reinforce the negative health behavior. This inconsistent nurturing behavior may be an example of intermittent reinforcement, which is positively rewarding behavior that is sometimes present and sometimes absent following a stimulus (Skinner, 1974). Inconsistent nurturing may, ultimately, strengthen the behavior of the substance abusive, eating disordered, violent, or depressed individual because intermittent reinforcement produces more long-term, nonextinguishable behavior than continuous rein-forcement (e.g., Burgoon, Burgoon, Miller, & Sunnafrank, 1981; Skinner, 1974). Clearly, the lack of caregiving by the relational partner or parent is likely an attempt to *punish*, or extinguish the undesirable behavior of the dependent partner or child; however, INC theory argues that the intermittent nature of this punishing behavior will actually *increase* the negative health behavior. Thus, relational partners and parents unwittingly strengthen the likelihood of substance-abuse behavior, disordered eating, violence, and depression through both intermittent reinforcement and intermittent punishment.

INC and the Substance-Abusive Individual/Romantic Partner Relationship

Given the above arguments, it is possible to contend that family members of substance-abusive individuals will be inconsistent in their use of reinforce-ment and punishment and that they will invest their self-esteem, identity, and self-worth in the ability to control and influence the substance-abusive behav-ior in their partners even when they are faced with adverse consequences. The number of individuals and partners affected by substance abuse is rising. In 2002, 22 million aged 12 and above were classified as substance dependent or substance abusive—9.4% of the total U. S. population (SAMHSA, 2007). This is an increase from 14 million in 2000 and 16.6 million in 2001. The costs and consequences associated with substance abuse are enormous. The National Institute on Drug Abuse (NIDA) estimates that overall economic costs (e.g., health care, productivity, police and corrections, legal expenses, social wel-fare, and so on) of substance abuse in 1998 were 143.4 billion, and these costs showed increases from 1992 to 1998 at a rate of 6% annually (NIDA, 2007). The consequences of substance abuse, however, are not solely economic—many relational and family problems are linked with drug and alcohol abuse as well. Research has shown that drug abuse is related to more communica-tion problems among partners (Fals-Stewart & Birchler, 1998; Kelly, Halford, & Young, 2002) as well as increased detachment and less desire for intimacy (Carroll, Robinson, & Flowers, 2002). Similarly, alcohol and drug abuse also are related to increases in partner verbal aggressiveness (Straus & Sweet, 1992) and physical abuse or violence (Quigley & Leonard, 2000).

INC theory argues that the contradictory nature of nurturing the sub-stance-abusive individual and controlling the substance abuse may translate into inconsistent attempts to curtail substance-abusive behavior. INC consid-ers the premise that most nonaddicted partners of substance-dependents are highly enmeshed and dependent upon their relationship with the chemical dependent and thus desire maintenance of the relationship (e.g., Wiseman, 1991). INC considers the additional premise that partners of drug dependent individuals often attempt to *control* their addicted partners by extinguish-ing deviant or drug dependent behavior. For example, wives of alcoholics are known to hide bottles, lock cabinets, and abscond with car keys (James & Goldman, 1971). Nurturing through times of crisis, or excessive substance use, may be perceived positively by both the substance-abusive individual and the relational partner (Le Poire, 1995). Over time, the partner's role as the nurturer-controller becomes a primary relational role. The premises of INC theory taken in combination lead to the logical conclusion that if partners actually control the substance-abusive, they lose their ability to utilize their nurturing resource base in response to the drinking/drugging behavior. In other words, even though partners fervently desire diminishment of this disruptive substance-abuse behavior of the chemical dependent, they may be driven by the fear that extinguishing the drinking/drugging behavior will decrease the substance-abusive individuals' dependency on them. Given this insight, it is not that surprising that the control attempts that the nonaddicted partner makes are not that effective at diminishing drinking/drugging behavior.

Nurturing and Controlling in Substance-abusive Relationships   In relationships between substance-abusive individuals and their romantic partners, INC theory predictions have been supported in both over-time changes in communication control strategies and in ongoing conversations about substance abuse. To consider how this inconsistency manifests itself within communication behavior over the life span of the relationship, Le Poire et al. (2000) investigated changes in partners' strategies to control substance abuse through in-depth interviews of couples including one substance-dependent individual and a non-substance-abusive partner. In this investigation, the researchers predicted and, found that partners typically cycled from reinforcing to punishing communication strategies following labeling of their substance-abusive partners as substance abusive. Specifically, this first study of INC theory hypothesized and found that functional partners (of both genders) changed their strategy usage over time, such that (a) they reinforced substance-dependent behavior more before their determination that the behavior was problematic than after; (b) they punished substance-dependent behavior more *after* they labeled the drinking/drugging behavior as being problematic than *before*; and (c) they reverted to a mix of reinforcing and punishing strategies, resulting in an overall pattern of inconsistent reinforcement and punishment (Le Poire et al., 2000). This cycling is central to the inconsistent nature of reinforcing or punishing communication strategies as postulated by INC theory. Such cycling clearly supports the expected inconsistent nurturing pattern in that it consists of nurturing, then punishing, then nurturing, then punishing communication behavior surrounding substance abuse behavior. Thus, as expected by INC theory, reinforcement is followed by punishment, which in turn is followed by reinforcement mixed with punishment.

Continued work examining relationships between substance-abusive individuals and their partners includes actual ongoing conversations in order to consider nonverbal and verbal communication behaviors that reinforce or punish substance abusive behavior during conversations about drug or alcohol abuse. These studies include couples in a simulated living environment re-enacting conversation to examine the extent to which control patterns illustrated in over-time changes across the relationship also manifest themselves within interpersonal conversations. The first of the interactional studies sought to determine the degree of nonverbal (i.e., kinesic and vocalic) and verbal reinforcement and punishment of substance abusive behavior during actual interactions influenced substance abusive individuals' recidivism and perceptions of nonusing partners' persuasive effectiveness (Duggan, Dailey, & Le Poire, 2008). These findings reveal consistent verbal punishment of substance abuse (e.g., threats, nagging) predicted lower relapse, whereas verbal reinforcement (e.g., telling the partner they are more fun when they use) predicted higher relapse. With regard to nonverbal communication, vocalic punishment and vocalic reinforcement predicted relapse and persuasive effectiveness (Duggan et al., 2008). Results suggest the combination of behaviors resemble intermittent reinforcement and punishment and should actually strengthen the substance-abusive behavior the partner is trying to curtail.

Analysis of nonverbal and verbal communication behaviors as predictors of health outcomes provides similar evidence for INC theory and the role of communication and codependency as a process. Recent examination of nonverbal communication behaviors (kinesic and vocalic involvement, pleasantness, and expressiveness) found that relapse was predicted by less vocal expressiveness, persuasive effectiveness was predicted less vocal expressiveness and more kinesic pleasantness, and goal attainment was predicted by more vocal pleasantness and more vocal involvement (Duggan, Le Poire, & Gaze, 2006). Results suggest social meanings of communication messages play a particular role in the dyadic nature of relationships such that indirect nonverbal cues serve as useful control strategies when verbal confrontation would be perceived as threatening. Similarly, analysis of verbal strategies in on-going conversations provides additional evidence for the dyadic nature of relationships between substance-abusive individuals and their romantic partners. Duggan, Dailey, and Le Poire (2008) found that persuasive effectiveness and goal attainment were best predicted overall by less content invalidation on the part of both substance abusers and partners, by nonabusive partners' increased self-assertion, other-accusation, and other-support. Implications for social meanings of communication messages suggest partners' investment in nurturing and controlling translates into competing goals. Finally, the authors predicted and found that changes in the process of communication over the course of the interaction suggest competing goals of nurturing and controlling. Specifically, couples reciprocated nonverbal communication associated with immediacy and altruism and verbal behaviors associated with validation and support. Conversely, couples diverged or compensated nonverbal communication associated with low immediacy, low altruism, and verbal strategies of assertion and defense (Duggan Le Poire, & Gaze, 2006).

Strategies of nurturing and controlling are also supported by a qualitative analysis of the strategies used by functional partners of substance abusers (Duggan, Le Poire, & Addis, 2006). Partners of substance-abusive individuals used several macro-level strategies that included both reinforcement and punishment. Specifically, they reported using verbal abuse, making rules pertaining to the addiction, punishment, getting a third party involved, threats, avoidance, ending the relationship, expressing personal feelings, withholding something from the partner as a punishment, supporting abuse by participation, demanding the partner stop/active involvement, and confronting (Duggan, Le Poire, & Addis, 2006). The use of these strategies approximates the hypothesized inconsistent and intermittent use of reinforcement and punishment of the substance abusive behavior, and is certain to strengthen the tendency to engage in alcohol or drug use. Although this patterning in and of itself was not found to be more predictive of greater relapse, patterns of reinforcement and punishment were linked to persuasive outcomes (Le Poire et al., 2000). Specifically, partners who were more consistent in punishing substance abuse and reinforcing alternative behaviors (e.g., encouraging attendance at AA meetings) had substance abusive partners who relapsed less. Moreover, more successful partners also reported less depression than those with partners who relapsed more. This is important for two reasons. First, partners of substance abusing individuals can help reduce their partners' recidivism. Second, this assistance can also translate into better mental health outcomes for the partners.

Many may be concerned that homogeny of family members regarding substance abuse status must be ruled out. In fact, Le Poire et al. (1998) undertook a study to explore this very issue in an investigation of reinforcing and punishing strategies based on the drug use status of the functional/persuading partners (past abuse, current abuse, current use, and nonuse). In terms of overall patterns of reinforcement and punishment, all partners appear to be inconsistent in their use of reinforcement and punishment of substance abuse, with past abusers punishing the substance abuse most before they labeled the drug use problematic, and current users and nonusers punishing the substance abuse the most following the labeling and in the post-frustration period. Additionally, current abusers were the most reinforcing of alternative behavior during every time period: a strategy which was most highly related to reduction in relapse (Le Poire et al., 2000). Further, with regard to a more qualitative analysis of strategy type, it appears that nonusers utilized the most indulgence and anti-drink strategies—strategies which clearly are in opposition based on their reinforcing and punishing natures. Past abusers additionally were rated as most persuasively effective by their partners, whereas nonusers were evaluated as the least persuasively effective. The substance use status of the persuading family member will be important to consider however, because modeling by parents and siblings (e.g., Hadelsman et al., 1993) has been known to be associated with greater substance abuse.

Communication and Improved Health   Evidence of this patterning of strategy usage supports the contention that family members intermittently reinforce and punish the behavior they are trying to extinguish. Of further interest is the effectiveness of the strategies exhibited. Learning theory would suggest that more consistent family members should be more effective in their influence attempts. Additionally, greater family involvement in treatment has been associated with abstinence, better family relations, and positive feelings about self (e.g., McCrady et al., 1986; McNabb, Der-Karabetian, & Rhoads, 1989). Further, Le Poire et al. (2000) found that consistently punishing substance abuse combined with consistently reinforcing alternative behavior was predictive of lesser relapse in a substance abusing sample, whereas Prescott and Le Poire (2002) found that consistently reinforcing alternative behavior predicted significantly higher perceptions of mothers' persuasive effectiveness in an eating disordered sample.

These patterns also have implications for the mental health of family members continuing to live with the substance-abusive individual. Implications can be drawn from the substantial anxiety experienced by spouses continuing to live with a partner who alternates between sobriety and drunkenness (Archer, 1979; Byrne & Holes, 1979; Cohen-Holmes, 1981; Conway, 1981; Howard & Howard, 1985). Further, wives with externalizing (acting out) husbands and husbands who drank outside the home had more state and trait anxiety, as well as depression, than did wives with internalizing (self-blaming) husbands. Since externalizing spouses and spouses drinking outside the home are less likely to be affected by the control attempts of their spouses (Beutler et al., 1993), it is possible to argue that spouses who are more effective at controlling their partners' drugging behavior also experience better mental health. This is consistent with the finding that the stress effects of living with an alcoholic partner diminish when the spouse makes attempts to control the other's excessive drinking (Edwards, Harvey, & Whitehead, 1973). Further, and most relevant, partners/spouses of substance abusers were less depressed when their partners relapsed less (Le Poire et al., 2000). Extrapolating to other family members, it is expected that parents, adult children and siblings who are successfully modifying their family members' substance abuse behavior will experience substantially less anxiety and depression as a result of greater predictability in the home environment.

INC and the Eating Disordered Daughter/Mother Relationship

Like partners of substance-abusive individuals, mothers of eating disordered daughters may subvert their own needs to inappropriately cater to the daughter, or they may deny, rationalize, project, or reframe negative relational implications related to the eating disorder. INC theory can inform the communication control process and the ways relational roles are dependent on continuing the eating disorder. Anorexia nervosa and bulimia represent severe disturbances in a female's relationship with food and with her own body image. Despite the fact that the media spotlight of the 1980s no longer focuses on these disorders, the prevalence continues to rise. In fact, the number of adolescents suffering from disordered eating has consistently increased over the past 50 years (H. Steiner & Lock, 1998)—and continues to do so. The two most prevalent eating disorders are anorexia nervosa and bulimia. Anorexia is characterized by extreme fasting, a refusal to maintain a normal body weight, an intense fear of gaining weight, and a significant disturbance in one's body evaluation. Bulimia involves cycles of binge-eating, followed by compensatory purging behaviors to prevent weight gain (APA, 1994). The American Psychiatric Association (1994) estimated the prevalence of eating disorders in the United States to be between 0.5% and 3% of the general population, with women outnumbering men 10 to 1. Researchers agree that anorexia and bulimia remain a persistent problem, particularly for young, middle-class, White women.

Despite the inability to isolate definitive etiological factors, research offers compelling evidence for four major categories of risk factors associated with eating disorders: biological (Wilson, Heffernan, & Black, 1996), psychological (Costin, 1997), sociocultural (Botta, 1999; Fredrickson & Roberts, 1997), and familial (Humphrey, 1989; Stern et al., 1989; Waller et al., 1990). Researchers suggest that these conceptually disparate factors work in combination, although there is little agreement as to which factor, ultimately, has more impact on the development of disordered eating behaviors. Although this work acknowledges the significant role that biology, psychology, and sociocultural factors play in contributing to eating disorders, this work focuses on the unique role the family plays in encouraging or discouraging disordered eating.

The connection of INC theory concepts to the issue of eating disorders has to do with what Kaffman and Sadeh (1989) termed the "emotional connotations of eating" that are most often present in traditional nuclear families (p. 34). A mother traditionally is the primary caregiver to the children in the family, and is therefore closely associated with food and its role in nurturing. When daughters engage in eating disordered behaviors, mothers seek to extinguish the eating disorder. In this case, mothers have competing goals of simultaneously *nurturing* and *controlling* the daughter while attempting to end a substance-abusive behavior. Mothers, by virtue of their role in the family, are expected both to nurture (i.e., provide love and affection) and to control (i.e., protect and impose restrictions upon) their children; however, mothers of eating-disordered daughters have been found to take these dual roles to the extreme. For instance, Humphrey (1989) found that mothers of anorexics were more nurturing and comforting than mothers in a control group, *and* were also more ignoring and neglecting than their control group counterparts. In essence, mothers cycle between approaching and avoiding behaviors toward and away from their daughters, in a pattern of extreme nurturing and controlling. Humphrey concluded that the excess nurturing undermines the daughter's efforts to individuate, and keeps her dependent on the family.

Concurrently, the excess neglect negates the daughter's developmental needs. Humphrey attributed the anorexic behaviors to this pattern of parental control and negation in that the daughter mirrors the conflicting messages with ambivalence about separating from home. The findings clearly demonstrate the association between a daughter's eating disorder and a pattern of disturbed family interactions.

Enmeshment and Eating Disorders   Minuchin, Rosman, and Baker (1978) asserted that the boundaries of family subsystems must be clear and without undue interference in order for the family system to function properly. Enmeshment occurs when distances between family boundaries decrease, and boundaries become blurred. In contrast, families become disengaged when intrafamily boundaries are overly rigid. According to Minuchin et al. (1978), all families fall somewhere between the enmeshment-to-disengaged continuum, with dysfunction defined as being extremely skewed to one end or the other. In their attachment research, Le Poire et al. (1997) confirmed role-reversal as one way in which parents and children perceive their relationships and is related to an overly enmeshing parent. Children who are role-reversed, or enmeshed, with their caretaker tend not to develop their own identities or to individuate from the parent. Humphrey (1989) found that mothers of anorexics were less asserting and more separating toward their daughters, an indication of unhealthy enmeshment between mothers and daughters. Lieberman's (1989) case study of a family in which all four children (2 sons, aged 25 and 15, and 2 daughters, aged 23 and 18) were bulimic found that the mother was morbidly jealous of her daughters' relationship with their father, accusing them of stealing his affections. The parents' marriage was fraught with conflict, and the mother often encouraged the girls to side with her against the father. The author surmised that bulimia was a means of releasing the tension created by the parents' marital discord and parental enmeshment. The mother's actions are consistent with another assumption of INC, that the functional partner is somehow dependent on the relationship with the afflicted.

Kadambari, Gowers, and Crisp (1986) found families of anorexics to be significantly overenmeshed and overprotective. Enmeshment is especially apparent in cases of dysfunctional marriages like the one cited by Lieberman (1989), whereby the mother-daughter bond becomes the center of the mother's life, with the eating disorder serving as the glue to ensure the continuation of the symbiotic relationship (Kaffman & Sadeh, 1989). Kaffman and Sadeh (1989) found that three quarters of their sample of anorexics and bulimics reported a mother-patient overinvolvement/overdependent relationship. This enmeshed relationship, which blocks the natural individuation and separation from the family or origin, was attributed in part to a peripheral-disengaged father. In essence, the mother substitutes the marital relationship with the mother-daughter relationship, fostering unclear and inappropriate boundaries. This is consistent with Humphrey's (1988) finding that mother's of anorexics

reported significant marital distress, describing their husbands as unaffection-
ate, unsupportive, sulky, withdrawn, and neglectful toward them. In the same
study, mothers reported positive relationships with their daughters, and the
daughters were found to be submissive toward their mothers—a relational scenario that provides fertile ground for mother/daughter enmeshment.

Reinforcement and Punishment of the Eating Disorder   In essence, the nurturing
provided by the mother may actually reinforce the disease, rather than extinguish
it. A child's fear of leaving home is thought to be one reason why the child
develops an eating disorder (Kaffman & Sadeh, 1989). Essentially, "becoming
sick" permits the child to prolong her stay at home, under the protective wing
of her mother. INC theory predicts that if the mother nurtures the afflicted
child when she exhibits signs of the undesirable behavior (i.e., refuses to eat,
or binges and purges), she may unwittingly reinforce the behavior, because the
child enjoys the protective nurturing the disorder evokes from the mother.
Since research has found that these same overly nurturing mothers tend also
to be extremely neglecting (i.e., Humphrey, 1989), the mother may suddenly
stop nurturing and start punishing the undesirable behavior—particularly
if she becomes frustrated in her attempts to end the behaviors. INC theory
predicts that this inconsistent pattern of behaviors will ultimately reinforce
the eating disorder. Initial investigations testing INC's assumptions in to the
domain of relationships between mothers and eating-disordered daughters
provide support for the application (Prescott & Le Poire, 2002). Specifically,
in-depth interviews with eating disordered daughters and their mothers
provide evidence for patterns of reinforcement and punishment predicted
by INC theory. In samples of both anorexic and bulimic daughters, analysis
suggests that mothers reinforced eating disorders more before they labeled the
behavior problematic, whereas they punished the eating disorders more after
labeling the negative health behavior problematic. Further, results indicated
that consistently reinforcing alternative behavior immediately following
labeling of the eating disorder significantly predicted higher perceptions of
the mothers' persuasive effectiveness. Finally, reinforcing the eating disorder
predicted greater amounts of relapse (Prescott & Le Poire, 2002). The most
important implication of these findings is that significant family members (i.e.,
mothers) use similar patterns of inconsistent reinforcement and punishment as
did partners of substance abusers.

Based on the empirical and theoretical literature reviewed, it seems
apparent that family relations play a central role in the development, maintenance—and possibly even the cure—of disordered eating behaviors. The
evidence converges to suggest overwhelmingly that eating disorders are not an
individual phenomenon. Anorexia and bulimia do not occur in a vacuum, nor
are they the result of a single, inherent defect within the girl who suffers from
disordered eating. In fact, the evidence suggests that eating disorders might be
characterized as interactional phenomena, which emerge and are sustained by

patterns within the family context. Treatment issues, therefore, could focus on the family as well as the individual. Such a model would necessitate that the family develop new ways of interacting with one another to the point that the eating disorder symptoms are no longer necessary for the family to function.

INC and the Violent Individual/Romantic Partner Relationship

Though it remains to be tested, INC theory may provide a useful theoretical framework to understand why victims of domestic violence maintain the relationship. Social scientific research over the past few decades has raised social awareness to the magnitude and severity of the problem of domestic violence. Domestic abuse is the leading cause of injuries to women ages 15–44 (Novello, Rosenberg, Saltzman, & Shosky, 1992). National surveys estimate that anywhere from 800,000 (Greenfield et al., 1998) to 1- (Bachman & Saltzman, 1995) or even 2-million (Copeland, 1987) women a year experience violence from an intimate. In addition, research suggests that most abuse is not a one-time occurrence, but a pattern of behavior (e.g., Infante et al., 1989; Pence & Paymar, 1993). For example, although 30% of female homicide victims were murdered by an intimate other (Greenfield et al., 1998), studies of women killed by a husband or boyfriend show that 90% of the victims had reported at least one prior incident of abuse (Berry, 1998).

Although research has been fruitful in identifying the scope of the problem, many questions remain unanswered about these complex relationships, however. For instance, despite suffering abuse, 40% of women who were the victims of dating violence continued their relationships (Henton, Cate, Koval, Lloyd, & Christopher, 1983). Sixty percent of a sample of married violent couples remained together 2 years following the initial interview (Jacobson, Gottman, Gortner, Berns, & Shortt, 1996). In addition, 23% of one sample of women who filed protective orders reported re-abuse once the injunction was in place (Carlson, Harris, & Holden, 1999). Being abused by a partner is an aversive and serious problem, yet these relationships prevail and endure.

Many researchers have identified reasons why women stay with abusive intimates; however, fewer have investigated the strategies and behaviors that women utilize in an effort to cope with abuse while maintaining a relationship that they feel compelled to continue. Given the complexity and severity of this interpersonal dynamic, abuse in intimate relationships is a serious issue. Although many forms of aggression (both verbal and physical) have been studied in the field of communication, few theorists have investigated abusive relationships from a communication perspective. INC is one theory that may inform the competing demands of ending the abuse but desiring to continue the relationship. For example, Walker (1979), Barnett and LaViolette (1993), and Rosen (1996) have attempted to explain why women stay in relationships after their attempts to end abuse fail, and INC theory adds to this research by focusing on the competing goals and resultant behaviors that drive them to sacrifice their own needs within the relationship. The battered woman's syndrome suggests that once women fall into a pattern of abuse, they lose sight of long-range planning, voice unrealistic expectations about recovery, and perceptions of alternatives are restricted or seem too dangerous to pursue (Walker, 1979). In contrast, learned hopefulness theory argues that women stay in violent relationships because they believe that their partner will change the abusive behavior eventually and also due to a responsibility placed upon them by society to maintain family relationships (Barnett & LaViolette, 1993). The theorists hypothesize that battered women learn to endure abuse largely because society creates a sense of female responsibility for the maintenance of the family. Walker (1979) argued that repeated beatings lead to learned help-lessness. That is, a woman begins to believe that there is little that she can do to bring about a predictable positive result. This leads to less help seeking or fewer escape attempts and brings about a self-perpetuating cycle in which the functional partner feels helpless about the relationship and that she cannot escape it; therefore, she becomes dependent upon the relationship and the abusive partner.

Specific relational dynamics and strategies are not investigated in the above theories on a micro-level nor on a macro-level across the life of the relationship. Rosen (1996) suggested that women experience competing goals in maintain-ing violent dating relationships. Women feel nurtured by, or desire to nur-ture, their partners who are charming at first. Once the abuse occurs, women reported that their presumably already vulnerable self-identities were fused to that of the relationship. To maintain these relationships, women reported the use of survival tactics, such as avoidance strategies, illusions of control, placa-tion, and isolation. As a solution to the theoretical problems related to particu-lar strategies (e.g., how did they act before they labeled the abuse as a problem as opposed to after), Inconsistent Nurturing as Control provides an alternative framework that integrates many of these perspectives to provide a more com-prehensive manner in which this phenomenon can be understood.

Paradoxical Injunctions in Violent Romantic Relationships   Competing goals of nurturing and controlling are consistent with reports indicate that women who stay with abusive partners because they love the partners and hope to be able to stop the abusive behavior (Rosen, 1996). Additionally, abusers often go through some remorse for their behavior, and that remorse can lead to a "contrition phase" in which the abuser may actually be extremely loving and caring as a way to "repent" for the previous behavior (Dutton, 1998; Walker, 1979). Thus, caring and nurturing are an important part of the relationship, but the functional partner also wants to control the violent behavior. Also consistent with assumptions of INC theory is the fact that partners are often dependent upon the relationship with the abusive individual, often by controlling the resources necessary for the women to leave or modify the relationship (Bograd, 1984). In addition, in the special case of domestic violence (as opposed to the addictive relationships originally posited in INC), the female partners may not so much depend upon the relationship, but may stay in the relationship due to risks of violent responses and personal safety (Strube, 1988).

It follows that, because functional partners are dependent upon the relationship, they want to maintain the relationship. Evidence also suggests that men with abusive personalities generate relational dynamics that make the women's attachment so strong that post-separation adjustment is difficult for the victims (Dutton & Haring, 1999). For instance, the link between social isolation and abusive relationships is well documented. More violence is present in relationships in which the abuser prevents the woman's contact with family and friends (Dutton, 1998). This, in turn, leads to the fewer social supports for the abused woman who may then perceive that she must depend upon her partner for care. Further, 88% of one sample of abused women possessed attachment patterns that involved a negative self-model (Henderson, Bartholomew, & Dutton, 1997). Typically, people with negative self-models believe they are not worthy of love and become overly dependent upon their partners for self-worth.

High vulnerability of the abuser may draw the partner into developing and maintaining the relationship. Research on resource theory suggests that men who feel a low sense of personal power often abuse their partners (Bersani & Chen, 1988). Families are power systems, and the spouse with the greater number of resources tends to have power over his/her partner. Loss of resources tends to threaten men's sense of control. Status inconsistency, when the husband who traditionally is expected to provide resources for his family does not or cannot, leads to frustration and aggressive behavior in relationships. Husbands who fail to adequately fulfill their role as resource provider, or are lower than their wives in education, occupation, or job skills (i.e., are status incompatible) are more likely to use violence to maintain dominance and control (O'Brien, 1971).

This low sense of personal worth and power can be an area of high vulnerability for which the partner is drawn to nurture the abusive individual. Thus, the emotional attachment may create more cognitive judgments of the abuse (e.g., it was an aberrant event; I am the key to helping him), which may result in continuing to nurture. Attribution research in this area supports this notion. The less negative attributions that women made about the internal causality and the intent of husband's abuse, the more likely they were to perceive efficacy for solving relational problems, as well as increased perceptions of husband provision of coping assistance, self-esteem support, cohesion, acceptance of emotional expression, and intimacy (Arias, Lyons, & Street, 1997). INC theory predicts that by pacifying the abuser, the afflicted will find the relationship highly rewarding (Le Poire, 1995). Social learning explanations of abusive behavior support this assumption. This perspective views behavior as shaped by the immediate reactions it generates. The absence of overt punishment constitutes "reward" for violent behavior. In addition, the violence may serve as an outlet for aversive tension and can produce a feeling of power and agency in the abuser (Dutton, 1998). Both failure to punish the abusive behavior and failure to follow up on punishments (e.g., threatening to call the police or leave the relationship, but never doing so) constitutes reinforcement for the abusive behavior, and may constitute the belief by the abuser that his behavior is acceptable. Once the pattern of interaction is established in a relationship, it often recurs in a predictable manner. Often, abused individuals can recount the pattern leading up to a violent outburst by their partner. Thus, the interactional patterns serve adaptive functions in that each individual fulfills a role in the relational system. Conversely, abused women undergo illusions of control in which they believe that they can control their partner's behavior (Rosen, 1996). Some women report fighting back against their partner's abuse (Barnett, Martinez, & Keyson, 1996; Gortner, Berns, Jacobson, & Gottman, 1997). The ongoing belief that the abusive partner will change often leads to maintaining violent relationships (Barnett & LaViolette, 1993).

If the partner succeeds in ending the undesirable behavior, the relationship may end. Abused women may simultaneously fear and desire their partner to leave. They want the abuse to end, but believe that they are incapable of living on their own without the resources (money, etc.) that their partner provides them, or they have fused their identities with that of the relationship, so that they believe that they more complete with the partner (Rosen, 1996). Similarly, abusive males often suffers from low self-esteem and low power issues and experience a "desperate love" syndrome in which they believe that they cannot live without their partner (Barnett & LaViolette, 1993). In addition, abusive men often are unreasonably jealous and use abusive behavior as a means of coercing their partner to stay with them (Dutton, 1998). As such, many abusive men may be scared that without intimidation, their partner may feel free to leave them, or may not be dependent upon them anymore.

Although data are not available to note whether stopping the violence ends relationships, findings about traumatic bonding may inform this proposition. Some studies suggest that traumatic bonding may occur for victims of intimate violence that is indicated by persistent attachment to the abuser, lowered self-esteem, and chronic trauma symptoms (e.g., depression and anxiety; Dutton & Painter, 1981, 1993a, 1993b). These women then idealize the abuser, which leads to more difficulties with post-separation adjustment (Dutton & Haring, 1999). Ideally, ending the abusive behavior should allow the couple to continue in a happier relationship. Ironically though, when abused women were asked to rate their current relationship and an ideal relationship, the differences between the two were not significantly different (Shir, 1999). The most important aspect of this assumption from an INC theory perspective is that the abused partner believes ending the violence may end the relationship. This conundrum may provoke inconsistent nurturing as control because the women desire to maintain the relationship. Because this inconsistency is likely to be ineffective at controlling or curtailing the violence, it is unlikely it will end and therefore more likely that she can maintain the relationship.

Intermittent Reinforcement and Undesirable Behavior   The romantic partner's reinforcement of the undesirable behavior may actually increase the probability that the behavior will recur. By either giving in to the abuser's demands or by not fighting back, the abused is appeasing or "nurturing" the abusive behavior. In doing so, the abusive individual learns that abuse can sometimes result in receiving rewards. A focus upon the positive aspects of the relationship would lead to increased nurturing behavior as it would reinforce the aspects of the relationship that are "primed" in the partner's mind. The systems approach to domestic violence supports this notion. Family violence is a product of the system rather than an individual pathology. Feedback in the family system generates stability or conflict, such as violence. If violent acts receive positive feedback, an upward spiral of violence emerges. If violence receives negative feedback, the violence remains within tolerable limits. In other words, if the abusive acts receive positive feedback, such as it serves as a catharsis or gets the functional partner to comply with the afflicted requests, an upward spiral of violence will continue.

The cycle of violence outlined by Walker (1979) identifies a pattern of tension building phase, in which the victim attempts to calm the partner—through nurturing, agreeable, and passive behavior—in an attempt to prevent the tension from building up to a breaking point. These behaviors resemble those of reinforcement. During the abusive phase, the victim's response is to protect the self in any way possible, including negative reinforcement by leaving the house or trying to calm the partner or overt punishment by calling the police or friends, or even self-defense. Finally, the contrition phase includes the violent individual's apologizes and attempts to win back the partner. Agreeing to stay or return, taking the partner back, or setting up counseling appointments all can be interpreted as reinforcing the abuse. Inconsistent nurturing, then, may combine with reinforcement and punishment to strengthen the violent behavior.

INC and the Depressed Individual / Romantic Partner Relationship

The romantic relationship with a depressed individual provides a rich forum for studying the communication patterns, and control dynamics in particular, between depressed individuals and their partners. Again from an INC perspective, several paradoxical injunctions make it likely that partners' attempts to control depression may backfire and actually increase or reinforce its occurrence. Explanations for etiology and maintenance of depression focus on intrapersonal processes (such as cognition; see, for example, Beck, 1973, 1976), and interpersonal problems (Segrin, 2000; Segrin & Abramson, 1994). Interpersonal models assume that dysfunctional relationships play a critical role

in the onset and maintenance of depression. Interpersonal problems associated with depression include social skill deficiencies (Lewinsohn, 1974) and an
inability to obtain positive reinforcement and avoid punishment in the social
environment (Segrin & Dillard, 1993). Similarly, the communicative acts of
the depressed individual seem to initially elicit reactions of sympathy and assistance but eventually lead to aversive experiences for relational partners who
begin to feel anxious and depressed themselves (Coyne, 1976).

Interpersonal models of depression suggest that depressed individuals engage
in more negative and less supportive communication with others and experience rejection from those in their social environment (Segrin, 1993; Segrin &
Abramson, 1994). Although rejection is not necessarily the result of a negative
mood induction in others (Segrin & Dillard, 1992), depressed individuals emit
more negative statements about themselves and their partners, and partners
respond in turn with more negative feedback (Vettese & Mongrain, 2000).
Depressed individuals use more aversive language in conversations (Strack &
Coyne, 1983), receive less social support, and experience and more problems
with intimate members of the social network (e.g., spouses and relatives; Wade
& Kendler, 2000) than do nondepressed individuals. Although general interpersonal models capture cycles of negativity in interpersonal relationships,
INC provides an explanation for partners' attempt to control depressive symp-
toms and the ways the relational roles become ingrained in depression.

Paradoxical Injunctions in Relationship with a Depressed Individual   Who is in
control? The first premise is that the nondepressed partner is in control of the
relationship. Premise two is consistent with premise one in that the dependent
(depressed) person is out of control of come aspect of his/her life, and thus out
of control of the relationship. Because the depressed behavior limits the options
for the nondepressed partner, however, the dependent (depressed) partner may
actually have ultimate control over the relationship. This conclusion directly
contradicts the first premise, because the behavior of the nondepressed partner
is ultimately reactive and limited to boundaries of the depressed individual.
Thus, the contradiction is that the nondepressed partner is not in control, but
instead the depressed individual is in control (Le Poire, 1992). The underlying
assumption is that the nondepressed partner is dependent on, and wants to
maintain, the relationship with the depressed individual.

Consider cognitive manifestations of depression as an example of the
paradox of control. Cognitive manifestations of depression include distorted
attitudes toward the self, his/her experiences, and his/her future. Although
partners' attempts to modify the distorted self-evaluations are met with considerable resistance at best, partners' refraining from attempts to modify modifying negative cognitions can be seen as reinforcing the distorted interpretations.
Although the depressed individual expects the worst and rejects any possibility of improvement, the nondepressed partner cannot agree with the negative
expectations. Often the nondepressed partner tries such strategies as encour-

aging psychotherapy or taking antidepressants, but these attempts at problem solving may be dismissed because the depressed individual believes they cannot help. The depressed individual thinks of a future that will continue or get worse, but the nondepressed partner is aware of more positive possibilities for the future. Suicidal thoughts or plans are correlated with more extreme cases of negative cognitions, so in the worst cases, the nondepressed partner sees it as his/her responsibility to limit options for suicide, which may mean never leaving the depressed individual alone.

Subordinating Needs Serves as Control   The second paradox suggests that partners' subordinating their own needs (e.g., during times of crisis) serves as a control mechanism long-term. Consistent with a norm of reciprocity, the depressed individual alters his/her behavior to return the obligation incurred by the self-sacrificing behavior of the nondepressed partner. The contradiction is that the nondepressed partner's "one down" behavior actually serves as "one up" in terms of control (Le Poire, 1992). Depleted motivations manifested in depression illustrate paradox two. As if taking a child's role, the depressed individual avoids responsibility and escapes problems rather than solving them, prefers dependence on others, and seeks immediate gratification in behaviors (Beck, 1973). Avoiding problems means leaving tasks to accumulate and retreating from family, friends, and professional obligations. The depressed individual often lacks positive motivation to the point that everyday tasks seem burdensome. The nondepressed partner subordinates his/her own needs so that during depressive episodes fewer tasks are accomplished, and the bulk of everyday tasks are done himself/herself. The nondepressed partner may do all of the housekeeping and errands, take care of the children and their schoolwork, and make excuses for why he/she and his/her partner missed social functions. Receiving help carries a special emotional meaning for the depressed patient. The depressed individuals' attempts at reciprocity may be framed as extremely costly for them. For example, when the depressed individual does his/her regular household chores, engages in conversation without mumbling or complaining of being tired, or attends a social function, he/she reminds the nondepressed partner of the great effort these behaviors entail. The depressed individual's expression of desire to reciprocate what his/her partner does to help and the special emotional connotations attached to helping behaviors are framed as grave attempts as reciprocity. Within the relationship, both receiving help and occasional attempts at giving back put the depressed individual in a "one up" position.

Relational Roles and Depression   The third paradox concerns ways the relationship itself is defined by the roles that result from depression. The codependent, nondepressed partners attempt to control the other individual by extinguishing deviant or negative behavior. For example, spouses of depressed individuals are known to engage in endless attempts to encourage the depressed individual to seek counseling, to take medication, to set life goals, to engage in any daily activities, and these spouses are willing to go to great lengths to support the depressed individuals in such endeavors. Nurturing is rewarding to the depressed individual in times of crisis and to the nondepressed partner, and successfully controlling the undesirable behavior (stops the depressive episodes), means that the nondepressed partner potentially loses the caregiving resource base (Le Poire, 1992).

If the caregiving behavior is one of the reasons the depressed individual stays in the relationship with the nondepressed partner, then the nondepressed partner may actually destroy the relationship by stopping the depression. The nondepressed partner may fear that curtailing depression will lesson the dependency. The emotional attachments that initially brought the couple together are replaced by emotional manifestations of depression that affect both the depressed individual and the nondepressed partner. Shared experiences and behaviors that define the earlier stages of relationship in which the couple enjoyed activities together, expressed love and kindness, set goals for their future, entertained family and friends, and experienced sexual intimacy are no longer gratifying to the depressed individual. Initially, the loss of satisfaction involves behaviors associated with responsibility, such as work productivity or contributions to everyday family life. Loss of emotional attachment parallels loss of gratification, and the loss of affections for family members or romantic partners is a major cause for concern within close relationships. In mild cases, the depressed individual may report feeling less intense love or affection for a romantic partner, but at the same time feeling more dependent on him/her. The loss of interest or positive feelings may progress to indifference. Thus, continued attachment, sharing, and intimacy have to be re-defined once emotional manifestations of depression set in. Shared experiences over the course of their relationship before depression was labeled as a problem can serve to prompt alternative ways to work through the relationship. Nurturing behaviors are rewarding for the depressed individual, and the same nurturing behaviors are among the ways nondepressed partners can encourage their spouse and feel a sense of connection with the depressed individual.

Evidence for Depression, Communication Strategies, and Health Outcomes   Patterns of control strategies originally tested in couples including one substance-abusive individual also applied to couples including one depressed individual. Specifically, partners of depressed individuals changed their strategies to curtail depression over time such that they reinforced depressive behavior more before their determination that the behavior was problematic, than after; they actively helped their partners get well and encouraged alternative emotional outlets more after labeling the depression problematic, than before; and they reverted to a mix of reinforcing and actively helping, after their initial control attempts proved unsuccessful (Duggan & Le Poire, 2006). Similarly, in contradistinction with nondepressed partners' goal to diminish depression, these sequences of actively helping and encouraging alternative emotional outlets intermixed with strategies that reinforce depression and reward withholding may reinforce the illness, rather than extinguish it. Thus, the mix of reinforcing and actively helping is likely to strengthen depression. Previous research provides some evidence for consistency and more positive mental health outcomes (less depression, fewer negative cognitions, and less anxiety), although the associations did not hold across the labeling periods (Duggan & Le Poire, 2006).

The depression data also provide evidence for the degree of over-time change being modified by sex. Female partners of depressed individuals actively helped their partners get well most before labeling depression problematic and reverted to a mixture of reinforcing depression and helping partners following the labeling (Duggan, 2007). Conversely, male partners of depressed individuals actively help partners following the labeling but decrease helping strategies and instead contribute to depressive behaviors and engage in more consistent sequences of negativity once they feel their helping attempts are unsuccessful (Duggan, 2007). Thus, the INC application to cycling through reinforcement and punishment explained both male and female partners' changes, but the patterns for proportions of strategies differed by sex.

Attribution for control in couples including one depressed individual differentiated between health outcomes in that individuals with more external attribution for control feel their partner's behavior is unpredictable and not influenced by what they say also use fewer strategies to curtail depression and instead use more strategies that reinforce depression and punish alternative behavior (Duggan, 2006). In couples including one depressed individual, poorer mental health and internal attribution for control were associated with more cohesiveness but less relational satisfaction; conversely greater mental health and external attribution in couples including one depressed individual predicts less cohesiveness but more relational satisfaction (Duggan, 2006). This pattern did not hold for comparison group couples who had not experienced a negative health behavior that interfered with everyday functioning. Comparison couples who reported more cohesiveness and relational satisfaction as they reported more internal attribution for control; comparison couples reported less cohesiveness and relational satisfaction as they reported more external attribution for control. Results from attribution research provides evidence for the importance of codependency, as high codependent partners are likely to engage in more attempts to control their partners than partners low in codependency.

Finally, to examine the degree to which partners use similar strategies in different kinds of relationships with individuals whose negative health behaviors interfere with everyday functioning, a qualitative analysis of the specific types of reinforcing and punishing strategies was conducted. Qualitative analysis identified themes and patterns among the strategies used by partners of substance abusers and partners of depressed individuals and revealed similar strategies across both contexts. These strategies include supporting the part-ners' problem, ignoring the problem, and helping the partner to end undesired behavior. Again, the use of reinforcing substance use strategies (supporting the partners' problem and ignoring the problem) and punishing substance use strategies (helping the partner to end undesired behavior) seem inconsistent (Duggan, Le Poire, & Addis, 2006). Used in combination, these inconsistent strategies are likely to be ineffective at terminating the substance abusive or depressive behavior and may reduce treatment efficiency.

Summary and Conclusions

INC theory attempts to understand relationships in which one relational part-ner tries to alter the behavioral patterns of a partner who is "at-risk" for health problems (or in the case of the violent partner, poses a health threat to others). This review of four relationships fitting this description—substance abusers and their partners, mothers and daughters with eating disorders, victims of vio-lence and their abusers, and depressed individuals and their partners—brings to light the unique power dynamics of helping-type relationships. Partners who try to change their partners' behavioral patterns are often nurturer-controllers (more commonly referred to as codependents). They simultaneously desire to care for and control their partners in the belief that change will enhance over-all health, improve their relationships, and enhance their own mental health. Ultimately, they have the best interest of their partners at heart, and yet, due to the paradoxes which exist in this type of relationship, they are likely to perform helping and controlling behaviors simultaneously. These mixed mes-sages frequently serve to intermittently reinforce and intermittently punish the substance abuse, eating disorders, and violent behavior. Unfortunately, this intermittent reinforcement and punishment should serve to strengthen the behavior they are trying desperately to extinguish.

There is hope, however. The research that exists using INC theory to study substance abusers and their partners showed that the inconsistency present in the relationship in and of itself did not adversely influence the continuation of the substance abuse (Le Poire et al., 2000). Alternatively, consistently punishing the substance abuse, while simultaneously consistently reinforcing alternative behaviors, did positively effect a reduction in the substance abuse. Moreover, partners who were more successful in assisting their partners' sobriety achieved better mental health in the form of decreased depression. Thus, what is clear is that partners of afflicted individuals can both help their partners and enhance their own mental health in the process. This type of relationship of persua-sive strategies and health outcomes of the afflicted partner and mental health outcomes for the functional partner needs to be explored more fully in the mother-eating disordered daughter- and violence victim-abuser- relationships. It is likely that consistently punishing eating disordered and violent behavior while simultaneously reinforcing alternative behavior could help reduce both eating disorders and violence. Further, mothers and victims who feel more successful are also likely to experience less anxiety and depression.

Of further note from the current analysis is the association between attachment patterns and helper-helpee relationships. Daughters with eating disorders often exhibit inappropriate boundaries with their mothers due to overenmeshment (anorexics) or detachment (bulimics). Additionally, physically abused women report strong and inexplicable attachments to their abusers. Thus, further study is called for to disentangle the complex attachment patterns that come into play in caregiving relationships. What is clear is that the paradoxes that exist in these types of relationships have had the ground work laid for them in past important relationships for both the functional and the afflicted partners.

Support for Codependency as a Communication Process

INC research and its application across the four relationships extends communication theory by combining and testing assumptions of codependency. Previous research provides evidence for codependency as a predictor of communication processes and relational outcomes under the condition of increased vulnerability. Facing illness or compulsive behavior that can in some way be attributed to the individual poses unique implications for relationships and communication. Researchers initially argued the position that codependency, like alcoholism, should be considered a disease entity and should be included in the DSM classification (Cermak, 1986; Schaef, 1986); however, the current empirical research and the examination of communication process and codependency suggest it would not necessarily be considered the illness in itself, but instead codependency is an important consideration in understanding the ways relational processes and roles shift when health is threatened. In particular, codependency is salient in relationships in which a negative health issue can be attributed in some way to the individual. In sum, results suggest support for INC theory in combination with codependency. Individual differences in codependency do not predict communication strategies or relational outcomes in isolation (Duggan, 2007). Consistent with theoretical predictions, this chapter describes studies that support the premise that negative health behavior limits the communicative and behavioral options within the relationship such that poorer mental health is likely associated with more attempts to control others.

Although, generally, interpersonal literature suggests lower relational satisfaction in nonreciprocal relationships, the implications of INC theory suggest a relational reward in continued dysfunctional behavior. The energy spent maintaining the relationship and dealing with depression may lead to intense interconnectedness that could be perceived as a symbol of relational strength and closeness. Thus, codependency in romantic relationships that include a depressed individual may extend interpersonal research on interdependence and emotional investment in romantic relationships more generally (i.e., Knobloch & Solomon, 2004). Romantic relationships that include one individual who engages in continued negative health behavior may be interpreted as more emotionally invested, because the communicative behavior of one partner may be more likely to stimulate emotional arousal in the other partner. Knobloch and Solomon (2004) described (greater) interdependence as including more influence, interference, and facilitation, and the salience of codependency in depressed individuals may be associated with exaggerated and overinvolved social influence processes.

Implications and Future Directions

INC theory suggests the threat of destroying the relationship by challenging expected roles may make salient codependent traits that would otherwise not be directly related to communication processes in romantic relationships. During substance abusive, eating disordered, violent, or depressive episodes, the parent or relational partner engages in continued attempts to encourage the individual and to nurture him/her through times of crisis. Nurturing behavior is rewarding to the afflicted individual because of the special emotional meaning the caretaking behavior carries, and so the partners' behaviors may unwittingly encourage continued codependency and the negative health behavior. Nurturing behavior is rewarding to the parent or partner because it provides an emotional connection that has come to redefine roles within the relationship after labeling the negative behavior problematic. Participants were representative of the complexity within a romantic relationship with a depressed individual and how codependency is inter-related with interpersonal issues and health. INC theory provides a framework to interpret the behaviors of couples when a particular behavior (or set of behaviors) was labeled problematic *after* the couple had committed to continuing the relationship, likely also helping eliminate potential blame parents or partners. Thus, the substance abuse, eating disorder, violence, or depression was identified as a problem once the relationship included already established patterns of communication, roles, shared experiences, and often lived through an extended period of time without the negative health behavior.

Future research in this area should focus on the sibling relationships in families with an individual who engages negative health behavior. The sibling subsystem is an almost entirely neglected area in the literature in substance abuse, eating disorders, domestic violence, and depression. Studies that do include sibling relationships tend to be those in which more than one child suffers from the negative health behavior; however, important questions regarding sibling relationships have yet to be addressed. For instance, why is it that in families with multiple children, only one develops the negative health behavior or engages compulsions? An investigation of what the other children are experiencing would give insight into how other family members are coping with whatever the family dysfunction might be. In other words, while one child develops an eating disorder, for example, is another a juvenile delinquent, or an obsessive overachiever? Additionally, research does not adequately address the issue of multiple dysfunctions *within* a given family.

Using INC as a theoretical framework, there are several possibilities for understanding communication implications when the negative behavior subsides. For example, evidence suggests that in some couples, physical abuse actually decreases over the years (e.g., Johnson, 1992), and substance abuse, eating disorders, and depression tend to be cyclic, such that there are times within the relationship free from the negative health behavior—however, what is not known is why. Did the violent individual engage in "spontaneous desistance" (Dutton, 1998)? Did the functional partner convince the substance abusive or depressed individual that he/she would leave if the behavior continued? INC can better inform the macro-patterns of behavior that occur across the life of the relationship as the functional partner attempts to manage and decrease/end the negative health behavior of the partner while maintaining the relationship.

Finally, the potential impact of dual-diagnoses should be considered. All of these relationships include individuals whose health problems may extend far beyond the symptoms they present to the relationship. For instance, a consistent finding is that at least 30% (Sheehan, 1993) of substance-dependent individuals are susceptible to dual-diagnoses including antisociality personality disorder (Lehman, Myers, Thompson, & Corty, 1993). Thus, it is important that future investigations consider the impact such personality disorders may have on communication behavior and on communication outcomes associated with the substance abuse, eating disorders, violence, and depression.

Note

1. Punishment is different from negative reinforcement in that punishment is an aversive stimulus presented in an attempt to extinguish the behavior it follows, whereas negative reinforcement is the removal of noxious stimuli following the presentation of a behavior that one is trying to maintain.

References

American Psychiatric Association. (1994). *Diagnostic and statistical manual of mental disorders* (4th ed.). Washington, DC: Author.

Amey, C. H., & Albrecht, S. L. (1998). Race and ethnic differences in adolescent drug use: The impact of family structure and the quantity and quality of parental interaction. *Journal of Drug Issues, 28,* 283–298.

Archer, N. S. (1979). Perceptions and attitudes of family members (Codependents): Pre- and post-treatment. *Labor-Management Alcoholism: Clinic and Journal, 9,* 75–80.

Arias, I., Lyons, C. M., & Street, A. E. (1997). Individual and marital consequences of victimization: Moderating effects of relationship efficacy and spouse support. *Journal of Family Violence, 12,* 193–209.

Asher, R. M. (1992). *Women with alcoholic husbands*. Chapel Hill: University of North Carolina Press.

Bachman, R., & Saltzman, L. E. (1995). *Violence against women: Estimates from the redesigned survey*. NCJ-154348. Washington, DC: Bureau of Justice Statistics.

Barnett, O. W., & LaViolette, A. D. (1993). *It could happen to anyone: Why battered women stay*. Newbury Park, CA: Sage.

Barnett, O. W., Martinez, T. E., & Keyson, M. (1996). The relationship between violence, social support, and self-blame in battered women. *Journal of Interpersonal Violence, 11,* 221–233.

Beach, S. R., & O'Leary, K. D. (1993). Marital discord and dysphoria: For whom does the marital relationship predict depressive symptomatology? *Journal of Social and Personal Relationships, 10,* 405–420.

Beck, A. T. (1973). *Depression: Clinical, experimental, and theoretical aspects*. New York: Harper & Row.

Beck, A. T. (1976). *Cognitive therapy and the emotional disorders*. New York: International Universities Press.

Berry, D. B. (1998). *The domestic violence sourcebook*. Los Angeles: Lowell House.

Bersani, C. A., & Chen, H. (1988). Sociological perspective in family violence. In V. B. Van Hasselt, R. L. Morrison, A. S. Bellack, & M. Hersen (Eds.), *Handbook of family violence* (pp. 57–88). New York: Plenum.

Beutler, L. E., Patterson, K. M., Jacob, T., Shoham, V., Yost, E., & Rohrbaugh, M. (1993). Matching treatment to alcoholism subtypes. *Psychotherapy, 30,* 463–472.

Bograd, M. (1984). Family systems approaches to wife battering: A feminist critique. *American Journal of Orthopsychiatry, 54,* 558–568.

Botta, R. A. (1999). Television images and adolescent girls' body image disturbance. *Journal of Communication, 49,* 22–48.

Burgoon, J. K., Burgoon, M., Miller, G. R., & Sunnafrank, M. (1981). Learning theory approaches to persuasion. *Human Communication Research, 7,* 161–179.

Byrne, M. M., & Holes, J. H. (1979). Co-alcoholic syndrome. *The Labor-Management Alcoholism Journal, 9,* 68–74.

Carlson, M. J., Harris, S. D., & Holden, G. W. (1999). Protective orders and domestic violence: risk factors for re-abuse. *Journal of Family Violence, 14,* 205–226.

Carroll, J., Robinson, B. E., & Flowers, C. (2002). Marital estrangement, positive feelings toward partners and locus of control: Female counselors married to alcohol-abusing and non-alcohol-abusing spouses. *Journal of Addictions & Offender Counseling, 23,* 30–40.

Cermak, T. L. (1986). *Diagnosing and treating co-dependence: A guide for professionals who work with chemical dependents, their spouses and children*. Minneapolis, MN: Johnson Institute.

Cermak, T. (1991). Co-addiction as a disease. *Psychiatric Annals, 21*(5), 266–272.

Cohen-Holmes, S. (1981). Patients in their own right, families of alcohol deserve equal attention in treatment. *Focus on Alcohol and Drug Issues, 4,* 5–6, 25.

Conway, J. (1981). Significant others need help too: Alcoholism treatment as important to rest of family. *Focus on Alcohol and Drug Issues, 4,* 17–19.

Copeland, L. (1987). Congressional reauthorization of federal domestic violence programs. *Response to Victimization of Women and Children, 10,* 20–21.

Costin, C. (1997). *The eating disorder sourcebook: A comprehensive guide to the causes, treatments, and prevention of eating disorders*. Los Angeles: Lowell House.

Cowan, G., Bommersbach, M., & Curtis, S. R. (1995). Codependency, loss of self, and power. *Psychology of Women Quarterly, 19,* 221–236.

Coyne, J. C. (1976). Toward an interactional description of depression. *Psychiatry, 39,* 28–40.

Duggan, A. P. (2006, June). *Attribution and interpersonal control strategies in couples including one depressed individual.* Paper presented to the International Communication Association at their annual meeting in Dresden, Germany.

Duggan, A. P. (2007). Sex differences in communicative attempts to curtail depression: An inconsistent nurturing as control perspective. *Western Journal of Communication, 71,* 114–135.

Duggan, A. P., Dailey, R. M., & Le Poire, B. A. (2008). Reinforcement and punishment of substance abuse during ongoing interactions: A conversational test of INC theory. *Journal of Health Communication, 13,* 417–433.

Duggan, A. P., & Le Poire, B. A. (2006). One down; two involved: An application and extension of inconsistent nurturing as control theory to couples including one depressed individual. *Communication Monographs, 73,* 379–405.

Duggan, A. P., Le Poire, B. A., & Addis, K. (2006). A qualitative analysis of communicative strategies used by partners of substance abusers and depressed individuals during recovery. In B. A. Le Poire & R. Dailey (Eds.), *Applied interpersonal communication matters: Family, health, and community relations* (pp. 150–174). New York: Peter Lang.

Duggan, A. P., Le Poire, B. A., & Gaze, J. (2006, November). *Nonverbal involvement, expressiveness, and pleasantness as predictors of relapse, persuasive effectiveness, and goal attainment in couples including one substance-dependent individual.* Paper presented to the Interpersonal Division of the National Communication Association at their annual meeting in San Antonio, TX.

Dutton, D. G. (1998). *The abusive personality.* New York: Guilford.

Dutton , D. G., & Haring, M. (1999). Perpetrator personality effects on post-separation victim reactions in abusive relationships. *Journal of Family Violence, 14,* 193–204.

Dutton, D. G., & Painter, S. (1981). Traumatic bonding: The development of emotional bonds in relationships of intermittent abuse. *International Journal of Victimology, 6,* 139–155.

Dutton D. G., & Painter, S. (1993a). Emotional attachments in abusive relationships: A test of traumatic bonding theory. *Violence and Victims, 8,* 105–120.

Dutton, D. G., & Painter, S. (1993b). The battered woman syndrome: Effects of severity and intermittency of abuse. *American Journal of Orthopsychiatry, 63,* 614–622.

Edwards, P., Harvey, C., & Whitehead, P. (1973). Wives of alcoholics, a critical review and analysis. *Quarterly Journal of Studies on Alcohol, 34,* 112–132.

Fals-Stewart, W., & Birchler, G. R. (1998). Marital interactions of drug-abusing patients and their partners: Comparisons with distressed couples and relationship to drug-using behavior. *Psychology of Addictive Behaviors, 12,* 28–38.

Fredrickson, B. L., & Roberts, T. (1997). Objectification theory: Toward understanding womens' lived experience and mental health risks. *Psychology of Women Quarterly, 21,* 173–206.

Gomberg, E. L. (1989). On terms used and abused: The concept of "codependency." *Drugs & Society, 3,* 113–132.

Gortner, E., Berns, S. B., Jacobson, N. S., & Gottman, J. M. (1997). When women leave violent relationships: Dispelling clinical myths. *Psychotherapy: Theory, Research and Practice, 34*, 343–352.

Greenfield, L. A., Rand, M. R., Craven, D., Klaus, P. A., Perkins, C. A., Ringel, C., et al. (1998). *Violence by intimates: Analysis of data on crimes by current or former spouses, boyfriends, and girlfriends* (NCJ-167237). Washington, DC: U.S. Department of Justice.

Hadelsman, L., Branchey, M. H., Buydens-Branchey, L., Gribomont, B., Holloway, K., & Silverman, J. (1993). Morbidity risk for alcoholism and drug abuse in relatives of cocaine addicts. *American Journal of Drug and Alcohol Abuse, 19*, 347–357.

Henderson, A. J., Bartholomew, K., & Dutton, D. G. (1997). He loves me; he loves me not: Attachment and separation resolution of abused women. *Journal of Family Violence, 12*, 169–191.

Henton, J., Cate, R., Koval, J., Lloyd, S., & Christopher, S. (1983). Romance and violence in dating relations. *Journal of Family Issues, 4*, 467–482.

Howard, D., & Howard, N. (1985). Treatment of the significant other. In S. Zimberg, J. Wallace, & S. Blume (Eds.), *Practical approaches to alcoholism psychotherapy* (pp. 137–162). New York: Plenum.

Hughes-Hammer, C., Martsolf, D. S., & Zeller, R. A. (1998). Depression and codependency in women. *Archives of Psychiatric Medicine, 12*, 326–334.

Humphrey, L. L. (1988). Relationships within subtypes of anorexic, bulimic, and normal families. *Journal of the American Academy of Child and Adolescent Psychiatry, 27*, 544–551.

Humphrey, L. L. (1989). Observed family interactions among subtypes of eating disorders using structural analysis of social behavior. *Journal of Consulting and Clinical Psychology, 57*, 206–214.

Infante, D. A., Chandler, T. A., & Rudd, J. E. (1989). Test of an argumentative skill deficiency model of interspousal violence. *Communication Monographs, 56*, 163–177.

Jacobson, N. S., Gottman, J. M., Gortner, E., Berns, S., & Shortt, J. W. (1996). Psychological factors in the longitudinal course of battering: When do the couples split up? When does the abuse decrease? *Violence & Victims, 11*, 371–392.

James, J. E., & Goldman, M. (1971). Behavior trends of wives of alcoholics. *Quarterly Journal of Studies on Alcoholism, 32*, 3773–3781.

Johnson, I. M. (1992). Economic, situational, and psychological correlates of the decision-making process of battered women. *Families in Society, 73*, 168–176

Kadambari, R., Gowers, S., & Crisp, A. (1986). Some correlates of vegetarianism in anorexia nervosa. *International Journal of Eating Disorders, 5*(3), 539–544.

Kaffman, M., & Sadeh, T. (1989). Anorexia nervosa in the kibbutz: Factors influencing the development of a monoideistic fixation. *International Journal of Eating Disorders, 8*(1), 33–53.

Kelly, A. B., Halford, W. K., & Young, R. M. (2002). Couple communication and female problem drinking: A behavioral observation study. *Psychology of Addictive Behaviors, 16*, 269–271.

Knobloch, L. K., & Solomon, D. H. (2004). Interference and facilitation from partners in the development of interdependence within romantic relationships. *Personal Relationships, 11*, 115–130.

Lehman, A. F., Myers, P., Thompson, J. W., & Corty, E. (1993). Implications of mental and substance use disorders: A comparison of single and dual diagnosis patients. *Journal of Nervous and Mental Disease, 181*, 365–370.

Le Poire, B. A. (1992). Does the codependent encourage substance dependent behavior? Paradoxical injunctions in the codependent relationship. *The International Journal of the Addictions, 27,* 1465–1474.

Le Poire, B. A. (1995). Inconsistent nurturing as control theory: Implications for communication-based research and treatment programs. *Journal of Applied Communication Research, 23,* 1–15.

Le Poire, B. A., & Cope, K. (1999). Episodic versus steady state drinkers: Evidence of differential reinforcement patterns. *Alcoholism Treatment Quarterly, 17,* 79–90.

Le Poire, B. A., Erlandson, K. T., & Hallett, J. S. (1998). Punishing versus reinforcing strategies of drug discontinuance: The effect of persuaders' drug use on persuasive effectiveness and relapse. *Health Communication, 10,* 293–316.

Le Poire, B. A., Hallett, J. S., & Erlandson, K. T. (2000). An initial test of inconsistent nurturing as control theory: How partners of drug abusers assist their partners' sobriety. *Human Communication Research, 26,* 432–457.

Le Poire, B. A., Haynes, J., Driscoll, J., Driver, B., Wheelis, T. F., Hyde, M. K., et al. (1997). Attachment as a function of parental and partner approach-avoidance tendencies. *Human Communication Research, 23,* 413–441.

Lewinsohn, P. M. (1974). A behavioral approach to depression. In R. J. Friedman & M. M. Katz (Eds.), *The psychology of depression: Contemporary theory and research* (pp. 157–178). Washington, DC: Winston-Wiley.

Lieberman, S. (1989). A family with four bulimic children. *International Journal of Eating Disorders, 8,* 101–104.

McCrady, B. S., Noel, N. E., Abrams, D. B., Stout, R. L., Nelson, H. F., & Hay, W. M. (1986). Comparative effectiveness of three types of spouse involvement in outpatient behavioral alcoholism treatment. *Journal of Studies on Alcohol, 47,* 459–465.

McNabb, J., Der-Karabetian, & Rhoads, J. (1989). Family involvement and outcome in treatment of alcoholism. *Psychological Reports, 65,* 1327–1333.

Minuchin, S., Rosman, B. L., & Baker, L. (1978). *Psychosomatic families: Anorexia nervosa in context.* Cambridge, MA: Harvard University Press.

Morgan, J. P. (1991). What is codependency? *Journal of Clinical Psychology, 47,* 720–729.

National Institute on Drug Abuse (NIDA). (2007). *Topics in brief.* Retrieved June 6, 2005, from http://www.nida.nih.gov

Novello, A., Rosenberg, M., Saltzman, L., & Shosky, J. (1992). From the Surgeon General, U.S. Public Health Service. *JAMA: The Journal of the American Medial Association, 267,* 3132.

O'Brien, J. E. (1971). Violence in divorce prone families. *Journal of Marriage and the Family, 30,* 692–698.

O'Gorman, P. (1993). Codependency explored: A social movement in search of definition and treatment. *Psychiatric Quarterly, 64,* 199–212.

Pence, E., & Paymar, M. (1993). *Education groups for men who batter: The Duluth model.* New York: Springer.

Prescott, M. E., & Le Poire, B. A. (2002). Eating disorders and the mother-daughter communication: A test of inconsistent nurturing as control theory. *Journal of Family Communication, 2,* 59–78.

Quigley, B. M., & Leonard, K. E. (2000). Alcohol, drugs, and violence. In V. B. Van Hasselt, & M. Hersen (Eds.), *Aggression and violence: An introductory text* (pp. 259–283). Needham Heights, MA: Allyn & Bacon.

Rosen, K. H. (1996). The ties that bind women to violent premarital relationships: Processes of seduction and entrapment. In D. D. Cahn & S. A. Lloyd (Eds.), *Family violence from a communication perspective* (pp. 151–176). Thousand Oaks, CA: Sage.

Substance Abuse and Mental Health Services Administration (SAMHSA). (2007). *Substance abuse and mental health statistics.* Retrieved June 6, 2005, from http://www.samhsa.gov

Schaef, A. W. (1986). *Codependence misdiagnosed-mistreated.* Minneapolis, MI: Winston Press.

Segrin, C. (1993). Interpersonal reactions to dysphoria: The role of relationship with partner and perceptions of rejection. *Journal of Social and Personal Relationships, 10,* 83–97.

Segrin, C. (2000). Social skills deficits associated with depression. *Clinical Psychology Review, 20,* 379–403.

Segrin, C., & Abramson, L. Y. (1994). Negative reactions to depressive behaviors: A communication theories analysis. *Journal of Abnormal Psychology, 103,* 655–668.

Segrin, C., & Dillard, J. P. (1992). The interactional theory of depression: A meta-analysis of the research literature. *Journal of Social and Clinical Psychology, 11,* 43–70.

Segrin, C., & Dillard, J. P. (1993). The complex link between social skill and dysphoria. *Communication Research, 20,* 76–104.

Sheehan, M. F. (1993). Dual diagnosis. *Psychiatric Quarterly, 64,* 107–134.

Shir, J. S. (1999). Battered women's perceptions and expectations of their current and ideal marital relationship. *Journal of Family Violence, 14,* 71–82.

Skinner, B. F. (1974). *About behaviorism.* New York: Alfred A. Knopf.

Springer, C. A., Britt, T. W., & Schlenker, B. R. (1998). Codependency: Clarifying the construct. *Journal of Mental Health Counseling, 20*(2), 141–158.

Steiner, C. M. (1974). *Scripts people live: Transactional analysis of life scripts.* New York: Bantam Books.

Steiner, H., & Lock, L. (1998). Anorexia nervosa and bulimia nervosa in children and adolescents: A review of the past 10 years. *Journal of the American Academy of Child and Adolescent Psychiatry, 37,* 352–259.

Stern, S. L., Dixon, K. N., Jones, D., Lake, M., Nemzer, E., & Sansone, R. (1989). Family environment in anorexia and bulimia. *International Journal of Eating Disorders, 8,* 25–31.

Strack, S., & Coyne, J. C. (1983). Social confirmation of dysphoria: Shared and private reactions to depression. *Journal of Personality and Social Psychology, 44,* 798–806.

Straus, M. A., & Sweet, S. (1992). Verbal/symbolic aggression in couples: Incidence rates and relationships to personal characteristics. *Journal of Marriage & the Family, 54,* 346–357.

Strube, M. J. (1988). The decision to leave an abusive relationship: Empirical evidence and theoretical issues. *Psychological Bulletin, 104,* 236–250.

Vettese, L. C., & Mongrain, M. (2000). Communication about the self and partner in the relationships of dependents and self-critics. *Cognitive Therapy and Research, 24,* 609–626.

Wade, T. D., & Kendler, K. S. (2000). The relationship between social support and major depression: Cross-sectional, longitudinal, and genetic perspectives. *Journal of Nervous and Mental Disease, 88,* 251–258.

Walker, L. (1979). *The battered woman.* New York: Harper & Row.

Waller, G., Slade, P., & Calam, R. (1990). Family adaptability and cohesion: Relation to eating attitudes and disorders. *International Journal of Eating Disorders, 9*(2), 225–228.

Watzlawick, P., Beavin, J., & Jackson, D. D. (1967). *Pragmatics of human communication.* New York: Norton.

Wegscheider-Cruse, S., & Cruse, J. R. (1990). *Understanding codependency.* Deerfield Beach, FL: Health Communications.

Whitfield, C. L. (1989). Co-dependence: Our most common addiction: Some physical, mental, emotional and spiritual perspectives. *Alcoholism Treatment Quarterly, 6*(1), 19–36.

Wilson, G. T., Heffernan, K., & Black, C. M. (1996). Eating disorders. In E. Mash & R. Barkley (Eds.), *Child psychopathology* (pp. 541–571). New York: Guilford.

Wiseman, J. P. (1991). *The other half: Wives of alcoholics and their social-psychology.* New York: de Gruyter.

Wright, P. H., & Wright, K. D. (1999). The two faces of codependent relating: A research-based perspective. *Contemporary Family Therapy: An International Journal, 21,* 527–543.

Chapter 12

Spirituality Provides Meaning and Social Support for Women Living with HIV

Jennifer L. Peterson

HIV typically is an anxiety-producing disease—partly because of its associations with illness and death, stigma, and uncertainty. The related sources of stress that people living with HIV may face include "health problems," "interpersonal conflicts," "stigma and disclosure fears," and "problems with the health care system" (Siegel & Schrimshaw, 2005, p. 229); caregiving for family members and/or partners, some who are also living with HIV (Hackl, Somlai, Kelly, & Kalichman, 1997); and the chronic medical, personal, and social uncertainty that an HIV diagnosis might bring (Brashers et al., 2003; also see Rintamaki, this volume). These stressors can impact both the mental and physical well-being of those living with the disease.

Because coping effectively with the stress of HIV illness can be associated with better adherence with treatments (Vyavaharkar et al., 2007), improved depressive symptoms (Remein et al., 2006), and slower disease progression (Ironson, Stuetzle, & Fletcher, 2006), understanding what defines "coping effectively" is critical. Some have examined differences between problem-focused and avoidant coping for example (Vyavaharkar et al., 2007), or between helpful and unhelpful forms of social support (Hays, Magee, & Chauncey, 1994). The mechanisms through which coping (including support) facilitates the management of stress and illness deserve sustained attention, however, as that effort is likely to enrich our understanding of why different coping strategies or processes are more or less effective (e.g., Brashers, Neidig, & Goldsmith, 2004).

An area that has begun to receive notice as a source of coping, but which remains relatively unexplored in communication research, is spirituality (Parrott, 2004). In HIV research, spirituality has been linked to frequency of received social support and psychological adaptation (Simoni, Frick, & Huang, 2006), and negatively related to stress, uncertainty, and psychological distress (Tuck, McCain, & Elswick, 2001). Exploring connections among spirituality, communication, and coping is important for explaining how, why, and for whom spirituality may be helpful, and how it is enacted for people coping with illness. The aims of this chapter, therefore, are (a) to describe the experience of spirituality for women coping with HIV, and (b) to explore how spirituality is connected to communication in this population.

It is especially important to study these issues among women living with HIV. Women are a quickly growing population of people living with HIV: Twenty-six percent of all HIV and AIDS cases in the United States are thought to be among women, with 80% of those attributed to heterosexual sexual contact (CDC, 2008). According to Center for Disease Control and Prevention (CDC) statistics, AIDS was the leading cause of death in 2004 for Black women between the ages of 25 and 34, and the sixth leading cause of death for all women in that age group. Moreover, women living with HIV tend to be more depressed than men with the disease, which can lead to immune system decline and increased mortality (Ickovics et al., 2001). In the following section, I set the stage for studying spirituality in this population.

Spirituality and Social Support

Researchers have described what spirituality means to people in general, and what specific implications spirituality has for those managing illnesses or other life crises. For example, Mattis (2000) interviewed women who defined religiosity as "organized worship" and spirituality as the "internalization of positive values" (p. 101). Tanyi (2002) similarly defined spirituality as "humans' search for meaning in life," whereas "religion involves an organized entity with rituals and practices about a higher power or God" (p. 500) and Meravigilia (1999) defined spirituality "as the experiences and expressions of one's spirit in a unique and dynamic process reflecting faith in God or a supreme being; a connectedness with oneself, others, nature or God; and an integration of all human dimensions" (p. 18). These definitions suggest that spirituality involves systems of values and meaning, connections between the self and a higher power or external force, and institutions and social networks that support these beliefs.

Researchers have associated spirituality and religion with mental and physical health outcomes. For example, people with life-threatening illnesses may have higher level of distress about death without the comfort of spirituality (Chibnall, Videen, Duckro, & Miller, 2002). Previous research, in addition, has indicated that spirituality and religion have been robust variables in predicting health-related outcomes including higher odds of survival (Hill & Pargament, 2003). For people living with HIV or AIDS, spirituality and/ or religious coping has been positively associated with better quality of life, greater social support, more effective coping (Tuck et al., 2001), lower levels of depression (Woods, Antoni, Ironson, & Kling, 1999a, 1999b), and longer survival (Ironson et al., 2002; Ironson et al., 2006). It also has been found to be a resource that enhances personal control, and provides a source of comfort, as well as a way of understanding and ordering the AIDS experience (Belcher, Dettmore, & Holzemer, 1989). Because of the potential of spirituality to promote positive health outcomes (Musgrave, Allen, & Allen, 2002), researchers even have encouraged practitioners to incorporate spirituality into treatment (Lauver, 2000).

The mechanism through which spirituality influences health outcomes is relatively unexamined. Some evidence suggests that aspects of religiosity or spirituality may be linked to important physiological regulatory processes such as the cardiovascular, neuroendocrine, and immune function (Seeman, Dubin, & Seeman, 2003); however, there has not been a clear explanation for why and how religion and spirituality might influence these health markers.

One step in the direction of better understanding how spirituality influences well-being is to note similarities in the functions attributed to spirituality and the functions ascribed to social support. Social support has been defined as "an umbrella term for a variety of pathways linking involvement in social relationships to well-being" (Goldsmith, 2004, p. 12). For example, the perception that support is available may foster less threatening appraisals of stressful events. Feeling valued and affirmed by others not only gives confidence in times of stress but also fulfills basic human needs. Social support may function as assisted coping, providing information, resources, and encouragement for solving problems and managing emotions in constructive ways. Involvement in a network of relationships can also regulate behavior and give meaning to life. These linkages between social support and well-being mirror some of the benefits of spirituality. Within the realm of HIV and AIDS research, Siegel and Schrimshaw (2002) found that the perceived benefits of spirituality include that it

> (1) evokes comforting emotions and feelings; (2) offers strength, empowerment, and control; (3) eases the emotional burden of the illness; (4) offers social support and a sense of belonging; (5) offers spiritual support through a personal relationship with God; (6) facilitates meaning and acceptance of the illness; (7) helps preserve health; (8) relieves the fear and uncertainty of death; (9) facilitates self-acceptance and reduces self-blame. (p. 91)

These benefits of spirituality are similar to definitions and benefits of instrumental, emotional, informational, and appraisal social support (see Albrecht & Goldsmith, 2003; Brashers et al., 2004; Goldsmith, 2004), suggesting that intersections between these concepts (spirituality and social support) might provide useful theoretical explanations for health outcomes.

Although some have suggested comparisons between social support and spirituality (Taylor & Chatters, 1988), there is need to further explore these concepts. There are at least two ways in which juxtaposing spirituality and social support may be useful. First, the comparison may encourage us to see social dimensions of spirituality. In contrast to viewing spirituality as primarily a system of beliefs, considering the similarities between spirituality and social support draws our attention to spirituality as relational (e.g., as a relationship to God or to a higher power, as relationships to a community of others who share this experience). This, in turn, yields opportunities to understand how spirituality is enacted in communication. Second, examining spirituality and social support may suggest interrelationships in the experiences of persons with HIV/AIDS. For example, can a strong spirituality help one cope with a lack of social support and with rejection from others? Does spirituality facilitate seeking and giving social support? To further explore issues such as these, I ask the following research question (RQ):

> RQ1:　What is the role of spirituality in the social support experiences of women living with HIV/AIDS?

A Study of Women Living with HIV

Audiotaped interviews of approximately 60 minutes each were used to examine the social support experiences as well as the communicative strategies and behaviors that women living with HIV utilize to seek or enact support. Before the interview, participants completed an informed consent document and a brief survey. Interviews were conducted at each of three sites in private offices. The author conducted a majority of the interviews; however, an additional researcher conducted eight of the 45 interviews and participated in the data analysis.

Instruments

Survey　Respondents were asked demographic questions such as their age, ethnic group, sexual orientation, and employment status. Health-related information (i.e., how long they had been diagnosed with HIV or AIDS, whether they were on medication for their illness or depression, and their current CD4 count and viral load) provided a health profile of the women in the study. The survey also included the Center for Epidemiological Studies Depression Scale (CESD). The CESD is a 20-item scale that has been used extensively in HIV/AIDS studies.

Interview Schedule　A semi-structured interview schedule was generated from the needs expressed in the literature on women living with HIV (e.g., Ciambrone, 2001, 2002) as well as literature on social support and HIV (e.g., Barroso, 1997). The first section of the interview schedule elicited information about the challenges the participant experienced as a woman with HIV or AIDS. The remainder of the interview focused on how social support functions for participants, what their experiences were seeking support, what support has been the most helpful and the most unhelpful, and how peer support compares to their other support experiences. Although there were no specific questions about spirituality, it spontaneously developed as a theme for many of the participants.

Participants

Participants were 45 women living with HIV or AIDS who were reimbursed $25. They were recruited through locations in three cities: (a) an HIV care facility in a very large midwestern city, (b) an AIDS service organization in a large midwestern city, and (c) an AIDS clinical trials unit (ACTU) in a large midwestern city. Intentional efforts were made to recruit a sample that reflected the wide variety of ages, races, and backgrounds of women with HIV. The average age of the participants in the sample was 39 years old (range = 19 - 64, SD = 8.79). Women reported their ethnic identity as African American (n = 36, 80%), Hispanic (n = 4, 9%), Caucasian (n = 2, 4%), or Bi-racial (n = 2, 4%). One woman (2%) did not answer the question. Three women (7%) reported being employed, 26 (58%) reported being on disability, and 5 (11%) women identified themselves as students. Twenty-six (58%) of the women reported having a partner with whom they were in a committed relationship. Thirty-nine (87%) of the women indicated that they had children. The number of children ranged from 0 to 7. Of these 39 women, 13 of them had children who did not live with them, and 11 of those had children under 18 who did not live with them.

The average time since diagnosis with HIV was 7 years (range = 0–16 yrs, SD = 3.96). Eleven (24%) of the women reported being diagnosed with AIDS. Those with AIDS reported an average time since diagnosis of five years (range = 1–7 yrs, SD = 2.12). The mean CD4 count, was 506 (range 8–1200, SD = 289.21). An additional indicator of the progression of HIV is the viral load, or the amount of virus in the blood stream. A viral load of 50 or less is considered to be undetectable for the purposes of this study. Because the range of viral loads was large (50–590,400), the median of 59 is a more accurate representation of the sample than the average of 29,437 (SD = 107,079.72).

Thirty-four (76%) of the women were taking medication to treat HIV. Twenty-five (56%) of the women were taking medication for depression. In this sample, the average score on the CESD was 23 (range 0–51, SD = 12.18). Scores on the CESD of 16 or above out of a possible 60 are considered to indicate significant depressive symptoms. Other studies have used a score of 23 to indicate significant depressive symptoms (e.g., Richardson et al., 2001). In this sample, raising the cut off to 23 lowers the number of women experiencing significant depressive symptoms to 23 (52%), which is still higher than in previous studies. Of the 42 women who completed both the CESD and the information on depression medication, 29 scored above 16 on the CESD. Twenty-one of those 29 whose scores indicated significant depressive symptoms reported taking medication for depression.

Data Analysis

This study employed a qualitative grounded theory approach (Charmaz, 2000; Strauss & Corbin, 1998). The research procedure included 11 steps. After transcribing the tapes, the transcripts were verified with the audiotapes. During the verification process, notes about general themes were taken. Once the transcripts were verified, they were re-read to look for specific themes and important issues. These themes were then examined for similarities and differences to group them under larger categories. The larger categories were then reviewed to make sure there were no overlapping or duplicated categories. At this point, the researcher who had participated in the interviewing process reviewed the transcripts and the categories. The transcripts were then coded according to the categories that were labeled with headings. The transcripts were re-examined to define and explain the categories in more detail. Quotations that were particularly representative of the categories were selected from the transcripts and reviewed by the additional researcher. The data analysis was then written and tied to relevant literature to explain the findings. Content validity of categories and themes was assessed through procedures that Lincoln and Guba (1985) described: (a) participants in the later interviews were used to validate categories and themes from earlier interviews and (b) a fellow HIV researcher reviewed transcripts to match categories and themes.

Results

This study grew out of a larger project focused on women's social support experiences, including the challenges and dilemmas of seeking and receiving support. From the interviews with women living with HIV, it became clear that religion or spirituality was intertwined with their experiences of social support. Of the women I interviewed, 58% mentioned spirituality, church, God, or religion in their interviews, despite the fact that there were no interview questions that mentioned these topics. Of the 26 women who discussed spirituality, 23 (88.5%) were African American, 16 (61.5%) had a partner with whom they were in a committed relationship, 22 (84.6%) had children, and 13 (50%) were taking medication for depression. It should be noted that previous research has indicated that spirituality is a more predominant coping resource for African Americans (Cotton et al., 2006; Sunil & McGehee, 2007; True et al., 2005). In particular, more African Americans report becoming more spiritual, whereas more Caucasians report feeling alienated from religious communities since being diagnosed with HIV (Cotton et al., 2006). These findings indicate that the results of this study may not reflect everyone's experience with spirituality; however, it did figure prominently in the support systems of the women in the study.

Those who spoke of spirituality described a strong sense of faith that they would be taken care of no matter what happened to them. Daisy, 32 years old, said, "God has given me many chances and he opened my eyes to the fact that there is a life with HIV and life goes on." Brianna, 40 years old, advised the best way to cope is, "Give your life to God and go to church." My interviewees seldom differentiated spirituality from religion except in those cases when a particular church had rejected them; consequently, in the analysis that follows, I interpret "spirituality" quite broadly to include both relationships to things spiritual as well as involvement in particular communities of faith.

This strong sense of spirituality had several functions described through the roles that God and the church played in the support system. In particular, spirituality or a connection to God offered the women an opportunity to develop meaning and perspective taking, to have a source of support, to provide control through a more powerful being, and to offer a path to community.

Develop Meaning and Perspective Taking

One of the functions of spirituality was that it helped women frame their HIV diagnosis as a positive, or at least inevitable, event. For some of the women in this study, spirituality served as a mechanism for perspective shifts. They believed that God had a plan for their lives, and that connecting spiritually to God as a higher being provided them a way to make sense of, and make changes to, their lives. Research has indicated that many women attribute a new or revived sense of spirituality because HIV infection encouraged them to take better care of themselves, or to get off of drugs (Goggin et al., 2001; Hall, 1998). For example, Judy, 37 years old, explained that "I have no issues with HIV. I believe in the Lord and I believe he will deliver me if I ask him. Because of my HIV, I am drug and alcohol free. I'd rather be HIV positive and drug and alcohol free than be positive and on drugs and not sober. That was hell." Judy recognized that, despite the challenges associated with being HIV positive, her life had changed for the better after breaking her addiction to drugs and alcohol. She attributed that change to her spirituality, which she articulates as a connection to God. Just as one might seek social support, Judy asked for deliverance from addiction. Judy also described how a relationship with God has led her to reframe everyday events: "Having God in my life is the best part. I can be miserable at myself and causing chaos but then I can be in His will and my day can go so smooth I can just be floating and smiling."

A spiritual connection also led women to see life in a new way. For some, that meant that spirituality also helped them make sense of events in the past. Discussing a tumultuous time from her past, Lauren, 56, commented,

> That was a trial from God. That was his way of telling me to slow down but I didn't listen, I didn't heed. They say that when you don't heed, trouble is right around the corner and I believe that now. I regret that sometime I have not been listening, as I should. I was walking around, but I was dead. I was no good to myself and I was no good to anybody else.

Lauren reframed her past in terms of her new understanding of a relationship with God: trouble derived from a failure to listen to what God was trying to tell her. With these new parameters, the women changed the way they approached living with HIV. Tammy, 42, explained, "God has given me many chances and he opened my eyes to the fact that there is a life with HIV and life goes on."

Becomes a Source of Emotional Support

Women in the study also described the acts of spirituality as a source of support. Just as communication with a supportive friend might be comforting, spiritual communication practices such as daily prayer and meditation were common ways the women calmed their stress and rejuvenated their mood. Lisa, 43 years old, explained the importance of prayer to her motivation: "First of all, I do pray. I stay positive and believe in the power of God. I do daily meditation and I try to stay focused on that." Spiritual activities have been negatively correlated with feelings of emotional distress (Sowell et al., 2000)—this relief from emotional distress was clear in many of the women's explanation of the role of spirituality in their lives. Edna, 43 years old, said, "I get a lot of support from reading my Bible and saying my prayers. I feel much better when I pray and talk to God." Doris, 39, exhibited this relief, "I get affected with loneliness and sadness. Some kind of enemy comes in and puts fear in my heart. I pray and God takes the fear away."

For some of the women, God provided a consistent/stable presence in their lives. That meant a sense of security in some cases, as Michelle, 52 years old, noted, "I feel secure because I know God is watching over me." In other cases, the women looked to God for reassurance and esteem support. Elizabeth, 35, summarized this support, "I love myself and God loves me." Maggie, 28, noted the sense of encouragement that prayer provides when she offered advice for other women, "For those that are living with it, I hope they keep their head up too and keep praying. The best thing to do is keep praying and don't give up. I'm not giving up."

Provides Control Through a More Powerful Being

For some of the women, God was a powerful force who could control elements of their lives that they could not, akin to perceived available instrumental support. Perhaps the most obvious way this was discussed is in terms of being cured of HIV/AIDS. For some, this meant being cured by God directly. Doris explained,

> I am having hope that God will give me that miracle. I really believe that God is going to heal me. I have been with God for ten years and when God says he is going to give me a miracle, I believe that he is going to give me a miracle. I won't have to take any more medicine when I get my miracle.

Similarly, Sheila, 38 years old, said, "I pray and I ask God because nobody can cure it but him. I have faith and trust in him." For others, God provides a cure working through others. Maggie commented, "I have faith in God that someone will come out with a cure." Emma added, "God has given the doctors the technology to do what they have done." Although some women looked to God to provide a cure through doctors, some women looked to God to dispute what doctors told them. Doris said, "I didn't listen to them doctors and I started praying and praying. I went to prayer every day. When the doctor said 'no,' God said 'yes.'"

Another portrayal of God was as the giver of life; as such, God has the power to decide who lives and dies. Sometimes this was reflected in a specific experience. Tammy recounted, "I had fear I thought I was going to die but for some apparent reason I didn't. I thank God for that." She went on to say, "God gave me this body and I'm going to take good care of it." Jane, 43, explained, "I told God that if he was going to take me to go ahead and do it now." Other times this was mentioned simply as God's power to give and take life. Sheila noted, "Getting up and thanking God that I am still alive," was the best part of everyday life.

In addition to the larger issues of life and death, God also was portrayed with power to direct various aspects of daily life. For example, God was seen as an entity that could provide or direct relationships. Doris explained, "It is just the grace of God that keeps me now. If God sees fit for me to have someone I will have someone." Lauren said, "God has sent me some beautiful friends, White and Black." God was also seen as having the power to direct the women to resources, or sources of support. When asked what she would tell a newly diagnosed woman, Lisa responded, "She needs to know that God loves her and that is why she was directed to this center."

Offers a Connection to Community

For some participants, ties to spirituality and to God meant church attendance and participation in church activities. For these women living with HIV, churches provided not only an environment to commune with God, but also offered opportunities for numerous types of social ties that might provide support opportunities; that is, churches are social networks in which one can readily find access to potentially supportive people. When first diagnosed, some women went to churches looking for help coping with their diagnosis. Lucy, 34 years old, explained,

> Basically I just went to a whole bunch of churches because I was devastated. I was searching for God and I just told a whole bunch of people that I needed help. I was in a real bad state of mind and somebody was able to take me under their wing and work with me and help me.

After diagnosis some women did not socialize much, but did feel comfortable among church members. Ruth, 28, said, "I don't hang out with people and if I'm not at group, I'm at home with my children or I'm at church." Others found support through churches. Kristen, 41, found, "I get support from people in church—my groups and even young adults."

Churches also provided the women with opportunities for ties to people who could provide more specific types of social support or assistance. For example, churches generally are led by a minister or pastor who can offer spiritual guidance while offering a confidential ear. Doris said, "When I get sick in my body, I go to church and my pastor prays for me and I feel better. I take my medication and he prays for me and I feel better." In addition to the minister, churches offer ties to those who are not necessarily living with HIV and in the same situation as these women. This provides exposure to people who might be more able economically and emotionally to provide support. Lucy noted, "I have a couple of friends from church who are in a better position than me that give me a lot of advice and help me out financially."

One unique aspect of community is the sense that it provides a group or collection of others wishing the best for the person and affirming him or her. Churches seem to be a useful source for this type of support. The notion that there is a larger entity praying for them provides the women with a feeling of hope. Doris said, "My church people prayed for me and I started feeling okay." Not only is there a group of people praying for them when they are facing challenges, but churches are also communities with which to share triumphs. Judy explained, "My church members are the same as I get from here. We moved from Elgin about two years ago. The devil was riding me and I felt like I wanted to use [drugs] but I didn't and the whole church was so happy that I didn't."

Participants also mentioned that an important feature of the church community is the opportunity to participate and give to others. Doris said, "I try to help people and I pray for people. I teach Bible study for people that don't know the Bible. I make calls for my church for different events we are going to have. I help clean the church sometimes and I help with the Food Pantry sometimes." The opportunity to participate in groups and offer others support through church programs enables women to reciprocate support, bolstering their self-esteem and preventing a sense of dependence (Siegel & Schrimshaw, 2002). Lucy said, "I'm in church now and I help a lot of people with it. They have to hear my story so they can come to me for help." Nikki, 42 years old, explained, "There is a large church here in town and they have support groups once a month. I go three or four times a year just to see everyone and meet new people and let everyone know who I am." Some churches that did not offer these types of services did offer help to those who wanted to provide them. Andrea, 38, explained,

No, but I'm a ministry leader and I am going to start my own program for halfway people. Today we are going to paint the place. My church gave us a place to run our HIV unit out of. Hopefully it will be running pretty soon. We'll be doing counseling, testing and support groups.

Although the women in this study reported predominantly positive experiences with their spiritual journeys, some reported that churches can be unwelcoming to those with HIV or AIDS. Emma had one such experience, "Talk about fear, rejection and bigotry. You are not going to find a more bigoted place than the house of God. It hurt me bad and I had to let go of that but I did not let go of God. I go to him and I find he does not judge me." Despite having this bad experience, God still functions a source of support and comfort to Emma through prayer. When asked what has helped her deal with her HIV infection, Emma replied,

> I do the God thing but I don't do the church thing. The God thing has been a good source of comfort and support for me. I go to the Word of God and not man's word because we know how man can take what God said and misconstrue it. Especially with HIV and people who are gay. I go to the Word of God and pray.

Some women, therefore, separated spirituality and God from organized religious activities, such as attending church.

Discussion

How women cope with the stressors associated with HIV has received more attention by researchers in the past decade. The women in this study faced various challenges to their adjustment to life with HIV—some reported past physical and/or sexual abuse in their lives. They also faced problems with drug and alcohol abuse. These experiences had a profound effect on how they reacted to their diagnosis as well as how they approached living with HIV. For some women, their HIV diagnosis was tied directly to their abuse, whereas for others it served as an additional source of stress and another roadblock to coping with HIV. No matter what challenges the women had faced or were facing, spirituality and/or God played a significant role in their lives, specifically in their support system. In fact, they perceived that spirituality was tied closely to their social support experiences.

Spirituality provided the women in this study with valuable support as well as a connection to a community. In this case, it might be important to consider that support from spiritual resources is support that is unattached to their illness. Spirituality is not a resource that is connected exclusively or specifically with HIV/AIDS; support derived from spirituality may also be useful for coping with the range of life stresses experienced by women in this sample. It is also bigger than, and independent of, the medical concerns that the women are experiencing, which may be a reason the women find it to be so vital. Likewise, supportive spiritual communities are not based on the common experience of living with HIV so membership is not limited by diagnosis. They are communities that family members and friends can engage in as whole members. Spiritual communities not only offer women the opportunity to find support for themselves, but offer the women the opportunity to care for and include family members in the support experiences at the same time.

Spirituality and Social Support

Based on the data in this study, there appears to be a strong connection between social support and spirituality. At a very basic level, the definition of social support and the perceived benefits of spirituality include similar concepts. Each of the four main themes that emerged from this analysis of spirituality are also main themes in research on social support. Through their relationship to God, women reported developing *new meanings and perspectives* on HIV, a function that resembles the processes of re-appraisal (e.g., Burleson & Goldsmith, 1998) and uncertainty management (e.g., Albrecht, Adelman, & Associates, 1987; Brashers et al., 2004), through which social support improves coping. The women in this study spoke of spirituality as a *source of emotional support and control.* Prayer and meditation entailed communication with a stable, supportive, affirming presence and a spiritual connection could be a powerful force capable of intervening to affect cures, extend life, and improve relationships. These themes resemble the provisions of social relationships, including emotional support and instrumental aid (e.g., Cutrona, Suhr, & MacFarlane, 1990). Finally, *connection to a spiritual community* provided opportunities for participation in a social support network. A spiritual connection to God facilitated entry into reciprocal ties of mutual aid and support with diverse others. Access to resources, reciprocity, and diversity have all been identified as important in theories of social support networks (e.g., see Cohen, Underwood, & Gottlieb, 2000) and they were also evident in women's talk about their participation in church.

It is also worth noting that just as social support may sometimes hinder coping, there is potential for the kinds of spirituality the women described to go against medical advice. A few women commented, for example, on experiencing rejection from a church community. Although none of these participants spoke of disappointed hopes for a cure, outside observers might note the potential tension when direction taken from spirituality is at odds with recommended medical regimens.

The relationship between social support and spirituality goes well beyond this similarity in definition. In what follows, I detail how spirituality facilitated access to a social support network and how spirituality functioned as a source of support.

Spirituality as Supportive Community

Churches serve as a context for network support and provide people with the opportunity to connect with others who share common beliefs. Community is an important source of support and comfort for people living with HIV, because it provides material and/or psychological safety and security (Adelman & Frey, 1997). Numerous studies have documented the importance of community for gay men. Developing a supportive community enhances social well-being (Somlai & Heckman, 2000) and a sense of belonging (Kraft, Beeker, Stokes, & Peterson, 2000). Community provides a way of re-establishing identity by connecting with other people living with HIV/AIDS (Lewis, 1999) and by providing a means to reactivate their social lives in a relaxed, informal setting (Katoff, 1992). Community also has an impact on individual-level behaviors (Brashers, Haas, Klingle, & Neidig, 2000). Many gay men actively seek out and become involved with community because they are empowered through group affiliation with peers, which permits the individual to challenge stigma and maintain a positive sense of self, while the community provides them with support, affirmation, and the knowledge that they are not alone (Lewis, 1999). Community facilitates accommodation to HIV status and helps educate people who are newly diagnosed about the illness and treatment options (Lewis, 1999).

It is clear that community provides gay men living with HIV important support resources. Although this was true for some of the women who were involved with women's peer groups, many of the women in this study did not feel they had adequate community resources. The feeling that there was not a community contributed to the feeling that support was not always available. The support that a community provides can be thought of as a safety net—when someone rejects an individual, there will always be someone to help. The women felt that it was very important to maintain the support resources they had because they did not have an illness community on which to rely. The feeling that there would be a social network of family and friends behind them no matter what happens was not part of these women's experiences.

For some of the women, then, spirituality provided their only sense of community. The women seek support from spiritual communities in which acceptance is given, in which there is relief from blame, and in which there is hope for the future. Finding support in these alternative communities provides the women with confidence and a foundation to seek additional support if they need it. In many cases, these people are willing to accept, listen to, and care for other members of their church.

The women mentioned supportive experiences with fellow church members including emotional, informational, and tangible support. In some cases, church members were included as support sources that could be called on if the woman was upset. In other cases, church members had provided school supplies for the women's children. Church membership connected these women to a community that provided emotional and tangible support. This experience reflects studies that have shown that people commonly receive emotional and tangible support from their congregations (Hill & Pargament, 2003). Previous research also has indicated that receiving instrumental support may enhance one's perception of support availability, which has been shown to be an important predictor of adjustment (Brashers et al., 2004). In this respect, being involved in a spiritual community provides the women with support, which is an important element in their adjustment to life with HIV.

Beyond the provision of tangible resources, the women also explained that support from spiritual outlets made them feel accepted and loved. This acceptance provided the women with the confidence to seek additional support. For example, one woman was encouraged by the reaction of her friends at church and felt that, with that support, she could seek out a support group designed for women living with HIV. By bolstering acceptance, spiritual-based support made it easier for some of the women to address more challenging requests, such as needing food, shelter, or help maintaining the family. Having the unconditional acceptance of their church community made the women feel more confident and more relaxed about disclosing their illness and accessing services available to them.

Perhaps just as important as the support a spiritual community can provide, is the opportunity it provides for the women to give support to others. Churches offer a unique environment in which there are few expectations about contributions in that any contribution is welcomed and appreciated. Being able to reciprocate or provide support to others is an important aspect for successful social support interactions. Although the opportunities might not always be available to directly reciprocate, participation in groups, Bible studies, and other church activities provides the women with a chance to give back to the church community.

Spirituality as a Supportive Relationship

In addition to being a context for support, spirituality also functions as a form of support all on its own. For some people, God is an entity who provides comfort, and God is a safe haven because he or she is a being who offers caring and protection in times of stress. Research indicates that a relationship with God will lead to greater comfort in stressful situations and greater strength and confidence in everyday life (Hill & Pargament, 2003), which is very similar to the buffering theories of social support. People who report a closer connection to God experience a number of health related benefits including less depression and higher self-esteem (Hill & Pargament, 2003).

One common way the women in this study engaged in a relationship with God was through prayer. Prayer is the most frequent spiritual behavior (Guillory, Sowell, Moneyham, & Seals, 1997). Prayer can have numerous benefits, similar to that of social support. Women living with HIV, who engage primarily in private forms of religion such as prayer, are less likely to engage in high risk behaviors, are more likely to perceive themselves as healthy, and more likely to feel they were in control of their health (Morse et al., 2000). Prayer offers women the opportunity to talk to someone who will listen without judgment. Many of the women incorporated prayer into a daily routine, as well as used prayer as a way to cope with being upset. Research supports the notion that spiritual activities such as prayer and meditation are useful coping strategies for people living with HIV (Reeves, Merriam, & Courtenay, 1999). Cassie, 38, commented that, "I get a lot of support from reading my Bible and saying my prayers. I feel much better when I pray and talk to God." One explanation for the effectiveness of prayer is that it is similar to disclosure. Prayers have been found to have similar linguistic characteristics to disclosures and may also be associated with the personal benefits that disclosure provides (VandeCreek, Janus, Pennebaker, & Binau, 2002). Disclosure can be beneficial because it helps people process events and experiences (Pennebaker & Keough, 1999). The women in this study frequently engaged in prayer and considered it to be an important source of strength and stability. Moreover, their descriptions of prayer and meditation reveal a relational dimension to spirituality as communication with One who accepts, guides, and acts.

Another role that God played in the lives of the women in this study was as a powerful other (i.e., God was a powerful being who was in control of events in their lives). Thus, they were comforted by their belief that there is an intrinsic benefit of having a relationship with God, because of the power that he/she has to control events and outcomes. Living with HIV/AIDS is a life filled with uncertainties and experiences that reinforce our lack of control as human beings. It is comforting that someone with whom one has a personal relationship through prayer and meditation has control over the events in one's life. When life events were too stressful or difficult for the women to think about, they often spoke of giving it to God or letting God work through them. Believing that someone else has control over your ultimate path provides the freedom to focus on the here and now and the care needed at the time. Being able to identify someone who has power over what is going on relieves burdens for some, and provides an outlet for hope. Some research has found that spirituality is positively associated with optimism (Biggar et al., 1999), which is a useful coping mechanism (Brashers, 2007) and can be an important aspect of depression care (Cooper, Brown, Vu, Ford, & Powe, 2001).

Spirituality also served as esteem support for many of the women in this study. Their faith provided esteem support because everyone is worthy of love and compassion in God's eyes. Spirituality provides a sense of acceptance and belonging that eases emotional tensions caused by their illness and the stigma attached to HIV. In this respect, spirituality can restore identity because it removes blame, provides perspective, and offers opportunities for reappraisal. For some of the women, spirituality had helped them believe there was a purpose to their diagnosis and that their faith would help them find that purpose, as well as sustain their health until a cure is found. Religion can provide people with a sense of their ultimate destinations in life by providing ultimate purpose and meaning even in disturbing life events (Hill & Pargament, 2003). In this case, the women are sustained in their coping efforts by this spiritual purpose and the support for reappraisal. Not only does spirituality provide network support, but it provides emotional and esteem support as well, making it an integral part of the support systems of these women living with HIV/AIDS.

Future Directions

The connections between social support and spirituality warrant further attention. Spiritual resources play such an important role in the lives of these women living with HIV that it seems impossible to separate it from their support experiences. When religion and spirituality have been studied, they typically have been included as secondary variables in the context of other research, primarily measured by church attendance, membership, or some type of religiosity scales (Hill & Pargament, 2003). Further research needs to develop communication specific measures of spirituality (see Egbert, Mickley, & Coeling, 2004) and to explain how and why spirituality affects health. One avenue for exploration in this case is the connection between spirituality and social support. Additional research to discover what women draw from their spiritual experiences and how those experiences impact their approach to or experience of support may provide insight into this connection. Insight into how and why spirituality functions as social support is important to understanding the support experiences of women living with HIV, as well as to discovering the connection between spirituality and health. In addition, the women in this study talked exclusively about God and Christianity as their connection to spirituality, but other forms of spirituality and religion (even nonreligious spirituality; see McGrath, 2005) may function differently for people living with HIV (see Persuad, 2007). Future studies, therefore, should investigate a wider range of spiritual and religious beliefs, and how they connect to the management of health and illness.

A focus on messages about spirituality also is an important direction. Robinson and Nussbaum (2004) examined doctor-patient interactions and found that 13% of their sample of interactions included mentions of religion/church attendance. Included in their discussions was the importance of church attendance for social support, and the implications that ill health (e.g., being homebound) had for church attendance. Another study demonstrated that talking about religion allowed people to integrate their religious, spiritual, and lay beliefs—for example, participants in their study reconciled scientific explanations for health and illness with spiritual explanations (Harris, Parrott, & Dorgan, 2004). Harris et al. found that participants in their study were able to develop understanding about genetic causes of disease that conformed with, or at least did not contradict, a religious framework. Some expressed uncertainty about the connection between God and genetic explanations, whereas others said that "God works through our genes" (p. 112). Additional research designed to explore messages about spirituality and health can further enhance our understanding of the role of spirituality and religion in beliefs about health, the connection between faith-based and medical-scientific explanations of health and illness, and the ways in which people manage health and illness.

Conclusion

The women in this study seemed to compensate for the lack of an HIV-related community with their connection to a spiritual community. Spiritual communities provide connections to other people who are potential sources of emotional and tangible support. Spirituality provides comfort and offers an opportunity for the women to disclose their stresses to an understanding and accepting other, as well as the confidence to cope with life with HIV. The multiple functions of spirituality in the lives of women living with HIV/AIDS make it a vital piece of their support systems.

Acknowledgment

This study was funded by the National Institute of Mental Health (MH65863).

References

Adelman, M. B., & Frey, L. R. (1997). *The fragile community: Living together with AIDS.* Mahwah, NJ: Erlbaum.

Albrecht, Adelman, & Associates. (1987). *Communicating social support.* Thousand Oaks, CA: Sage.

Albrecht, T. L., & Goldsmith, D. J. (2003). Social support, social networks, and health. In A. Marshall, K. I. Miller, R. L. Parrott, & T. L. Thompson (Eds.), *Handbook of health communication* (pp. 263–284). Mahwah, NJ: Erlbaum.

Barroso, J. (1997). Social support and long-term survivors of AIDS. *Western Journal of Nursing Research, 19,* 554–582.

Belcher, A. E., Dettmore, D., & Holzemer, S. P. (1989). Spirituality and sense of well-being in person with AIDS. *Holistic Nursing Practice, 3,* 16–25.

Biggar, H., Forehand, R., Devine, D., Brody, G., Armistead, L., Morse, E., et al. (1999). Women who are HIV infected: The role of religious activity in psychosocial adjustment. *AIDS Care, 11,* 159–199.

Brashers, D. E. (2007). A theory of communication and uncertainty management. In B. Whaley & W. Samter (Ed.), *Explaining communication theory* (pp. 201–218). Mahwah, NJ: Erlbaum.

Brashers, D. E., Haas, S. M., Klingle, R. S., & Neidig, J. (2000). Collective AIDS activism and individuals' perceived self-advocacy in physician-patient communication. *Human Communication Research, 26,* 372–402.

Brashers, D. E., Neidig, J. L., & Goldsmith, D. J. (2004). Social support and the management of uncertainty for people living with HIV. *Health Communication, 16,* 305–331.

Brashers, D. E., Neidig, J. L., Russell, J. A., Cardillo, L. W., Haas, S. M., Dobbs, L. K., et al. (2003). The medical, personal, and social causes of uncertainty in HIV illness. *Issues in Mental Health Nursing, 24,* 497–522.

Burleson, B. R., & Goldsmith, D. J. (1998). How the comforting process works: Alleviating emotional distress through conversationally induced reappraisals. In P. A. Anderson & L. K. Guerrero (Eds.), *Handbook of communication and emotion: Research, theory, applications, and contexts* (pp. 245–280). San Diego, CA: Academic Press.

Centers for Disease Control (CDC). (2008). HIV/AIDS among women. Retrieved August 2008, from http://www.cdc.gov/hiv/topics/women/resources/factsheets/women.htm

Charmaz, K. (2000). Grounded theory: Objectivist and constructivist methods. In N. K. Denzin & Y. S. Lincoln (Eds.), *Handbook of qualitative research* (2nd ed., pp. 509–536). Thousand Oaks, CA: Sage.

Ciambrone, D. (2001). Illness and other assaults on self: The relative impact of HIV/AIDS on women's lives. *Sociology of Health and Illness, 23,* 517–540.

Ciambrone, D. (2002). Informal networks among women with HIV/AIDS: Present support and future prospects. *Qualitative Health Research, 12,* 876–896.

Chibnall, J. T., Videen, S. D., Duckro, P. N., & Miller, D. K. (2002). Psychosocial-spiritual correlates of death distress in patients with life-threatening medical conditions. *Palliative Medicine, 16,* 331–338.

Cohen, S., Underwood, L. G., & Gottlieb, B. H. (2000). *Social support measurement and intervention: A guide for health and social scientists.* New York: Oxford University Press.

Cooper, L. A., Brown, C., Vu, H. T., Ford, D. E., & Powe, N. R. (2001). How important is intrinsic spirituality in depression care? A comparison of White and African American primary care patients. *Journal of General Internal Medicine, 16,* 634–638.

Cotton, S., Tsevat, J., Szaflarski, M., Kudel, I., Sherman, S. N., Feinberg, J., et al. (2006). Changes in religiousness and spirituality attributed to HIV/AIDS: Are there sex and race differences? *Journal of General Internal Medicine, 21,* S14–S20.

Cutrona, C. E., Suhr, J. A., & MacFarlane, R. (1990). Interpersonal transactions and the psychological sense of support. In S. Duck (Ed.), *Personal relationships and social support* (pp. 30–45). London: Sage.

Egbert, N., Mickley, J., & Coeling, H. (2004). A review and application of social scientific measures of religiosity and spirituality: Assessing a missing component in health communication research. *Health Communication, 16,* 7–27.

Goldsmith, D. J. (2004). *Communicating social support.* New York: Cambridge University Press.

Goggin, K., Catley, D., Brisco, S. T., Engelson, E. S., Rabkin, J. G., & Kotler, D. P. (2001). A female perspective on living with HIV disease. *Health & Social Work, 26*(2), 80–89.

Guillory, J., Sowell, R., Moneyham, L., & Seals, B. (1997). An exploration of the meaning and use of spirituality among women with HIV/AIDS. *Alternative Therapies, 3*(5), 55–60.

Hackl, K., Somlai, A. M., Kelly, J. A., & Kalichman, S. C. (1997). Women living with HIV/AIDS: The dual challenge of being a patient and caregiver. *Health and Social Work, 22,* 53–62.

Hall, B. A. (1998). Patterns of spirituality in persons with advanced HIV disease. *Research in Nursing & Health., 21,* 143–153.

Hays, R. B., Magee, R. H., & Chauncey, S. (1994). Identifying helpful and unhelpful behaviors of loved ones: The PWA's perspective. *AIDS Care, 6,* 379–392.

Harris, T. M., Parrott, R., & Dorgan, K. A. (2004). Talking about human genetics within religious frameworks. *Health Communication, 16,* 105–115.

Hill, P. C., & Pargament, K. I. (2003). Advances in the conceptualization and measurement of religion and spirituality: Implications for physical and mental health research. *American Psychologist, 58,* 64–74.

Ickovics, J. R., Hamburger, M. E., Schoenbaum, V. D., Schuman, P., Boland, R. J., & Moore, J. (2001). Mortality, CD4 cell count decline, and depressive symptoms among HIV-seropositive women: Longitudinal analysis from the HIV epidemiology research study. *Journal of the American Medical Association, 285,* 1466–1474.

Ironson, G., Solomon, G. F., Balbin, E. G., O'Cleirigh, C., George, A., Kumar, M., et al. (2002). The Ironson-Woods Spirituality/Religiousness Index is associated with long survival, health behaviors, less distress, and low cortisol in people with HIV/AIDS. *Annals of Behavioral Medicine, 24,* 34–48.

Ironson, G., Stuetzle, R., & Fletcher, M. A. (2006). An increase in religiousness/spirituality occurs after HIV diagnosis and predicts slower disease progression over 4 years in people with HIV. *Journal of General Internal Medicine, 21,* S62–S68.

Katoff, L. (1992). Community-based services for people with AIDS. *Primary Care, 19,* 231–243.

Kraft, J. M., Beeker, C., Stokes, J. P., & Peterson, J. L. (2000). Finding the "community" in community-level HIV/AIDS interventions: Formative research with young African American men who have sex with men. *Health Education & Behavior, 27,* 430–441.

Lauver, D. R. (2000). Commonalities in women's spirituality and women's health. *Advances in Nursing Science, 22*(3), 76–88.

Lewis, J. (1999). Status passages: The experience of HIV-positive gay men. *Journal of Homosexuality, 37,* 87–115.

Lincoln, Y. S., & Guba, E. G. (1985). *Naturalistic inquiry.* Thousand Oaks, CA: Sage.

Mattis, J. S. (2000). African American women's definitions of spirituality and religiosity. *Journal of Black Psychology, 26,* 101–122.

McGrath, P. (2005). Developing a language for nonreligious spirituality in relation to serious illness through research: Preliminary findings. *Health Communication, 18,* 217–235.

Meravigilia, M. G. (1999). Critical analysis of spirituality and it empirical indicators. *Journal of Holistic Nursing, 17,* 18–33.

Morse, E., Morse, P. M., Klebba, K. E., Stock, M. R., Forehand, R., & Panayotova, E. (2000). The use of religion among HIV-infected African American women. *Journal of Religion and Health, 39,* 261–276.

Musgrave, C., Allen, C. E., & Allen, G. J. (2002). Spirituality and women of color. *American Journal of Public Health, 92,* 557–560.

Parrott, R. (2004). "Collective amnesia:" The absence of religious faith and spirituality in health communication research and practice. *Health Communication, 16,* 1–5.

Pennebaker, J. W., & Keough, K. A. (1999). Self and identity in adaptation to stress and emotion. In R. Ashmore & R. Contrada (Eds.), *Self and identity: Vol. 2. Interdisciplinary explorations in physical health* (pp. 101–124). New York: Oxford University Press.

Persuad, R. (2007). Spirituality and HIV disease progression. *Journal of General Internal Medicine, 22,* 1220.

Reeves, P. M., Merriam, S. B., & Courtenay, B. C. (1999). Adaptation to HIV infection: The development of coping strategies over time. *Qualitative Health Research, 9,* 344–361.

Remein, R. H., Exner, T., Kertzner, R. M., Ehrhardt, A. A., Rotheram-Borus, M. J., Johnson, M. O., et al. (2006). Depressive symptomatology among HIV-positive women in the era of HAART: A stress and coping model. *American Journal of Community Psychology, 38,* 275–285.

Richardson, J., Barkan, S., Cohen, M., Back, S., FitzGerald, G., Feldman, J., et al. (2001). Experience and covariates of depressive symptoms among a cohort of HIV infected women. *Social Work in Health Care, 32,* 93–111.

Robinson, J. D., & Nussbaum, J. F. (2004). Grounding research and medical education about religion in actual physician-patient interaction: Church attendance, social support, and older adults. *Health Communication, 16,* 63–85.

Seeman, T. E., Dubin, L. F., & Seeman, M. (2003). Religiosity/Spirituality and health: A critical review of the evidence for biological pathways. *American Psychologist, 58,* 53–63.

Siegel, K., & Schrimshaw, E. W. (2002). The perceived benefits of religious and spiritual coping among older adults living with HIV/AIDS. *Journal for the Scientific Study of Religion, 41,* 91–102.

Siegel, K., & Schrimshaw, E. W. (2005). Stress, appraisal, and coping: A comparison of HIV-infected women in the pre-HAART and HAART eras. *Journal of Psychosomatic Research, 58,* 225–233.

Simoni, J. M., Frick, P. A., & Huang, B. (2006). A longitudinal evaluation of a social support model of medication adherence among HIV-positive men and women on antiretroviral therapy. *Health Psychology, 25,* 74–81.

Somlai, A. M., & Heckman, T. G. (2000). Correlates of spirituality and well-being in a community sample of people living with HIV disease. *Mental Health, Religion & Culture, 3,* 57–70.

Sowell, R., Moneyham, L., Hennessy, M., Guillory, J., Demi, A., & Seals, B. (2000). Spiritual activities as a resistance resource for women with Human Immunodeficiency Virus. *Nursing Research, 49,* 73–82.

Strauss, A. L., & Corbin, J. M. (1998). *Basics of qualitative research.* Thousand Oaks, CA: Sage.

Sunil, T. S., & McGehee, M. A. (2007). Social and religious support on treatment adherence among HIV/AIDS patients by race/ethnicity. *Journal of HIV/AIDS & Social Services, 6,* 83–99.

Tanyi, R. A. (2002). Towards clarification of the meaning of spirituality. *Journal of Advanced Nursing, 39,* 500–509.

Taylor, R. J., & Chatters, L. M. (1988). Church members as a source of informal social support. *Review of Religious Research, 30,* 193–203.

True, G., Phipps, E. J., Braitman, L. E., Harralson, T., Harris, D., & Tester, W. (2005). Treatment preferences and advance care planning at end of life: The role of ethnicity and spiritual coping in cancer patients. *Annals of Behavioral Medicine, 30,* 174–179.

Tuck, I., McCain, N. L., & Elswick, R. K., Jr. (2001). Spirituality and psychosocial factors in persons living with HIV. *Journal of Advanced Nursing, 33,* 776–783.

VandeCreek, L., Janus, M. D., Pennebaker, J. W., & Binau, B. (2002). Praying about difficult experiences as self-disclosure to God. *International Journal for the Psychology of Religion, 12,* 29–39.

Vyavaharkar, M., Moneyham, L., Tavakoli, A., Phillips, K. D., Murdaugh, C., Jackson, K., et al. (2007). Social support, coping, and medication adherence among HIV-positive women with depression living in rural areas of the Southeastern United States. *AIDS Patient Care and STDs, 21,* 667–680.

Woods, T. E., Antoni, M. H., Ironson, G. H., & Kling, D. W. (1999a). Religiosity is associated with affective and immune status in symptomatic HIV-infected gay men. *Journal of Psychosomatic Research, 46,* 165–176.

Woods, T. E., Antoni, M. H., Ironson, G. H., & Kling, D. W. (1999b). Religiosity is associated with affective status in HIV-infected African American women. *Journal of Health Psychology, 4,* 317–326.

Chapter 13

Multiple Discourses in the Management of Health and Illness

Why Does It Matter?

Roxanne Parrott

> Time was represented in the physicians' narratives as a valuable and scarce commodity. The value emerged as a justification for negative attitudes which physicians showed toward any activity that took too much of the precious resource. Physicians resented activities that took too much time. (Vanderford, Smith, & Harris, 1992, p. 149)

Communication in the management of health and illness coalesces around identifying the boundaries and scope of a condition, person, professional, or situation associated with health or health care, and giving meaning to health status by "naming and defining its cause" (Thompson, 2000, p. 3). In doing so, the communication reflects the reality suggested in the opening quotation. There are outcomes which emerge from communication about health and illness management that, in turn, constrain communication about health and illness management. Time as a resource is one such example. The meanings of resources such as time are constructed through three overlapping discursive fields of influence that blend in indistinguishable ways without persistent efforts to identify them (Parrott, 2004).

Communication about health and health care sometimes focuses on the allocation and use of scarce resources, such as dollars for research, monies for health care delivery, and time, which reflects how we communicate as a society about health. This communication is shaped by political, religious, and organizational agendas in the derivation and delivery of health knowledge and services to the American public. Communication about health and health care that focuses on the understanding and use of the derived or expert information and knowledge about health and health care is often, but not always, easier to identify. These efforts to communicate the science of health inform, motivate, and may make profit for those involved in its use. Communication about health and health care that focuses on the understanding and use of more indigenous knowledge sources and experiential information regarding health and health care is such a persistent reality in our daily lives that we may forget or neglect to acknowledge it. This lay discourse is derived from cultural, social, and individual arenas that guide individual behavior with health and health care outcomes (e.g., Parrott & Polonec, 2007).

Whether communicating as a society about health, communicating the science of health, or communicating our experiences with health, there are a number of consistent outcomes with different implications for public health, medical, and self-management realms of health and illness management but with persistent realities relating to health. Some of these are explicitly discussed in the literature about communication and health; some only implicitly. Few are systematically considered in terms of the multiple discursive fields in which they take on unique meanings. This volume highlights a number of these areas. This chapter considers 15 such outcomes. Table 13.1 includes definitions of these outcomes: (a) resource allocation; (b) gate-keeping; (c) identity formation and/or maintenance; (d) comprehending and comparing; (e) uncertainty; (f) fear; (g) accountability; (h) effort; (i) excuse and/or justification accounts; (j) stereotypes; (k) compliance; (l) hope and/or optimism; (m) guilt, embarrassment, and/or shame; (n) sanctions; and (o) policy and/or behavior change. Their persistence and universality forms a framework for understanding the power that advocacy efforts may have in shaping health care reform.

Communicating as a Society about Health

Communication about health often says something about a society in terms of its values and priorities. We do not guarantee access to health care in the United States, yet we do value "life, liberty, and the pursuit of happiness." Tensions around these seemingly inconsistent ideas are evident in political debates, religious dogma, and organizational rules and priorities. These societal discussions influence decisions about how resources will be allocated for medical research and the delivery of health care. What research is funded forms the foundation of scientific evidence we have to communicate when guiding individuals and institutions about how to manage health and illness. The knowledge becomes a type of gate-keeper at the institutional level to guide the establishment of protocols regarding who receives what care and who will pay for it. The communication is then so integrally involved with how we define health and what options we have for managing illness that it is recognizable largely only by our personal effort and intention. For example, prior to the mapping of the human genome, no efforts could be formed around genetic predispositions linked to drug efficacy. With funding of research to seek answers to the question, "Do genes affect drug efficacy?" doctors may vary both the drugs prescribed and dosages based on the results of genetic tests. We can recognize that not very many years ago, such knowledge did not exist, and such options were not available.

The case of fetal health illustrates the significance of how society communicates about health and health care on how health and illness will be managed (Parrott & Condit, 1996). For example, prior to the medical research

Table 13.1 Outcomes of Communicating about Health and the Management of Illness

Resource Allocation: decisions about where time, money, and people will be directed to achieve health and health care.

Gate-keeping: the restriction versus admission of conditions, people, professionals, and sites to classifications and categorizations relating to health and health care.

Identity Formation and/or Maintenance: the ways in which health and health care define the core nature of individuals, professionals, and institutions.

Comprehending and Comparing: the understanding and ability to see differences and similarities between symptoms, diseases, and health care providers, options, and treatments.

Uncertainty: an increase, decrease, or stability in thoughts about health, health care sites, and personnel available to administer care.

Fear: the presence or absence of this negatively valenced emotion in relation to health and illness management.

Accountability: the direct or inferred "chain-of-blame" associated with health and health care; may assign responsibility and/or liability to individuals, professionals, and institutions in more or less formal ways.

Effort: the amount of energy and other resources an individual, professional, or institution will devote to health and health care.

Excuse and/or Justification Accounts: explanations for why an individual, professional, or institution is behaving with regard to promoting health and/or health care which may include acceptance of responsibility while denying culpability.

Stereotypes: preconceived views about individuals or institutions relating to health and health care.

Compliance: individual and/or institutional adherence to expected standards of conduct.

Hope and/or Optimism: individual and/or institutional predisposition to expect the best outcome.

Guilt, Embarrassment, and/or Shame: emotions related to individual and institutional acknowledgment of behavior inconsistent with the expected standards of conduct.

Sanctions: strategies designed to enforce or endorse standards associated with health and health care for individuals and institutions.

Policy and/or behavior change: individual and/or institutional initiative to address an identified shortcoming in the form of rules, laws, or actions

---

which confirmed that substances consumed by a woman cross the placenta and affect the fetus, women were often told that the womb was a place where the developing fetus sat growing in comfortable and safe isolation. Corresponding with the societal discourse that contributed to the science of prenatal care, new institutional identities formed as sites emerged for providing prenatal care, and professional identities formed in terms of providers of prenatal care. Institutional and professional comprehension of and comparison between users and nonusers partly sorted around outcomes relating to user and nonuser (Daniels & Parrott, 1996). Accountability was conveyed in societal discourse that asserted the need for better access to prenatal care and more compliance among women with use of care. Sanctions were even discussed at the societal level in terms of noncompliant women who used substances harmful to the fetus (Kline, 1996; Lemieux, 1996).

Several communication research programs suggest the significance of understanding and translating knowledge about how communicating as a society contributes to the range of outcomes considered in this chapter. For example, technical arguments relating to maternal and fetal health have been used in discussion to develop policies relating to reproductive health in this nation. Political arguments based less on medical science and more on values and morals have also been used to debate the formation of these policies. The former contributes to health policies associated with "choice," whereas the latter is more aligned with "control" over these decisions (Stearney, 1996). Changes in the organization of health care have been based on societal discourse which includes discussions about the bioethics of managed care and citizen rights relating to health care, the latter established not to be guaranteed in the Constitution (Bracci, 2001).

Framing the debate about euthanasia as a matter of conscience leads to quite different reflections than framing the debate in terms of end-of-life decision making. The latter opens a space for comprehension and comparison of alternatives, whereas the former already presumes that a decision to make such a choice is a violation of values and unconscionable (Hyde & Rufo, 2000). Debates about environmental tobacco smoke and subsequent policy illustrate the tension between communicating about the public good versus personal autonomy (Moore, 1997). Similar insights emerge about communicating the environmental risks relating to geological radon (Sandman, Weinstein, & Klotz, 1987). In these analyses, the reality that the agenda setting role of media often parallels the public health agenda emerges (e.g., Pratt, Ha, & Pratt, 2002).

Beyond an examination of debate which contributes to medical research agendas and health policies, it is societal discourse that reflects how decisions were made to organize to deliver health care in the United States in the ways that we do (and how that has implications for communication in health care encounters, see contributions in this volume from Lammers & Barbour; Real & Street; Waitzkin). The study of political discourse about Medicaid illustrated the fact that the resources allocated to support asthma research, for example, preceded policies associated with treatment (Gillespie, 2001). This is a persistent reality, as debate about the allocation of resources to medical research contributes to knowledge about disease diagnosis and treatment, and efforts to translate this to improve lives often lead to new debates and decisions about the provision of care. An analysis of free market discourse and its relation to health care reform provides a provocative starting place for understanding gaps in individual citizen comprehension and ability to make comparisons relating to health care (Conrad & Millay, 2001).

Communication about advance care planning research also reveals intersections between policies and organizational practices that ultimately affect how individuals cope with medical uncertainties (Hines, 2001), as does communication to parents about the care of their hospitalized children (Adams

& Parrott, 1994). An examination of the discourse associated with the ideology versus practice of medical education (Scheibel, 1996) demonstrates gaps between the ideals expressed as goals and the realities translated into educational settings. These research findings may be justified, excused, or contribute to change. Similarly, published communication research makes apparent the importance of hospital-based organizational communication for the formation of nurses' understanding of their roles and accountability (Apker, 2001). The impact of managed care settings on community health initiatives also reveals the pathways between the societal activity of organizing and models of delivering care in terms of such outcomes as resource allocation, gate-keeping, accountability, and effort (Medved et al., 2001). The communication processes associated with interdisciplinary health care teams (Ellingson, 2003) illustrates how individual team member efforts combine to improve the management of patients' health. The organization and formation of these care models contributes to accountability and effort. Other research has demonstrated that a supervising physician may manage difficult patient situations and contribute to cost savings, a resource outcome, which supports the practice of having supervising physicians (Pomerantz, Fehr, & Ende, 1997). Communication networks within nursing homes (Sachweh, 1998) also reveal the importance of accountability through roles and rules within these organizational settings. These issues have additional implications as considered in the chapter by Pescosolido, Croghan, and Howell in this volume.

Self-management discourse at the societal level has been examined in published research about environmental advocacy (Cantrill, 1993), revealing citizen efforts to manage the environment as a backdrop for well-being. Communication research also has demonstrated the importance of advocacy efforts of AIDS care partners in unlocking the gate, so to speak, in the management of living with AIDS (Miller & Zook, 1997). Bathhouse communication has been found to contribute to compliance with condom use (Elwood, Greene, & Carter, 2003). On the other hand, work-family policies have been shown to exist, giving the appearance of support for self-management of well-being within families, but organizational norms often inhibit use, contributing to embarrassment (Kirby & Krone, 2002). Communicating about health as a society thus clearly demonstrates links to the development of health policies linked to public health, medicine, and self-care. These reciprocally relate to the evidence base we have for communicating the science of health.

Communicating the Science of Health

How we communicate about medical research findings provides opportunities to improve health and manage illness. Efforts to communicate the science of health become content for scientific journals and dissemination into practice settings. As the science evolved to reveal a role for women's behaviors, nutrition and otherwise, on fetal development, for example, corresponding efforts to communicate with women about prenatal care occurred both formally during medical interaction and public health communication campaigns designed to promote prenatal care (Parrott & Daniels, 1996). The uncertainty about pregnancy outcomes, according to much public health communication and often medical interaction, could be reduced by following the prescriptions related to use of prenatal care based on the focus for fetal outcomes in the funded research. The science has now evolved to a point in which preconception care is viewed as the more efficacious approach to fetal health, with neural tube disorders associated with a woman's folic acid deficits being translated to efforts to communicate this new science to women and doctors, as well as the public (Weisman et al., 2006).

The reality that an evolving state of knowledge based in medical science contributes to the necessity of communicating the information in ways that may improve lives is revealed across many situations. With knowledge about organ donation come novel approaches to communicate about this need, sometimes linking to individual identity, sometimes addressing fears about premature decisions to harvest organs, and sometimes assessing the gate-keeping function associated with receipt of donated organs (Kopfman & Smith, 1996; Kopfman, Smith, Ah Yun, & Hodges, 1998; S. E. Morgan & Miller, 2002). Not only does the current state of knowledge suggest what topics will be addressed in communication about health and illness management, it suggests that questions outside the parameters of this knowledge may be treated as an *absence* of relationships for groups not included in research, or an absence of illness in patients with symptoms outside the parameters of definitions of illness. Women and heart disease is an apt example. Just because women were not included in early research to assess their risk for heart disease did not mean that women are not at risk for heart disease, which was one way of translating the lack of evidence about such risk, and communicating about it.

The science linking overexposure to the sun and skin cancer has contributed to efforts to support ways to adapt to this risk, and still maintain employment and/or leisure activities, thus attending to individual realities associated with resource allocation (Parrott, Monahan, Ainsworth, & Steiner, 1998). It is also evident that comprehending the personal relevance of the environment for one's own well-being relates to perceptions of regional ecosystem management (Cantrill, 1998). In part, because public health communication so often arouses fear to unproductive ends, efforts to understand how communicating the science of health relates to this outcome, sometimes contributing to motivation and other times impairing comprehension. These efforts have demonstrated the attributes of messages that contribute to perceived risk (Trumbo, 2002) or perceptions of susceptibility, severity, and efficacy (Dorsey, Miller, & Sherer, 1999; Rimal, 2001; Rimal & Real, 2003; Roberto, Meyer, Johnson, & Atkin, 2000).

The sensation value of antidrug PSA message features (public service announcements; S. E. Morgan, Palmgreen, Stephenson, Hoyle, & Lorch,

2003) and the use of fear appeals to promote performance of testicular self-exam (Morman, 2000), responsible drinking (Slater, Karan, Rouner, & Walters, 2002), and immunizations (Smith, 1997) have considered compliance and behavior change as outcomes. Strategic efforts have also focused on resistance to persuasion, or efforts to help audiences bombarded with messages to avoid behavior changes which contribute to negative health outcomes (Pfau & Van Bockern, 1994; Pfau, Van Bockern, & Kang, 1992). This focus leads to efforts to understand counterarguments and messages included in alcohol advertising (Snyder & Blood, 1992) and tobacco (Altman, Slater, Albright, & Maccoby, 1987; Weis & Burke, 1986), as well as visual communication about appearance and body image distortions (Myers & Biocca, 1992), and sexual etiquette in teen magazine narratives (Garner, Sterk, & Adams, 1998). These studies also raise questions about accountability.

An examination of the importance of the channel used to communicate about health implicitly acknowledges a role for media as gate-keeper, with efforts to reach individuals with forms of media most often used illustrated by radio messages about gun trigger-lock use, (Roberto, Myers, Johnson, Atkin, & Smith, 2002), coaches as role models, and youth sun protection (Parrott & Duggan, 1999), as well as worksites to promote organ donation (S. E. Morgan and Miller, 2002). Beyond this public health communication site for communicating the science of health, medical interaction research illustrates the value of parents negotiating the problem presentation during pediatric encounters (Stivers, 2001), a reflection of their effort and a contributor to the reduction of their uncertainty. The ways that physicians transition to physical exam from history-taking (Robinson & Stivers, 2001) or how providers define the "doctorability" of patient claims of symptoms (see Heritage, this volume) also plays a significant role in participants' comprehension and behavior. Patients benefit from skills training to increase competence during medical interaction (McGee & Cegala, 1998), with results relating to comprehension which in turn affects such outcomes as compliance and behavior change.

Medical interaction depends upon physicians' and patients' abilities to keep pace with the science. Who has access to the information? Medical interpreters may increase individual ability to use health information, as discussed in Hsieh's chapter, this volume. Identities form in response to public health communication that, although conveying information intended to increase comprehension and shape behaviors designed to promote health and the management of illness, also creates views about accountability and blame (see Rintamaki, this volume). Emotions, as discussed by Haskard, Williams, and DiMatteo in this volume, are a critical link to patient outcomes, ranging from hope to fear to embarrassment or guilt. Some research finds that when individuals feel guilty about sexual experiences, they are less likely to use contraception (Moore & Davidson, 1997). Identities form in response to medical interaction as well, as suggested in Lambert, Levy, and Winer's chapter in relation to medications prescribed and used in psychiatry.

Nonverbal communication also contributes to these outcomes. Patients' perceptions of physicians' professionalism has been linked to their nonverbal emotional displays (J. E. Morgan & Krone, 2001). Physicians may better comprehend patients' suffering through attention to nonverbal behaviors (Heath, 2002). Patients may feel stigmatized and stereotyped based on provider behaviors in response to information given about HIV status (Agne, Thompson, & Cusella, 2000), and disclosure about sexual abuse (Beach & LeBaron, 2002). Physicians' talk, gaze, and body orientation direct doctor-patient consultation during openings (see Heritage, this volume; Robinson, 1998) and thus contribute to the management of uncertainty. Nonverbal communication may also motivate patients to provide information about insurance and psychosocial concerns, further contributing to a greater likelihood of compliance if barriers have been addressed (Duggan & Parrott, 2001).

Communicating the science of health also has an important role for our ability to manage well-being as well. The Internet has been found to satisfy stay-at-home moms' health information needs (Tardy & Hale, 1998), highlighting their ability to bypass formal gate-keepers of health information. Other research questions the informational adequacy of Internet content to provide the means to manage well-being (Dutta-Bergman, 2003). Information fulfills one form of social support and, when combined with emotional and instrumental forms, has been found to help breast cancer survivors manage uncertainty in their daily lives (Ford, Babrow, & Stohl, 1996) and women with AIDS negotiate the medical, social, and personal complexities of the illness (see Peterson, this volume). The absence of social support, on the other hand, has been directly linked to psychosocial problems (Segrin, 2003), which may range from feelings of hopelessness to guilt. Linking these two realms, Internet access and social support, it is perhaps not too surprising that an increasing number of cancer patients have been found to go online to seek social support (Wright, 2002), once more bypassing gate-keepers of information. Older adults' coping has also been found to be enhanced by computer-mediated social support (Wright, 2000), with strategic efforts designed to develop optimal match between support needs and computer mediated communication support communities (Turner, Grube, & Meyers, 2001). Such meanings overlap with individual experiences, including cultural and familial contingencies (see Duggan, Le Poire, Prescott, & Bahan's discussion of codependency and its influence on health and health outcomes in this volume).

Communicating Our Experiences with Health

We know too little about how we talk to one another about health or about how parents, for example, talk about health habits to their children. For some time, efforts have been made to understand how health and the management of illness relate to our social networks. Continuing the example relating to pregnancy, we do not know how women talk to other women about experiences such as pregnancy. Women may talk to their own mothers to compare their knowledge levels, understanding, and experiences. The availability of the grandmother, the grandmother's favorable reaction to the pregnancy, the grandmother's respect for her daughter's autonomy, and the grandmother's willingness to reminisce about her own pregnancy have been found to predict positive experiences, such as less fear about labor, for a woman's acceptance of the motherhood role (Mercer, 1986). Mothers of pregnant women are potentially important sources of information who will affect pregnant women's decision-making across all areas of pregnancy. In fact, we lack any research to suggest whether mothers who were pregnant in an era prior to the discovery of how substances cross the placenta tell their daughters that they smoked, consumed alcohol, or behaved in ways counter to current knowledge.

Behavior and the ability to resist drugs are affected by social networks (Hecht, Trost, Bator, & MacKinnon, 1997). Social norm expectancies relating to alcohol consumption (e.g., Rimal & Real, 2003) also suggest that even when we may understand the science being communicated about a role for alcohol consumption on health, beliefs about what our friends expect may contribute to our behavior more than such awareness. In a similar vein, when young adults perceive alcohol PSAs to be realistic, matching their experience with their friends, this contributes to comprehension via the motivation to process messages (Andsager, Austin, & Pinkleton, 2001). Comprehension is also predicted by such attributes as sensation-seeking among adolescents (Greene, Krcmar, Rubin, Walters, & Hale, 2002; Sheer, 1995). This has proven invaluable for understanding outcomes associated with anti-marijuana media messages (Stephenson, 2003; Stephenson et al., 1999).

Families contribute to cancer patients' psychosocial adjustment as well (Gotcher, 1993), but also pose dialectical tensions for adult survivors of sexual abuse (Ford, Ray, & Ellis, 1999). Not surprisingly, families also predict dietary behavior more often than awareness of the science about healthy eating (Rimal & Flora, 1998). Partners importantly contribute to maintenance of sobriety (Le Poire, Hallett, & Erlandson, 2000). Individual religious beliefs impact illness causation perceptions (Parrott et al., 2004), with likely implications for the exposure to and effectiveness of health messages. Motivation for verbal communication, which may be related to cultural or social experiences, has been found to impact medical interaction (Kim et al., 2000). Media use patterns have demonstrated that reading sports magazines positively relates to body satisfaction for adolescent females aged 10–19 years whether they participate in sports or not (Harrison & Fredrickson, 2003). Media consumption also relates to eating disorders (Harrison, 2000; Harrison & Cantor, 1997), body image (Botta, 1999; David & Johnson, 1998), and pessimism about health care in the United States (Culbertson & Stempel, 1985).

As Charmaz in this volume observes, an absence of disclosures about suffering in patients' subjective stories about serious chronic illness should *not* be assumed to reflect an absence of such experience. It may instead reflect a response to the emphasis of communicating about health in this society. As spokespersons repeat time and again, great strides have been made in extending the lives of those who have these chronic conditions. Those who would complain about their suffering or distress may be concerned that they appear to lack appreciation for life-extending therapies, reflecting on their identity construction out of the societal discourse (see Rintamaki, this volume, for an explication of social identity development), and contributing to an absence of this type of talk but not this type of experience. These outcomes suggest the vital role that public health advocacy and patient advocacy may have in advancing agendas relating to each, a reality suggested by the contributors and work included in this volume.

Public Health and Patient Advocacy: If Not Now, When? If Not Us, Who? If Not Here, Where?

There are more than 150,000 articles about medical research published each month in more than 20,000 biomedical journals (Levin, 2001). Despite this tremendous resource to improve health, as we entered the 21st century, the United States ranked 12th out of 13 industrialized countries when judged by 16 health indicators (Starfield, 2000). Ahead of the United States were Japan, Sweden, Canada, France, Australia, Spain, Finland, the Netherlands, the United Kingdom, Denmark, and Belgium. Only Germany followed the United States on the list. The indicators for which we ranked so poorly are important ones. They convey the very essence of life in concrete terms. We ranked last in low birth weight, neonatal mortality, and infant mortality rates. For post-neonatal mortality, the United States crawls up to an 11th place ranking due largely to the amazing technological resources used to keep alive premature and low birth weight babies (Starfield, 2000).

We also ranked last in years of potential life lost, excluding external causes, which is an indicator of how many people in the United States died before living to an average life expectancy. The remaining indicators are all about life expectancies: at 1 year, 15 years, 40 years, 65 years, and 80 years, together with an age-adjusted mortality indicator. Variances exist relating to gender in these age-related measures, with males ranked worse than females at the age of 1 and 15 years, females ranked worse than males at the age of 40 years, and then no gender differences at the age of 65 when we ranked 7th; no differences emerged for 80 year olds, for which we ranked 3rd (Starfield, 2000).

There is a hidden story in these numbers. It relates to major modifiable causes of death in the United States, which contribute to premature loss of life for millions of Americans. Smoking, poor diet and physical inactivity, alcohol consumption, microbial agents such as influenza and pneumonia (excluding HIV), toxic agents including pollutants and asbestos, motor vehicle accidents, firearms, sexual behavior including HIV, and illicit use of drugs (CDC, 2004). Survive those, and the technology and resources of the best health care system in the world kick in. Life extending medical tests and therapies contribute to improved rankings the older we get. But the final indicator, age-adjusted mortality, for which we ranked 10th, is a sad testament to our overall health status as a nation. We can do better. We will only do better, however, if each of us takes seriously our role in understanding and using communication about health and the management of illness. This will likely require the development and use of advocacy skills.

Advocacy skills include the ability to communicate one's needs effectively and to negotiate with employers, insurers, and health care providers (Walsh-Burke, 1999). Advocacy efforts may be undertaken by individuals on behalf of their own or a loved one's well-being. AIDS patients' experiences with and involvement in advocacy efforts, for example, contribute to a greater likelihood of obtaining information to make informed decisions (Brashers, Haas, Klingle, & Neidig, 2000). Public health professionals and practitioners may undertake advocacy efforts as well. Using an example which relates to one of the modifiable causes of morbidity and mortality in the United States, injury prevention faculty from Johns Hopkins became a source of information to support the passage of a law in Maryland to limit the availability of certain types of handguns (Teret, Alexander, & Bailey, 1990). Although such organizations as the police, the medical community, and many civic groups favored passage of the law, they lacked data about the public health problem related to the issue. The public health experts provided the data contributing to the ability to refute effectively arguments raised by the pro-gun groups. Nonprofit organizations also may form to advocate for members, with rights as social welfare organizations to engage in nearly unlimited lobbying with lawmakers, arguing for a position on relevant legislation (Vernick, 1999).

Although self-care or self-help programs have been in and out of favor in the United States, the term entered the National Library of Medicine publication "Index Medicus" in the early 1980s. The Centers for Disease Control and Prevention solicited proposals to assess self-care educational programs in the United States, and one project to emerge from the work focusing on usual activities. Of the 773 programs identified, half included the development of advocacy skills related to health care as an objective (DeFriese, Woomert, Guild, Steckler, & Konrad, 1989). A review of self-management programs designed to facilitate patients living with chronic diseases such as arthritis and diabetes did not include advocacy skills as a component, which may represent an absence of such content in most of these programs (Warsi, Wanger, LaValley, Avorn, & Solomon, 2004). Advocacy efforts have found positive effects across the discursive domains, with the National Psoriasis Foundation, for example, functioning as a patient advocacy organization with lobbying and advocacy efforts contributing to the development of a psoriasis gene bank and acceptance of psoriasis therapies by government and insurers (Gordon, 2005).

How we communicate as a society about health and the management of illness is so often just the backdrop against which everything else exists that we fail to acknowledge how significant it is in setting the stage for what we know and what we do. From the allocation of resources for medical research to the alignment of institutional and individual identities to support this allocation, our cognitions, emotions, and behaviors align with this reality. As researchers and practitioners, advocacy research and practice adds another dimension to translational research, the pursuit of efforts to apply what we have learned in basic research in order to improve lives. The typology of outcomes relating to communicating as a society about health, communicating the science of health, and communicating our experiences with health is far-reaching in scope. It thus heightens the urgency around which efforts to promote public health and patient advocacy skills center, thus enhancing both research and practice designed to improve health and the management of illness.

References

Adams, R. J., & Parrott, R. (1994). Pediatric nurses' communication of role expectations to parents of hospitalized children. *Journal of Applied Communication Research, 22,* 36–47.

Agne, R., Thompson, T. L., & Cusella, L. P. (2000). Stigma in the line of face: Self-disclosure of patients' HIV status to health care providers. *Journal of Applied Communication Research, 28,* 235–261.

Altman, D. G., Slater, M. D., Albright, C. L., & Maccoby, N. (1987). How an unhealthy product is sold: Cigarette advertising in magazines, 1960–1985. *Journal of Communication, 37*(4), 95–106.

Andsager, J. L., Austin, E. W., & Pinkleton, B. E. (2001). Questioning the value of realism: Young adults' processing of messages in alcohol-related public service announcements and advertising. *Journal of Communication, 51,* 121–142.

Apker, J. (2001). Role development in the managed care era: A case of hospital-based nursing. *Journal of Applied Communication Research, 29,* 117–136.

Beach, W. A., & LeBaron, C. D. (2002). Body disclosures: Attending to personal problems and reported sexual abuse during a medical encounter. *Journal of Communication, 52,* 617–639.

Botta, R. A. (1999). Television images and adolescent girls' body image disturbance. *Journal of Communication, 49,* 22–41.

Bracci, S. L. (2001). Managing health care in Oregon: The search for a civic bioethics. *Journal of Applied Communication Research, 29,* 171–194.

Brashers, D. E., Haas, S. M., Klingle, R. S., & Neidig, J. L. (2000). Collective AIDS activism and individuals' perceived self-advocacy in physician-patient communication. *Human Communication Research, 26,* 372–402.

Cantrill, J. G. (1993). Communication and our environment: Categorizing research in environmental advocacy. *Journal of Applied Communication Research, 21,* 66–95.

Cantrill, J. G. (1998). The environmental self and a sense of place: Communication foundations for regional ecosystem management. *Journal of Applied Communication Research, 26,* 301–318.

Centers for Disease Control. (2004). *Fact sheet: CDC's prevention activities that target actual causes of death.* Retrieved March 3, 2009, from http://www.cdc.gov/od/oc/media/pressrel/fs040309b.htm

Conrad, C., & Millay, B. (2001). Confronting free market romanticism: Health care reform in the least likely place. *Journal of Applied Communication Research, 29,* 153–170.

Culbertson, H. M., & Stempel III, G. H. (1985). "Media malaise:" Explaining personal optimism and societal pessimism about health care. *Journal of Communication, 35,* 180–190.

Daniels, M., & Parrott, R. L. (1996). Prenatal care from the woman's perspective: A thematic analysis of the newspaper media. In R. L. Parrott & C. M. Condit (Eds.), *Evaluating women's health messages: A resource book* (pp. 222–233). Newbury Park, CA: Sage.

David, P., & Johnson, M. A. (1998). The role of self in third-person effects about body image. *Journal of Communication, 48*(4), 37–58.

DeFriese, G. H., Woomert, A., Guild, P. A., Steckler, A. B., & Konrad, T. R. (1989). From activated patient to pacified activist: A study of the self-care movement in the United States. *Social Science & Medicine, 29,* 195–204.

Dorsey, A. M., Miller, K. I., & Sherer, C. W. (1999). Communication, risk behavior, and perceptions of threat and efficacy: A test of a reciprocal model. *Journal of Applied Communication Research, 27,* 377–395.

Duggan, A. P., & Parrott, R. L. (2001). Physicians' nonverbal rapport building and patients' talk about the subjective component of illness. *Human Communication Research, 27,* 299–311.

Dutta-Bergman, M. J. (2003). Health communication on the web: The roles of web use motivation and information completeness. *Communication Monographs, 70,* 264–274.

Ellingson, L. L. (2003). Interdisciplinary health care teamwork in the clinic backstage. *Journal of Applied Communication Research, 31,* 93–117.

Elwood, W. N., Greene, K., & Carter, K. K. (2003). Gentlemen don't speak: Communication norms and condom use in bathhouses. *Journal of Applied Communication Research, 31,* 277–297.

Ford, L. A., Babrow, A. S., & Stohl, C. (1996). Social support messages and the management of uncertainty in the experience of breast cancer: An application of problematic integration theory. *Communication Monographs, 63,* 189–207

Ford, L. A., Ray, E. B., & Ellis, B. H. (1999). Translating scholarship on intrafamilial sexual abuse: The utility of a dialectical perspective for adult survivors. *Journal of Applied Communication Research, 27,* 139–157.

Garner, A., Sterk, H. M., & Adams, S. (1998). Narrative analysis of sexual etiquette in teenage magazines. *Journal of Communication, 48*(4), 59–78.

Gillespie, S. R. (2001). The politics of breathing: Asthmatic Medicaid patients under managed care. *Journal of Applied Communication Research, 29,* 97–116.

Gordon, K. (2005). Patient education and advocacy groups. *Archives of Dermatology, 141,* 80–81.

Gotcher, J. M. (1993). The effects of family communication on psychosocial adjustment of cancer patients. *Journal of Applied Communication Research, 21,* 176–188.

Greene, K., Krcmar, M., Rubin, D. L., Walters, L. H., & Hale, J. L. (2002). Elaboration in processing adolescent health messages: The impact of egocentrism and sensation seeking on message processing. *Journal of Communication, 52,* 812–831.

Harrison, K. (2000). The body electric: Thin-ideal media and eating disorders in adolescents. *Journal of Communication, 50*(3), 119–143.

Harrison, K., & Cantor, J. (1997). The relationship between media consumption and eating disorders. *Journal of Communication, 46*(1), 40–68.

Harrison, K., & Fredrickson, B. L. (2003). Women's sports media, self-objectification, and mental health in black and white adolescent females. *Journal of Communication, 53,* 216–232.

Heath, C. (2002). Demonstrative suffering: The gestural (re)embodiment of symptoms. *Journal of Communication, 52,* 597–616.

Hecht, M., Trost, M. R., Bator, R. J., & MacKinnon, D. (1997). Ethnicity and sex similarities and differences in drug resistance. *Journal of Applied Communication Research, 25*(2), 75–97.

Hines, S. C. (2001). Coping with uncertainties in advance care planning. *Journal of Communication, 51,* 498–513.

Hyde, M. J., & Rufo, K. (2000). The call of conscience, rhetorical interruptions, and the euthanasia controversy. *Journal of Applied Communication Research, 28*(1), 1–23.

Kim, M. S., Klingle, R. S., Sharkey, W. F., Park, H. S., Smith, D. H., & Cai, D. (2000). A test of a cultural model of patients' motivation for verbal communication in patient-doctor interactions. *Communication Monographs, 67,* 262–283.

Kirby, E. L., & Krone, K. J. (2002). "The policy exists but you can't really use it": Communication and the structuration of work-family policies. *Journal of Applied Communication Research, 30,* 50–77.

Kline, K. (1996). The drama of in utero drug exposure: Fetus takes first billing. In R. L. Parrott & C. M. Condit (Eds.), *Evaluating women's health messages: A resource book* (pp. 61–76). Newbury Park, CA: Sage.

Kopfman, J. E., & Smith, S. W. (1996). Understanding the audiences of a health communication campaign: A discriminant analysis of potential organ donors based on intent to donate. *Journal of Applied Communication Research, 24*(1), 33–49.

Kopfman, J. E., Smith, S. W., Ah Yun, J. K., & Hodges, A. (1998). Affective and cognitive reactions to narrative versus statistical evidence organ donation messages. *Journal of Applied Communication Research, 26,* 279–300.

Le Poire, B. A., Hallett, J. S., & Erlandson, K. T. (2000). An initial test of inconsistent nurturing as Control Theory: How partners of drug abusers assist their partners' sobriety. *Human Communication Research, 26,* 432–457.

Lemieux, R. (1996). Illicit drug use and the pregnant woman: Prevalence, social impact effects, and legislative action. In R. L. Parrott & C. M. Condit (Eds.), *Evaluating women's health messages: A resource book* (pp. 49–60). Newbury Park, CA: Sage.

Levin, A. (2001). The Cochrane collaboration. *Annals of Internal Medicine, 135,* 309–312.

McGee, D. S., & Cegala, D. J. (1998). Patient communication skills training for improved communication competence in the primary care medical consultation. *Journal of Applied Communication Research, 26,* 412–430.

Medved, C. E., Morrison, K., Dearing, J. W., Larson, R. S., Cline, G., & Brummans, B. H. (2001). Tensions in community health improvement initiatives: Communication and collaboration in a managed care environment. *Journal of Applied Communication Research, 29,* 137–152.

Mercer, R. T. (1986). *First-time motherhood: Experiences from teens to forties.* New York: Springer.

Miller, K., & Zook, E. G. (1997). Care partners for persons with AIDS: Implications for health communication. *Journal of Applied Communication Research, 25,* 57–74.

Moore, M. P. (1997). The cigarette as representational ideograph in the debate over environmental tobacco smoke. *Communication Monographs, 64,* 47-64.

Moore, N. B., & Davidson, J. K. (1997). Guilt about first intercourse: An antecedent of sexual dissatisfaction among college women. *Journal of Sex Marital Therapy, 23*(1), 29–46.

Morgan, J. E., & Krone, K. J. (2001). Bending the rules of "professional" display: Emotional improvisation in caregiver performances. *Journal of Applied Communication Research, 29,* 317–340.

Morgan, S. E., & Miller, J. K. (2002). Communicating about gifts of life: The effect of knowledge, attitudes, and altruism on behavior and behavioral intentions regarding organ donation. *Journal of Applied Communication Research, 30,* 163–178.

Morgan, S. E., Palmgreen, P., Stephenson, M. T., Hoyle, R. H., & Lorch, E. P. (2003). Associations between message features and subjective evaluations of the sensation value of antidrug public service announcements. *Journal of Communication, 53,* 512–526.

Morman, M. T. (2000). The influence of fear appeals, message design, and masculinity on men's motivation to perform the testicular self-exam. *Journal of Applied Communication Research, 28,* 91–116.

Myers, P. N., & Biocca, F. A. (1992). The elastic body image: The effect of television advertising and programming on body image distortions in young women. *Journal of Communication, 42*(3), 108–133.

Parrott, R. L. (2004). Emphasizing 'communication' in health communication. *Journal of Communication, 54,* 751–787.

Parrott, R. L., & Condit, C. M. (1996). *Evaluating women's health messages: A resource book.* Newbury Park, CA: Sage.

Parrott, R. L., & Daniels, M. (1996). Promoting prenatal care to women: Promises, pitfalls, and pratfalls. In R. L. Parrott & C. M. Condit (Eds.), *Evaluating women's health messages: A resource book* (pp. 205–221). Newbury Park, CA: Sage.

Parrott, R., & Duggan A. (1999). Using coaches as role models of sun protection for youth: Georgia's "Got Youth Covered" project. *Journal of Applied Communication Research, 27,* 107–119.

Parrott, R. L., & Polonec, L., (2007). Preventing green tobacco sickness in farming youth: A behavior adaptation approach. In K. B. Wright & S. D. Moore (Eds.), *Applied health communication: A sourcebook* (pp. 341–359). Creskill, NJ: Hampton.

Parrott, R., Monahan, J., Ainsworth, S., & Steiner, C. (1998). Communicating to farmers about skin cancer: The behavior adaptation model. *Human Communication Research, 24,* 386–409.

Parrott, R., Silk, K., Weiner, J., Condit, C., Harris, T., & Bernhardt, J. (2004). Deriving lay models of uncertainty about genes' role in illness causation to guide communication about human genetics. *Journal of Communication, 54,* 105–122.

Pfau, M., & Van Bockern, S. (1994). The persistence of inoculation in conferring resistance to smoking initiation among adolescents: The second year. *Human Communication Research, 20,* 413–430.

Pfau, M., Van Bockern, S., & Kang, J. G. (1992). Use of inoculation to promote resistance to smoking initiation among adolescents. *Communication Monographs, 59,* 213–230.

Pomerantz, A., Fehr, B. J., & Ende, J. (1997). When supervising physicians see patients: Strategies used in difficult situations. *Human Communication Research, 23,* 589–618.

Pratt, C. B., Ha, L., & Pratt, C. A. (2002). Setting the public health agenda on major diseases in sub-Saharan Africa: African popular magazines and medical journals, 1981–1997. *Journal of Communication, 52,* 889–904.

Rimal, R. N. (2001). Perceived risk and self-efficacy as motivators: Understanding individuals' long-term use of health information. *Journal of Communication, 51,* 633–654.

Rimal, R. N., & Flora, J. A. (1998). Bidirectional familial influences in dietary behavior: Test of a model of campaign influences. *Human Communication Research, 24,* 610–637.

Rimal, R. N., & Real, K. (2003). Perceived risk and efficacy beliefs as motivators of change: Use of the Risk Perception Attitude (RPA) framework to understand health behaviors. *Human Communication Research, 29,* 370–399.

Roberto, A. J., Meyer, G., Johnson, A. J., & Atkin, C. K. (2000). Using the extended parallel process model to prevent firearm injury and death: Field experiment results of a video-based intervention. *Journal of Communication, 50*(4), 157–175.

Roberto, A. J., Myers, G., Johnson, A. J., Atkin, C. K., & Smith, P. K. (2002). Promoting gun trigger-lock use: Insights and implications from a radio-based health communication intervention. *Journal of Applied Communication Research, 30,* 210–230.

Robinson, J. D. (1998). Getting down to business: Talk, gaze, and body orientation during openings of doctor-patient consultations. *Human Communication Research, 25,* 97–123.

Robinson, J. D., & Stivers, T. (2001). Achieving activity transitions in physician-patient encounters: From history taking to physical examination. *Human Communication Research, 27,* 253–298.

Sachweh, S. (1998). Granny darling's nappies: Secondary baby talk in German nursing homes for the aged. *Journal of Applied Communication Research, 26*(1), 52–65.

Sandman, P. M., Weinstein, N. D., & Klotz, M. L. (1987). Public response to the risk from geological radon. *Journal of Communication, 37*(3), 93–108.

Scheibel, D. (1996). Appropriating bodies: Organ(izing) ideology and cultural practice in medical school. *Journal of Applied Communication Research, 24,* 310–331.

Segrin, C. (2003). Age moderates the relationship between social support and psychosocial problems. *Human Communication Research, 29,* 327–342.

Sheer, V. C. (1995). Sensation seeking predispositions and susceptibility to a sexual partner's appeals for condom use. *Journal of Applied Communication Research, 23,* 212–229.

Slater, M. D., Karan, D. N., Rouner, D., & Walters, D. (2002). Effects of threatening visuals and announcer differences on responses to televised alcohol. *Journal of Applied Communication Research, 30,* 27–49.

Smith, S. L. (1997). The effective use of fear appeals in persuasive immunization strategies: An analysis of national immunization intervention messages. *Journal of Applied Communication Research, 25,* 264–292.

Snyder, L. B., & Blood, D. J. (1992). Caution: Alcohol advertising and the Surgeon General's alcohol warnings may have adverse effects on young adults. *Journal of Applied Communication Research, 20,* 37–53.

Starfield, B. (2000). Is U.S. health really the best in the world? *Journal of the American Medical Association, 284,* 483–485.

Stearney, L. M. (1996). Sex control technology and reproductive "choice": The conflation of technical and political argument in the new science of human reproduction. *Communication Theory, 6,* 388–405.

Stephenson, M. T. (2003). Examining adolescents' responses to antimarijuana PSAs. *Human Communication Research, 29,* 343–369.

Stephenson, M. T., Palmgreen, P., Hoyle, R. H., Donohew, L., Lorch, E. P., & Colon, S. E. (1999). Short-term effects of an anti-marijuana media campaign targeting high sensation seeking adolescents. *Journal of Applied Communication Research, 27,* 175–195.

Stivers, T. (2001). Negotiating who presents the problem: Next speaker selection in pediatric encounters. *Journal of Communication, 51,* 252–282.

Tardy, R. W., & Hale, C. L. (1998). Getting "plugged-in": A network analysis of health information seeking among "stay-at-home moms." *Communication Monographs, 65,* 336–357.

Teret, S. P., Alexander, G. R., & Bailey, L. A. (1990). The passage of Maryland's gun law: Date and advocacy for injury prevention. *Journal of Public Health Policy, 11*(1), 26–38.

Thompson, T. (2000). The nature and language of illness explanations. In B. B. Whaley (Ed.), *Explaining illness: Research, theory, and strategies* (pp. 3–40). Mahwah, NJ: Erlbaum.

Trumbo, C. W. (2002). Information processing and risk perception: An adaptation of the heuristic-systematic model. *Journal of Communication, 52,* 367–382.

Turner, J. W., Grube, J. A., & Meyers, J. (2001). Developing an optimal match within online communities: An exploration of CMC support communities and traditional support. *Journal of Communication, 51,* 231–251.

Vanderford, M. L., Smith, D. H., & Harris, W. S. (1992). Value identification in narrative discourse: Evaluation of an HIV education demonstration project. *Journal of Applied Communication Research, 20,* 123–161.

Vernick, J. S. (1999). Lobbying and advocacy for the public's health: What are the limits for nonprofit organizations? *American Journal of Public Health, 89,* 1425–1429.

Walsh-Burke, M. C. (1999). Self-advocacy training for cancer survivors: The cancer survival toolbox. *Cancer Practice, 7,* 297–301.

Warsi, A., Wanger, P. S., LaValley, M. P., Avorn, J., & Solomon, D. H. (2004). Self management education programs in chronic disease: A systematic review and methodological critique of the literature. *Archives of Internal Medicine, 164,* 1641–1649.

Weis, W. L., & Burke, C. (1986). Media content and tobacco advertising: An unhealthy addiction. *Journal of Communication, 36,* 59–69.

Weisman, C. S., Hillemeier, M. M., Chase, G. A., Dyer, A. M., Baker, S., Feinberg, M., et al. (2006). Preconceptional health: Risks of adverse pregnancy outcomes by reproductive life stage in the central Pennsylvania women's health study (CePAWHS). *Women's Health Issues, 16,* 216–224.

Wright, K. (2000). Computer-mediated social support, older adults, and coping. *Journal of Communication, 50,* 110–118.

Wright, K. (2002). Social support within an on-line cancer community: An assessment of emotional support, perceptions of advantages and disadvantages, and motives for using the community from a communication perspective. *Journal of Applied Communication Research, 30,* 195–209.

Index

Page numbers in italics refer to figures or tables.